Rock The Nation

Rock The Nation
Latin/o Identities and the Latin Rock Diaspora

Roberto Avant-Mier

continuum

Published by the Continuum International Publishing Group
The Tower Building   80 Maiden Lane
11 York Road   Suite 704
London   New York
SE1 7NX   NY 10038

www.continuumbooks.com

Copyright © 2010 by Roberto Avant-Mier

All rights reserved. No part of this publication may be reproduced or transmitted in any form or by any means, electronic or mechanical, including photocopying, recording or any information storage or retrieval system, without prior permission from the publishers.

First published 2010

Library of Congress Cataloging-in-Publication Data
Avant-Mier, Roberto.
Rock the nation : Latin/o identities and the Latin rock diaspora / Roberto Avant-Mier.
    p. cm.
  Includes bibliographical references and index.
  ISBN-13: 978-1-4411-6897-9 (hardcover : alk. paper)
  ISBN-10: 1-4411-6897-4 (hardcover : alk. paper)
  ISBN-13: 978-1-4411-6448-3 (pbk. : alk. paper)
  ISBN-10: 1-4411-6448-0 (pbk. : alk. paper) 1. Rock music—Latin America—History and criticism. 2. Rock music—United States—Latin American influences. I. Title.
  ML3534.6.L29A83 2010
  781.66089'68—dc22   2009051407

ISBN: 978-1-4411-6897-9 (Hardback)
        978-1-4411-6448-3 (Paperback)

Typeset by Pindar NZ, Auckland, New Zealand

Contents

Foreword vii
Author's Note x

Introduction — On Latinos/Hispanics in the United States: 'Latino/as,' the US Census, and Other Foundational Concepts 1

1. *Heard it on the X*: Border Radio as Public Discourse, the Latin/o Legacy in Popular Music, and the Roots of Multicultural America. . . 29

    Interludio 1° (first interlude) 52

2. The Missing Links: Zoot Suits, Original Chicanos, and Diasporic Latin/o Connections 55

    Interludio 2° (second interlude). 83

3. Latinos in the Garage: Latin/o Presence and Influence in Garage-Rock . . . and Other Rock and Pop Music 87

    Interludio 3° (third interlude). 110

4. *Las Ondas de José Agustín*: The Birth of Rock in México and the Latin/o Rock Diaspora (1970–1990) 112

    Interludio 4° (fourth interlude) 142

5. Transnational Punk(s): On the Transnational Character of the Latin/o Rock Diaspora 146

    Interludio 5° (fifth interlude) 176

Conclusion — Alter-Latino: The Latin/o Rock Diaspora and New *Latinidades* 179

Bibliography 205
Permissions 217
Index 219
Acknowledgments 227

Para mi familia

(To my family)

Y para...

Juanita, who taught me how to sing out loud; Eileen and Belinda, who taught me how to dance; for 'Homer,' for letting me use his stereo, and for the gift of a CD player; Andy, who introduced me to Black Sabbath, Ozzy Osbourne, Judas Priest, Iron Maiden, Led Zeppelin and The Beatles, and who also taught me to appreciate album covers and liner notes; Tiny, who introduced me to lowriders and Van Halen; all my family who dance *cumbias* and cry when they hear *mariachis*; Tilo, who got me into Metallica and Slayer and invited me everywhere ('damn Mexicans'), and Ray for friendship and all the fun and the laughs; Olguita, who talked with me about '*rock en español*' and who lets me sing the blues; Adrian and Derek, who asked questions and always wanted to hear more; Mi tía Elena, who would talk '*tírili*' with you, if you could handle it; Mi tía 'Pumpkin,' whose cassette-tape collection probably exceeds my music collection; for my kids, who sing and dance with me; for all my other friends like Russ, Curt, Tom, Dick P., another Russ ('Que Viva Irony Man!'), Terry, Dan the Man, Steve, Hal, Sean, Dennis, Phil, Jimmy, Rick, Zach, and many others with whom I've talked about music over the years; other friends and acquaintances who have talked with me about music and favorites, gave me ideas or suggestions, and sometimes even gave me music; people I met at conferences who gave me ideas or suggested books; for the woman who cried at my conference presentation years ago; for all my students and classes with whom I've talked about music and theories; for the Mexis in America; for the Mormon that loves Los Tres; for the Chicana that digs Nirvana; for the Latina with the Chuck Taylor Converse sneakers; for the *gabacha* that loves '*rock nacional*'; for the Irish guy who speaks Spanish; for all the other Latinophiles who 'get it' (you know who you are); and for every other person who, like these people, lives the contradictions. *No hay pureza.*

Foreword

Roberto Avant-Mier's book inspired me to think about the role music has played in my own life: as a mechanism through which I have articulated different aspects of my identity, especially upon becoming a part of the Mexican, or Latin American, diaspora. I was born in Mexico City, and my parents belong to a generation whose participation in the student movements of 1968 and 1973 marked their political and cultural development. The music associated with social activism in Latin America, known as *nueva canción latinoamericana* has been, for me, a point of reference from an early age. Interestingly, the American and British rock 'n' roll records my father left behind upon moving to the United States were also central to the development of my identity. While these two forms of music were often pitted against each other — the former expressing the ideas and sentiments behind Latin American movements for national sovereignty, while the latter was often linked to American cultural hegemony — in actuality, they coexisted as the generation born between the 1940s and 1950s embraced modernization, the loosening of social restraints, and the democratization of Mexican society.

I moved to the United States to attend high school and, almost immediately, I began to grasp how musical expression serves as a tool for normalizing racialized identities in this country. My schoolmates, particularly those of Latin American background, told me that that the music I listened to and the aesthetic preferences I had developed since my childhood in México were 'White.' Wanting to adjust to a new social context, I began to listen to hip-hop instead of rock, synth-pop, and *nueva canción*, but whenever I traveled to México I brought back music by bands like Café Tacuba and, ironically, reacquainted myself with the world of US and British rock. I traveled back and forth between A Tribe Called Quest and Caifanes, or Blur, Nirvana, and Gang Starr. Then, in the mid 1990s, when I was a sociology student at Berkeley, something interesting happened. A solid underground scene, closely linked to transnational bohemian and activist circles, began to grow in the San Francisco Bay Area. I would not consider what I am beginning to describe as a Latino scene, but rather a rock movement composed of recent migrants from working- and middle-class urban centers of Latin America, who consciously rejected US-based racial, or ethnic, identities, and favored not only national but regional identities. It was not just about being a Mexican or an Argentinean rocker, but, rather, a subject from specific neighborhoods in Mexico City, Guadalajara, or Buenos Aires where punk, indie, or grunge had been adopted as local identities.

As the scene continued to develop in the United States, there was on the one hand a growing interest in the genre on the part of transnational record labels, music publications, and international concert promoters who recognized the commercial potential of bands from the Spanish-speaking world. On the other hand, many rock musicians had become involved with political movements such as the Zapatista uprising in southeastern México, the various mobilizations against the processes of economic restructuring associated with globalization, and supporting the rights of migrants and refugees across the world. Thus, bands like Santa Sabina from Mexico City played free shows in the Mission District of San Francisco during pro-immigrant-rights festivals. California-based groups like Los Super Elegantes played along international acts like La Lupita, Tijuana No! or Aterciopelados at parties such as *La Rockola* at the now defunct Berkeley Square, as well as warehouse spaces and popular rock venues. Interesting dynamics played out at the concerts and spontaneous after-parties, where it was common to hear discussions about the state of Latin American music, culture, and politics between musicians and their fans.

Paradoxically, the growth of an increasingly globalized mass media and the commercial interest on the part of music conglomerates allowed Latin American rock musicians to travel throughout the word and showcase their music. US-based market research firms developed simplistic frameworks categorizing Hispanic youth and their bicultural and bilingual music tastes and growing interest in *rock en español*. Many large-scale promoters did not know, nor understand, the music, and were used to a 'traditional' Latino market in which class and national differences were simply erased. For many of us — artists, college students, writers, independent promoters, activists, and music fans who had migrated for various reasons to the US — there was no rigid distinction between rock produced in Latin America and rock produced in the English-speaking world. Our record collections included bands like Café Tacuba, Massive Attack, and Garbage. We spoke Spanish to each other, felt at home in Mexico City, Tijuana, New York, or San Francisco and often ran into each other in these various cities. We did not understand our musical tastes in racialized or ethnic terms and attended these shows because we formed part of the same culture that produced the music.

The particular perspective that I have described above has a socio-historical experience grounded in both México and the United States. For this reason, I find Roberto Avant-Mier's analysis of the sounds and subcultures linked to diasporic Latino populations, and the experiences that have given rise to cultural expressions as varied as Pachuco Boogie and Chicano garage-rock so important. His book provides a historical context to further explore why trends in music hold such different meanings for music fans and performers alike. Furthermore, Avant-Mier confronts the notion of a monolithic and monolingual American culture by uncovering the contribution of Latinos and Latin American immigrants to American popular music. Simultaneously, he explores the influence of many of these musicians on the thinking of early Anglo-American rockers and consequently, places Latino and Latin American rock in direct conversation with the most significant developments in American popular music since the 1940s.

In the tradition of thinkers such as Eric Zolov and George Lipsitz, Avant-Mier's diasporic analysis of rock highlights the potential for music to disrupt official discourses of nation, race, and ethnicity, and brings our attention to the hidden intercultural and transnational realities that trigger musical innovation. His examination of the similarities, differences, identity politics, and commercial practices found behind categories such as *rock en español*, Chicano rock, and Latin rock is crucial for an understanding of why musical acts with similar preoccupations and influences can end up in different symbolic and real spaces, such as in different rows in a record store, or under different categories in the Grammy or MTV Music Awards.

Many exciting musical developments have taken place in Latin America since the mid 1990s. But despite the large number of Latinos living in the US, commercial success remains elusive for most Latin American rock and electronic acts, especially when traditional or identifiable Latin sounds are not made salient in their music, or when they choose to sing in languages other than Spanish, or skip vocal content altogether. This is due in part to the current state of the music recording industry itself, but also to a general indifference, or plain ignorance, on the part of US music fans and culture industries when it comes to the non-English-speaking world. But it is also due to an apparent disconnection between the specific cultural yearnings and needs of Latinos living in the US, and the desires and musical interests of rock musicians living in cities like Buenos Aires, Santiago, or Mexico City. In other words, popular music remains a space in which tensions related to identity unfold and also, where artistic innovation and commercial demands intersect with, and contribute to, these tensions. Avant-Mier's analysis of the Latin rock diaspora is helpful if we wish to go beyond typical Black/White binaries in the study of American popular music, and, also, if we seek to understand how a music scene can be so closely related to the complexities implicated in the construction of our constantly shifting identities.

Oscar León Bernal
Doctoral student in Anthropology at the CUNY Graduate Center
New York City, 2009

Author's Note

This book began as a study of Latino/a identity signifiers, and it developed into the story of the Latino/Hispanic engagement with rock music. Thus, it became two books in one. It started as an account of Latino/as, identity constructs, and how both Latino/as and identity constructs matter in contemporary culture. Beginning with my graduate work, I set out to study Latino/a identity and how identity signifiers had meaning and made meaning, as well as how those meanings are and were constructed. As my research expanded, one of the locations of shifting meaning pertaining to Latino/Hispanic identity terms was in popular music and, later, in Latin/o rock music (generally speaking) and various subgenres such as Latin rock, Chicano rock, *rock en tu idioma*, *rock en español*, rock Latino, Latin alternative, *rock alternativo*, and *Latino alternativo* — all terms that in one way or another signify Latino/a people recording and/or performing in the rock idiom or somehow relating to the rock music genre. For example, in tracing the Latino/Hispanic identity signifiers of various bands and artists, I quickly noticed that bands and artists were sometimes referred to as 'Hispanic' while others might say 'Latin.' Likewise, in searching article keywords or book indexes, one might not find anything under 'Latin' but might find something under 'Latino,' or vice versa. Likewise, 'Spanish,' 'Mexican,' 'Chicano,' and several other terms came to mind, and became part of the problem in researching Latino/Hispanic music.

At the same time, I set out to investigate Latino/a identity, as it related to music, and I wanted to avoid the typical associations of Latino/Hispanic people with salsa, *merengue*, *bachata*, *ranchera*, 'Mexican regional' music, 'tropical' music, and various other (stereotypical) associations. In other words, I wanted to avoid the typical ways in which Latino/Hispanic people are defined, how they are represented, and the music genres with which Latino/as are most often associated. Thus, my investigation of identity issues in rock music developed in order to subvert and disrupt Latino/Hispanic stereotypes and associations that are even further symbolized through cliché words, phrases, and metaphors such as 'spicy,' *sabroso, caliente*, tropical, hot-tempered, passionate, salsa, salsa-dancing, etc. These are all stereotypes and ideologically loaded discourses that, in my opinion, continue to marginalize Latino/Hispanic people in the US, continue to mark them as racial others, and, yet, continue to define them in popular culture. Granted, salsa, *merengue*, 'Mexican regional,' and other music genres are all important (and valid) aspects of Latin/o culture(s). I, however, was interested in pushing the boundaries of definitions of Latin music and testing the limits of the meaning of 'Latino' and 'Hispanic,' which all resulted in my search for Latino/a identity within the rock genre.

Thus, from an intentional focus on rock music, this project also turned into the story of how Latino/as have engaged rock 'n' roll, rock, and other rock subgenres (what I call 'rock formations'). From early Latin rhythms, sounds, and instruments . . . to the people that played those instruments or injected American popular music with those sounds . . . to lyrical themes by non-Latino/as that indicated interaction with Latino/as or Latino/a culture(s) . . . to the ways that Latino/a culture has influenced trends and mainstream youth culture in the US and elsewhere . . . what I discovered was that chronicling the trends, issues, and changes in Latin/o rock music (in its various subgenres) was the same as chronicling the trends, issues, and changes in Latino/Hispanic identities in the US, that it was demonstrating the ways in which Latino/as communicate and interact with each other (e.g., how they assimilate and acculturate to mainstream US culture), and that it was speaking to Latino/a identities beyond mainstream US culture (e.g., how they assimilate to African Americans and to other Latin Americans beyond the US).

As one brief example, I can point toward the song 'Donna' by Ritchie Valens. While Valens is most famous for 'La Bamba,' a song that virtually any person can name as a song with Latin resonance, the song 'Donna' was actually a bigger hit during its time. More important, from my perspective, is what 'Donna' illuminates. As one historian revealed, 'Donna' was a love song written by Ritchie Valens when he was forbidden from dating a White girl (Donna was her name) by her father, who disapproved of Ritchie for being 'Mexican.' In other words, songs like 'Donna' illuminate intercultural tensions and conflicts, while various other songs demonstrate inter-ethnic alliances and communication. To put it another way, songs and music, when read as discourse, can and should be understood as evidence of assimilation, acculturation, integration, marginalization, and resistance. Thus, as my research continued and one discovery led to another, I developed a sense that studying rock music's connections to Latino/as was a way of studying the complications and nuances of Latino/a identities, and vice versa.

Finally, such investigations convinced me that research about Latino/as and rock music was also the same as research about nations, nationality, and national identities. For example, as I studied Latin/o influences in US popular music, it was rather striking that Latino/as do not figure more prominently in mainstream narratives about national culture in the US. As I discovered how rock music had grown and developed in countries such as México and Argentina, I learned that rock music in other countries had more to do with the nation-state as rock music served official uses for inculcating youth with nationalist ideologies, and as youth challenged hegemonic national culture through rock music. Although different, this was another instance of how Latinos/Latin Americans 'rocked' the nation with their music. Ultimately, I discovered yet another way in which rock music by Latin Americans/Hispanics further rocked the nation by challenging simplistic notions of national identities and by disrupting prevalent notions of the primacy of nation-states, and this discovery influences the analysis toward the end (see

Chapter five and the Conclusion). In summary, there are many different ways that Latino/as, through rock music, have rocked the nation.

My title therefore, *Rock the Nation*, reflects a focus on nation-states and how a study of Latin/o rock music and Latino/a identity signifiers contributes to academic discussions and political conversations about what nations mean, and how we can better understand the constructions of nations and national culture(s) in popular culture. In this context, my emphasis on nations is based on my position that Latino/as can and should be considered part of American history, and that Latino/as deserve recognition for contributions and influences on mainstream American culture. Moreover, my emphasis on nations reflects the realization that Latino/as have always been a part of the disruptive force that challenges the Black/White racial binary that both challenges mainstream narratives about American history and what it means to be an American, and therefore represents an antiracist impulse. In other words, emphasizing nations in this study and challenging the primacy of nation-states is not intended as antinational, and if there is any sense that disrupting the primacy of the national is antinational, it should be recognized as a testament to the ways in which national cultures are often coupled with racialized discourses. Rather, the focus on nations in this book is more of an intentionally antiracist perspective, and, therefore, I hope that what I see as challenges to race and racism will be given attention throughout this investigation.

Roberto Avant-Mier, Ph.D.
El Paso-Juárez/Salt Lake City/Boston
c/s 'y que!'

Introduction

On Latinos/Hispanics in the United States: 'Latino/as,' the US Census, and Other Foundational Concepts

> ...the efficacy and social significance of mass media do not lie primarily in the industrial organization and the ideological content, but rather in the way the popular masses have appropriated the mass media and the way the masses have recognized their identity in the mass media.[1]

> Well I've never been to Spain, so don't call me a 'Hispanic.'[2]

In 2000, the United States Census determined that Latino/as (and/or Hispanics)[3] in the US now constitute its largest minority, accounting for at least 12.5 per cent of the total US population.[4] This news was significant in different ways, one being that Latino/as surpassed African Americans as the largest minority group in the US. Other important findings were that the Latino/Hispanic population had increased

---

1   Martín-Barbero, 'The Processes: From Nationalisms to Transnationals,' 346.
2   Lyrical excerpt from 'Never Been To Spain' by El Vez; For more on El Vez, see Habell-Pallán, 'El Vez Is "Taking Care of Business": The Inter/National Appeal of Chicano Popular Music,' and Saldívar, *Border Matters: Remapping American Cultural Studies*.
3   The 2000 Census uses the category of 'Spanish/Hispanic/Latino.' However, throughout this book I will employ the term 'Latino' to denote a more neutral identifier that approximates the Census category of 'Spanish/Hispanic/Latino' or perhaps, 'Latin American.' As such, my use of 'Latino' reflects a pan-American, pan-Latin view of culture, without regard for nationality. Further, following others, 'Latino/a' will be used here consistently, emphasizing the masculine and feminine forms together in order to 'avoid androcentric interpretation of the term'; see Johnson, *Speaking Culturally: Language Diversity in the United States*, 167. Thus, throughout the rest of this research the term 'Latino/a' will indicate people from various Latin American (Central American or South American) nations, although it is important to reiterate that I also use the term 'Latino/a' to indicate a person from the United States. In other words, I will employ the term 'Latino/a' irrespective of national citizenship. For more on the term 'Hispanic' and 'Hispanic peoples' see Johnson, *Speaking Culturally*. In 'The Mexican Diaspora,' Rinderle also provides an excellent literature review of the uses and origins of various labels such as 'Hispanic,' 'Latino,' 'Chicano,' 'Mexican American'; See Rinderle, 'The Mexican Diaspora: A Critical Examination of Signifiers.'
4   Census, *The United States Census 2000*; Guzmán, 'Census 2000 Brief: The Hispanic Population.'

by 57.9 per cent between 1990 and 2000 and that the Latino/Hispanic population now represents much of the total youth population (under 18) in the US.[5]

Worth noting for the 'Latino' umbrella category, the 2000 Census was the first to include the category 'Latino' as opposed to 'Spanish/Hispanic' of the previous Census. The salience of this fact is that it reflects a discursive shift in our national constructions of race and ethnicity. Of course, such discursive shifts have been a consistent part of the US Census for decades. Census categories prior to 1970, for example, did not even include 'Hispanic.' Moreover, the censuses of 1950 and 1960 considered only 'persons of a Spanish surname,' and the 1930 Census treated 'Mexican' as a racial category instead of the more specific national origin category that it is today.

Other issues surrounding the 2000 Census included the meanings of categories such as 'Spanish,' 'Hispanic,' and 'Latino'; these three markers are collapsed as a single category in the most recent Census (i.e., 'Spanish/Hispanic/Latino'). This is problematic in that within our national discursive constructions, 'Spanish' is supposed to mean the same as 'Hispanic' and/or 'Latino,' and yet people of these groups often differentiate them. A person who calls her/himself 'Spanish' often does so specifically because she/he dislikes other terms like 'Hispanic' and/or 'Latino.' Likewise, some people dislike the term 'Hispanic' either because it essentializes or because it is a word that exists only in US English, whereas others dislike the term 'Latino' for its essentializing nature or because it is a word more commonly used in Spanish. Further complicating this situation, some people eschew either 'Hispanic' or 'Latino' in favor of more specific identity signifiers and markers. For example, some would disagree with such terms, opting for more specific ethno-national markers such as 'Puerto Rican,' 'Cuban,' 'Nicaraguan American,' or perhaps 'Mexican American' (to name just a few). Still, others like myself might call ourselves 'Mexicans' (despite being US citizens, and for several generations), simply because it refers to one's ethnic heritage, to the cultural background of one's family, or more simply, to identifications which one learned to use in everyday life. Nonetheless, some prefer to call themselves 'Mexicans' or 'Mexican Americans' even though others in their own family refer to themselves as 'Chicano' (or 'Chicana').

Yet another consideration is that these identity markers shift and change their meanings. In one context, a 'Spanish' person might be defined literally as someone from Spain or with family ties to Spain. However, for a person living in a major city along the US East Coast, 'Spanish' more likely signifies a person with Caribbean origins — a Puerto Rican, Cuban, or Dominican. In the US Southwest, a 'Spanish' person does not mean either of the above, but a person born in, living, and residing in the US — most likely in New Mexico, Colorado, or Texas. Used synonymously with 'Hispano,' a 'Spanish' person in this context of signification prefers to be called Spanish in order to avoid being called a 'Mexican' or being associated with 'Mexicans' and/or 'Mexican Americans.' Through this identity marker, a person emphasizes identification with Spanish heritage and the legacy

---

5   Ibid.

of Spanish and European colonialism, differentiates from the stigma attached to 'Mexicans' (presumed to be immigrants or illegal aliens perhaps), and thereby suggests claims to ownership and belonging in the US. One implication of all of this is that in the wake of the increasing Latino/Hispanic presence in the US, identity politics have become quite complex; expressions of ethnic identity are becoming increasingly complicated.

Aside from the official data reported in the latest US Census, some scholars suggest that the real number of Latinos/Hispanics in the US is difficult to quantify given that Hispanics and Latino/as sometimes identify as 'White,' 'Black' or otherwise, probably in order to avoid the rigid (often binary) constructions of US identity categories. One scholar argues that legal migration for seasonal agricultural work has combined with illegal immigration to such an extent that most of the recent counts of Latino/as and Hispanics are impossible to determine,[6] and adds that most estimates of Hispanics in the US are likely to be conservative. The point here is that although actual numbers of Latino/as in the US are difficult to ascertain, there is no question that they are much higher than ever before. I propose that both the increasing presence of Latino/as in the US and the complications of Latino/a identity provide an impetus for research on Latino/a identity constructions.

Moreover, in the context of this proposal to study Latino/a identity, my research reveals that the complexity of Latino/a identity begins to move beyond ethnic identity and toward questions of race, race relations, racial tension, stereotyping, intercultural fear, assimilation, and resistance. Examples of the difficulty of Latino/a identity and its articulation to these larger social issues, for example, can be found in recent political controversies. With regard to the 2000 US elections, some scholars recall how candidates, popular media, and pundits have only superficially recognized and ultimately failed to engage 'what is possibly the most important minority community in contemporary history.'[7] Likewise, with the (in)famous 2003 California recall election, the complexity of Latino/a identity reared its head in questions of political blocs.

The 2003 recall election revealed some of these problems when candidates were presented with the question of how to appeal to Latino/a voters. Arnold Schwarzenegger was playing up his immigrant past, presumably to appeal to immigrant-friendly Latino/as in California, and meanwhile Lieutenant Governor (and supposed favorite with Latino/as) Cruz Bustamante, was questioned on his identity as a 'Chicano' and his affiliation with MEChA, a university student organization founded on *Chicanismo*.[8] While Cruz Bustamante might have gained

---

6   Portales, *Crowding Out Latinos: Mexican Americans in the Public Consciousness*.

7   Pineda, 'Book review of R. O. de la Garza and L. DeSipio, "*Muted Voices: Latinos and the 2000 Elections*,"' 52.

8   MEChA stands for *Movimiento Estudiantil Chicano de Aztlán*, 'The *Aztlán* Chicano Student Movement' or 'The Chicano Student Movement of *Aztlán*.' The organization's birth was closely related to the wider Chicano-movement activities of the late 1960s. MEChA was founded on the principles of justice, civil rights, cultural awareness and pride, and political activism for Mexican Americans and Mexican-origin people in the US, and has directly contributed to educational reforms in education such as the development of Chicano Studies programs and departments. It has also been criticized

points with Chicano/as and other Mexican Americans for refusing to renounce his membership in MEChA, he probably lost points with Hispanics or other Latino/as who associate Chicano/as with radical political ideologies or perhaps a lower social class. Given the results of the recall election, Bustamante apparently lost favor with Anglo-Americans, African Americans, and other minority groups in California as well. Likewise, although Bustamante might have gained points with Latino/as for being the grandson of immigrants, Schwarzenegger was himself an immigrant to the US.

However, what if being an immigrant didn't matter to voters in California? What does it matter that Latino/as didn't vote as a single, monolithic political bloc as was assumed (or hoped) by political scientists? Further, what is the value of being an assimilated Hispanic in the US? What does it mean, politically, to be a 'Chicano' in contemporary times? Moreover, given the currency of 'Latino' and 'Hispanic,'[9] is there really no difference between these latter signifiers? In other words what does it mean, politically, to say one is a 'Latino'? How does that compare to 'Chicano' as an identity signifier? These are some of the questions that motivate this intellectual project.

Further underscoring the significance of such questions, the complexity of Latino/a identity has surfaced recently in scholarly fora such as *Foreign Policy* where Harvard University professor and political scientist Samuel P. Huntington argued that Latino/as threaten to divide the United States. Framing the Latino/a identity issue through metaphors of war, Huntington employs discourse of 'invasion,' 'beach-heads,' 'entrenchment,' and 'turf wars' to make the claim that Latino/a peoples' refusal to assimilate is a *major threat* to life and culture in the US[10] (emphasis added). According to Huntington, in other words, signifiers like 'Latino' or 'Chicano' are dangerous because they signify an emphasis on cultural identity and a symbolic refusal to assimilate. Ideologues, such as Huntington, would obviously favor 'Hispanic,' which connotes assimilation to mainstream US culture and speaking English.[11]

Nonetheless, I argue that if Latino/as appear threatening to anybody because of the presumption that they will not, do not, or cannot assimilate to English and mainstream US culture, then it follows that Latino/a identity warrants further investigation. Given Huntington's ethnocentric statements and inflammatory discourse, and many others such as those voices in contemporary 'talk radio' programs, I propose that Latino/a identity is not properly understood and I take

by people who note its antiassimilationist views, ethnic nationalism, and radical political views. It continues today as a student organization in hundreds of colleges and universities throughout the US.

9   See Flores, 'Constructing Rhetorical Borders: Peons, Illegal Aliens, and Competing Narratives of Immigration'; Grieco and Cassidy, 'Census 2000 Brief: Overview of Race and Hispanic Origin'; Guzmán, 'Census 2000 Brief: The Hispanic Population.'

10   Huntington, 'The Hispanic Challenge.'

11   It is important to note that Huntington has been critiqued elsewhere. See, for example, Said, 'The Clash of Ignorance'; Capetillo-Ponce, 'From "A Clash of Civilizations" to "Internal Colonialism": Reactions to the Theoretical Bases of Samuel Huntington's "The Hispanic Challenge"'; and Loza, 'Assimilation, Reclamation, and Rejection of the Nation-State by Chicano Musicians.'

up the challenge to provide further understanding on the subject. In order to do this, I propose to study Latino/a identity as a discursive construction and mediated production. Moreover, thinking about the symbolic effects of Latino/a identity provides only a first line of thinking for this undertaking. Before pursuing it more deeply, I will suggest another important line of thinking for this book. Since the first focuses on the symbolic effects of Latino/a identity, the other focuses on the relation of Latino/a identity to material effects.

Through my preliminary research on popular rock music as it relates to Latino/as, I discovered that the problem of Latino/a identity(ies) goes beyond politics and that shifting discourses of identity within the Latino/a community pose problems in other social contexts. One such context is that of the problematic and inconsistent (and often inaccurate) categorizing and labeling related to popular music and music industry categories. In music stores, for example, retailers are faced with the question of where to place certain CDs. According to established marketing strategies, a rock music CD should be placed in sections such as 'rock' or 'rock/pop.'

However, in the late 1990s, during my first forays into researching Latin/o rock music (or *rock en español*, as one of its forms has been called), I searched various record stores in the United States seeking new music by popular Latin/o rock bands and artists. I discovered that the latest album by Café Tacuba, an internationally prominent rock/pop band, cannot be found under 'rock' or 'pop.' Although triggered by the fact that Café Tacuba had recently won a Latin Grammy in the 'Best Rock/Alternative Album' category, I learned that Café Tacuba was not included in the 'rock' section of the store. Oddly, the CD was available in the 'Latin' section, and, likewise with other contemporary Latin(o) rock bands, one will be more likely to find such music in the category of 'Latin' (if in stock at all). Apparently, Café Tacuba's Spanish lyrics and Mexican origins warrant its categorization as 'Latin' instead of rock, and, by extension, the very sounds of the music appear irrelevant — in spite of such music being called '*rock en español*' (literally, rock in Spanish)! Music scholar Deborah Pacini Hernández tells us more about this:

> When one goes to a music store like Tower Records, Chicano rockers such as Santana, Malo, and Los Lobos will be found in the rock section, even when they sing in Spanish, while *rock en español* artists will be in the Latin section. Even contemporary Chicano rockers Voodoo Glow Skulls' Spanish-language version of their CD *Firme* is stocked in the rock section.[12]

For some this might seem like an unproblematic distinction based on the use of Spanish-language lyrics, the record label, or even the respective national identity of these bands (i.e., Mexican Americans or Chicano/as in the 'rock' section and Mexicans/other Latin Americans in the 'Latin' section), but it is worth noting examples like Carlos Santana. Santana, for one, was actually born in México and migrated to the US as a teenager; he had considerable success with rock songs in

---

12   Pacini Hernández, 'A Tale of Two Cities: A Comparative Analysis of Los Angeles Chicano and Nuyorican Engagement with Rock and Roll,' 79.

Spanish (e.g., 'Oye Como Va'), and, perhaps, can even credit his lengthy career to such. Noting his prominence in the US rock scene of the late 1960s and early 1970s, Santana's music is often categorized in music histories as 'Latin rock,'[13] and yet still gets placed in the 'rock' section. Similarly confounding, Santana's Latin rock sound is often included on compilations for the best of Chicano rock. One recent *Billboard* magazine article further underscores the ambiguous placement of Latino/a recording artists and the problems it might pose for consumers, noting,

> Even retailers, who are acutely aware of cross-market appeal (that Latinos are big buyers of R&B music, for example), are limited in what they can do in stores beyond placing bin cards referring customers to alternative sections where they can find an album.[14]

In other words, in the logic of North American racial and ethnic categories, it is apparent that Latino/as continue to fall somewhere in between the dichotomous Black/White racial hierarchy that is so pervasive in US culture. Furthermore, the difficulty that Latino/a identities pose for the music industry extends beyond potentially confused customers. Such a situation grows more complicated when one considers Latino/a recording artists' complaints about record companies proposing to market them as 'Latin' acts. This occurs in spite of the fact that many second-, third-, or fourth-generation US Latino/a artists, often do not speak Spanish or have any affiliation with México or any other Latin American country. Other articles in *Billboard* indicate that for many of these Latino/as, their primary identity is simply American, and yet they struggle with being stereotyped as a Latin, Mexican, or Hispanic act. In another egregious example, Latino/a studio musicians are often paid less for the same work, depending on the degree of Latin-ness that is accorded to the music they are playing. As Pacini Hernández notes on this problem,

> Given the international orientation of the Latin music industry, however, bicultural, bilingual Latino musicians and fans will continue to be confused with their Latin American counterparts, and continue to find themselves located on the fault lines between the 'Latin' and mainstream markets — and the cultural assumptions associated with each of them.[15]

This problem is compounded when one considers that some US citizens do identify as Mexicans, Chicanos, or Latino/as, and consciously relate their identities to their music preference(s).

Within the music industry, yet another problem arises from the correlation of artists with music industry awards for which they are or are not eligible. For

---

13   Appell and Hemphill, *American Popular Music: A Multicultural History*; McCarthy and Sansoe, *Voices of Latin Rock: The People and Events that Created this Sound*.
14   Cobo, 'Latin Crossover's New Twist,' para. 31.
15   Pacini Hernández, 'The Name Game: Locating Latinas/os, Latins, and Latin Americans in the US Popular Music Landscape,' 57.

example, although American bands like Los Lobos are already multi-Grammy winners, I have never seen them nominated for a Latin Grammy Award. Although these latter examples relate to the artist/bands' national origins, it is important to note that similar identity complexity often exists on the side of consumers, which pushes the issue further beyond the relatively simple problem of buying recorded music. In other words, the complexity of Latino/a identity(ies) has larger implications. In other contexts, the complications of Latino/a identities can be extended to questions of stereotyping, ethnocentric assumptions, assimilation to mainstream US culture versus resistance to it, the value of bilingualism, problematic race relations, racialization and racism, intercultural conflict, transnationalism, and globalization. Ultimately, examples such as these demonstrate how Latino/a identity signifiers challenge contemporary social constructions of ethnicity and race in the US, and, specifically, how Latino/a identity signifiers challenge constructions of national identity(ies).

Moreover, the issues I am addressing are multifaceted. Identities are a problem for cultural outsiders like Samuel P. Huntington who perceive connections to how people are or are not assimilating, and to questions about how identity markers signify deeper political (and ideological) investments. Yet, the task is likely as daunting for a cultural insider. For example, the issue can grow quite complex when considering the range of signifiers between Latino/a groups within the US.

Delgado, for instance, discusses the complications of Latino/a identity politics between and among groups that are (stereo)typically seen as one essentializable Hispanic or Latino community by mainstream constructions in the US. As demonstrated in letters to the editor of *Lowrider* magazine, however, Delgado considers the expression of identity by Latino/as in the United States who identify as 'Raza,' 'Tex-Mex,' 'New Mex,' 'Mexicana/o,' 'Hispana,' 'Hispano,' 'Tejano,' and 'Aztec Chicano-Americana' in addition to 'Chicano,' 'Latina/o' and 'Hispanic.'[16] He concludes that communication scholars have only begun 'to explore the ways in which the local discourses of marginalized groups reflect these groups' experiences, identities, and perceptions of their environment.'[17]

Jensen and Hammerback taught us about the community of people in South Texas, as just one group of Latino/as in the US, who also encountered difficulty and have struggled with this issue at least since the 1800s. Over the years, people in the area have used 'Mexican,' 'Mexican American,' 'Spanish,' 'Spanish American,' 'Hispanic,' 'Hispano,' 'Chicano' and several other labels.[18] Other scholars shed additional light on this problem as well: Hispanics or Latino/as in South Texas often do not even use terms like 'Hispanic' and 'Latino' or even 'Mexican American' and 'Chicano,' but instead identify themselves and others as 'batos' (vatos), 'bolillos,' 'pochos,' 'pelados,' and 'mojados.'[19] Likewise, in far west Texas, there is an even

---

16 Delgado, 'When the Silenced Speak: The Textualization and Complications of Latina/o Identity,' 420.
17 Ibid., 420.
18 Jensen and Hammerback, 'Radical Nationalism among Chicanos: The Rhetoric of José Angel Gutiérrez.'
19 Richardson, *Batos, Bolillos, Pochos, and Pelados: Class and Culture on the South Texas Border*.

more confusing situation with 'immigrants,' 'nationals,' 'Juarenses,' 'Juareños,' 'Fronterizos,' 'Chilangos,' 'Mexicans,' 'Northern Mexicans,' 'Southern Mexicans,' 'Mexican Americans,' 'Americans,' 'Pochos,' and 'Chicanos.'[20] Although the constitution of each category could necessitate its own research entirely (in these cases, lines are drawn with regard to regional identity and local identities), it is safe to say that the problem of Latino/a identity in the US exposes many layers of complexity.

Nevertheless, the problem of trying to understand the nuances of Latino/a identity(ies) is not limited to Mexicans, borderlands, or the southwestern US. Even in unlikely places, like small bars in Northwest Ohio, Latino/as attending 'Latino Night' at the local bar find themselves in circumstances where the differences among 'Mexicans,' 'Puerto Ricans,' 'Spanish,' 'Hispanics,' 'Americans,' and 'Nicaraguans' are greater than the similarities. Often, these groups find commonality only in the Spanish language, and at times the language itself is not even enough to supplant the differences between them. As Willis-Rivera indicates, these differences in identities can be extended to differences in music listening and dancing preferences, as well as other discursive and non-discursive practices during such 'Latino Night' gatherings.[21]

The significance of these illustrations is that there are ongoing identity struggles significant enough for people to attend to, and, more importantly, that there is something at stake in these ongoing questions of culture and identity. I contend that these ongoing struggles loom larger in how they come to be articulated with ongoing power struggles and contemporary political relationships. One might reconsider, for example, Samuel Huntington's inflammatory argument that Latino/as pose a threat to US culture when they 'refuse to assimilate' to mainstream US culture (and English). As Huntington suggested, Latino/a identity signifiers that imply cultural retention rather than assimilation are a 'major threat' to US culture. Moreover, if the diversity and range of Latino/a identities pose difficulties in such political questions, then attempting to understand Latino/a identities is crucial. As one scholar recently noted about the need to better understand Latino/a identity,

> Such understanding is paramount not only if Latina/os are to engage the political system on even terms, but also if they are to feel a sense of legitimacy in this engagement... The often overlooked and often scapegoated Latina/o community deserves this attention.[22]

Following this perspective, I recognize that many current social issues, such as emerging political blocs and changing election strategies — this could also include marketing assumptions, popular culture and media representation, the state of the economy, globalization, and even terrorism — are related to Latino/as in complex ways. For political blocs, the important question is about whether Latino/as can

---

20 Vila, *Crossing Borders, Reinforcing Borders: Social Categories, Metaphors and Narrative Identities on the U.S.-Mexico Frontier.*
21 Willis-Rivera, '"Latino Night": Performances of Latino/a Culture in Northwest Ohio.'
22 Pineda, 'Book Review of R. O. de la Garza & L. DeSipio, *"Muted Voices: Latinos and the 2000 Elections,"* 54.

ever take advantage of the political potential of a unified 'Latino' minority group; for elections, the question is about how to appeal to Latino/a voters; for marketing, the question is also about appeal; for popular culture and media representation, questions arise about whether Latino/a actors can move beyond ethnic stereotypes and how industries will respond to a burgeoning segment of Latino/a consumers; with regard to the economy, debates rage about the necessity of cheap labor and a flow of immigrants for a healthy economy; for globalization, Latino/as symbolize (in different ways) the worldwide phenomenon of cultural flow, transculturation, and transnationalization; and for issues of terrorism, Latino/as feel scapegoated when confronted with reactionary policies that call for closing borders and constructing walls along borders in order to secure them. Importantly, these salient contemporary issues are often discursively linked to Latino/as. Therefore, it might also follow that the complexity of Latino/a identity politics points toward some of the most pertinent questions of our time.

Overview, Premise, and Theoretical Foundations

I take the position here that current forms of popular rock music can contribute to understanding the multilayered complexity of identity, signification, and communication. The aforementioned examples of Latino/a artists who get placed in different bins ('rock' vs. 'Latin') provide some interesting examples of the problems with genres, but also of the shifts by identity signifiers (another kind of genre) in media contexts. This research has its basis in the premise that the 'Latino' and 'Chicano' rock subgenres of popular music provide a valuable data set for analyzing the politics of identity that extend to ethnicity, language, border, nation, and politics. As Kohl observes, 'As an artistic and cultural form music can be a valuable tool for reading ideological intentions and the changing political and economic tenor of the times.'[23]

By articulating Latino/a identity questions to popular music research, I argue that in some contexts, Latin/o music, people, and culture have been central to the development of rock music, and if placing Latino/as at the center of rock music seems unusual, I contend that this is a result of North American racial logic that marginalizes Latino/as as outsiders, foreigners, and always exotic. Pushing the analysis further, I also argue that the Latin/o rock diaspora illuminates the role that rock music has played in the cultural development of other nations, and illustrates interesting paradoxes with regard to identity politics, especially with regard to nationalism. For example, in some contexts Latino/as have utilized rock music to mediate their assimilation into mainstream North American culture. In Latin America, rock music in Spanish has been used to resist English and the hegemony of mainstream US culture. Yet, in other contexts, singing in English and adopting US popular culture has allowed youth to resist the hegemonic nationalisms of their own countries (i.e., countering notions of US cultural imperialism). Thus, throughout the Americas, rock music demonstrates how Latino/as utilize music and popular culture for assimilation into mainstream national culture(s), for

---

23   Kohl, 'Reading Between the Lines: Music and Noise in Hegemony and Resistance,' 3.

resistance to the hegemony of dominant culture(s), and otherwise for mediating the negotiation of Latino/a identities. By linking rock from the US to rock music from Latin America, I ultimately conclude that the similarity of 'Latino/a' and 'Latin American' rock music is an example of how ethnic identity and subjectivity are not fixed, stable and essential, but, rather, a specific circumstance where ways of expressing cultural, political, linguistic, and ideological investments intersect in discourse in ways that further problematize contemporary constructions of fixed identity categories.

Put differently, my specific interest here is in the identity-related functions of popular music. Therefore, I do not intend to investigate the music itself, but rather the discourse(s) of identity in relation to popular music. My objects of study are songs, rhythms, instruments, lyrics, albums, album cover artwork, liner notes, live performances, interviews, newspaper articles, magazine articles, on-line articles, websites, academic articles, academic books, lectures and conference presentations, other studies on Latin/o rock music, life stories, literature, and any other discursive material that I have come across in several years of research. Overall, my methodology is genealogy, in the Foucauldian sense of 'genealogy.' Thus, this book represents my conscious effort to disrupt facile notions of 'rock' music and popular music history (based on outdated notions of Black and White people), as much as it signifies my effort to challenge mainstream histories by foregrounding the stories of the marginalized, under-acknowledged, and ignored — of which Latino/as represent one such group.

In other words, this is not a musicological study. Rather, it is an analysis of discourses of identity found in Latin/o rock music, and of the use of popular music in constructing Latino/a identities. Thus, instead of viewing music as the object of study, my object of study is cultural identity, and music is conceptualized as a discursive mode for expressions of identity, ethnicity, language, borders, and nations. Therefore, I am conceptualizing this book primarily as a study of identity and a study of the articulation of identity to popular music. My objective is to investigate how identity works for and against 'Latino/as,' 'Chicano/as,' and 'Hispanics' in contemporary popular culture. Specifically, my driving questions are: (1) What are the relationships between signifiers like 'Latin' and 'Chicano' as ethnic identity markers in relation to how they are articulated to popular music discourse? (2) How can popular music discourse (songs, rhythms, instruments, album covers, liner notes, etc.) contribute to an understanding of the ways in which identities are articulated? (3) How has the history of the uneven and complex development of different subgenres of rock music throughout the Americas contributed to cultural processes of assimilation and resistance? (4) How are those developments articulated with issues of language, culture, identity, and nationality? (5) How does Latino/a identity, as discursively constructed, constrain and enable the social, cultural, and/or political status of individuals and particular groups? And finally, (6) Are nation-states still the best way to organize popular music?

Media and the Construction of Nationalism(s)

For Latin America, the communication scholar at the forefront of the connection between media and Latin American nationalism has been Jesús Martín-Barbero. Martín-Barbero has shown specifically how mass media were used in forging connections between different races, classes, and political entities throughout Latin America. As he argues, '... the efficacy and social significance of mass media do not lie primarily in the industrial organization and the ideological content, but rather in the way the popular masses have appropriated the mass media and the way the masses have recognized their identity in the mass media.'[24] This use of media is what he explicitly calls the political function of the media.

In what Martín-Barbero calls 'the clearest and most identifiable expression of Latin American nationalism and mass, popular culture,' the national culture for México was created by Mexican cinema. In México, a long and bloody revolution had taken its toll between 1910 and 1921 and resulted in factions, and it could be argued that after the Mexican revolution it was film that formed the Mexican populace into a national body. What cinema did for México was bridge the gaps and mediate conflicts between the rural peasantry and the urban masses. Viewing films that featured heroic deaths of rebels, rich mystifications of *haciendas* and *rancheros*, chauvinistic attitudes, a revolutionary *machismo* (not at all unrelated), and other images that positioned revolutionaries as national heroes, Mexican cinema from the 1930s to the 1950s was able to bridge gaps between people and bring the masses together as a 'nation.' The gaps bridged, however, were ambiguous; people often saw themselves as moving upwards by gaining equal footing with another class or group of people. As Martín-Barbero notes about México, achieving equality and realizing nationality in that sense were, paradoxically, a way of getting back and revisiting previous revolutionary ideologies as well as their loyalties to revolutionary leaders and heroes.

In my opinion, what is even more remarkable in the context of Mexican cinema is its egregious use by directors and producers for propagandistic images of military heroes and leaders. The revolutionary general 'Pancho' Villa actually sold, to the (in)famous US filmmaker D. W. Griffith, the rights to film various revolutionary battles, in order to gain public support and change opinions of North American stakeholders and interest groups about who Pancho Villa 'really' was. As Tovares notes, 'Pancho Villa had an exclusive contract with Mutual Film. The money he earned from this deal was used to buy arms in the United States.'[25] In sum, cinema in México was used for the purposes of disseminating propagandistic narratives and in the case of Pancho Villa, the money from his exclusive movie deal was used to buy arms to further his 'national' cause.[26]

Radio was also used in the mediated production of Mexican nationalism, and

---

24   Martín-Barbero, 'The Processes: From Nationalisms to Transnationals,' 346.
25   Tovares, *Manufacturing the Gang: Mexican American Youth Gangs on Local Television News*, 43.
26   For more on the historical legacy of Mexican cinema and transnational capitalism, see Fein, 'Myths of Cultural Imperialism and Nationalism in the Golden Age of Mexican Cinema.'

Joy Hayes has examined the intersection of communication, popular culture, and nationalism in México. Hayes reveals not only how radio was used to advance political ideologies, but also how radio's history coincided with US interventionism and political interests in México.[27] Hayes' insight into the history of radio in México is significant insofar as it reveals both the use of radio in constructing Mexican nationalism as well as the dual positioning and paradoxical nature of radio and nationalism in México.

In Argentina, in addition to the emergence of the tango as a form of national culture and popular export, a form of nationalism was also created through radio and radio theatre. In ways similar to México, Martín-Barbero argues, 'The true importance of radio theatre in Argentina was its bridging role between the cultural traditions of the people and mass culture.'[28] With its own mystifications of *gauchos* as outlaws, themes of social protest and demands, the historical flavor in Argentine radio theatre provided popular archetypal characters to celebrate and heroes and heroines of the independence movement with whom to identify. The importance of this connection between radio and nationalism in Argentina cannot be overstated. As Martín-Barbero remarks, 'Before becoming Peronism, Argentine populism was a way of plugging mass culture into a wide family of existing expressions of popular culture. How significant it is that Evita became much more than just an actress through her role in a radio theatre company!'[29] Eva Duarte, of course, parlayed her popularity as an actress and eventually became Evita Perón, the wife of President Juan Perón. She became heavily involved in Argentine politics herself and was given the title of 'Spiritual Leader of the Nation' before her death in 1952, and became the stuff of legend.

Continuing the connection between media and nationalism in Latin America, Martín-Barbero identifies the function of the music, dance, and physical expression of Black peoples in Brazil that led to the acceptance of Blacks first on an economic level, then later to the crossing of other ideological barriers in order to be part of the national culture in Brazil. In yet another example, national identifications in Chile were made through the popular press. Political ideologies and alliances were not separate from identity and nationalism, and were fostered through newspapers functioning as political propaganda. The work of Martín-Barbero reveals the specific ways media in Latin America functioned as 'mediators between the state and the masses.'[30] More relevant for this study is the recognition that media play both ideological and political roles in social change and in the construction of nationalist sensibilities and identifications.

Revealing deeper connections, Eric Zolov extends the connection between mass media and nationalism. In *Refried Elvis*, Zolov analyzes the rise of rock 'n' roll music in México and documents the attempts by the Mexican government to co-opt rock 'n' roll music for furthering a nationalist agenda. As Zolov notes,

---

27 Hayes, *Radio Nation: Communication, Popular Culture, and Nationalism in Mexico, 1920–1950*.
28 Martín-Barbero, 'The Processes: From Nationalisms to Transnationals,' 348.
29 Ibid., 349.
30 Ibid., 352.

the Mexican government in the 1950s and 1960s saw rock 'n' roll music as a way to inculcate youth with Mexican nationalism.³¹ Artists were encouraged to sing in Spanish, to sing 'safe' love songs and to serve a nationalist hegemony. Consequently, forms of social protest included singing in English, singing political songs, or both. As a result, certain artists/bands were favored and even promoted by the Mexican government while others were censored, marginalized, harassed, physically beaten, and jailed. In Argentina, the articulation of rock music to politics takes on similar significance. Vila and others note that the history of rock music in Argentina is similarly colored with complex issues of individual identity, political associations, and class conflict that also resulted in censorship, harassment, jail, and even death.³² In other Latin American nations, as well, the history of rock music is one that often reveals political implications and, sometimes, dire consequences (speaking literally).

Furthermore, I include the United States here in a conversation about Latin America and nationalism, and I rely on existing research that articulates media to nationalism in the US. For example, Lawrence Grossberg et al. remind us that because of large numbers of immigrants during the late 1800s and early 1900s, communities throughout the US appeared ethnically divided, and politicians and other leaders understood that a popular culture was needed. So media were used to establish unity, assimilate immigrants, create a common popular culture, and unite an 'American' populace.³³ In other words, it is important to note that during the early decades of the twentieth century, US media were actively used to establish and promote a singularly 'American' national identity.

As with the other examples mentioned above, a case can be made for cinema as nationalist propaganda in the US. A prominent example is D. W. Griffith, whose legacy in US film history is remembered as brilliant and masterful. Yet some argue that Griffith's silent film *The Birth of a Nation* (1915) should really be seen for its racist representations and stereotypes of African Americans and for its sympathetic portrayal of the Ku Klux Klan. As Rhodes notes, 'In fact, *Birth of a Nation* was part of an era in which historians . . . reinforced the image of blacks as inferior, slavery as benevolent, and Reconstruction as a failure.'³⁴ In this context, the overwhelming popularity of *The Birth of a Nation*, and of D. W. Griffith himself, can be contextualized as a nod to a pre-Civil War idealized construction of Americanness and nationhood. Meanwhile, other examples of media and nationalism in the US are films like *Rocky* in the 1970s and *Rambo* in the 1980s and their resonances with the political tenor of the Reagan administration. Scholars connect US nationalism with the post-Vietnam era yearning for success in war and national pride, in conjunction with a post-Carter administration longing for masculine heroes and leaders like actor John Wayne — for which former actor Ronald Reagan made

31 Zolov, *Refried Elvis: The Rise of the Mexican Counter-Culture*.
32 Semán and Vila, 1992 [1987]. 'Rock Chabón: The Contemporary National Rock of Argentina'; Vila, '*Rock Nacional* and Dictatorship in Argentina.'
33 Grossberg et al., *Mediamaking: Mass Media in Popular Culture*.
34 Rhodes, 'The Visibility of Race in Media History,' 37–8.

a great comparison.³⁵ What is significant about these examples of cinema in the US is how media and popular culture have been instrumental in constructing, reconstructing, or reinforcing ideologies of 'the nation.'

Returning to the conversation about popular music as a form of mass media and public discourse, comparisons can be made between US cinema and popular music. In *Audiotopia* Josh Kun reminds us of some of the earliest articulations of music to ideological notions of a unified nation-state. Kun discovers that one of the earliest examples is Walt Whitman, whose 1860 poem 'I Hear America Singing' (from *Leaves of Grass*) stands as a lasting sentiment about music and the nation-state. As Kun observes about Whitman, 'He believed that it was music that was loved and shared by all Americans; it was music that could bring the nation together.'³⁶ Beginning with Walt Whitman in 1860, the nation is a sounded terrain and a musical construction, and the notion of 'America' depends on patriots whose 'Americanness' is defined through the singing of patriotic songs. Political and cultural citizenship for others requires the reception of and listening to such songs; 'the poem posits a direct relationship between musical performance and the formation of a national identity.'³⁷

Kun further demonstrates how Whitman's poem ushered in an era of debate about US nationalism and the changing character of the nation in which music became the principal metaphor for different perspectives within the debate. The debate stretched from the nineteenth into the twentieth century, and what followed Whitman's poem was a 'virtual obsession' by writers and intellectuals with defining the ethno-racial character of 'America' and the continual use of music and musical metaphors to make claims, cases and arguments for what the nation was and should be.³⁸ There were plays by Israel Zangwill as early as 1908 that introduced the metaphor of the US as a 'melting pot,' a reaction to a spike in the US foreign-born population from 1901–1920. Within a year, Rabbi Judah Magnes rejected the idea of the melting pot and continued Whitman's debate. Later Horace Kallen introduced the notion of 'cultural pluralism' in a 1915 article that compared the American 'symphony' to the American 'orchestra.' Not long after, John Dewey responded to Kallen's article, both agreeing and disagreeing with it.³⁹ Kun further notes that by 1915, D. W. Griffith had produced *The Birth of a Nation* and pseudo-scientific books about the human 'races' appeared as best-sellers, and how Waldo Frank's notion of 'the symphonic nation' in 1924 and his 1929 response to Kallen further fueled the political discussion of music and nationalism, altogether continuing the discourse about race and ethnicity in 'America.'

Some writers and intellectuals took the position that assimilation of ethnic groups into a monolithic 'American' culture was the ultimate goal, and of course, assimilation to 'American' culture meant total assimilation to Anglo-Saxon culture and speaking English. Meanwhile, some in this debate questioned whether

---

35 See, for example, Jeffords, *Hard Bodies: Hollywood Masculinity in the Reagan Era*.
36 Kun, *Audiotopia: Music, Race and America*, 31.
37 Ibid., 30.
38 Ibid., 41.
39 Ibid., 41–3.

complete assimilation was possible, and others questioned whether it was even desirable. Few took the position that assimilation could happen in other ways.

Other scholars note how the 1927 film, *The Jazz Singer* (the first motion picture with sound) featured Al Jolson performing in blackface, tapping into the tradition of minstrelsy:

> For many white Americans at the time, minstrelsy music was linked to a sense of patriotism, and its popularity reflected an attempt to fashion a new American identity that rejected the sentimentality of British parlor songs. [...] a shared feeling of superiority to blacks was one of the few things that unified a nation of immigrants, many of them more recent arrivals than the African Americans they mocked.[40]

Kun explains that by the 1930s, the (White) bandleader Paul Whiteman starred in the play *King of Jazz* and further promoted metaphors of US melting pots and symphonies.[41]

According to Kun, the long-standing debate that articulated music to the nation's character reached its zenith just a few decades later with the 1964 LP record, *America, I Hear You Singing*, an album that featured Frank Sinatra, Bing Crosby, and Fred Waring, and which celebrated US history and the ideas upon which the country was founded. The album's producer commented, '... the album [is part of] a tradition of using music as "propaganda" in order to "stimulate a strong nationalistic spirit among our citizens."'[42] Kun notes further how Walt Whitman's debate resurfaced with the 1975 release of *I Hear America Singing*, an overtly patriotic album about the US that included various popular songs as well as 'The Star-Spangled Banner' and even included a picture of Walt Whitman in the accompanying booklet, and he concludes that the debate could possibly include the 1999 release of 'Sing America,' a benefit CD compilation for the preservation of the symbols of American heritage and culture.[43] I would add that the debate could be extended to more recent examples such as the nationalistic resonance within debates about music by contemporary country music stars Toby Keith and the Dixie Chicks, as well as the CD release of 'The Star-Spangled Banner' in Spanish and its ensuing debates in 2006.

Of course, as Kun astutely observes, Walt Whitman's famous poem and the ensuing timbre of nationalist discourse that followed did not seek to include Frederick Douglass, who himself had written about music and the national character of the US around the same time as Whitman. Nor did it include Duke Ellington and other African American musicians who were taking jazz to unprecedented heights and worldwide popularity. Nor did it include Native Americans and their music, or any 'Tejanos,' Mexican Americans and other US Latino/as whose music and culture preceded the westward expansion of the US. Nor did it include the

---

40   Appell and Hemphill, *American Popular Music*, 37.
41   Kun, *Audiotopia*, 45.
42   Ibid., 34–5.
43   Ibid., 31.

many Cuban, Puerto Rican, French/French Antillean Creole, or Spanish musical influences that were well established in the US prior to 1850. Nor did the musical debate on nationalism include the Rev. Dr. Martin Luther King Jr., or, for that matter, Little Richard, Ray Charles, Fats Domino, or James Brown. It is not a coincidence, in other words, that Whitman's musings on music and the nation were repeatedly adapted to fit corresponding political turmoil with regard to various cultural shifts and changing ethno-racial relations. As Kun observes about the 1964 LP, *America, I Hear You Singing*, that pictured Sinatra, Crosby, and Waring on its cover, in the midst of much civil rights turmoil in the US,

> [It] put their three smiling white faces on its cover next to the American flag and above a map of the United States, calling them the 'most representative Americans in the entertainment world,' and 'Right before our ears, listening has become a method of enacting Americanness, a mode of cultural citizenship.'[44]

These articulations of music with the nation-state and ethno-racial relations provide a rich background for my current questions on music and nationalism. As Kun warns, it is important to note the preeminence of White, European Americans in such mediated productions. The corresponding absence of African Americans is probably more telling of how public discourses frame US nationalism; nationality is often discursively constructed through race. Furthermore, these articulations of music with nationality contextualize US nationalism, but they do not actually address the place of Latino/as in the US.

In *Audiotopia*, Kun emerges as an important scholar with regard to the absence of Latino/a groups in the conversation of US nationalism. As he suggests about *rock en español* and other articulations of Latino/as with rock music, Walt Whitman's treatments of US nationalism through music could not possibly comprehend such music. He writes, 'The identities the music both produces and is produced by, and the national spaces it both inhabits and travels across, together refuse conventional, bounded mappings of the nation.'[45] Following Kun, I contend that the absence of Latino/a groups in such conversations is just as salient in terms of how it reveals symbolic formulations about the place of Latino/as within the US nation-state. Likewise, I submit that the conversation about rock music and Latino/a identity that follows in this book contributes to an understanding of how media are implicated in ideological constructions of nationalism, and how rock music continues to parallel cultural, social, and political changes.

The notion that rock 'n' roll music could have political, social, and cultural ramifications is a mere footnote in US history; long gone are the days when any form of rock music had any serious impact or political efficacy in North America. Yet, for Latin Americans in the examples above, the articulation of rock music to identity politics takes on greater significance that continues into the present. Rock music continues to have an impact on Latino/as, and in various Latin American

---

44   Ibid., 34–6.
45   Ibid., 185–6.

nations as well as in the context of rock music by Latino/as within the US, rock music continues to have significant implications for Latino/a identity. Those implications are not only about the character of nations, but also about assimilation to dominant cultures versus cultural retention, about complex issues of linguistic nationalism and linguistic colonialism, and about new spaces for interrogating culture and identity.

Identity and Border Theory

As Delgado tells us about studying Latino/a identity from a communication perspective, 'The goal is to re-center an alternative set of realities, experiences, and identities: to see and represent from the perspective of the Other.'[46] Following this call, this book re-centers Latino/as in US culture. By placing Latino/a identity at the center of US popular culture, a more comprehensive and nuanced study of rock music can engage the identity politics of language, ethnicity, and nationality. A goal of this book is to better understand the tensions involved in cultural and linguistic assimilation and resistance as they pertain to citizen and immigrant populations in the US. Therefore, this book places borders — literal and figurative zones of contact, hybridity, and mixture — at the center of the discussion rather than at the margins. Instead of viewing a 'pure' culture at the center and hybrid cultures at the margins, this book assumes hybridity as the norm and cultural purity or isolation as the marginal, if such a notion even exists at all. The significance of this perspective is best explained through the 'border studies paradigm.'

Within a border studies paradigm, cultures can and should be analyzed in the context of their similarities as much as their differences.[47] Further, just as important as the critical differences between cultures are the critical sites of commonalities. The idea that Western theories put Western culture(s) at the center, and that other ideas of marginalized, minority, and/or disenfranchised groups are situated at the periphery can be questioned. In the border studies paradigm, the center becomes the margin and the margin becomes the center. Yet, noting problems with such a straightforward reversal, the significance of the border studies paradigm might lie in how it decenters culture, rather than how it reverses margin/periphery. The decentering is one that implies that people living on the border (literally and figuratively), people who live in the in-between spaces of culture(s), and people who are more accurately identified by intersectional aspects of their gendered, sexed, raced, and classed identities better define the critical points of inquiry on which scholarship should turn. As recent trends in US culture have shown, it may no longer be possible to speak of cultures as pure, isolated, or in any way unaffected by the aesthetics of various cultural groups. People and culture(s) currently at the center are problematized rather than remaining fixed (essentialized) constructions of identity, identification, and cultural practice.

The pachuco/cholo/chicano/mexicano/hybrid/mestizo/mixteco/border jumper/performance artist Guillermo Gómez-Peña notes:

---

46   Delgado, 'When the Silenced Speak,' 420.
47   Singh and Schmidt, 'On the Borders Between U.S. Studies and Postcolonial Theory.'

Artists are talking about the need to create a structure parallel to NAFTA — a kind of Free Art Agreement — for the exchange of ideas and noncommercial artwork, not just consumer goods and hollow dreams. If formed, the task of this network of thinkers, artists, and arts organizations from Mexico, the United States, and Canada (and why not the Caribbean?) would be to develop models of cross-cultural dialogue and interdisciplinary artistic collaboration. Through multilingual publications, radio, film, video, and performance collaborations, more complex and mutable notions of 'North American' cultures and identities could be conceived.[48]

Gómez-Peña's call to develop more complex models of culture(s) and identities that are more pertinent to the times can certainly be reconciled with the border studies paradigm. Similarly, other notions of 'diaspora' as articulated by other critical scholars,[49] the idea of a 'Greater México,' the state of 'liminality' and the extended '*frontera*,'[50] and the idea of a postcolonial, pan-American consciousness are also relevant.

In *The Dialectics of Our America*, for example, Saldívar reframes the notion of an 'America' and attempts to redirect hegemonic Eurocentric notions of nationality and consciousness with a postcolonial, pan-American consciousness. Central to Saldívar's thesis are the suggestions of transgeography, postcolonialism, polyvocality, hybridity, pan-ethnicity, transnationalism, and cross-culture within and between 'Hispanics' and other 'Latina/os' in the western hemisphere.[51] In similar fashion, Limón alludes to a 'Greater México' that points to the commonalities as well as the differences between people on both sides of the border.[52]

Latino/as and Diaspora

Given the complex realities of global and transnational cultures, it is important to question Western theoretical assumptions in order to generate new theoretical lines of inquiry that are more responsive to the times. I therefore proceed here with a brief note about my rationale for diaspora, or a diasporic view of Latino/a culture. To make a brief note of my operational conception of 'diaspora,' a *diaspora* simply involves the scattering of people far from their homeland. It is known that when people migrate, their relationship to their places of origin does not necessarily end; people remain connected to their homelands, often transmitting cultural and economic resources back and forth. Gilroy's notion of the Black diaspora is illuminating as it indicates how people of African origin, scattered throughout the Americas and around the Atlantic ocean, took with them their musical traditions, and contributed to developments in music in their new locales — the result being that diasporas speak to points of commonality for the various national,

---

48   Gómez-Peña, *The New World Border: Prophecies, Poems & Loqueras for the End of the Century*, 9.
49   Clifford and Marcus. *Writing Culture: The Poetics and Politics of Ethnography*; Gilroy, *The Black Atlantic: Modernity and Double-Consciousness*.
50   Saldívar, *Border Matters: Remapping American Cultural Studies*.
51   Saldívar, *The Dialectics of Our America: Genealogy, Cultural Critique, and Literary History*.
52   See Limón, *American Encounters: Greater Mexico, the United States, and the Erotics of Culture*.

regional, and cultural groups that they would otherwise make up. In other words, 'Black diaspora' serves as a container for the musical traditions and tendencies that many Africans shared and took with them around the world. Music, in this light, emerges as one of the most significant types of media that are used for communication by peoples as they are dispersed and travel throughout the world, either through the contexts of slavery, colonialism, capitalism, immigration, transnationalism, or globalization.

With regard to my view of a 'Latin diaspora,' or a 'Latin rock diaspora,' I focus on how the study of music as cultural practice (and music as discursive practice) can be expanded to include the capacity of music to create space, re-create place, and to remap certain cultural spaces, as well as to reconstruct, preserve, and maintain identities. More specifically, I attempt to illuminate the continuities and commonalities between and among Latino/as around the world in order to make sense of how (US) 'Latino/as' and other 'Latin Americans' can be understood in contemporary cultural geographies. In doing so, I introduce some tenets that inform my conception of *diaspora*.

First, it is important to note to recognize the value of popular music for diasporic analysis; popular music and its production is often deeply rooted in a diasporic past and often an intercultural present, a fact that highlights the hybridity of music as well as its potentially disruptive capacities. Second, to focus on *diaspora* here is to focus on reciprocal interactions between people, intertwining influences, and intercultural communication. Third, to speak of *diaspora* is to switch to a discursive mode that focuses on the transnational perspective on culture, politics, history, etc.; *diaspora* moves beyond the nation-state as the primary unit of analysis, foregrounding globalization, transnationalism, im/migration, and the movement of people and culture. Fourth, I am compelled to mention what I wish would be an obvious caveat — that *diaspora* must still be contextualized through gender, class, ethnicity, sexual orientation, etc., and I do, in fact, include some contextualizations in this research endeavor.[53] Finally, I wish to add another caveat — that analyzing culture through a diasporic lens (i.e., my use of 'Latin/o' to signify Latin Americans and US Latino/as) is to combat the flattening out for the sake of the complex. I am proposing a diasporic view of Latin/o culture(s), which is in itself a simplification and essentialism, all in order to combat the persistent and prevalent Black/White dichotomy in popular music research as well as in other areas of study. As Valdivia notes, 'too often when ... scholars think about or approach issues of race and ethnicity, they still think in binary terms of black and white. Latino/as fall out of the picture.'[54] In other words, my view of the Latin diaspora in rock music can be considered a strategic essentialism, or a research heuristic, that serves the purpose of permitting an alteration in research, and, as

---

53 Much of this work is beyond the scope of this chapter due to constraints on length, although I have taken up these requisite contextualizations in other work; See Avant-Mier, 'Of Rocks and Nations: A Critical Study of Latino/a Identity through Latino/a Rock Discourse.'

54 Valdivia, 'Is My Butt Your Island? The Myth of Discovery and Contemporary Latina/o Communication Studies,' 4.

Valdivia notes, has the potential to unsettle established areas of research but also signifies the promise to create new ones.[55]

The implications of this research, I propose, go beyond contributing knowledge about Latin/o rock diaspora music, and such analyses can contribute to the growing body of work in Latino/a communication studies, cultural studies, ethnic studies, Latino studies, and Latin American studies. As Valdivia argues, 'Expanding the geographic reach of the Latina/o diaspora serves to strengthen the field and make more connections to overlapping areas of study.'[56]

Music as Communication

As I will demonstrate, recorded music is a medium for mass communication, a mode of public discourse, and can be used as an instrument for nationalist ideology. As one anthropologist argues about media, 'One enduring concern is the "power" of mass media, and in particular their roles as vehicles of culture.'[57] Following this perspective and others, however, I am not interested in a view of this vehicle of mass communication as directly causal or as one that goes unidirectionally from a sender to a receiver. My interest is in pursuing questions that can be addressed in a similar fashion to James Carey's approach. One of the field's greatest scholars, Carey argued that scholars of communication can now view the process of communication from a different perspective, one that no longer focuses on an oversimplified, linear model of transmission. Carey argued that the 'transmission view' of communication was relevant when communication was viewed in geographic, place-to-place terms. Yet, according to Carey, a 'ritual view' of communication 'is directed not toward the extension of messages in space but toward the maintenance of society in time; not the act of imparting information but the representation of shared beliefs.'[58] Carey noted,

> If the archetypal case of communication under a transmission view is the extension of messages across geography for the purpose of control, the archetypal case under a ritual view is the sacred ceremony that draws persons together in fellowship and commonality.[59]

Carey's view of communication, therefore, lends itself to analyses and questions that complement border studies and diaspora. As Carey posited, 'Communication is a symbolic process whereby reality is produced, maintained, repaired, and transformed.'[60] Such a view also squares itself with Stuart Hall's work on identity, and cultural studies more broadly. The strength of this approach to understanding identity and nationalism in contemporary discourse(s) is the ability to use media history in conjunction with the legacies of Latin/o rock to investigate both the

---

55 Ibid., 11.
56 Ibid., 9.
57 Spitulnik, 'Anthropology and Mass Media,' 294.
58 Carey, 'A Cultural Approach to Communication,' 240.
59 Ibid., 241.
60 Ibid., 243.

politics of identity and the construction of nationalisms and identities through their contemporary discursive formations.

Furthermore, as I approach a deeper evaluation of various Latin(o) rock music trends, a more sustained discussion at this point requires moving beyond the notion of recorded popular music as communication, but more specifically as discourse. In other words, can recorded music or popular songs be regarded as discourse? To answer this question, it is necessary theoretically to frame mass-mediated processes such as the dissemination of popular music as an element of a larger cultural dialogue.

In *Speaking into the Air*, for example, Peters posits a perspective on communication whereby a move from interpersonal dialogue to mass-dissemination is not unbridgeable. As Peters argues, dissemination can surely become dialogue in the sense that dissemination can be viewed as a kind of 'suspended dialogue,' suspended in time.[61] In other words, disseminated seeds of (mass-) communication are relevant in that they can take root and later lead to dialogic processes. Discourses can be transmitted and disseminated in ways that have effects many years after their first articulations, and in different places. Likewise, George Lipsitz has probably been the foremost scholar in applying the concept of dialogue to popular music, and he adds that popular music is 'the product of an ongoing historical conversation in which no one has the first or last word.'[62]

Continuing this idea of popular music as a dialogic space, another useful concept in popular music research comes from Cooper and Haney. In their analysis, the 'answer song' emerges as relevant for a discussion of cultural dialogue involving popular music. They argue that, 'Answer songs are tunes that respond to direct questions or continue specific themes, ideas, or melody patterns from earlier songs,' and also note,

> [Answer songs] invariably provide contrasting positions — personal and political — to previously stated viewpoints; they offer interesting, sometimes unexpected story-continuing options; and they often translate common phrases, domestic problems, or personal concerns into a popular cultural contest.[63]

Within this line of thinking, an important point to make is that answer songs and responses, contests, and concerns in popular music and other public 'dialogues' are examples of discourse(s). Thus, 'answer songs' and 'popular music as cultural dialogue' are at the base of the following examination of the Latin/o rock diaspora. Finally, I follow Alvarez in viewing Latino/a youth culture as 'an arena of inter-ethnic relationships,'[64] and therefore pay special attention to instances of intercultural dialogue and communication throughout this study.

---

61   Peters, *Speaking into the Air: A History of the Idea of Communication*, 62.
62   Lipsitz, *Time Passages: Collective Memory and American Popular Culture*.
63   Cooper and Haney, *Rock Music in American Popular Culture II: More Rock 'n' Roll Resources*, 13.
64   Alvarez, 'From Zoot Suits to Hip Hop: Towards a Relational Chicana/o Studies,' 55.

On Defining 'Rock' Music

If the sliding signifiers of identity are difficult to engage, I also recognize that the term 'rock' music is itself an equally difficult term given its tendency to exemplify discursive slippage. Like 'Latino/a' identity markers and signifiers, the term 'rock' music is itself problematic, fragmented, loaded with incongruities, and requires further explication in terms of how it will be used throughout this book. Nevertheless, since I propose to study Latin and Latino/a 'rock' music in this study, an important question to consider is what separates rock music from a broader definition of pop music, or other genres? Given its tendency to be subsumed by popular culture, by the mainstream and by capitalist culture industries, how is a 'rock' band different from pop group or bands in any other genres in popular music? What are the markers that signal which musician, artist or performer can be considered part of rock music's canon? How can it be defined? How will I use it in this research?

In order to engage 'rock' as a critical term for this study, I am aware of other literature that defines rock music through its electrified guitar instrumentation.[65] As one scholar notes,

> The key symbol of rock 'n' roll from the very outset was the electric guitar. The guitar reflected its folk roots in Southern blues and country music; the electric amplification reflected its power, vitality, and youthfulness [...] It took something like rock 'n' roll, unencumbered by tradition and too youthful to care much for the rules, to exploit the new possibilities of electrical sound.[66]

Similarly, other scholars argue that the guitar has been the 'main expressive vehicle of rock music.'[67] Interestingly, another scholar focuses on the symbolism of the electric guitar for rock music, although others define rock by its rhythm section composed of bass and drums.[68]

For this project, however, I am not necessarily interested in determining a fixed musicological definition of rock music. As one prominent music and communication scholar argues,

> ... rock itself has a history which cannot be reduced to the history of its sonic register. Although an account of rock cannot ignore its musical effectivity, it is also the case that rock cannot be defined in musical terms. There are, for all practical purposes, no musical limits on what can or cannot be rock ... Its musical limits

---

[65] For example, see Albrecht, *Mediating the Muse*; Bannister, '"Loaded": Indie Guitar Rock, Canonism and White Masculinities'; Perrone, 'Changing of the Guard: Questions and Contrasts of Brazilian Rock Phenomena.'
[66] Albrecht, *Mediating the Muse*, 159–60.
[67] Corona and Madrid, 'Introduction: The Postnational Turn in Music Scholarship and Music Marketing,' *Postnational Musical Identities*, 13.
[68] Avelar, 'Defeated Rallies, Mournful Anthems, and the Origins of Brazilian Heavy Metal.'

are defined, for particular audiences at particular times and places, by the alliances constructed between selected sounds, images, practices and fans.[69]

Noting this, I do not profess to be conducting a musicological investigation. Rather, what I am interested in is the ideological role that music plays in the construction of linguistic, regional, ethnic, political, and national identities. Thus, I will move away from seeking a precise musicological definition, toward a more fluid definition of rock that parallels the cultural circumstances that I am investigating in this research project — emphasizing the heuristic value of signifiers for this research.

Likewise, I am mindful of previous scholarship on rock and other international music currents in México, and especially how 'rock' is defined. Stigberg, for example, employs phrases such as 'rock-derived ensembles with electric guitars' and 'a rock-derived rhythm section' to reflect on the amalgamation of rock 'n' roll music with *balada*, *balada romántica*, and *cumbia* in México.[70] I borrow this working definition, 'rock-derived,' in response to how, within a single composition with many layers, it would be impossible to differentiate diverse musical styles from one another. Employing 'rock-derived' reflects a view that a song or composition can be called 'rock' because of how it borrows from and builds upon previous music in the tradition of rock, which is to say that singular compositions by pop artists do not qualify as rock music. As Stigberg argues, the definition of a style can be understood 'in terms of its continuity with the past' and how it 'extends' the tradition.[71] This notion is not only useful for defining rock, but in fact serves the following chapters heuristically, allowing me to focus this study on Latino/a identity within a single genre of popular music. Defining rock music as derivative of various styles is another crucial point to make in forging a definition of 'rock' music. Nonetheless, as much as I would like to rely on a concept like 'rock-derived,' it is worth remembering Stigberg, who notes that in rock music, 'linkages between musicians and styles across traditional boundaries are easily made and severed.'[72]

Related to this fact, there is another issue that complicates such an attempt to arrive at a clear definition of 'rock' music. As one *Newsweek* article noted, the conversation about Latin/o rock is not just about rock 'n' roll music, '. . . but all the different strains that feed into and spin off from it, from reggae and ska to hiphop and hard core.'[73] This is to say that a precise definition of rock is virtually impossible because of historical evidence that it does not confine itself to any one particular sound or style. As this article further noted, 'rock music' can probably best be defined in terms of a point on a map with various intersections that

---

69 Grossberg, *We Gotta Get Out of This Place: Popular Conservatism and Postmodern Culture*, 131.
70 Stigberg, 'Foreign Currents during the 60s and 70s in Mexican Popular Music: Rock and Roll, the Romantic Ballad and the Cumbia,' 176.
71 Ibid., 176.
72 Ibid., 177.
73 Hayden and Schoemer, 'Se Habla Rock and Roll? You Will Soon: A Musical Invasion from South of the Border,' 70.

collectively form some kind of nexus and the appearance of a location that could be called rock music, without preoccupation with fixed definitions. The divergent streams that make up the intersections are African and African American musics like blues and R&B, Anglo-European styles like Appalachian ('hillbilly') folk musics, western swing, and country and western, and the marriage of those to various Latino/a influences (which have been undervalued and hardly acknowledged in mainstream rock histories) that all came to be known as 'rock 'n' roll.'[74] Heavy metal, punk, rockabilly, folk rock, progressive rock, and southern rock all, in one way or another, have some connection in their origins in 'rock 'n' roll' music. This point, of course, leads the discussion of defining rock to the point of recognizing its hybridity and acknowledging the reality that 'rock' is at once a combination of all of these, some of these, a few of these, or at times, just one of these styles.

As Grossberg asserts, however, 'rock is perhaps the only musical culture in which the identity of its audience (perhaps even more than that of its producers) bleeds into the music.'[75] Perhaps then, another way to define rock is through its historical associations with rebellion and counter-culture. With regard to the *rock en español* movement, one article observes that it is 'packed with the same kind of musical irreverence, sonic anarchy, and establishment-baiting ingredients that has characterized rock in rawest form since its birth more than 40 years ago.'[76] This definition is true of rock music from the shocking reality of White youth listening to Black music and Elvis Presley's hip gyrations that created so much public controversy in the 1950s, to ideas of free love and an emphasis on using drugs for experimentation in the 1960s, to the rise of punk and heavy metal in the 1970s, to the Parents Music Resource Center who focused their attention on rock music for offensive lyrics during the 1980s, to the accusations in the late 1990s that Colorado's Columbine High School shootings happened because the two perpetrators were listening to the music of Marilyn Manson, to whatever present cultural shifts and musical events will be remembered in the future as transgression and counter-culture. All of these are but a few of the many examples where rock music has defined itself by its marginalization with respect to dominant or mainstream cultural ideals. This aspect of rock music's legacy can be related to its origins in lower-class and/or working-class communities,[77] and surely the working-class face of rock music is itself another way to arrive at a working definition of rock.

Rather than defining rock music, however, Grossberg analyzes the concept of 'rock cultures,' which refers to articulations or alliances of rock with cultural practice (e.g., images of performers and fans, economic relations, aesthetic conventions, styles of language, appearances, media representations, and ideological commitments).[78] As Grossberg observes, however, 'Rock cannot be identified with any single alliance, for such an identification would merely normalize one

---

74   'Rock 'n' roll' is also known as 'rock 'n' roll,' 'rock 'n roll,' 'rock and roll,' or 'rock & roll.'
75   Grossberg, *We Gotta Get Out of This Place*, 133.
76   Holston, '*Rock en Español*: A Youth Market Comes of Age, but Record Executives Turn a Blind Eye,' 46.
77   Lipsitz, *Time Passages*; Lipsitz, *Rainbow at Midnight*.
78   Grossberg, *We Gotta Get Out Of This Place*.

alliance as the "proper" definition of rock.'[79] Furthermore, another key concept is the idea of 'rock formations,' referring to significant colonized spaces related to daily life (e.g., television, film, advertising, etc.) in contemporary society to which rock music is articulated.[80]

Moreover, it is worth noting that the focus of this study, rock's connection(s) to Latino/as, reveals that the Latin/o rock diaspora also recognizes connotations of rock as rebellion, the articulation of rock to working-class sensibilities, Latin/o 'rock cultures,' and Latin/o 'rock formations.' It is therefore apropos for this project that a definition of rock music might be related to its legacy and to its history in rebellion antiestablishment politics, socio-economic (working class) origins and politics, and various Latino/a cultural practices. In my view, these historical and contextual factors are instrumental in getting at the question of how to define 'rock' music, rather than relying on fixed musicological definitions.

In sum, what I wish to suggest is that I am not necessarily interested in arriving at a fixed definition of rock music, and I have to question whether one is at all possible. Noting the similarity of the rock conversation to this larger project of investigating identity, I specifically employ the term 'rock music' as a heuristic that allows me to conduct my analysis of Latin/o rock music. My use of the term 'rock music' in this research is based on a broad notion of 'rock' that encompasses many styles, and acknowledges various significations related to it.

Perhaps there is something about rock music that allows its significations to float freely among various marginal groups, their individual members and their cultural practices. It defies precise classification because each marginal group defines and inhabits its own variation of a 'rock nation' out of a common pattern of sound, rhythm, and storytelling. Frequently, rock music celebrates marginality itself even as it is constantly being subsumed into the cultural mainstream, and rock music renews itself with a continuous search for marginal status. As such, it is almost a parody of the politics of identity; one's signifiers are loaded with connotations that are problematic for another. Nevertheless, defining 'Chicano' and/or 'Latino' rock might be possible, but perhaps this is an act of appropriation that misses rock music's essential dynamics of defiance. I contend that, just like Latino/a identity, rock's identity is always moving on.

Chapter Previews and Concluding Remarks

To continue this exploration of Latin/o rock music, I would like to reiterate some working assumptions that will guide this study. I have sketched some social, historical, and situational information about various Latino/a groups in the United States. My sketches, which consider everything from culture to musical expression, focus on the US and México, and, more importantly, on the borderlands where these two cultures meet. By focusing on borderlands, I intend to enter into current debates about borders, language, culture, ethnicity, identity, and specifically

79 Ibid., 132.
80 Ibid., 132–3.

national identities. My historical, contextual, theoretical, and methodological assumptions are therefore part of a larger cultural studies matrix.

This undertaking is an analysis of US/México border culture that integrates both cultures into a larger, transcultural space of borderlands. Consequently, this effort is a contribution to American cultural studies as articulated to borderland theory. Second, this research informs the growing interest in Latino/as and popular culture. Third, it speaks to a gap in the literature where rock music has been ignored in discussions of 'ethnic' musical expression; preliminary research reveals that studies of Latin/o music rarely analyze rock music and often equate Latin music with salsa or other popular music categories such as 'tropical' music, and often with Spanish-language music only. Fourth, this project combines a critical approach with a border studies paradigm. And, finally, students of culture and identity, scholars in cultural studies, people interested in Chicano/a and Latino/a studies, professionals in communication, and fans of rock music will find this investigation useful.

Following this introduction are five middle chapters and a conclusion. This introduction establishes the rationale for and the significance of my book research, and poses the questions that drive the study. In doing so, it introduces the relevant literatures and theoretical frameworks for understanding Latino/a identity. Chapter one introduces the topic of 'border radio' and how the border radio era demonstrates the cross-cultural fertilization between the US and México. This chapter revisits rock 'n' roll's origins, and expands the discussion by including Latino/as in the conversation about rock 'n' roll's influences. It articulates blues legends, country music history, and rock 'n' roll lore to Latin/o connections, contributions, and influences. What follows accordingly is an extension of my argument that Latino/as are important for understanding contemporary identities and cultures in the US. Thus, this first chapter closes with a return to the discussion of the place of Latino/as in mainstream US culture.

In Chapter two, I revisit the 'Pachuco Boogie' era, which provides a rich historical background and another perspective on early Latin/o influences in North American popular music, and, specifically, on styles that were fermenting and would eventually be called rock 'n' roll. Using the recent *Pachuco Boogie* compilation as an entry point, the chapter analyzes music, clothing, and slang to understand the intercultural flavor of the era. Moving into an analysis of the lives of Don Tosti and Lalo Guerrero as noteworthy artists of the period, this chapter demonstrates how Latino/as in this era were in an ambiguous place with regard to politics of assimilation to the mainstream, resistance to dominant culture, and in between identity categories such as 'Chicano' and 'Latino,' and, further, how rock music is further articulated to issues/questions of identity, culture, and language. Also in this chapter, we witness critical moments in cultural history where Latino/a cultural influences are adopted by various youth who employ fashion and styles that will contribute to the eventual rock 'n' roll aesthetic that quickly followed the *pachuco* (zoot suiter) era. This chapter also continues a rock 'n' roll (or 'rock') timeline that organizes this book, and closes with some residual effects of the 'Pachuco Boogie' era in contemporary popular culture.

Chapter three begins with a conversation about the relevance of contemporary Latin/o cultural expressions in the North American mainstream, but extends the trajectory of the previous chapters through an analysis of the 'garage-rock' phenomenon of the mid 1960s. More specifically, this chapter discusses the significance of the garage-rock moment while simultaneously reading trends related to garage-rock music such as garage-rock's reliance on Latin/o music, rhythms, influences, and contributions. It continues the diasporic view of Latino/as by focusing the analysis on US-based Latino/Hispanic contributions to rock and how those articulations also demonstrate the identity, culture, and language issues that were revealed in previous chapters. Chapter three concludes with an analysis of recent trends in popular music and how they relate to Latino/a identity.

In Chapter four, I continue the conversation on Latin/o rock connections by addressing the story of the birth of rock in México in the 1950s and 1960s as told by José Agustín and Javier Batiz (and others). Throughout this chapter, I reflect on Agustín's life story in order to get to inter-connections and cross-fertilization(s) between the music genre called *Onda* and the significance of a literary trend called *Onda*. This chapter further chronicles the history of rock in México through following decades as well as discussing significant Latin/o rock articulations north of the border. In the concluding section, I offer some points about the relevance of rock music in Mexican music's history as well as how the significance of rock in México provides alternative perspectives on the nature of US–México relations.

Therefore, in Chapter five I attempt to map another perspective of Latin/o rock by discussing rock's development in Argentina as political discourse. Beyond Argentina's early rock, one of the figures to emerge from the dark days and political turmoil was Gustavo Santaolalla, who would make his way to the US in the late 1970s, and can be connected to LA's punk-rock scene in the 1980s as well as much of the recent and contemporary *rock en español* music in the 1990s and 2000s. Furthermore, this chapter's analysis avoids a dichotomous view (i.e., US vs. others) of Latin/o rock and focuses on the intersections, artist collaborations, and other points of interconnection throughout the Latin/o rock diaspora.

In the conclusion for this book I briefly discuss some of the most recent trends, events, moments, and important artists from the late 1990s to the early/mid 2000s. The Conclusion closes with a return to the discussion of Latino/a identity issues and a summary of themes throughout various chapters. I conclude this project with a review of the heuristic value of 'Latino' as an essentializing racial category and commentary regarding the ways that Latino/as present disruptions of racial hierarchies, as well as how popular (rock) music challenges us to reconsider the primacy of nation-states as organizing categories for people and culture. Moreover, this book signals an effort to reclaim rock music and its history for Latino/as, in order to raise the question of how Latino/as fit in with regard to our narratives of 'nation' and national culture.

Conclusion

Portales tells us that 'Spanish-speaking Americans' currently comprise one out of every nine citizens (and could number even more if Portales' arguments about seasonal migration and illegal immigration are true).[81] An implication of such facts is that as many as one in five people in the US could be considered a Latino/a. In spite of the fact that Latino/as were projected to emerge as the largest minority group in the United States in the next 15–25 years, Latino/as have already surpassed African Americans as the largest minority group in the US, as indicated by the latest Census. And in spite of the problems of Latino/a identity markers and signifiers, Latino/as appear to be in an unprecedented position to influence mainstream US culture; Latino/as in the US constitute a group with growing importance for scholars and cultural research. This book is an effort to articulate popular cultural expressions to the tensions of identity, language, culture, nationality, and borders as they relate to both immigrant and nonimmigrant 'ethnic' populations that are now more highly visible than ever.

81 Portales, *Crowding Out Latinos: Mexican Americans in the Public Consciousness.*

1

Heard it on the X: Border Radio as Public Discourse, the Latin/o Legacy in Popular Music, and the Roots of Multicultural America

> ... *democracies, I fear, must content themselves with commercial, popular art that informs the culture and noncommercial, academic art that critiques it [...] These answers of course, tend to confirm my own predisposition to regard recorded popular music as the dominant art form of this American century. My point is that Pollock and Warhol do not exploit the lumpen vernacular, they redeem it — elevating its eccentricities into the realm of public discourse.*[1]
>
> *Borders... what borders?*[2]

In December of 2007 I received a 'check this out' email from a family member about a fascinating newcomer to the popular music scene. The email included a link to a YouTube video clip in which a teen phenomenon, named Vince Mira, appeared on the *Ellen DeGeneres* TV program and fired up the talk-show host and her studio audience with a solid rendition of the Johnny Cash classic 'Ring Of Fire.' Able to mimic Cash's famous baritone voice and playing an acoustic guitar, the teenager Vince Mira even imitated the 1950s rockabilly style with his blue jeans and cowboy shirt, his short slicked-back hair, and thin frame.

As I watched the young man work through the classic song and listened to the audience roar thereafter, I got a sense of the power of popular music to stir people to emotion. Yet, as I listened to the studio audience cheering loudly for the live performance, I began to read the comments that were attached to the email message, from those who had forwarded the email before it arrived in my own email inbox. Comments were also posted on the video's page on YouTube. Those comments ranged from praise and excitement about the rising star of Vince Mira to jeers and virtual disgust about how Mira was 'ripping off' the rock and country

---

1 Hickey, *Air Guitar: Essays on Art & Democracy*, 99–100.
2 Quotation by Louie Perez of Los Lobos, in liner notes to *Rock en Español Vol. One* by Los Straitjackets.

Vince Mira. Photo by: John Keatley

music legend Johnny Cash. Most interesting to me, however, was the fact that the young Vince Mira appeared 'Latino,' and how he revealed in the interview with Ellen that he started playing and singing 'Spanish songs' with his family before switching to English pop songs and Johnny Cash.

I then began to wonder whether race and ethnicity had something to do with how people were receiving the 'viral video' in which a skinny young man, with 'Latino' looks and stories of singing Spanish songs, was rearticulating the music of a legendary and iconic figure in the history of North American popular music. As I saw it that day on my computer screen, people must have misunderstood Vince Mira's articulation of Latino/as to 'Ring Of Fire' as unauthorized appropriation, or, perhaps, cultural theft. At the very least, the jeers must have come from a place of ignorance about the various Latin/o cultural contributions to North American popular music, and, more specifically, to ignorance about the cultural connections specific to the Johnny Cash song 'Ring Of Fire.'

While recent changes in Census categories for Latinos/Hispanics reveal how US culture is ambivalent about where Latino/as fit in and about how to deal with a burgeoning US Latino/a population, in this chapter I steer the conversation toward specific instances of Latino/a influence in North American popular music through sounds, lyrics, instruments, or other aspects. In the following sections I will use *Heard it on the X*, a 2005 compact disc release by Los Super Seven, as an entry point into the conversation about Latino/as and American culture, as well as the role of border radio as public discourse that informs the discussion.

Revisiting the 'X' Stations and Border Radio

The 'X' radio stations, as they were known, were the high-powered AM radio stations whose call letters began with X because they were Mexican radio stations, and they broadcasted from the Mexican side of the US/México border from high-powered transmitters that would have made them illegal in US territory. Sometimes reaching as much as a million watts of radio power, the X stations such as XER (which later became XERA), XEG, XERB, XERF, XEAW, XEMO, XEMU, XEAK, XTRA, and XELO were among various 'outlaw' X stations, considered as such because of how they defied the logic of borders and other practical limitations for broadcasting in a time when radio practices were still being defined.

According to one anecdote by country music legend June Carter Cash, when she and her family lived in Del Rio, Texas, the X stations blasted so much wattage that you didn't even need a radio to listen in, and you could hear border radio 'on any barbed wire fence in Texas.'[3] Whether that story is true or not, however, is not really important; the stations were known to be so powerful that they could blast radio power far beyond the Texas/México border and far up in the US plains states, into the Midwest, and almost 'anywhere in the nation.' Some attest that the X stations reached as far away as Canada, Europe, Japan, and New Zealand while others jokingly suggest that the stations were putting out so much wattage that they affected birds as far away as Australia, Finland, and Java. A more interesting fact, I contend, is that the X stations played music that could not be heard on mainstream radio stations in the US. Aside from the religious orientation and commercial pitches for many outlandish products that dominated airtime on the X stations, the X stations exerted a different kind of power when they began to play music to attract listeners and became the first radio stations on earth to play 'western' and 'hillbilly swing,' along with blues, R&B and other 'race' music. Likewise, regional Mexican and other Latin American music was sometimes heard as well, and the fact that listeners were exposed to all of these contributed fundamentally to new popular music genres that resulted (e.g., country and rock 'n' roll).

In the spring of 2005, the Grammy Award-winning super-group Los Super Seven released a compact disc as a tribute to border radio, or the X stations. *Heard it on the X* was the third album by Los Super Seven, and the title was culled from a somewhat famous but now forgotten song from 1975 called 'Heard it on the X' by the Tex-Mex rock/blues band ZZ Top:

> Do you remember, back in 1966?
> Country Jesus, hillbilly blues, that's where I learned my licks.
> Oh, from coast to coast and line to line, in every county there,
> I'm talking 'bout that outlaw X, that's cutting through the air.
> Anywhere y'all, Everywhere y'all,
> I heard it, I heard it, I heard it on the X.[4]

While the collaborative effort of Los Super Seven acknowledged ZZ Top through liner notes, the version by the contemporary super-group is more noteworthy as the lasting acknowledgment of and testament to the role of border radio for the

---

3   Fowler and Crawford, Liner notes to *Heard it on the X* [compact disc], no pagination.
4   ZZ Top, 'Heard it on the X,' from 1975's *Fandango!*

community of listeners that were formed by it between the 1930s and 1960s, as well as to border radio's lasting impact on American culture.

Whereas the details and implications of border radio have been discussed previously in radio studies,[5] the current analysis focuses on *Heard it on the X* as a contemporary cultural text and a form of intercultural public discourse that further illuminates the Latino/a legacy in American popular music as well as illuminating the impact that border radio had on the radio listening community and even race relations in the US. Widely acclaimed and much loved, the most remarkable aspect about *Heard it on the X* by Los Super Seven was the disc's focus on paying tribute to the influence of border radio on country and rock 'n' roll music (and other popular music), and on US culture in general. As Bentley notes about the disc,

> The dozen songs on the album cover the entire breadth of the lone star state in such a way that listeners get a direct blast of history from artists that helped create it, as well as those who learned from its roots. The way those lessons are taught is musical heritage at its most heartening.[6]

As *Heard it on the X* suggests, and as the following analysis reveals, the 'X' border radio stations were integral to the changes of an ever-growing and rapidly changing US culture between the 1930s and 1960s and a great deal of popular music that followed. Featuring the music of poor and working-class Whites along with African Americans and Latino/as, the X stations helped radio to become the first mass medium that was truly multicultural, and therefore allowed border radio to have a significant and lasting impact on North American culture.

Radio scholar Michael Keith describes the role of radio in the US, '... the world's first electronic mass medium had performed a unique, if not profound, role in the life of Americans for three quarters of a century,'[7] and Rothenbuhler and McCourt tell us that, 'By providing new venues for expression of regional, class, and ethnic identities, radio played an instrumental role in a series of major transformations, if not revolutions, in American culture.'[8] Likewise, Benedict Anderson argues about radio and nationalism,

> Invented only in 1895, radio made it possible to bypass print and summon into being an aural representation of the imagined community where the printed page scarcely penetrated. Its role ... generally in mid-twentieth-century nationalisms, has been much underestimated and understudied.[9]

It could be said, therefore, that border radio deserves further attention as a public

---

5   Fowler and Crawford, *Border Radio: Quacks, Yodelers, Pitchmen, Psychics, and Other Amazing Broadcasters of the American Airwaves*; Kahn, 'The Carter Family on Border Radio,' 205–17.
6   Bentley, Liner notes to *Heard it on the X* [compact disc], no pagination.
7   Keith, 'The Long Road to Radio Studies,' 531.
8   Rothenbuhler and McCourt, 'Radio Redefines Itself, 1947–1962,' 368.
9   Anderson, *Imagined Communities: Reflections on the Origin and Spread of Nationalism*, 54.

discourse that was produced by a multicultural setting in Texas as much as it anticipated, and likely contributed to, multiculturalism and intercultural communication in the US in the decades that followed. The implications, of course, are that *Heard it on the X* represents a radio-listening community that anticipated the end of the Jim Crow South and preceded the integration of US culture and society, and thus signifies the lasting impact of the sound medium of radio on 'American' life.

Moreover, a deeper analysis of the recent *Heard it on the X* release (and the border radio that it commemorates) reveals significant connections to Latino/a music and culture. I propose a corollary that what also should be recognized is how Los Super Seven's *Heard it on the X* simultaneously recalls the Latin legacy in American popular music and culture as it was mediated through radio. Thus, *Heard it on the X* also provides an opportunity to reconsider the history and role of Latino/as in US culture. In a time of burgeoning significance of Latino/a peoples in the US — from the emergence of Latino/as as the nation's largest minority to irrational fears about a growing number of Spanish speakers (and 'losing English'), from political efforts to capture Latino/a voters to the building of border walls, from heated debates about immigration reform to questions about the value of ethnic assimilation in a time of intense globalization — *Heard it on the X* illuminates an important radio community (an integrated cultural space predating modern country music, rock 'n' roll, and other popular music genres, scenes, and movements), serves as a vital corrective to radio and popular music history with regard to the contributions of Latino/as and Hispanics, and also provides a rich background for the conversation about the place of Latino/as in the US.

Los Super Seven

All-star super-groups have been around for decades in popular music and bands like Blind Faith in the 1960s, Bad Company in the 1970s, the Traveling Wilburys in the 1980s, the Texas Tornados and Damn Yankees in the late 1980s/early 1990s, Audioslave in the late 1990s, and recent bands like Velvet Revolver in the 2000s continue to be well received by fans. Most of those bands received much critical acclaim and made mountains of cash in the process, yet music critic Ed Ward describes Los Super Seven as 'the only supergroup that doesn't suck.'[10] While such a candid characterization might be based upon esoteric aesthetic judgments, I would suggest that if such a statement has any merit, it might be related to Los Super Seven's far-reaching musical range as well as the diversity of artists and musicians that are part of the collective. While Los Super Seven could actually be called Los Super Twenty-five-or-so, their musical styles include country, blues, folk, Tex-Mex rock, *corrido, cumbia, mariachi (ranchera), norteño, jarocho, bolero, son*, and many others.

Los Super Seven began in 1998 with the release of their self-titled first disc, which featured the first lineup of seven main artists.[11] Among the thirteen songs

---

10   Ward, 'SWSX Records: Los Super 7 — Heard It on the X,' no pagination.
11   The original Los Super Seven lineup included: Joe Ely, Freddy Fender, David Hidalgo, 'Flaco'

on the first album that were mostly in the vein of regional Latin music that ranged from *cumbia, ranchera, conjunto norteño, tejano*, and combinations thereof, the artists blended the sound of different Latin music genres into a contemporary musical effort that recognized the importance of traditional music and important artists of the past.[12] For the second album by Los Super Seven, *Canto* (released in 2001), producers reshuffled and came up with another all-star lineup.[13] As a result of the addition of three international music stars, the twelve songs on the second disc by Los Super Seven featured a more expanded version of Latin music to include Brazilian, Peruvian, Cuban, and other Latin American songs in addition to the regional Mexican styles that were already part of the super-group's repertoire. Likewise, the influence of US country music remained strong as did the tendency toward genre-blending.

When *Heard it on the X* was released in 2005, Los Super Seven all but gave up the façade of being an all-star band of just seven members. Not only did they reshuffle the deck once again, but previous members returned while the new lineup included more Super Seven newcomers (but established stars).[14] The result was a list of at least ten Super Seven members, although that number also underreports the numerous other musicians, producers, and contributors that were part of the *Heard it on the X* project. And this fact, I contend, looms large in significance given the fact the tribute disc invokes a radio community that was impacted by border radio and Tex-Mex culture that included Latin music alongside hillbilly and western swing music and even blues. In the following pages, I describe some important songs from *Heard it on the X* that reveal intriguing connections to Latino/as in US culture, and simultaneously signify the place of Latino/as in contemporary US culture.

Blues Music and Tex-Mex Culture

One of the important social-cultural connections illuminated on 2005's *Heard it on the X* is a song by the aging blues musician Clarence 'Gatemouth' Brown, who

Jimenez, Ruben Ramos, Cesar Rosas, and Rick Treviño.
    12   Likewise, one important stand-out track on the first album was a thoughtful and sorrowful cover of an old folk song by folk legend Woody Guthrie about immigrants and deportation, 'Plane Wreck At Los Gatos (Deportee),' which seemed to commemorate Woody Guthrie and US folk music at the same time that it did the plight of immigrants and migrant workers.
    13   While David Hidalgo, Cesar Rosas, Ruben Ramos and Rick Treviño remained from the original Los Super Seven lineup, the new Super Seven included the international pop music superstar Caetano Veloso from Brazil, whose extensive legacy included decades worth of MPB (Música Popular Brasileira), *Tropicália, bossa nova*, folk and rock as well as international fame, political activism, and a reputation as one of the most important Brazilian musicians of all time. Another piece of the Super Seven puzzle was the Peruvian Susana Baca, whose contributions stemmed from her background as a contemporary interpreter and proponent for Afro-Peruvian music and culture. The final piece of the puzzle was the US country star Raul Malo, whose time as a frontman of The Mavericks placed him in one of the most successful and popular country acts of the 1990s. Interestingly, since the late 1990s Malo had increasingly focused his musical efforts on Cuban and Latin music, and therefore, on his Cuban American culture and identity.
    14   Among the returning Super Seven members for *Heard it on the X* were Joe Ely and Freddy Fender, while the new additions included Delbert McClinton, John Hiatt, Lyle Lovett, Rodney Crowell, and Clarence 'Gatemouth' Brown.

covers the song 'See That My Grave Is Kept Clean.' While the musicians and producers of *Heard it on the X* were wise to include Clarence 'Gatemouth' Brown, as an important link to blues music and African Americans on border radio of years past, they were likely unaware that the significance could be extended beyond to include the Mexicans and Latin Americans that influenced early blues artists. While the predominant influence of African/African American culture is obvious in blues music history, a lesser-known fact remains that early blues musicians were also influenced, albeit ever so slightly, by Mexican culture.

For example, history also teaches us that in decades past, Mexicans were much closer to Blacks than to Whites. As one Black cotton picker commented on their proximity around 1920,

> The Negroes and Mexicans mix some if the Negroes can speak Spanish. They come to some of our dances and dance with our girls if we will let them. They used to, more than they do now. They won't let us dance with their girls, so now our boys won't let our girls dance with them.[15]

Although also suggesting developing intercultural tensions, we are informed in this short statement of life in the 1920s that Mexicans and Blacks in Texas were interacting socially and culturally, that they were familiar with each other's music and dance culture, and that they were involved with each other at some level through music and dance practices. Facts such as this help explain why some early bluesmen hinted at Mexican (and perhaps Spanish) influences.

For example, the famous song 'See That My Grave Is Kept Clean' (which is covered on *Heard it on the X*) was actually written by Blind Lemon Jefferson, one of Texas' original blues musicians, and Jefferson is considered one of the main figures in 'country blues,' one of two central figures of 'Texas blues,' and one of the earliest and most important bluesmen of the 1920s. At the same time, Jefferson himself suggested that various unknown guitarists among Mexican workers in the rural Texas area where he was raised likely influenced him, and scholars have noted that those Mexican musicians probably played intricate flamenco guitar, playing patterns that became part of Blind Lemon Jefferson's unique playing style that suggested 'the influence of jazz and flamenco.' As scholars note, such influence likely resulted from Jefferson's proximity to Mexican *vaqueros*[16] (Mexican cowboy types) since Blacks and Mexicans are known to have worked alongside each other in cotton fields and elsewhere. Of course, other scholars note that it was Mexican *vaqueros* who introduced the guitar to the US in the first place.[17]

Supporting such significance, the twelve-string guitar furthers the blues connections to Mexicans beyond the standard guitar. For example, the twelve-string is known to have Mexican origins, and is also known as the *bajo sexto* that is commonly associated with *norteño*, *tejano*, and 'Tex-Mex' music. Interestingly, other

---

15   Taylor, *An American-Mexican Frontier: Nueces County, Texas*, 269.
16   Davis, *The History of the Blues*, 116.
17   Ibid., 116.

Texas bluesman such as 'Leadbelly' (Huddie Ledbetter), born in the late 1800s, played the twelve-string guitar, and it even became his signature instrument. Likewise, bluesmen such as Blind Willie McTell and Lonnie Johnson[18] were also famous for playing the twelve-string guitar.

As I recalled these historical footnotes about Blind Lemon Jefferson and Leadbelly, I was reminded that when it comes to the legacy of African American and Latin influences and the multicultural dialogue that defines US popular music, some historical clues shift the conversation to include the legacy of Robert Johnson. The blues legend is known to have had tremendous influence on popular music in the US and especially rock 'n' roll,[19] although he is probably best known for the Faustian legend of having sold his soul to the devil 'at the crossroads' in exchange for being the world's greatest blues guitarist. Yet, historical evidence surrounding some of his recordings tells us that Johnson can also be considered important for how he forged his own dialogue with Latin/o music culture in South Texas through the late 1920s/early 1930s.

Several years ago, I took notice of a small part of Robert Johnson's musical legacy, a 1930s song titled 'They're Red Hot,' in which Johnson can actually be heard singing about a traditional Mexican (and Latin American) food — hot *tamales*. 'They're Red Hot' is a song that has been performed and recorded countless times by blues artists, so on the surface, Johnson's interpretation sounds like another version of a timeless blues classic that has been reworked and recorded by several different musicians over several decades. However, it is intriguing that in spite of this question about Johnson, 'hot *tamales*' does not appear in other renditions by other artists. In other interpretations of 'Red Hot,' the line 'Hot *tamales* and they're red hot' is changed to 'My gal is red hot.'[20] So for others, 'red hot' was a reference to the physical beauty of the singer's 'gal,' while for Johnson, 'red hot' was a reference to hot *tamales*. To this day, the song can be heard with 'hot *tamales*' in more recent renditions that follow Robert Johnson such as Eric Clapton's recent tribute to Robert Johnson, *Me and Mr Johnson* (2004). Nevertheless, I continued to wonder why Johnson was singing about hot *tamales*, and other questions emerged. Why would Johnson, a Black man from Mississippi who played blues, be singing about traditional Mexican food (*tamales*)? What could account for Johnson's lyric — using a Spanish word denoting Mexican food in a blues song? Is there is any explanation for the change in the lyrics?

To put these questions in better light through an interesting connection to border radio and the X stations, Fowler and Crawford recall how former Texas Governor W. Lee 'Pappy' O'Daniel actually used border radio to further his

---

18 Aside from his mastery of the twelve-string guitar, Lonnie Johnson had other Latin connections such as the strains of Latin and Caribbean music that became part of New Orleans music (and eventually 'jazz') which itself characterized Johnson's music.

19 Marcus, *Mystery Train: Images of America in Rock 'n' Roll Music*; Garofalo, *Rockin' Out: Popular Music in the U.S.A.*

20 It has been noted, for example, that versions such as Billy 'The Kid' Emerson's 1950s song 'Red Hot' were tributes of a sort to Robert Johnson's 'They're Red Hot,' in spite of their own lyrical changes and some musical differences, and by then were being used as a schoolyard taunt.

campaigns for governor in the 1930s. As Fowler and Crawford note, it was quite natural that public figures with access to high-powered radio stations drifted into politics.[21] 'Pappy' O'Daniel made his fortune through radio but also used border radio to get elected. He was known all over as 'Pass the Biscuits, Pappy' O'Daniel because of his association with Hillbilly Flour products that were heavily advertised on radio at the time.[22] Since he used his own border radio station for political advantage (broadcasting from México to circumvent US regulations), it was suggested that his famous phrase should be changed from 'Pass the Biscuits, Pappy' to 'Pass the Tamales, Pappy.'[23] In other words, for Texans of the 1930s *tamales* were part of a discursive index that reminded people of 'México' and must have resonated the political and socio-cultural implications of border radio. Still, the question remains: Why did the Mississippian Robert Johnson write a song about hot *tamales*?

As far as Johnson's connection to *tamales*, a clue exists in the liner notes to Johnson's *Complete Recordings* collection (1990), indicating that he traveled to San Antonio and Dallas, Texas, for recording sessions in 1936 and 1937. The recording sessions listed in the *Complete Recordings* reveal how Johnson recorded his Texas sessions between the sessions of Tex-Mex/Tejano artists like Las Hermanas Barraza, Andres Berlanga, Francisco Montalvo and others. Could it be that Johnson may have interacted with these artists and later changed a line or two in his songs — as blues musicians were prone to do? Eric Rothenbuhler reminds us that for those early blues artists picking up on regional variations in musical style, assimilating multiple styles, and adapting to one's locale and audience were all standard practices. Likewise, the art of entertaining a crowd, lyrical improvisation, and being clever with the audience were all critical parts of being a blues entertainer.[24] Moreover, Rothenbuhler's recent research suggests that Johnson even learned from records and radio, revealing that the radio medium and records likely influenced Robert Johnson through the various musical styles that he was exposed to but also that Johnson composed his music and lyrics 'for' the radio and records.[25] The significance of these details, however, is in the fact that the supposed grandfather of blues and the great-grandfather of rock 'n' roll had contact with Mexicans and/or Mexican Americans in South Texas and through 'They're Red Hot,' provides evidence of how some blues lyrics were changed as a result of interaction with Tex-Mex culture.

Moreover, as one hip-hop scholar notes, blues music can be distinguished from other genres by its obsession with the theme of mobility, a fitting obsession given its development during the (post-slavery) Jim Crow era and upsurge during the Great Migration (1910–1930). Blues music constantly referenced trains, railroad tracks, crossroads, highways, movement, wandering, and the 'right of mobility'

---

21   Fowler and Crawford, *Border Radio*, 159.
22   Dempsey, 'The Light Crust Doughboys Are on the Air!,' 107–25.
23   Fowler and Crawford, *Border Radio*, 183.
24   Rothenbuhler, 'For-the-Record Aesthetics and Robert Johnson's Blues Style as a Product of Recorded Culture,' 68–71.
25   Ibid., 65.

(and still does).²⁶ Yet, as much as the blues referenced roads, movement, and mobility, another theme that also emerged was of going to México, where one might escape the shackles of, if not slavery then Jim Crow-era circumstances, and to perhaps start a new life. Where leaving for good is demonstrated in famous blues songs like 'Delta Slide' in which Mississippi John Hurt sang 'I'm goin up the country, and I ain't comin' back no more,' the emergent theme of going to México is best demonstrated in songs such as 'Key To The Highway' by Big Bill Broonzy (1941) in which he referenced going 'to West Texas' and then 'down to the border,' to get away from his troubles. Of course, 'Key To The Highway' was performed and recorded by other blues artists and by several other bands/artists, including many in the rock genre throughout the 1960s and 1970s, and Big Bill Broonzy would eventually be recognized as an influence on rockers such as Jimi Hendrix. Meanwhile, other Broonzy songs such as 'San Antonio Blues' told of going to San Antonio where 'people make you feel at home.' Given the historical proximity of Blacks and Mexicans, as well as the interaction between bluesmen like Robert Johnson and other Mexican ensembles, songs like these by Broonzy and other artists demonstrate both a level of assimilation between Blacks and Mexicans as well as how México lingered as a place of hope and promise for many poor and rural African Americans, and especially for the bluesmen who voiced some of their experiences.

This proximity between Mexicans and African Americans and the theme of going to México help to explain why more famous bluesmen like Bo Diddley recorded songs with titles such as 'Spanish Guitar' (1960) and 'Aztec' (1961), both guitar instrumentals that became hits, and why other famous bluesmen such as Long John Hunter actually moved to México and became a fixture of the music scene in Juárez. Hunter, of course, was so famous throughout the West Texas region that Buddy Holly crossed the border just to see him, and Bobby Fuller — an El Paso, Texas rock 'n' roller — was even known to have been Long John Hunter's protégé before he became famous in the mid 1960s for hits such as 'Let Her Dance' and 'I Fought The Law.'

Furthermore, the fantasy of going to México and its thematic legacy in the blues carried on through widely popular R&B songs such as 'Down In Mexico' by The Coasters (1956) and through early rock 'n' roll songs such as the unfortunate 'Mexico' by Elvis Presley (1963),²⁷ as well as many other rock songs that followed such as 'Louise' by The Yardbirds (1964), 'Have Love Will Travel' by The Sonics (1965), 'Hey Joe' by Jimi Hendrix (1966),²⁸ 'Going to Mexico' by the

26   Cobb, *To The Break of Dawn: A Freestyle on the Hip Hop Aesthetic*, 25; See also, Rotella, *Good With Their Hands*, 63–4.
27   And various other Elvis songs; Moreover, it is also worth noting that Presley's 'Mexico' is actually part of the soundtrack to the feature film *Fun In Acapulco*, which featured various other Mexican and Mexican-themed songs (e.g., 'Guadalajara,' 'Marguerita,' and 'El Toro') as well as other Latin-themed songs such as 'Bossa Nova Baby' and 'No Room To Rhumba In A Sports Car.'
28   While the song 'Hey Joe' was not written by Jimi Hendrix and has been covered by other bands and artists, I am listing Jimi Hendrix here because his version is the most famous and most popular. Also, Jimi Hendrix would have had a stronger connection to the blues legacies that I am describing here than other artists in the rock era.

Steve Miller Band (1970), 'Baby, Let's Go To Mexico' by the Sir Douglas Quintet (circa 1970), 'Goin' Down To Mexico' by ZZ Top (1970), and 'Across The Border' by Electric Light Orchestra (1977). Of course, Doug Sahm and the Sir Douglas Quintet released other Mexican-themed songs such as 'Nuevo Laredo' (1970) and 'Michoacan' (1971), but, unfortunately, this thematic legacy is also evident in other songs like 'Mexican Blackbird' by ZZ Top (1975) which characterized México through blatant sexism and racism. While early bluesmen sang of going to México to get away from Jim Crow or to start a new life (i.e., leaving troubles behind), the going to México theme had been transformed by bands in the 1970s like ZZ Top who misunderstood the significance of leaving troubles behind and could only conceptualize going to México as a pretense for adventure, partying, and sexual exploits.

Logically, such sexism and racism can be understood as a precedent for other rock songs such as 'Sexy Mexican Maid' by the Red Hot Chili Peppers (1989) and 'Juarez' by Mark Lanegan (1990), and likely many others in the rock genre. Alternative-rocker Mark Lanegan, in fact, also recorded other Mexican-themed songs such as the popular 'Borracho' (1994) and 'El Sol' (1994), while other recent rock songs on the México theme include 'Soul to Squeeze' by the Red Hot Chili Peppers (1993), 'Mexico' by Cake (1998), 'Mexico' by Incubus (2001)[29] and 'Atlanta' by Stone Temple Pilots (2004), in which singer Scott Weiland laments his real-life breakup with his Mexican American girlfriend through discourse comparable to his predecessors (e.g., 'visions of Mexico seduce me' and 'the Mexican princess'). Meanwhile, México continues to serve as a muse for other rock artists, even as they drift toward folk music. For example, Mexican geography, borders, and western lore are evident in Bruce Springsteen's folk albums *The Ghost of Tom Joad* (1995) and his recent *Devils & Dust* (2005).

Aside from the Mexican theme in blues, the acoustic twelve-string guitar, which in previous decades was associated with Mexican music and some southern bluesmen, became common in rock music through The Beatles (played by George Harrison), The Byrds (by Roger McGuinn), The Who (by Pete Townshend), Led Zeppelin (by Jimmy Page), Queen (by Brian May), and the Eagles (e.g., 'Hotel California'). In the 1980s, it was heard through Tom Petty and the Heartbreakers (played by Tom Petty and Mike Campbell) who sometimes follow the folk/country-rock sound of The Byrds, and by the mid 1980s, the twelve-string was still used in 'alternative-rock' songs by REM (played by Peter Buck), The Cure (by Robert Smith), and The Smiths (by Johnny Marr), and hard-rock/heavy metal bands like Guns n' Roses (by Slash).

Of further significance, Leadbelly's heavy blues sound became influential for some 1990s grunge-rockers, such as Mark Lanegan and Kurt Cobain, and is evident in the example of Nirvana's famous 'Where Did You Sleep Last Night?' (in which Kurt Cobain artfully covered Leadbelly's 'In The Pines'). The electric twelve-string was employed by a new generation of hard-rockers in the 1990s, such

---

29 The band Incubus has other connections through Mexican American drummer Jose Pasillas and songs with Spanish titles such as 'Pistola' (2004).

as Rage Against the Machine and System of a Down. Most recently the twelve-string guitar has become a staple instrument for some of the best contemporary indie-rock bands, such as The Decemberists.[30]

Moreover, the Spanish/acoustic-guitar style is more obvious and audible in famous rock songs such as 'Malagueña' which was covered by various artists in country and rock 'n' roll over the decades (e.g., Roy Clark, Chet Atkins, Ritchie Valens, Bill Haley and the Comets, Dick Dale, and Brian Setzer), 'Greensleeves' and 'Beck's Bolero' by guitar virtuoso Jeff Beck (1968), 'Laguna Sunrise' (1971) and 'Fluff' (1972) by Black Sabbath, 'Spanish Fly' (1979) and 'Little Guitars (Intro)' (1982) by hard-rock heroes Van Halen, 'Cohesion' (1984) by punk-rock band the Minutemen, 'Obsession Confession' (1994) by former Guns n' Roses guitarist Slash, as well as in recent productions such as different songs (e.g., 'Muleta' in 2000 and 'El Gatillo/Trigger Revisited' in 2008) by Calexico, 'Weird Divide' (2001) by indie-rock favorites The Shins, and most recently, in 'An Interlude' (2009) by The Decemberists.

Therefore, although Clarence 'Gatemouth' Brown's cover on the *Heard it on the X* album was just a cover of an old blues classic by Blind Lemon Jefferson, the significance is such that Brown's recording connected him and the other artists on *Heard it on the X*, as well as a larger community of listeners of the border X stations, to the earliest of African American blues musicians, but also to forgotten Mexican and Latin American musical influences. Worth noting, the blues legends mentioned here are but a few brief examples of the many blues artists that had some form of interaction or engagement with Mexicans or other Latino/as in the US, and these examples only demonstrate a few of the ways in which Black–Mexican connections are discernable. What this evidence suggests, is that Latino/as can lay claim to having played some part in the formation of US popular music, whether through musical notes and instrumentation, as in Jefferson's case and Leadbelly's, or through lyrics, as in Johnson's case,[31] or through the significance of the 'going to México' theme that is evident throughout blues and rock music's history, or in the prevalence of acoustic (or electric) twelve-string guitar that has character-ized so much of rock music that it is virtually unnoticeable in today's popular music. Moreover, such facts allows me to construct a history of popular music in terms of a cultural dialogue with Latino/as and other multicultural influences, and that avoids typical dichotomous histories of popular music that feature only Black and White streams of influence. Beyond this, I contend that when these dormant features of early twentieth-century life were mediated through radio, the interracial and intercultural nature of border radio and the various X stations awakened a multicultural spirit in popular culture and fomented the integrated, multicultural character of a rapidly changing US culture — a culture that always

---

30   For more on the twelve-string and its Mexican origins see Simmons, 'The Origins of Twelve-String Power.'
31   Interestingly, famous New Orleans artist Buckwheat Zydeco released 'Hot Tamale Baby' in 1987.

included Latino/as and in which Latino/as played a significant role with regard to disrupting the racial order of the time.

Western, Hillbilly Swing and Country

In addition to blues music, other genres that are commemorated in Los Super Seven's *Heard it on the X* album are 'western swing' and 'hillbilly' music, and a direct correlation can be made between the emergence of border radio and the roots of country and western music in the 1930s and 1940s. As Kahn avers, 'The earliest stations to showcase hillbilly music were in the United States, but by the early 1930s, stations began broadcasting hillbilly music from just across the Mexican border.'[32] Although music was not being regularly broadcast over US networks during this period, by the late 1930s hillbilly and gospel were a great part of what was coming across from border radio broadcasting and were becoming more popular.[33]

Related to this fact, one of the greatest contributions by Mexican radio stations and border radio to popular music in the US was the way it contributed to the careers of the famous Carter family. As Kahn recognizes, 'The Carter Family is one of the most famous recording groups to emerge from the American country music scene' of the 1920s, 30s, and 40s.[34] What is not commonly known is that The Carter Family's fame resulted from their recording career in conjunction with their radio performance career that aided in spreading their music and fame.

While their recording career began in the late 1920s it continued through the 1930s, their broadcast days on Mexican radio lasted until 1942. For a time, The Carter Family actually lived in San Antonio, Texas and traveled to places like Del Rio, Texas and Monterrey, México (in the state of Nueva León) and several other border stations that dotted the Mexican–American border. It was around this time that their family began to grow and included several Carter children who would carry on the Carter legacy in country music.[35] Critical to the success of The Carter Family was the innovation of recording their shows, instead of relying on live performances. According to Kahn, because radio shows were usually performed live, the earliest recordings and re-broadcasting of radio shows began on border radio in order to save the artists and announcers from early morning performances and, of course, early morning commutes to the stations on the Mexican side of the border. Although it was precipitated by the very nature of border radio stations — traveling across distance and national borders — this practice eventually spread throughout the entire broadcasting industry after World War II.[36]

In addition to such innovations in the radio broadcasting industry, The Carter Family's fame also contributed to working out a power struggle that was occurring between the US and México over broadcast frequency allocation. In this sense, not only did border radio contribute to the fame and success of early country music

---

32 Kahn, 'The Carter Family on Border Radio,' 206.
33 Ibid., 207.
34 Ibid., 205.
35 Ibid., 209
36 Ibid., 208.

pioneers, it also contributed to popular music in different ways, such as recorded programming, and forced the US and México to work out solutions to frequency allocation problems at the time most critical to radio as a mass medium.[37]

In yet another articulation of early country music to border radio and Latino/a music and culture, another significant cut from the (2005) *Heard it on the X* album is the song 'My Window Faces The South,' featuring Lyle Lovett's vocals on a cover version of an old 1940s tune by the pioneering country music act Bob Wills and His Texas Playboys. According to Starr and Waterman, an important part of the 'western' element in country music was the western swing music-style that amalgamated Texas cowboy songs, German and Czech polkas, and Texas-Mexican *corridos*, *conjunto acordeon*, and Mexican *mariachi* music.[38] As Starr and Waterman note, the most famous figure in western swing music was Bob Wills, who achieved success as the bandleader for Bob Wills and His Texas Playboys. Starr and Waterman also remind us that the Texas Playboys' biggest hit was a 1941 song called 'New San Antonio Rose,' which was a hit on both the country and pop charts. 'New San Antonio Rose' was later covered by Bing Crosby and went even higher on the pop charts, but the Texas Playboys version included a trumpet duet 'in the style of a Mexican *mariachi* band.'[39] As Starr and Waterman attest, the incorporation of such Latin American musical influences is part of what allowed western swing to exert a permanent influence on country music and Bob Wills to be considered one of the pioneers in country and western music.[40]

Reconsidering such a Latin (and more specifically *mariachi*) tinge in country music helps to understand why the 1959 song 'El Paso' by Marty Robbins became such a huge hit for Robbins as well as a significant part of country music's history. Released in 1959, 'El Paso' was the first song to rule the pop charts as the 1960s were ushered in, and propelled Marty Robbins to critical acclaim (e.g., a Grammy Award) and major commercial success. In fact, Marty Robbins was so successful with 'El Paso' that it eventually spawned two popular sequel songs, 'Faleena' and 'El Paso City,' more Grammy Awards for Robbins and other accolades, and eventually helped Robbins get elected to the Country Music Hall of Fame. Of course, of relevance for this analysis, 'El Paso' was a Mexican *corrido* translated into English, and beyond the obvious outlaw/gunfighter narrative that puts it squarely within Mexican *corrido* tradition, the vocalizations by Marty Robbins left no doubt that he was mimicking México's *ranchera* (or *mariachi*) singing style. Nonetheless, 'El Paso' was so significant that it eventually resurfaced in rock music as a cover by the Grateful Dead and others.

---

[37] In yet another noteworthy connection for border radio and popular music history, radio DJ Wolfman Jack, who became famous in rock 'n' roll lore for his hoots, howls, and gravel-throated voice, actually began his radio career through border radio in Del Rio, Texas. Already the subject of much fame and notoriety in early rock 'n' roll history, Wolfman Jack was immortalized in the feature film *American Graffiti* that documented the emergence of rock 'n' roll. Yet it was on border radio in the 1950s that Wolfman Jack got his start and began broadcasting early rock 'n' roll and jazz music and became famous for his 'Wolfman' antics.

[38] Starr and Waterman, *American Popular Music: From Minstrelsy to MTV*, 149.

[39] Ibid., 151.

[40] Ibid., 151.

Moreoever, the early *mariachi* influence by Bob Wills and His Texas Playboys (and others) on the emerging country sound can also be extended to what eventually became known as 'rockabilly' — something between country music and rock 'n' roll — and the music of country music and rockabilly legend Johnny Cash; the *mariachi* influence is probably best remembered in the exploding trumpets that drive the 1963 song 'Ring of Fire' by Johnny Cash. However, the sound of *mariachi* trumpets would surface elsewhere in the 1960s and 1970s.

The use of *mariachi* trumpets, Mexican/Spanish guitar, marimbas, *bolero* beats, and other 'Latinized country rhythms' that began with western swing music in the 1930s and 1940s and survived through country and western music, can be found in many examples that followed in the late 1960s and into the 1970s. Concerning this 'Latin tinge' in North American popular music, scholars cite the examples of several tracks on the 1968 album, *I Believe In You*, by Mel Tillis, and throughout the 1970s in various songs like The Amazing Rhythm Aces' 'Third Rate Romance, Low Rent Rendezvous,' Lind Hargrove's 'Mexican Love Songs,' Maria Muldaur's 'Say You Will,' Captain Hook's 'Making Love and Music,' and Michelle Phillip's 'There She Goes.' Roberts adds that there were more subtle examples of the Mexican tinge in Hoyt Axton's 'The No No Song,' 'When the Morning Comes,' and 'Flash of Fire' as well as Crystal Gayle's 'Someday Soon,' 'Talking in Your Sleep,' 'Too Good to Throw Away,' and 'Wayward Wind.'[41] Of course, the Mexican influences on country and country-rock music were even more obvious in the music of the Eagles as well as in the music by Latino/as Linda Ronstadt, Johnny Rodriguez, and Freddy Fender.[42] Freddy Fender's 'country' music is often cited as 'country-rock,' 'South Texas Rock,' and 'Tex-Mex rock-and-roll.'[43]

Although not in the country genre (or rock 'n' roll), not lost on popular music history is Herb Alpert, whose signature sound was defined by *mariachi* trumpets and who scored several pop music chart hits by tapping into the *mariachi* legacy in American music. Alpert, of Jewish-Ukrainian heritage, was classically trained in the trumpet and could have easily focused on other music styles like classical or jazz and had even dabbled in rock 'n' roll. Thus, it is noteworthy that he chose the *mariachi* aesthetic to give his own music some Latin flavor. Scholars note how Alpert actually traveled to Tijuana, México to record bullfighting sounds that were later overdubbed onto his signature song 'The Lonely Bull.'[44] He then started billing himself as 'The Tijuana Brass,' and 'The Lonely Bull' ended up at #6 on the charts in November 1962. As one tells it, by 1966 Herb Alpert and the Tijuana Brass were 'more pervasive than any British rock group,' scoring top-selling albums and winning Grammy Awards, and they would eventually go on to score a string of hits throughout the 1960s and 1970s and even produced other *mariachi* pop acts.[45]

Returning to rock 'n' roll lore, Johnny Cash's 'Ring of Fire' can be connected

---

41 Roberts, *The Latin Tinge: The Impact of Latin American Music on the United States*, 196–8.
42 Ibid., 198.
43 Lipsitz, *Dangerous Crossroads*; Mendheim, *Ritchie Valens: The First Latino Rocker*; Roberts, *The Latin Tinge*.
44 Otfinoski, *The Golden Age of Rock Instrumentals*.
45 Ibid., 182–3.

to other notable examples of blaring trumpets through songs like 'Rocks Off' by the Rolling Stones, which was released on their 1972 album *Exile on Main Street*. Whereas this album remains a rock classic and is often cited as a favorite of rock 'n' roll aficionados, 'Rocks Off' is not often remembered for *mariachi* trumpets and comes off as an otherwise unremarkable rock music piece. However, the Rolling Stones are known to have used other Latin music in their own 'British Invasion' productions, such as 1964's 'Not Fade Away' (based on the *clave* rhythm), 1965's 'Get Off of My Cloud' (a *cha-cha-chá* rhythm), and 1968's 'Sympathy for the Devil' (a mambo construction that also features prominent conga drums).[46]

'Rocks Off' can thus be contextualized in light of its Latin connections, and *mariachi* trumpets in 'Rocks Off' can be linked in a genealogy that connects Bob Wills, Johnny Cash, the Rolling Stones, Herb Alpert, Bing Crosby, Patti Page, Elvis Presley (and many others) to more recent and contemporary country, rock, alternative-rock, alt-country, and indie-rock acts such as The Neutral Milk Hotel, Calexico,[47] Cake, DeVotchka, Sufjan Stevens, The Raconteurs, Spoon, Wilco, and The White Stripes[48] (among countless others that feature prominent trumpet-rock sounds). Further, while contemporary artists such as DeVotchka and Sufjan Stevens likely feature more than just trumpets in their music and likely register various other (folk) musical influences, it is worth considering that their antecedents in popular music were songs like 'Ring of Fire' by Johnny Cash, 'Rocks Off' by the Rolling Stones, and other songs in the genealogy. In other words, without those musical antecedents, how would we understand the use of a blaring trumpet, a seemingly insignificant instrument in rock traditions, in contemporary rock music?

Moreover, there were many other bands throughout the 1960s and 1970s that also featured trumpets prominently in their music, and synthesizers that were so much a part of pop and new-wave music throughout the 1980s mimicked the background tones that trumpets made in decades past. Nevertheless, as this analysis demonstrates, songs like 'Ring of Fire', 'Rocks Off' and others are linked in an important genealogical chain that extends far back into the days of border radio, attesting further to the impact of border radio on American culture. Meanwhile, Cash's 'Ring of Fire' has been covered by Latino/a acts such as *tejano* accordionist Mingo Saldivar (as 'Rueda de Fuego' in 1992), Los Vaqueros del Oeste (as 'Rueda de Fuego/Ring of Fire' in 2000), and also by contemporary punkers Girl In A Coma in live performance, while Cash's other major hit 'Walk The Line' was recorded by Texas rockers Los Lonely Boys (in 2004), all of which suggests that Latino/as themselves understand some of Cash's 'country' music as Latin-influenced or Latin-inspired.

---

46   On this point see Sublette, 'The Centrality of Cuban Music.'

47   Interestingly, Calexico actually features *mariachi* horns during their live performances, and, perhaps fittingly, Calexico were actually included in the *Heard it on the X* project, playing on at least seven of the disc's twelve cuts.

48   On their latest LP release in 2007, The White Stripes cover Patti Page's 1950s song 'Conquest,' featuring trumpets that sound similar to Page's original recording, which suggests that Patti Page's music can also be included in a list of *mariachi*-influenced US pop music.

Girl In A Coma. Photo by: Adam Stockstill

Moreover, the literal and metaphorical allusions to 'going to México,' Mexican women, and Mexican *cantinas* that are found in classic blues and rock music have also surfaced, and then resurfaced, in country music. One might note the Mexican themes in classic country songs such as the 1983 version of 'Pancho & Lefty' by Merle Haggard and Willie Nelson (a cover of the 1973 original by Texan country/folk singer Townes Van Zandt, who in turn cited Texas bluesmen such as Blind Willie McTell and Lightnin' Hopkins as influences) and other songs such as 'The Seashores Of Old Mexico' by Merle Haggard (1987), which was also covered by George Strait (in 2006), and perhaps even songs such as 'The Gulf Of Mexico' by pop-country star Clint Black (1990).[49] I submit that such songs (and countless others) provide an alternative perspective on US popular music that illuminates the dialogues between Mexican and Latino/a culture and defining genres of North American popular music.

Buddy Holly's Latin Connections

For further connections between the radio community invoked by the *Heard it on the X* release and Latino/a culture, one does not need to look very far. The 2005 tribute to border radio also featured a rendition of 'Learning the Game,' sung by country artist Rodney Crowell and performed by several other Super Seven artists. 'Learning the Game,' however, is actually an old tune by Buddy Holly. Buddy Holly, a West Texas rock 'n' roller, is acknowledged as a pioneer in the development of rock 'n' roll because of his use of electric guitars (revolutionizing the popular music industry in the 1950s), although I submit that the music of Buddy Holly might have been more influential in other ways. Holly provides yet another link between *Heard it on the X*, border radio X stations, and the unknown history of popular music that further elucidates the impact of Latino/as on American culture.

First, the life (and death) of Buddy Holly can be connected to none other than Ritchie Valens (Richard Valenzuela), the Mexican American/Chicano artist most famous for the 1959 hit 'La Bamba.' Valens and Holly were making hits at the same time and touring together in 'The Winter Dance Party' of January 1959. They also boarded a plane together on 3 February 1959 of that same year, a plane that crashed in an Iowa cornfield and took the lives of both in addition to The Big Bopper (J. P. Richardson). Interestingly, like Valens, Buddy Holly was said to have injected rock 'n' roll with Latin influence. Although many note how Holly's music had a unique sound that nobody could account for or explain, and others state that 'not even the performers could explain just what it was or where it came from,'[50] several scholars recall the fact that Holly was considered to have a 'Tex-Mex' sound that some speculate was a result of his West Texas roots.[51] As mentioned above, it is known that before Holly became famous he had traveled further into West Texas, into El Paso, and then crossed over into Juárez, México to see the blues artist Long John Hunter. It is interesting to consider the possibilities of his exposure to Mexican music during this period. Sublette also notes how Buddy Holly's West Texas style 'had a lot of Afro-Cuban feel,' and how country music legends such as Buck Owens recall playing *rumbas*, tangos, sambas, and Bob Wills' music (which all suggest a dialogue with Latin music).[52]

Buddy Holly's 'Tex-Mex' sound is evident in hit songs like 'Brown-Eyed Handsome Man.' Although Holly's was a cover of a Chuck Berry song where Berry

---

49   While the latter sounds more like an ode to the beach and a sea/sailing vacation, the lyrical references to 'ladies' and 'yesterdays,' and the music suggesting acoustic Mexican guitar are unmistakable links to the previous examples here.
50   See, for example, the Buddy Holly biography by Goldrosen and Beecher, *Remembering Buddy: The Definitive Biography*, 160.
51   See, for example, Geijerstam, *Popular Music in Mexico*.
52   Sublette, 'The Kingsmen and the Cha-Cha-Chá,' 84.

was also insinuating a brown-skinned handsome man,[53] the guitar riff that Buddy Holly applied in his version of 'Brown-Eyed Handsome Man' sounded much more like the Tex-Mex sound for which Holly was known. Perhaps not coincidentally, the riff in 'Brown-Eyed Handsome Man' sounds much like the riff for the 1958 song 'Tequila' by The Champs — another early rock 'n' roll song with an obvious connection to Mexican culture, but also a Latin rhythm.[54] In other hit songs by Buddy Holly such as 'Not Fade Away' — a rock 'n' roll classic which has been covered countless times by rock and country artists, most famously perhaps by the Rolling Stones and the Grateful Dead — one can hear a 1–2–3 . . . 1–2 rhythm commonly known as the 'Bo Diddley beat.' Yet research reveals that although Bo Diddley is usually given credit as the originator of the famous 'Bo Diddley beat,' the beat is actually a product of more Latino/a influence on North American music. Musicologists have noted its basis is the five-beat *clave* rhythm associated with Afro-Cuban music, and musicologist/historian Ned Sublette notes how maracas can be heard in songs like 'Bo Diddley' and how track sheets from the recording session listed a cut that only said 'Rhumba' further contextualize the Latin influences in early rock 'n' roll music.[55] Meanwhile, others extend the origination of the 'Bo Diddley beat' to African rhythms or Moorish influences in music from Spain.[56]

Exact origins are obviously difficult to ascertain, but I suggest that what matters more is that Buddy Holly's connections to Latin American music can be seen through more than just one song. In the same vein, not lost to history is the fact that Holly married Maria Elena Santiago shortly before his death. In Holly's biography, Santiago revealed that when the couple were living in New York, Buddy had been playing Latin American and Spanish records and trying to copy the music and guitar riffs. Santiago also adds that Buddy was learning Latin American songs with the intention of recording them, and that Buddy even wanted to learn Spanish.[57]

As rock historians know very well, the tragic death of Buddy Holly deprived the world of the foremost practitioner of the Tex-Mex sound in rock 'n' roll. In the same plane crash, rock enthusiasts also lost Ritchie Valens, who was not only a contemporary of Holly, but perhaps even an influence. Together, they might have been the champions of Latin-influenced rock 'n' roll music, perhaps even the fathers of what much earlier could have been called Latin rock music or even *rock en español*. These historical facts are reiterated here not merely to suggest that

---

53   See also Lipsitz, *Time Passages*, 115; This point is a mere suggestion about how Buddy Holly may have identified with the song. Holly was likely able to identify with the song because of the reference to brown eyes but also with brown-skinned minority populations. Moreover, it is worth noting that such changes in lyrics have happened with other songs in rock 'n' roll history such as Van Morrison's 'Brown-Eyed Girl,' where Van Morrison's original lyrics were about a brown-skinned girl. Not coincidentally, 'Brown-Eyed Girl' has also been linked to Latin music through its rhythm and instrumentation.
54   Garofalo, *Rockin' Out*; Otfinoski, *The Golden Age of Rock Instrumentals*; Mendheim, *Ritchie Valens*; Sublette, 'The Kingsmen and the Cha-Cha-Chá.'
55   Sublette, 'The Kingsmen and the Cha-Cha-Chá,' 83.
56   I have noted this in my own research; see footnotes in the following chapter on Latino connections to 1960s garage-rock (Chapter three).
57   Goldrosen and Beecher, *Remembering Buddy*, 123.

Buddy Holly should be remembered as a Latino rocker, but rather, that Holly's connection to Ritchie Valens, along with his Tex-Mex sound and his interest in Latin music is all an indication that the Latin/o connection to rock 'n' roll music began quite early in the genre's history, and in fact, much earlier than mainstream accounts are willing to acknowledge.

Unfortunately, the Valens and Holly stories ended in tragedy, but their music and influences have not been forgotten. Not only did their music retain lasting significance, but their stories reveal intriguing articulations to Latin/o culture(s) and perhaps even investments in Latino/a identity (even though they remain ambiguous due to their untimely deaths). By connecting rock 'n' roll with Latin/o music, they solidified the connection between Latino/as and rock 'n' roll music that would reach beyond the 1950s — and across national borders. Ironically, the example of Buddy Holly presents us with the case of Latino/a music influences that were upon Buddy Holly, who in turn put his own influences on the vast community of border radio listeners, who were themselves listening to radio waves that originated on Mexican soil. It was a case of a dialogic cross-cultural and intercultural communication that happened at the level of public discourse and was mediated through radio.

As music scholar George Lipsitz argued about popular (rock 'n' roll) music that was fermenting during this time, such mediated productions should be seen as political expressions. As Lipsitz put it,

> If one views politics as only the public struggle for political power, then rock-and-roll songs were apolitical. But if one defines politics as the social struggle for a good life, then these songs represent politics of the highest order.[58]

Interestingly, when Los Super Seven included their homage ('Learning the Game') to Buddy Holly's West Texas music and his 'Tex-Mex' rock 'n' roll sound, they simultaneously connected all of the Super Seven artists, musicians and collaborators to a larger community of African Americans/Blacks, various working-class Whites, and various other Tex-Mex/Tejano/Mexican Americans throughout Texas and elsewhere that were so profoundly impacted by border radio and the various cultures that came together via its frequencies.

Conclusion

For purposes of time and space, my analysis of *Heard it on the X* and of the connections between border radio and Latino/as (and the lasting impact of both on American culture) ends here. However, it is worth noting that the Latin/o resonance in Los Super Seven's tribute to border radio could go even further. Other examples included on *Heard it on the X* are a cover of 'Let Her Dance,' an original song by Bobby Fuller, a native of El Paso, Texas who also championed the Tex-Mex sound and paralleled the life of Buddy Holly with his own early and tragic death; a cover of 'Talk To Me,' a song that was made famous on border radio through

---

58   Lipsitz, *Rainbow at Midnight*, 327.

Sunny and the Sunliners, another rare example of Mexican Americans in rock 'n' roll although further success in the rock genre so eluded them that the band returned to performing *tejano* and *norteño* music thereafter; and 'I'm Not That Kat (Anymore)' and 'The Song of Everything,' two songs that were written by the Texan Doug Sahm who achieved success with 'the Sir Douglas Quintet' by posing as an English rock band and hiding the fact that several band members were Mexican Americans and denying their obvious Mexican and Latin/o musical influences;[59] and of course, the title song 'Heard it on the X,' a song written by Texas blues-rockers ZZ Top who themselves were both impacted by border radio enough that they wrote a song about it but also provide many important links to Mexican or Latin/o culture through their own musical and lyrical references. Likewise, other 'Super Seven' stories that deserve further attention are the story of Raul Malo, the singer/frontman for The Mavericks (one of the most popular and top-selling country music acts of the 1990s), who can be seen as negotiating his connections to country music at the same time as his Cuban and Latin American heritage. Another interesting Super Seven story would be that of Mexican American country star Rick Treviño, who has been an integral part of every Super Seven album and can be seen as negotiating his own country music identity with regard to his own Mexican American identity and Latino/a heritage.

In sum, the evidence provided by the example of *Heard it on the X* stands as a testament to Latin-influenced blues artists, to *mariachi*-influenced western swing music, and to Tex-Mex-influenced rockabilly and rock 'n' roll. Given such examples, it is remarkable that significant Latin/o contributions to mainstream US culture and popular music continue to go unrecognized and under-acknowledged, and also remarkable that the Black/White dichotomy of mainstream imaginations of rock 'n' roll are so persistent. Nevertheless, *Heard it on the X* further underscores my assertion of American culture's debt to Latino/a influence in popular music through border radio, but also to the lasting impact of different Latino/a cultural influences on rock 'n' roll and American popular music. Furthermore, whereas my contention has been that Latino/a influences on North American music have been minimized, this latter point illustrates my argument that Latino/a connections to American popular music can be articulated to issues of identity and the preliminary remarks that I set out with in the introduction of this book, with regard to questions about the place of Latino/as in contemporary US culture and issues and tensions related to assimilation.

The incorporation of Mexican *mariachi* sounds into country and western and rock 'n' roll reflect a significant trend in US culture throughout the first half of the twentieth century (i.e., cross-assimilation and increasing intercultural communication). Rather than decry sounds as particularly 'ethnic,' artists and musicians were able to parallel the acculturation processes that were happening in wider cultural contexts. Adopting and using Mexican sounds was not only recognition of the presence of another community of people in Texas, evidence of interaction

---

59   Also available as Avant-Mier, 'Latinos in the Garage: A Genealogical Examination of the Latino/a Presence and Influence in Garage Rock, Rock and Pop Music.'

with them, and perhaps even an appreciation for them and their culture. It could be said that the example of *mariachi*-influenced country music reflects a tendency in mainstream US culture to minimize 'ethnic' characteristics in order to make them more palatable to mainstream audiences. While Elvis Presley's co-optation of African American music is remembered as an early example of this, and rapper Eminem can be seen as a recent example, the case of *mariachi* trumpets in country and western and hillbilly music recalls how this has been happening since much earlier in US history. Otherwise, the Mexican influences in blues music demonstrate how African Americans assimilated Latin/o culture and influences, although these continue to be forgotten, ignored, or just deemed irrelevant (or perhaps coincidental?) in most histories of African Americans and blues.

In conclusion, I argued in the beginning of this book that the question of Latino/a identity and how it serves as a reminder that mainstream US culture reveals ambiguity about what Latino/as are, who they are, by what signifiers they should be called, and how they can be understood. Yet, even after further analysis, new questions are raised about the role of radio and the possible impact(s) of radio and other mass media on the future relationship with Latino/a culture. First, how will formatting changes in recent decades impact ethno-racial relations in America's future? And since Latino/as now constitute emerging radio markets, how will new radio formats impact American culture in decades to come? Will Latino/as be further assimilated through mass media like radio? Or, will emphasis on local, regional, and ethnic markets hinder assimilation? Similarly, in the age of niche marketing, narrowcasting, and market segmentation for many different media, could current industry trends possibly result in less interaction between Latino/as and other Americans and foster an environment of mediated tribalism instead of intercultural communication? And finally, will Latino/as ever be recognized for their lasting impact on American culture and will they ever be included in conversations about mainstream US culture, rather than always being positioned as threatening outsiders, aliens, immigrants, and invaders?

I submit that if xenophobia and intercultural conflict and fears had won during the days of border radio, North Americans would have feared that their children would lose blues music, or hillbilly swing to Mexican and Latin American music. And like current fears about too many Mexicans and other Latino/a immigrants and/or losing English, border radio listeners in the US might have feared that future generations of youth would be forced to play in *mariachi* bands. However, analyzing contemporary cultural texts like *Heard it on the X* and revisiting the story of border radio, as well as radio's lasting impact on American culture, tells us that what actually happened was something much more interesting.

As border radio historians Fowler and Crawford recently reminded us in the *Heard it on the X* liner notes, 'Today, hispanic broadcasters dominate la frontera. Gringo broadcasting outlaws have migrated to cable television, the internet, and satellite radio. But the spirit of the X lives on, echoing through the universe...'[60] Likewise, the effects of border radio and Latin/o influences in popular music

---

60 Fowler and Crawford, Liner notes to *Heard it on the X* [compact disc], no pagination.

continue, echoing through America's sound waves as well as through much of our contemporary popular music.

Interludio 1° (first interlude)

It is noteworthy that, by 1991, heavyweights of the *rock en español* movement (see following chapters) such as México's Maldita Vecindad y Los Hijos del Quinto Patio (or just, 'Maldita Vecindad') were using trumpets in some of their most popular songs, one example being 1991's 'Toño.' While this may not seem surprising for a Mexican band to utilize a prominent trumpet sound in their music, I would argue again that trumpets have been an unusual instrument for rock 'n' roll, even for *rock en español*. I would therefore argue that the use of trumpets in this form of rock music also puts Maldita Vecindad's song 'Toño' within the genealogy that I am describing in Chapter one. In other words, rather than viewing 'Toño' as an isolated *rock en español* song, only in dialogue with Mexico's *mariachi* traditions, one can also view it as part of the longstanding dialogue between mainstream rock 'n' roll (or various rock formations) and Mexican and/or Latin American musical traditions.[1]

In similar fashion, the 2005 song 'Borracho' by Monterrey, México band Genitallica begins with slow-tempo acoustic guitar strumming, progresses to a hard-rock/metal fusion with traditional *mariachi* music, and includes lyrics of drinking tequila that conjure moments of celebration. Characteristically, the song also features prominent trumpets, and the video features the mohawked and dreadlocked band members dressed in *mariachi* uniforms as well as people dancing wildly at a party and even hitting a piñata. As with Maldita Vecindad, Genitallica's Mexican rock fusion should be obvious given their origins. However, it is likely that the band and fans (and scholars of popular music) are unaware that the *mariachi*-rock productions are also the legacy of mainstream North American rock.

Furthermore, just north of the Rio Grande/Río Bravo, *mariachi* trumpets in alternative/indie-rock music can still be traced in recent and contemporary music such as Spoon's 2007 hit song 'The Underdog,' a widely popular song that continues to be played on alternative/indie-rock radio throughout the US, and a song that actually featured real *mariachis* in the accompanying video; or in moments such

---

1   More interesting, perhaps, is the fact that the lyrics of Maldita's 'Toño' convey the image of a trumpeter who plays every night in a crowded slum of Mexico City that everybody in the neighborhood knows. The discursive register is such that the young man 'Toño' would likely be a trumpeter in a *mariachi* band, or perhaps a young person with hopes of joining a *mariachi* band in the future, in the hope of grinding out a living in the crowded capital; For more on the issues connected to rock music in Mexico City, see Hernández, 'Breaking the Mold of Contemporary Working-Class Mexican Masculinity'; Hernández, 'Chronicles of Mexico City Life: The Music of Rockdrigo González'; and Solórzano-Thompson, 'Performative Masculinities: The *Pachuco* and the *Luchador* in the Songs of Maldita Vecindad and Café Tacuba.'

Genitallica. Photo by: Alex Luster

as Calexico's live performances, which feature various songs with Mexican-style trumpets and other Latin music influences, and also a Mexican touring member who is actually given 'solo' opportunities and also even in Spanish; or perhaps in recent productions like alternative-rock artist Beck's re-release of 'Burro,' a song from the acclaimed and commercially successful *Odelay* album from 1996,[2] which was reproduced and re-released in a *mariachi* (*ranchera*) style in 2008, complete with acoustic guitars, high-pitched trumpets, and Beck singing in Spanish; or in the recent music by The White Stripes such as (a) 2007's 'Icky Thump,' a song with lyrics about México that seem to sympathize with the plight of Mexicans as immigrants to the US, (b) the song 'Conquest' on the same album, which features a kind of duel between electric guitars and piercing trumpets, (c) the 2008 re-release of the same song as an EP version titled 'Conquest (Acoustic Mariachi Version),' complete with the obvious acoustic guitars, more prominent *mariachi* trumpets and a slower tempo, and (d) the subsequent re-release of the original song as 'Conquista (Spanish Version),' in which singer Jack White sings in Spanish and is backed up by a *mariachi* chorus;[3] furthermore, in early 2009 new-wave/alternative-rock star Morrissey released his new album, *Years of Refusal*, with the song 'When Last I Spoke to Carol,' a song that begins with acoustic Spanish-guitar strumming and progresses to prominent *mariachi*-style trumpets that clearly link Morrissey to the genealogy in Chapter one as

---

  2   In the original 1996 *Odelay* album, the song was titled 'Jackass' and had English lyrics, while the 2008 version was titled 'Burro' and featured a complete translation of the lyrics into Spanish.
  3   The articulation of Jack White (and music by The White Stripes) to Mexican music and the plight of Mexican immigrants is perhaps not surprising at all, given that White grew up in the 'Mexicantown' neighborhood of Detroit.

well.[4] Yet another significant *mariachi*-rock connection happened in 2009 when a hardcore-punk-rock band from LA called 'The Bronx' changed their name to 'Mariachi El Bronx' and recorded their album of the same name. In a recent story on National Public Radio, the band members describe the project as a genuine tribute to *mariachi* tradition and to the Mexican music traditions that they heard throughout their lives and that they love and respect. Underscoring the not-so-unnatural Latin rock connections that I am mapping here, one of the members of Mariachi El Bronx quipped that the new *mariachi* album was actually 'the punkest thing in the world' and 'the punkiest thing we could ever have done.'[5]

As all these examples attest, some of the most innovative, most 'hip,' most popular and most successful contemporary punk-rock, alternative-rock, and indie-rock artists and bands continue the North American dialogue with the *mariachi* sound and with Mexican and other Latin American music, and as the evidence presented in Chapter one recalls, to view it as mere 'fashion' or coincidence is at best short-sighted, and at worst ignorant. In other words, to consider the lasting significance of border radio and its impact on American culture is to recognize the various Latin/o cultural influences on contemporary popular music. Similarly, to recognize Latin/o cultural influences in American popular music is to consider questions of identity related to Latino/as.

Selective Discography and Tracks Listed Here and in Chapter One:

Beck. 'Burro,' *Odelay (Deluxe Edition)* (Geffen Records Inc., 2008).
Cash, Johnny. 'Ring Of Fire,' *Ring of Fire: The Best of Johnny Cash* (Columbia Records/Sony Music Entertainment Inc., 1963).
Clapton, Eric. 'They're Red Hot,' *Me & Mr. Johnson* (Warner Music, 2004).
Johnson, Robert. 'They're Red Hot,' *Robert Johnson: The Complete Recordings* [Longbox] (Columbia Records/Legacy, 1990).
Maldita Vecindad (y Los Hijos del 5° Patio). 'Toño,' *Lo Mejor de: Maldita Vecindad* (BMG Entertainment, 2001).
Mariachi El Bronx. 'Cell Mates,' *Mariachi El Bronx* (Swami Records/White Drugs, 2009).
Morrissey. 'When Last I Spoke To Carol,' *Years of Refusal* (Decca, 2009).
Neutral Milk Hotel. 'Holland, 1945.' *In the Aeroplane, Over the Sea.* (Merge Records, 1998).
Rolling Stones. 'Rocks Off,' *Exile On Main St.* (Virgin Benelux B. V., 1972).
Spoon. 'The Underdog,' *Ga Ga Ga Ga Ga* (Merge Records, 2007).
Los Straitjackets. 'Ana,' *Rock en Español Vol. One* (Yep Roc, 2007).
Los Super Seven. *Heard it on the X* (TELARC International Corporation, 2005).
_____. *Canto* (Sony Music Entertainment Inc., 2001).
_____. *Los Super Seven* (BMG Entertainment, 1998).
The White Stripes. 'Conquista (Spanish Version),' 'Conquest (Acoustic Mariachi Version),' [singles] (Warner Bros./Third Man Records, 2008).
_____. 'Conquest,' *Icky Thump* (Warner Bros., 2007).
ZZ Top. 'Heard it on the X,' *Fandango!* (Warner Bros., 1975).

---

4 Formerly of the 1980s band The Smiths, Stephen Patrick Morrissey has also been known to have other connections to Latino/as. See, for example, Arellano 'Their Charming Man: Dispatches From the Latino Morrissey Love-In' and/or Klosterman, '1,400 Mexican Moz Fans Can't Be (Totally) Wrong.'
5 See NPR, 'Mariachi Punk: At Home in L.A.'

2

The Missing Links: Zoot Suits, Original Chicanos, and Diasporic Latin/o Connections

It is not simply that people retain the capacity for fantasy and self-expression in the face of depersonalization and dehumanization, but even more that the very mechanisms of domination provoke expressions of opposition, alterity, resistance, and transcendence.[1]

The present day pachuco refuses to die![2]

The border radio period that I described in the previous chapter essentially lasted from the 1930s to the 1960s, but radio's reach was materializing elsewhere. In 1938, for example, at XEJ radio in Ciudad Juárez, México (in the northern border-state of Chihuahua, just south of El Paso, Texas), the Mexican comic/film star German Valdes performed as a *pachuco* character, where he dressed in zoot suits and spoke in 'Spanglish,' in what was basically a humorous caricature about zoot suiters of the time that also functioned as a denigrating stereotype about their culturally poor, '*pocho*' (i.e., North Americanized) cousins who had lost their 'real' Mexican culture. Valdes later introduced the *pachuco* to Mexican popular culture by performing as Tin Tan on XEW radio in Mexico City.[3] As Tin Tan he would eventually become a major film star in México in the 1940s and a famous popular culture icon thereafter,[4] but part of his legacy relates to how he popularized the *pachuco* character in México through his performances on radio, effectively making *pachucos* (in)famous.

Where, in the previous chapter, I revisited the history of border radio and the outlaw X stations that unwittingly created a fertile ground for intercultural sensibilities that would in turn develop further to create new, hybrid sounds and result in further innovation and various new genres in popular music, in this chapter I turn my focus toward the 'Pachuco Boogie' period as an important moment in

---

1 Lipsitz, *Footsteps in the Dark*, 261.
2 Liner notes for the 1968 album *Cruising with Ruben and the Jets*, by Frank Zappa and the Mothers of Invention.
3 Varela, Liner notes to *Pachuco Boogie*, 6–7.
4 For more on Tin Tan and *pachucos*, see Monsiváis, *Mexican Postcards*.

popular music history with far-reaching implications for Latin/o music that would follow, but also for other mainstream popular music in the US. Moving forward from Chapter one, in which I also traced a brief genealogy of Latin/o influences in mainstream popular music in the US within different genres, I continue the deconstruction of the rock genre as simply a Black/White phenomenon, and further pursue the formation of a new perspective that includes Latino/as and Latin/o culture in the history of rock music. As I argue, Latin/o culture should be recognized for its various influences on blues, country, rock, and pop music, and this knowledge requires us to rethink what we know about rock music and demonstrates how we can view the rock genre and its eventual subgenres in terms of its Latino/a articulations. More important for this chapter, however, those developments altogether mark the transition from early connections between Latino/as and mainstream popular music to fully fledged hybrid productions that, not coincidentally, also mark changes in the way Mexican Americans saw themselves in addition to marking specific identity categories such as *Pachuco, Chicano*, and eventually others.

This chapter therefore begins with a brief review of the meaning of zoot suits and *pachuco* culture in order to get to a 2002 compact disc release of *Pachuco Boogie* by Arhoolie Records, an important chronicle of the *pachuco* era as well as of 'Pachuco Boogie' music, that altogether launches the analysis that will follow in the rest of the chapter. I move forward by further exploring the significance of *pachucos*, the lives and music by Don Tosti and Lalo Guerrero as important artists of the period, and some discursive elements of the subculture as they relate to the *Pachuco Boogie* release and specific songs, and into an analysis of the life and music of Lalo Guerrero as an important transitional artist whose music, life, and work point to emerging Latino/a identities. In the chapter's closing remarks, I map the zoot suiter and 'Pachuco Boogie' influences throughout the rock genre in order to demonstrate how counter-minstrelsy, zoot suit culture(s), and *pachuco* style would all have influences on the rock 'n' roll aesthetic for several decades beginning in the 1950s and on through the 1960s and 1970s. Finally, I conclude this chapter by illuminating the far-reaching influences of the era and the significance of its impact on rock 'n' roll and other popular music up to the present.

Zoot Suits, *Pachucos* and 'Pachuco Boogie'

It is known that the *pachuco*'s origins with Mexican nationals and Mexican Americans from the US was in a subculture evolving along the El Paso-Juárez border[5] in which Mexicans and Mexican Americans (hereafter, 'Mexicans')[6]

---

5   As some scholars have noted, El Paso, Texas is considered the birthplace of *pachucos*. A guy from 'El Paso' was an 'El Pachuco,' although eventually the name was applied to anybody of the subculture. It is interesting that to this day, El Paso is sometimes referred to by locals as 'El Pachuco,' 'El Chuco,' or 'Chuco town,' and remnants of *caló* (*pachuco* slang) are still audible in working-class slang on both sides of the Juárez-El Paso border.

6   On this point, I follow Paredes in his seminal treatise on Texas-Mexican border culture and musical expression. As Paredes put it, 'Mexican' (with quotation marks) is to be understood in a cultural sense, without reference to citizenship or to 'blood'; see Paredes, *With His Pistol in His Hand: A Border Ballad and Its Hero*, 'Introduction' (no pagination). My use of 'Mexicans,' therefore,

participated in a subculture of rebellion that materialized in three main forms of expression — clothes, music, and slang[7] — that either consciously or unconsciously negotiated the tensions of urban versus rural circumstances and identities.[8] The *pachuco* style was the material embodiment of emergent identities in which urban versus rural, English versus Spanish, and 'American' versus 'Mexican' were some of the prominent tensions. Informed by African American culture and images of urban 'hep cats,' the *pachuco* style came to symbolize an identification that was similar to that of African Americans; Mexicans and Mexican Americans were quite aware of their lower-class status and their condition as second-class citizens in the US. Moreover, as they identified with the position of African Americans in North American social hierarchies, urbanized hipsters began to wear zoot suits in the fashion of jazz star Cab Calloway and other African Americans in major US cities.[9] Not coincidentally, they were also influenced by the music that was in vogue — jazz and swing.

The third form of cultural expression, the hip street slang, also mimicked African Americans, but 'Mexicans' had more to draw from linguistically. Where Black zoot suiters created a hip, jive-talking style that was still English, the *pachuco* slang could borrow from that hip slang in English, but also translate it to Spanish. They could even change words to 'Spanglish,' and often, the patois could include *caló*, a marginal Spanish slang that didn't qualify as Spanish for Mexican elites or at best was considered a lower-class form of Mexican Spanish for the uneducated and uncultured. *Pachucos*, then, had several linguistic options to draw from — from proper English and hep cats' jive slang to proper Spanish, 'Spanglish,' and *caló* — which in combination resulted in a richer, more complex, and often indecipherable argot that practically required in-group status for comprehension. Thus, in order to participate in the subcultural discourse, one had to be at least bilingual, but it also helped to be quick-thinking, humorous, and inclined to play with language.

In fact, *pachuco* style also demonstrated a counter-cultural sensibility in language that could also be considered for how it simultaneously isolated cultural outsiders. In this sense, *pachuco* style reflected the values of all of their zoot suiter counterparts, whether they were Black, Latino, White, Filipino, or other Asian Americans. As Rubin and Melnick argue, the zoot suit culture,

> . . . is a fascinating example of an important paradigm of popular culture: the ability of its consumers to subvert familiar symbols and thereby imbue them with new, altogether different, meanings [. . .] a kind of counter-minstrelsy.[10]

I will provide some examples further below in order to demonstrate

---

is a reference to Mexican Americans as well as Mexican nationals who found themselves in the US and in border spaces such as El Paso, Texas, and emphasizes the interaction between such groups.

7   Rubin and Melnick, *Immigration and American Popular Culture: An Introduction*, 72.
8   For more on *pachucos, caló*, and the meaning of zoot suits see Barker, *The Mexican Experience in Arizona*, and Monsiváis, *Mexican Postcards*.
9   Rubin and Melnick, *Immigration and American Popular Culture*, 62–4.
10 Ibid., 61.

counter-minstrelsy and symbolic subversion in practice, as well as some of the nuances of *caló* street slang. However, for the purpose of clarity and organization in this chapter, it is important first to introduce the 'Pachuco Boogie' era that provides the backdrop for the analysis that follows in the rest of this chapter.

'Pachuco Boogie'

As scholars have noted, the 1930s and 1940s were decades of great innovation and hybridization in American popular music. The Latinization of jazz and other popular music, for example, resulted in further hybridization and new forms of expression. As Roberts notes, the mambo was highly influential on 'jump blues' and other forms of Black popular music in the 1940s.[11] Likewise, in the United States' Southwest and in locales such as Southern California, orchestras playing mambo and tropical music; and local ensembles playing *mariachi* music, tango, *rumba*, and even Spanish *flamenco* dances were alive and well in the 1940s. Artists such as Edmundo Tostado ('Don Tosti') as well as Eduardo 'Lalo' Guerrero, Chico Sesma, Raul Díaz, and Eddie Cano were in the beginning of their respective careers. All had various levels of involvement with jazz, swing, jump blues, and boogie woogie bands during this era — Don Tosti had played with the Tommy Dorsey Orchestra and Eddie Cano had worked with Charles Mingus in 1945. For various reasons such as these, it should not be surprising that the mambo and musical expressions such as 'jump blues' or the 'jump-type shuffle' would also be found in Mexican/Mexican American 'Pachuco Boogie' music, and that this new music perhaps most signified the intercultural exchange that was happening throughout the southwest in the mid to late 1940s.

While White artists like Greek American Johnny Otis, who passed as Black, were big in Los Angeles, playing swing and jump blues to large crowds of Mexican Americans from LA's Eastside and contributing to the fermenting scene that would eventually become rock 'n' roll, also playing the jump-type shuffle was established Mexican American artist Don Tosti (with Raul Díaz and their band The Pachuco Boogie Boys) who had a local hit in the Los Angeles area in 1948 with 'Pachuco Boogie,' an up-tempo boogie track that featured the bilingual street slang of the *pachucos* and became one of the first million-selling 'Latin' songs.[12] Interestingly, those 'Mexican' musicians achieved wide success through 'Pachuco Boogie' in spite of communicating what was a very specific ethnicity and culture through their music that was somewhat isolating for cultural outsiders and those with more mainstream values.

For a contrasting view of the cultural issues of the time, one can look toward another Latino contemporary of *pachucos*, who was also appearing in North American popular culture in the 1940s. Also popular in the post-World War II period was a singer named Andy Russell, a singer who capitalized on the thirst for all things Latin, who reached #1 in the US with 'Bésame Mucho,' and who went on

---

11 Roberts, *The Latin Tinge*, 136.
12 See Macías, *Mexican American Mojo: Popular Music, Dance, and Urban Culture in Los Angeles, 1935–1968*, 126.

to become a multi-million record seller and an international star. Andy Russell was actually a Mexican American, born Andrés Rábago Pérez to immigrant parents from northern México, who adopted the anglicized stage name Andy Russell. In spite of his Mexican background, Andy Russell was more of an English speaker in his youth, and he was uncomfortable with Spanish and didn't like Mexican music much. Nevertheless, he began singing in Spanish at the urging of a bandleader.

In interviews, Russell eventually attributed his phenomenal success to the fact that his light skin and European features allowed him to pass as Anglo- or European-American.[13] His signature song 'Bésame Mucho' was later recorded by other artists including The Beatles in 1962 (marking another intersection of rock 'n' roll music with Latino/as), but the case of Andy Russell also reminds us of social structures that often required Latino/as to perform whiteness in order to have any chance of success in the mainstream music business. When whiteness wasn't possible, Latino/as returned their focus to Latin/o music, singing in Spanish, and remaining local in their aspirations.

Thus, a major part of the significance of 'Pachuco Boogie' music for rock 'n' roll history was how it signified an emerging post-war consciousness by 'Mexicans' who started to see themselves as 'Americans,' mixing mambo and other Latin rhythms and singing in Spanish, English, 'Spanglish,' and *caló*.[14] More significant perhaps was the fact that the references to the *pachuco* subculture outwardly expressed the zoot suiter's sensibility of marginalization. As Anthony Macías notes,

> ... the pachuco boogie songs lent instant visibility to an entire generation of Mexican Americans who not only enriched popular culture but also made it their own. The popular pachuco party songs powerfully articulated an identity and a dialect at odds with the square, monolingual dominant society.[15]

Don Tosti

All along the border country (e.g., crossroads like Juárez/El Paso), there were many young men who were part of the developing subculture that Tin Tan was mimicking in México's popular culture. One of those young men from El Paso was the aforementioned Edmundo Martínez Tostado, born in 1923, who hailed from El Paso's tough *segundo barrio* neighborhood and grew up speaking *caló*, the *pachuco* street slang of the period. In spite of humble beginnings, he was a musical prodigy and became successful at a young age. After a family move to Los Angeles, Tostado became a session musician with modest success until he got lucky breaks in both touring with famous jazz bands and later with recording, eventually becoming

---

13 Loza, *Barrio Rhythm: Mexican American Music in Los Angeles*, 142–50.
14 While the place of 'Pachuco Boogie' in rock 'n' roll's legacy is probably more tangible, Guevara mentions the possibility of 'Pachuco Boogie' as another candidate for the title of the first rap record; see Guevara, 'The View from the Sixth Street Bridge: The History of Chicano Rock,' 117.
15 Macías, *Mexican American Mojo*, 131.

famous as Don Tosti.¹⁶ More important however, is that Don Tosti became known as the creator of what came to be called 'Pachuco Boogie' — the amalgamation of jazz, swing, and boogie woogie with other popular Latin American rhythms (e.g., *danzón*, mambo, and *guaracha*) and Mexican American street culture (e.g., Spanish, 'Spanglish,' and *caló* slang).¹⁷

Don Tosti and his band cut the song 'Pachuco Boogie' in 1948 and followed with other songs such as 'Güisa Gacha,' 'Wine-O Boogie,' and 'El Tírili,' creating the sound and commemorating the 'Pachuco Boogie' era.¹⁸ And while Tosti is often cited as the inventor and creator of 'Pachuco Boogie,' he was joined by other luminary figures such as Lalo Guerrero, another young man of the time who was also a transplant to Southern California, also spoke *pachuco* and was familiar with the subculture, and was cutting records as a newcomer in the music industry.

Lalo Guerrero

Elsewhere in the borderlands, Eduardo 'Lalo' Guerrero was born to immigrant parents in Tucson, Arizona in 1916. As Lalo told it in his biographies, he was born into what was basically a segregated 'Mexican' community in Tucson where Whites lived on one side of the tracks and 'Mexicans' on the other. While his father worked for the railroad, his mother stayed home to raise the children, and it was his mother who taught him to play guitar. Lalo grew up listening to and singing the latest Mexican songs in Spanish, but he was also a fan of some American songs in English that he heard on the radio. In his autobiography and in interviews, Lalo confessed that his childhood dream was to be an English-language crooner and to cross over into the pop music market, singing mainstream 'American' music and singing in English.

Guerrero's situation, however, was that he was a Mexican American from, of all places, Tucson, Arizona, and he was born to Mexican immigrant parents. In fact, Guerrero also added that he looked 'very Mexican' and 'very much Indian,' so he saw the issue quite simply — he was barred from entry into the English-language pop music market because of his 'Mexican' physical features. As he reported, 'I saw I wasn't going to make any money. [So . . .] I reverted to singing Mexican music.'¹⁹ So, after not being able to get work, and after being encouraged by producers to sing Spanish and produce music for the local Latin music market, he made the switch to the Spanish-language market. As an 'American,' this went against his first

---

16 The change to the name Don Tosti is interesting in itself. While Varela provides an anecdote about how the last name Tostado was shortened to Tosti to fit on a poster for an event, Macías relates the name change to a trend in LA where Mexicans were trying to make their names sound ethnically Italian (to which Don Tosti eventually attributed his relative lack of success with Mexicans), further revealing the complexity of the identity-related cultural politics of the time; see Varela, Liner notes to *Pachuco Boogie*, 8; Macías, *Mexican American Mojo*, 132.

17 A musicological definition of 'Pachuco Boogie' music is offered by Macías who notes how 'Pachuco Boogie' was basically boogie woogie blues, and further as, '[a] bouncing ostinato figure of continuously repeating two-pulse bass patterns played by the left hand, and its 'rhythmically and melodically playful' jazz phrases improvised by the right hand'; See Macías, *Mexican American Mojo*, 123-33.

18 Varela, Liner notes to *Pachuco Boogie*, 8-9.

19 Loza, *Barrio Rhythm*, 159.

inclinations and childhood dreams. Yet, as a 'Mexican' growing up in the times of the *pachucos*, he was able to make the transition to the Mexican music market and eventually found himself in Southern California doing Latin music and mixing it up with the burgeoning 'Pachuco Boogie' music scene. In a recent documentary on Lalo Guerrero, Chicano actor/activist Edward James Olmos recently addressed the *pachuco* era and the prominence of Lalo Guerrero within it:

> It's Spanish, but it isn't Spanish. It's caló. It's pachuco. It was a whole way of life. It was a subculture within a culture. And Lalo grabbed it and really understood it to the fullest, and became the voice of that period in time.[20]

It is also interesting, of course, that Guerrero's career moves were initiated by the racial tenor of the era and the intercultural relations of the day. It was only out of sheer necessity that Guerrero began to sing and perform in Spanish and *caló*.[21]

In the following section, I extend this analysis toward a recent compilation titled 'Pachuco Boogie,' that included the music of both Don Tosti and Lalo Guerrero (and many others), that provides insight into the 1940s culture, and that speaks to the cultural contributions of the 'Pachuco Boogie' era. Likewise, I will further address the life of Lalo Guerrero, the culture that spawned the music, and new Latino/a identities that followed.

The 'Pachuco Boogie' Era

In 2002, Arhoolie Records released a compact disc titled *Pachuco Boogie, Featuring Don Tosti — The Original Historic Recordings* as the tenth volume of their *Historic Mexican-American Music* series. To hear the *Pachuco Boogie* compilation is to step into a time-machine, stepping back into the 1940s and into a rich musical culture that begins with jazz and mambos, and moves along into swing, boogie, and *guaracha* mixing with brass horn explosions and scat-singing, then to slow-tempo acoustic *tejano* duets, full-*mariachi corridos*, acoustic guitar jams, blues (in Spanish), *rhumba*, *danzón*, up-tempo accordion instrumentals, and piano blues (in Spanish). As the name suggests, the disc chronicles the *Pachuco Boogie* era through its music. In the disc's liner notes Chuy Varela states that it is a 'missing link' and that, '[t]hese recordings are the earliest documentation of a burgeoning Chicano musical subculture that set a foundation for future stars . . . in the Chicano musical continuum.' However, I submit here that the album also provides another level of conversation on Latino/a connections to what later became rock 'n' roll as well as discursive evidence about the evolution of Latino/Hispanic identities. As Varela further states, 'it was a musical transition that also ushered in a quest for identity and political power.'[22]

While the music is as brilliant as it is diverse, the lyrics aptly capture the

---

20 Edward James Olmos, quoted in Guerrero & De los Santos, *The Original Chicano* [documentary].
21 Loza, *Barrio Rhythm*, 159.
22 Varela, Liner notes to *Pachuco Boogie*, 12.

sensibilities of the time — bicultural, bilingual Mexicans and/or Mexican Americans (hence, 'Mexicans') who negotiated their identities within and performed their identities through popular music. Among many other words and phrases that document the language, the culture, and the times, throughout many of the songs of 'Pachuco Boogie,' men are referred to as *vatos* or *batos* (dudes), while women are referred to as *hainas* and *güisas* (chicks) and *pachuquitas* (female *pachucos*), and references are made to *chanclear* (literally, to throw a sandal; meaning, to dance) and to the *volteón* (literally, the turning or spinning; meaning, the dance).[23]

In one illuminating example, in the opening number 'Pachuco Boogie' by Cuarteto Don Ramon Sr.,[24] the singer's chorus is interrupted by another voice speaking the hip *caló* street slang: 'Where you goin' man?'[25] to which another youth replies,

> 'No way, I'm not going man. I'm coming. I'm coming from "The Pass" man. I'm comin' from El Paso dude. I came here to "Losca" to show off my rags cuz it's cool here man. See?' (Author's translation)[26]

Part of the culture's significance here lies in the always playful, often nonsensical, and somewhat untranslatable *caló*. In the song, the second speaker is saying he is from 'The patience' if translated literally to English. However, because in Spanish 'The patience' is actually uttered as *El paciente* in the song (see previous footnote), it is worth noting that the alliterative parlance '*El paciente*' begins with the same sounds as 'El Paso' (the city in Texas) which is what was actually meant. In other words, the alliterative sounds alone could connote some of the meaning that was intended. So, in this line, the unwritten rules of the subculture virtually require the playfulness with language so that one might first rhyme a few syllables without really saying what is really meant. As a follow up in the dialogue, the speaker might say 'El Paso' (what was really meant) as the *pachuco* does in this song, or simply continue with other jargonistic banter that would convey meaning through its context. For example, it could have also been left unsaid: In Spanish '*Paciente*' begins with the first syllable 'Pac' (for 'Paz') which alone could be used to signify place. To an insider, the sound 'Paz' can convey meaning such as 'The Pass' simply because 'Paz' (in Spanish) sounds like 'Pass' (in English) but also because 'The Pass' is a famous nickname for El Paso — 'The Pass of the North' — and in fact, the origins of its historical name in Spanish, '*El Paso del Norte*.' Moreover, as the speaker tells the others that he 'came here' to 'Losca,' 'Losca' is a shorthand reference for Los Angeles, California (i.e., Los CA). In other words, without a sense of the nuances

---

23   From the Spanish, *voltear* (to turn).
24   As *Pachuco Boogie* liner notes reveal, Cuarteto Don Ramon Sr. was actually Don Tosti and his band, who were using a different name to circumvent local musicians' union rules.
25   In *caló*, 'Ese, onde la lleva pues?'; similar to Spanish, 'A donde la llevas pues?'
26   'Nel, ese. Pues no voy ese. Vengo, del paciente. Ve? Es un lugar que le dicen El Paso. Nomas que de allá vienen los pachucos como yo. Eh? Me vine aquí a "Losca." Ve? Me vine a parar garra, porque aquí está bote de aquella, ese.'

of the argot, the discourse would not make sense. The phrases make no more sense in proper Spanish than they do in English, and more significant perhaps, is that without English/Spanish bilingual abilities that operate simultaneously, the dialect is virtually untranslatable. Examples such as these thereby illuminate the prevalence of intercultural communication within the subculture and demonstrate the complexity of the evolving identities of the time.

As the song continues the jive-talking *pachuco* further interrupts the band, prompting the singer to begin scat-singing, and eventually interrupting again to talk about getting '*tírili*' which is also the title of the album's fourth track. The word '*tírili*' serves as another valuable example here, since the word demonstrates hidden meanings and flexibility. In one context, it was a reference to an ability to speak like a hipster. So, to speak *tírili* could simply mean to speak the street slang. In other contexts *tírili* meant something like 'being wasted.' For example, one might say, 'Me puse bien *tírili*' to mean, 'I got really wasted.' Yet, 'being wasted,' in turn, had its own set of double-meanings. For some it connoted a state of being drunk on alcohol, while for others 'being wasted' meant being high on marijuana. Yet, in other expressions, such as those heard in the song 'El Tírili,' it meant the guy, the dude, or the person himself (e.g., the *pachuco*). On yet another level, 'El Tírili' could simply mean the guy, or it could refer to a marijuana-smoking guy (i.e., like 'pothead'), or to a 'wino' (i.e., drunkard or bum). So one could be a *tírili* (i.e., for acting like a *tírili*), in a condition of *tírili* (i.e., for behaving like a *tírili*), or simply speaking *tírili* (i.e., for talking like a *tírili*). The exact meaning of the word, of course, was understood through its context. As *pachucos* of the day said it, one could either speak *tírili* (like a *pachuco*) or one couldn't, and to speak it was as much of a cool-test as it was a facility with language.

Words such as *tírili* and the *pachuco* subculture have been analyzed elsewhere. For example, in *Mexican American Mojo* Anthony Macías carefully records significant aspects of the culture and the time as well as many other examples of the discourse through personal interviews and historical research. I will therefore suspend my analysis of *caló* in order to return to the 2002 *Pachuco Boogie* compilation by Arhoolie Records that registers the cultural shift(s) that followed.

For example, as much as the *pachuco* discourse reflected multilingual wit, it also required biculturalism and even intercultural competence. In one instance, the disc's second track 'Güisa Gacha' (mean chick), a romping mambo containing humorous lyrics, tells of a youth dancing with a 'mean chick' who is mean precisely because she eventually reveals that she's just '. . . waiting for my boyfriend to come back.' Most significant in this track is the linguistic code-switching that occurs. The song switches from Spanish/*caló* to English, and the final humorous flip (revealing that she's just dancing with another right now because she's waiting for her boyfriend) is in English, although delivered with a slight accent. So, in this song, English is employed as a discursive device to bring the song to its humorous conclusion.

In other examples, such as the song 'Wine-O Boogie,' the title and chorus use the word 'wino' (a drunk, drunkard, or bum) instead of an equivalent word in Spanish or *caló*, and tells about how he and his 'chick' got drunk on '*el wine*' (instead of *el vino*, in Spanish). Meanwhile, in other songs such as 'Los Blues' by Don Tosti y su Trío, the singer tells others to '*wachar*' (from English, to watch or to look), and in 'El Tírili' the singer talks about how some guys '*Luego luego quieren fight*' (right away want a 'fight') using Spanish in combination with the English word 'fight' to convey meaning. While seemingly insignificant on a surface level, it is important to note that song lyrics such as these depend upon at least a basic level of English comprehension, revealing the extent to which intercultural communication was a part of the subculture. Without a certain level of intercultural competence, meanings would be lost, nuances could be missed, and the subculture could be stripped of its meaning and robbed of its loftiest social significance — subcultural protest through counter-minstrelsy and symbolic subversion.

In all of these examples, and the many more that could be provided, what is being revealed is the culture. Through linguistic analysis of various discursive elements, one gets a picture of the importance of the music, dancing, and the clothing that were core elements of the subculture, but also of the street slang that itself reveals class, race, gender norms, sexism, fights, the prevalence of alcohol in the party scene, and, often, the habitual use of marijuana to 'get high' or have a good time.

Interestingly, one of the constant themes running through the *Pachuco Boogie* music was that of using marijuana recreationally, and in terms of identity politics, this theme is highly significant. For, as Macías avers on this theme,

> Given that the dominant society had used 'loco weed' as a pretext to deport Mexicans in the early 1930s, and had federally criminalized it in 1937 with the Marihuana Tax Act, Mexican Americans' mores were countercultural, particularly regarding a plant with such a long history of use in Mexico and the U.S. Southwest. Indeed, because of the strong connection between marijuana and Mexicans, many African American jazz musicians referred to joints as 'Mexican cigarettes.'[27]

Without a doubt, to publicly celebrate an identity that overtly expressed criminalizing practices was a potential risk. Likewise, to communicate an identity that denied the legitimacy of the dominant culture and expressed a counter-cultural, marginal, or minority group perspective should also be understood as highly significant identity politics through symbolic subversion and (musical) public protest.

Indeed, the identity issues are further illuminated when considering the fact that the 1930 Census treated 'Mexican' as an entirely separate racial category. This, in turn, was a response to previous attempts by the US government from the 1850s to the 1920s that counted Mexicans as 'Whites.' Which is to say that by the racial codes of that time period, by not being Black, Mexicans were considered White by default. Peculiar in its own right, it was a kind of *de facto* whiteness. By the late 1920s, different campaigns had been launched to officially classify Mexicans

---

27 Macías, *Mexican American Mojo*, 129–30.

as non-Whites, and then as the Great Depression began in 1929, and xenophobia and anti-immigrant sentiment worsened; 'Mexican' then became a racial category.

This early period, from the 1920s–1930s, is an interesting and significant moment for a conversation about Latin/o influences in US popular music and especially about rock 'n' roll. It was a moment when 'Mexicans' and other 'Hispanics' went from legally White, at the same time that they were also victims of Jim Crow-like segregation (so, by association, Black), to being an entirely separate racial category. And yet, one might logically conclude that in spite of all of this ambiguity, the significance was that 'Mexicans' and other Latino/as were ever-present and numerous enough to precipitate discourse about what to call 'them,' as well as somewhat influential in the culture.

Moreover, as Eric Zolov suggests in *Refried Elvis*, the Mexican connection to marijuana use might also be responsible for the practice of using marijuana in rock 'n' roll scenes and movements that developed later.[28] In this case, the articulation of Mexican youth to marijuana use that is revealed in 'Pachuco Boogie' music provides yet another example of influences on what became the rock 'n' roll style, but, more significantly, reveals an example of the merging of popular music with contestatory, shifting, and evolving identity categories.

To consider another example, the final cut on the *Pachuco Boogie* compilation is the 1948 song 'Chicano Boogie' by Don Tosti's Quartet, which moves from scat-singing to instrumental piano jazz music backed by rhythmic percussion, to bilingual jive-talk that takes over as the lyrical accompaniment to the music. What's most interesting is the use of the term 'Chicano.' From the beginning of the spoken discourse, the song's male narrator (Don Tosti) addresses the issue of what 'Chicano Boogie' means. As Don Tosti tells us in the hip *caló* street slang,

> Hey dudes. You guys have heard the 'Pachuco Boogie' right? Well, this 'Chicano Boogie' is crazier. If you haven't heard it man, that sucks. Yeah, you can boogie to it . . . you can move those big hips and the big sandals brotha. Cuz, check it out man . . . it's in rhumba time AND its boogie dude. Get crazy, man. Listen big daddy . . . here comes the boogie with the rhumba![29]

Without resorting to a musicological analysis on boogie and *rumba*, what the narrator is suggesting is that 'Chicano Boogie' is something like a step-up from 'Pachuco Boogie' or an evolutionary step forward (literally, 'crazier' than 'Pachuco Boogie'). In other words, whether talking about the music or the dance or the song, this discourse suggests 'Chicano' as a term evolving out of *pachuco* cultural sensibilities, and just as the narrator affirms the combination of boogie with *rumba*,

---

28 See Zolov, *Refried Elvis*.
29 Author's translation of 'Chicano Boogie' from Spanish and *caló*; Original lyrics are as follows: 'Esos vatos, usted nunca ha oído el 'Pachuco Boogie' verdad? Este 'Chicano Boogie' ta más loco. Si no han oído hermano, gacho. Le puede vailar el boogie . . . y le puede mover la caderota y la guarachota hermano. Porque wachen . . . tiene el tiempo de rumba y tiene el de boogie, ese. Póngase locote hermano. Oiga, ese vatote . . . ahora aquí viene el boogie y la rumba'; 'Chicano Boogie' appears in *Pachuco Boogie, featuring Don Tosti — The Original Historic Recordings*.

specifically that something can be both, the discourse employs the term 'Chicano' in order to suggest combining elements or, at least, that 'Chicano' is about being both of something — even though they don't seem like they can go together.

What is more intriguing about this discourse is that it registers an unusual use of the word 'Chicano' in 1948, at a time where it was still something of a pejorative term in the culture. As Macías notes on this subject, some people did use the term, but 'some people were offended' by the term 'Chicano.'[30] For many Mexicans and Mexican Americans of this time period, the term 'Chicano' was not yet articulated to social movements or fashionable politics, and often the term was used as an insult of sorts. Thus, its use in the 'Pachuco Boogie' era makes its appearance somewhat surprising and rather remarkable as an early use of the identity marker 'Chicano.'

In all these examples, an important element that is revealed is the extent to which biculturalism, multilingualism, and intercultural competence were standard aspects of the subculture's norms. On another level of significance, the songs on the compilation not only document the vernacular, but also demonstrate how the language reflected the sensibilities of the time and the emergent identities that followed. Furthermore, such examples illustrate the relationship between emergent identities and expression(s) in popular music.

'Pachuco Boogie' to 'Original Chicanos'

In *Barrio Rhythm*, Steve Loza examines the impact of Lalo Guerrero who was part of LA's 'Mexican' music scene in the 1930s and 1940s as it emerged from of a difficult trade relationship between the US and México. As Loza notes of the time, trade regulations prohibited the importation of records from México while other laws prevented Mexican companies from recording in the US.[31] While such restrictions with music might have seemed like a curse for some people at the time, for Mexican American musicians in California it turned out to be a blessing in disguise. What resulted was the growth of a music scene in Los Angeles in which songs were transmitted by word of mouth and bands hearing each other live. Loza argues that local musicians were actually vitalized by these circumstances; they were forced to become masters of their craft in spite of being unable to obtain recorded music.[32] Another unintended result was the emergence of independent record companies founded in LA that were to have a lasting impact on the local community by establishing networks, bars, nightclubs, and social scenes that centered on music. The impact on rock 'n' roll music is evident when one considers that many of the early African American and Mexican American rock 'n' roll musicians from LA and Southern California were able to sustain their careers because of a solid Mexican American fan base that formed around local clubs and the already-existing music scene.[33]

30   Macías, *Mexican American Mojo*, 106–7.
31   Loza, *Barrio Rhythm*, 69–77.
32   Ibid., 69–70.
33   See Macías, *Mexican American Mojo*; Macías, 'Rock con Raza, Raza con Jazz: Latinos/as and Post-World War II Popular American Music'; M. Garcia, 'The "Chicano" Dance Hall: Remapping

In yet another connection between Latino/as and the early rock 'n' roll scene, Loza's research into the early recording industry informs us that several Black musicians, like Fats Domino, T-Bone Walker, and other artists who performed R&B music, were in fact made famous on the Imperial Records label. Yet, none of this happened until Imperial Records had earned enough profits from Mexican artists in the 1940s to implement reinvestment strategies and shift their emphasis to the Black audience and 'rhythm and blues' or, later, 'R&B.'[34] R&B music, of course, would resurface in the 1950s through what was then being called rock 'n' roll music, and figures such as Fats Domino would become some of its earliest icons.

'Mexican' Music

Returning to Lalo Guerrero, I alluded above to how his music career in Spanish began out of necessity when he was not accepted as a viable English-language performer, but the details of his early career provide more interesting facts and other material worthy of consideration here. For example, some time in the 1930s Guerrero wrote one of his most famous songs, 'Canción Mexicana,' which became popular in México once it was recorded by famous singer Lucha Reyes. It has been widely considered a classic Mexican song ever since then, and was eventually covered by major Mexican figures, such as Javier Solís, Lola Beltrán, Trío Los Panchos, and countless others in México. This part of the story alone is quite remarkable given that Guerrero was in fact from Tucson, Arizona and had a difficult time breaking into the Mexican music industry specifically because he was an 'American.'

However, another side of the story reveals how 'Canción Mexicana' was actually written by Guerrero, when he was just seventeen and before he had ever set foot in México, during the time of lingering poverty from the Great Depression in the US.[35] Guerrero later revealed that he wrote the song as a tribute to Mexican music, to try to lift the spirits of the local Mexican people he knew who were having a difficult time due to the effects of the Great Depression. As he said, 'It was a kind of gift to the people of my old *barrio* to remind them that, even if we were poor, we had something to be proud of.'[36] During this time of depressed economy, many Mexicans were forcibly removed from the US and returned to México, although Guerrero's family returned to México by their own volition. However, his family was so Americanized that they didn't like their new life in México and quickly returned to their life in Arizona as 'Americans.' Interestingly, Guerrero's early success as a Mexican music composer and songwriter were colored by the political, economic, social, and cultural effects of the time, as well as the intercultural dimensions of his life.

Public Space in Post-World War II Greater Los Angeles'; Reyes and Waldman, *Land of a Thousand Dances: Chicano Rock 'n' Roll from Southern California*.
   34   Loza, *Barrio Rhythm*, 77.
   35   Guerrero and Mentes, *Lalo: My Life and Music*, 53–4.
   36   Ibid., 54.

Humor, or Political Commentary?

Aside from his early attempts to break into popular music markets, another significant period in Lalo Guerrero's career featured humorous music and fun music for children. Although not altogether separate from the days of witty slang of the 'Pachuco Boogie' era, the humorous music gave Guerrero an entirely different edge. Whereas his 'Pachuco Boogie'-era songs such as 'Los Chucos Suaves' (1949), 'Muy Sabroso Blues' (1949/1950), and 'Chicas Patas Boogie' (1950) must have appeared humorous on some level, Guerrero eventually took his humor to an entirely different level. He eventually began to use humor to make a point, and in this next stage, Guerrero walked the line between humor and political commentary.

Guerrero once said that he could 'Mexicanize' anything for fun and that for him, doing such comically, silly songs was just tapping into a very Mexican tradition. One example, 'Pancho Lopez,' appeared in 1955 and was sung to the tune of the famous song 'Davy Crockett,' which was popular at the time. Guerrero claimed that 'Davy Crockett' was everywhere — on the radio, in the streets, in elevators — and one just couldn't get away from it. After hearing some street children singing about the Mexican revolutionary icon Pancho Villa, Guerrero decided to rewrite the famous 'Davy Crockett' song but replaced the Anglo name with a Mexican name. Avoiding the still-popular figure of Pancho Villa, he made up the name 'Pancho Lopez' and wrote a song about a Mexican character from Chihuahua who was born on a serape under a tree, was very fat, could eat twelve tacos as a three-year-old, shot a gun, rode his *burro*, would run away to avoid work, slept a lot, swam across the Rio Grande, moved to Los Angeles, and began to sell his 'tacos, and beans with cheese.'[37]

Surprisingly, 'Pancho Lopez' became wildly popular and quickly sold nearly a million records. The song at this point was Guerrero's most popular English-language song and his biggest hit in the US, and it eventually propelled him to star status in the US after he appeared on various television shows, including *The Tonight Show*, and as a result of write-ups in magazines like *Time*.[38] The song even reached #3 on the nation's Latin music charts, indicating how the song was popular with Latino/as as well as with other American audiences. In retrospect, however, it seems rather unfortunate that the song was so popular in the US. Without a doubt, the song's resonance in the popular imagination must have had something to do with the stereotypes it conveyed. The song essentially confirmed beliefs about Mexicans that must have been rampant at the time.

Noting this, Guerrero later clarified that the song was intended to spoof the original 'Davy Crockett' song and to convey some of what many Mexican Americans were feeling at the time about the relationship between México and the US and the glorified popular culture narrative of the American takeover of Mexican land. One scholar notes, however, that:

---

37 Kun, *Audiotopia*, 56.
38 Ibid., 124.

Humor was a device for Lalo Guerrero to find himself within popular culture, but also keep a little bit of a critical distance... he also could see as a Mexican American who was aware of prejudice and aware of the way his people were treated by the culture, and ignored by the culture, or stereotyped by the culture... and you know, in that sense humor has been used by all ethnic groups. Lalo, he was able to set it to music.[39]

Kun also notes the significance of using humor in music and cultural productions such as these: 'These melt-resistant *audiotopias*–long since derided as either forgettable novelty items or embarrassing portraits of ethnic self-hate ... enact a refusal of de-ethnicized Americanness through a defiant sounding of [ethnic] difference.'[40]

In the aforementioned documentary about Guerrero's life and music, *The Original Chicano*, the famous Chicana leader and activist Dolores Huerta commented that the song was 'healing' in a way because it was humorous and non-violent, and that it allowed Mexicans and Chicanos to vent and express anger about the history between México and the US and the loss of land to the US by México.[41] Confirming this sentiment, musician Louie Perez of Los Lobos commented on the significance of Lalo Guerrero for other Mexican Americans. As he recalled about Guerrero's humor, 'Lalo was revolutionary because he was the first person that made it okay for Chicanos or Mexicans to make fun of themselves.'[42] As Josh Kun avers on the use of ethnic humor and music, 'Parody is not quiet. Part of the task of [ethnic] parody is to be noticed, to leave a mark and make a statement, to commit an aggressive, guerilla crime of reversal and takeover.'[43]

From Humor to Chicano Consciousness

Thus, if the music of Lalo Guerrero is instructive for the conditions of its production, for the tenuous identities connected to the music, or for the way humor in music could be understood as political discourse, it also takes on further significance. In a particularly salient example from 1968, Guerrero penned the song 'Corrido de Delano' about striking workers near the town of Delano, California, as part of the fundraisers for the work of Chicano activist César Chávez in organizing migrant workers to strike against the atrocious conditions of their labor, and to 'let people know what was happening there.'[44] The song became an anthem for the Chicano movement, since that time and for years thereafter, and it remains an important artifact for the Chicano movement to this day. Guerrero even followed up later with another Chicano-themed song called 'Himno Chicano' (The Chicano Hymn) which he wrote to try to encourage Mexican Americans to register and vote. Through these examples, we learn how Lalo Guerrero was

---

39   Tom Waldman, as quoted in Wilkman, *Chicano Rock!: The Sounds of East Los Angeles*.
40   Kun, *Audiotopia*, 56.
41   Guerrero, *The Original Chicano*, quotation by Dolores Huerta.
42   Ibid., quotation by Louie Perez.
43   Kun, *Audiotopia*, 73.
44   Guerrero and Mentes, *Lalo: My Life and Music*, 139–41.

directly involved in the Chicano movement and how his music served multiple functions as a medium of communication: the music reported the poor working conditions, called for the need for protest, chronicled the times and the movement, and registered a symbolic 'Chicano' identity.

Dolores Huerta also comments on this significance. She remembers that Lalo's song 'Corrido de Delano' was the first song by a major artist about César Chávez, the first recorded song about the movement, and that 'he got the whole spirit of the movement in that song.'[45] And in 1992 César Chávez, the Chicano leader/activist/hero/icon, himself commented on Lalo Guerrero's significance for Chicano/as: 'Lalo has the very special talent for chronicling and recording the major advances of our community for throughout all these 60 years. No one has done the job that he's done.'[46]

Moving forward several years, Guerrero maintained his iconic status as a 'Chicano' hero by continuing his compositions of humorous/political music. In the 1980s he recorded the song 'No Chicanos On TV,' a silly take on the astute realization that there were very few examples of Latino/a representation on mainstream television programming, and Dolores Huerta recalled that the song had some impact. According to Huerta, 'After the song came out people started asking, 'Why aren't there Chicanos on television?' and articles were written about it.' Meanwhile activist Chicano/as and Latino/as formed committees and started contacting the television stations and owners to ask them about the issue of lack of representation.[47] So once again, what began as a mundane spoof by Lalo Guerrero, albeit through his own cultural/political inclinations, eventually became political discourse and even initiated political action.

Emerging Identities

To close this analysis of Lalo Guerrero, I propose two other ways in which Lalo Guerrero looms large as an important figure of the 'Pachuco Boogie' era, and for Latino/as in mainstream popular culture in the US. One manner should appear obvious given the information provided in the previous section, the use of the identity term 'Chicano.' The other can be heard in the resonance of Guerrero's past, and in the reverberations related to those identities that were less obvious but also suggest identities of the present and future.

The first of these, using 'Chicano,' has been mentioned previously in this chapter. As I argue above, the appearance of 'Chicano' as a self-ascribed identity marker is interesting in itself, but so also is the fact that it was being used by people like Lalo Guerrero in popular songs of the time. Others have commented on this. For example, Chicano actor and activist Cheech Marin recently commented on this fact:

What [Lalo Guerrero] does is he chronicles that experience, that Chicano experience,

---

45   Guerroro, *The Original Chicano*, quotation by Dolores Huerta.
46   Ibid., quotation by Cesar Chavez.
47   Ibid., quotation by Dolores Huerta.

before there was even a term 'Chicano' or the notion that there was a separate 'Chicano' identity' [...] Lalo has been in the mix, in defining what 'Chicano' is and [...] with putting 'Chicano' as a term of creativity, and pride, and going forward, and it takes the onus off of being kind of a derogatory term by Mexicans to other Mexicans. I was very proud of being Chicano, and hearing Lalo's songs even furthered that feeling.[48]

Further noting Guerrero's significance for Chicano/as is playwright Luis Valdez who produced the famous play *Zoot Suit*, an artifact of the Chicano/a movement and the eventual movie of the same name, that chronicled the infamous 'Sleepy Lagoon' murder case and the discriminatory practices of the legal/justice system as they pertained to Mexican Americans. Not coincidentally, the soundtrack for *Zoot Suit* prominently featured the 'Pachuco Boogie' music of Lalo Guerrero. According to Valdez, 'The memory of Lalo Guerrero is something that will be maintained as the memory of our people, because he became then, a living symbol of "the *Raza*" on the march.'[49]

Thus, if Guerrero's music and life can be understood in terms of the implications for Chicano/a identity, I submit that Guerrero's music was also significant for how it reconciled 'Latino' identities and suggested an early 'Latino' identity. For example, the mere possibility that a pan-American, pan-Latin, 'Latino/a' identity can be brought forth by Lalo Guerrero's music was suggested by Linda Ronstadt who said recently,

> What I really love about Lalo's diversity is that he can write a *bolero*, he can write a Mexican indigenous rhythm, he can write a *cha-cha*, he can write anything, that came from the greater Latin world, with equal authenticity.[50]

While an obviously personal perspective and seemingly anecdotal, I contend that this perspective is supported when considering other aspects of Lalo Guerrero's life and music that allowed him such 'Latin' authenticity.

For example, throughout his early life Guerrero was exposed to popular music in English and in Spanish, and was in fact a fan of both. The specific music that he was taught by his mother was already Spanish and Mexican, but it was also mixed with Texan music traditions, some of which were reflections of Polish, German, and Czech musical traditions in Texas. This, of course, demonstrates Guerrero's predispositions toward cultural openness and intercultural communication through music, whether he was conscious of it or not. Moreover, he was also a product of the jazz era — which prominently included African Americans but was essentially multicultural. So, from the very beginning, Guerrero can be understood through his cross-racial and multicultural background and identifications.

As his music career progressed, the move from 'Mexican' to 'Latin' became

---

48   Ibid., quotation by Cheech Marin.
49   Ibid., quotation by Luis Valdez.
50   Ibid., quotation by Linda Ronstadt.

visible. Guerrero noted in his autobiography how by the late 1930s, club music was changing so that his band then included congas, *danzón*, and *música tropical* from Mexico's Caribbean coast and from other Caribbean nations. With the popularity of movies, the music began to include samba from Brazil, tango from Argentina, and more *boleros* — romantic songs that tend to be popular throughout Latin America.[51] As he observed, by the late 1940s, the bands had to be able to play more *música tropical* such as the *pachanga*, the *cha-cha-chá*, and the mambo, which were all eventually incorporated into his orchestras.[52] As musicologist/historian Ned Sublette has noted on musical shifts in this period, the mambo was first popularized in México City, led by the Cuban bandleader Pérez Prado and Cuban singer Benny Moré, followed by New York City where many of the players were Puerto Rican. As Sublette argues about this moment, 'we have to speak now, not of Cuban, but of "Latin" music.'[53]

Moreover, Guerrero's songs, such as the Spanish-language spoof 'Elvis Perez' were popular in México and Latin America, but also in Spain and Portugal. Another song, 'Lola,' was quite popular in Uruguay and Argentina, and other records were popular in Cuba, Chile, Peru, Argentina, El Salvador, Uruguay, and Colombia.[54] His 'Las Ardillitas' (The Squirrels) children's records were also phenomenally popular in México, and allowed him a mainstream popularity in México that he never achieved in the US. More relevant perhaps is the fact that his entire life and career seemed to represent an ambiguous relationship between the US and México, between being Mexican and being American, between speaking Spanish and speaking English, and between wanting success in the US pop market and fortuitously scoring hits in México.

As Luis Valdez said about Lalo Guerrero, 'He became a voice of not just his generation, but for several other generations that came after him. You're talking about 70 years here. You're talking about seven decades of work.'[55] Given such reverence and the rest of the analysis presented in this chapter, I propose that Lalo Guerrero might therefore also be viewed as one of the earliest transnational 'Latino' successes and understood in terms of how his music contributed to emerging 'Latino/a' sensibilities.

In 1980 Lalo Guerrero was named a 'National Folk Treasure' by the Smithsonian Institution, and honored by Bill Clinton in 1997 with the National Medal of Arts:

> For a distinguished music career that spans over sixty years, two cultures, and a wealth of different musical styles. With humor, passion, and profound insight, he has entertained and enlightened generations of audiences, giving power and voice to the joys and sorrows of the Mexican American experience.[56]

---

51 Guerrero and Mentes, *Lalo: My Life and Music*, 66.
52 Ibid., 97.
53 Sublette, 'The Centrality of Cuban Music.'
54 Ibid., 129–31.
55 Guerrero, *The Original Chicano*, quotation by Luis Valdez.
56 Guerrero and Mentes, *Lalo: My Life and Music*, 169.

Of course, Guerrero's accomplishments can be extended beyond the genres with which he is most often associated. In relation to rock 'n' roll, specifically, Lalo Guerrero can be credited as an influence for musicians associated with LA's 'Eastside Sound,' major Chicano/a rock artists like Los Lobos, Linda Ronstadt,[57] and his own son Mark Guerrero, a rock songwriter who recorded with A&M and Capital Records.[58] In the concluding section of this chapter, I point to some other notable productions in rock 'n' roll that demonstrate how far-reaching *pachucos*, *pachuco* style, and 'Pachuco Boogie' music were, and how they continue to be in contemporary expressions of rock music.

From 'Pachuco Boogie' to Rock 'n' Roll

Moving forward from the 'Pachuco Boogie' era of the late 1940s/early 1950s, there are many songs that reveal the era's resonances throughout American popular culture. For example, in 1952, African American Chuck Higgins recorded a tenor saxophone instrumental called 'Pachuko Hop' that made him a local star in the Los Angeles area, especially among Mexican Americans. As Macías reminds us, not only was Higgins a popular figure among Mexican Americans, but he also recorded other Mexican-themed songs over the next two years, such as 'Tortas,' 'Boyle Heights,' 'Beanville,' 'Bean Hop,' 'El Tequila,' 'El Toro,' 'Pancho,' and the unfortunately titled 'Wetback Hop,' all of which illustrate the lingering popularity of *pachuco* subculture as it blended with jump blues as well as the intercultural relations and dynamics that nurtured jump blues and rhythm and blues (which eventually informed R&B and later, rock 'n' roll) in LA and Southern California. Meanwhile Jack McVea, another African American, recorded another memorable saxophone instrumental called 'Tequila Hop' in 1954 to appeal to his increasingly 'Mexican' audiences.[59] Macías further mentions how Little Richard (Richard Wayne Penniman), one of the major figures in early rock 'n' roll, was also part of the LA music scene in the early to mid 1950s, a scene that provided him valuable career experience and early success. Meanwhile, his signature song 'Tutti Frutti' is another interesting story connecting Little Richard to Latin America. The song is known to be a graphic depiction of sex and gay community slang, but it actually originated with camp icon Carmen Miranda who wore a 'Tutti Frutti' hat.[60] Yet, perhaps Little Richard's 'Latin' credentials are not just a coincidence. After all, in another historical footnote, Little Richard's birth name was allegedly 'Ricardo.'[61]

By 1955, blues artists such as John Lee Hooker recorded songs like 'Mambo

---

57 The Guerrero–Ronstadt connection is interesting in that during the Depression era Guerrero associated with Gilbert Ronstadt, father of Linda, in Tucson, Arizona. Linda Ronstadt began her career as a singer for the rock band The Stone Ponies, she later moved into the country music genre, and by the 1980s recorded traditional Mexican *mariachi* music and even recorded some of Lalo Guerrero's original songs.
58 Loza, *Barrio Rhythm*, 165.
59 Macías, *Mexican American Mojo*, 151.
60 Mehr, 'In the Beginning was the Word . . .,' 92.
61 See Kirby, *Little Richard: The Birth of Rock 'n' Roll*, 30.

Chillun' to capitalize on the Latin trend, with some success,[62] although more prominent R&B examples include Elvis Presley's 'Hound Dog' in 1956 (originally recorded by Big Mama Thornton in 1952) which was based on a mambo or habanera-mambo rhythm.[63] As the song was covered by several artists prior to Elvis and in the years following his major hit, 'Hound Dog' itself demonstrates the extent to which Latin music was circulating in American popular music and was influencing early rock 'n' roll sounds. Back in the LA scene, Handsome Jim Balcom recorded another popular, upbeat, sax-and-guitar instrumental in 1958 titled 'Corrido Rock,' furthering the Latinization of R&B and the nascent rock 'n' roll scene that had begun much prior to Ritchie Valens and his hits in 1958 and 1959.

Big Jay McNeely was a White saxophonist of the time who faced some measure of discrimination because of the multicultural tenor of the music scene, and later said about the period that multicultural interaction was looked down upon and limited by authorities.[64] These examples are reminders that sometimes the music itself wasn't the only thing of importance but so also were the intercultural relationships that the music fostered as well as the multicultural identities that it spawned.

'Doo Wop'

An important hit in 1960 was 'Memories of El Monte,' a doo wop tune that commemorated the inter-ethnic and interracial dances of the late 1950s at the famous El Monte Legion Stadium in LA. Although 'Memories of El Monte' was recorded by The Penguins, who were most famous for the song 'Earth Angel' (the flipside of which was another Latin-themed song called 'Hey, Señorita' that some connect to the Ritchie Valens song 'Cry, Cry, Cry'), not lost on history is the fact that 'Memories of El Monte' was actually co-written by Frank Zappa, who in turn had his own set of Latino/a cultural connections and credentials. Zappa once told about how in the late 1950s he was such a fan of Ritchie Valens, that he stole money from his father to buy a ticket to a Valens show.[65]

Zappa might also be considered a beneficiary of the Ritchie Valens/'La Bamba' legacy. After the tragic death of Valens, producer and Del-Fi Records owner Bob Keane sought to release music of artists that he believed could capitalize on Valens' success and perhaps become the next Valens.[66] Refocused with a new studio and capital, Keane released Chan Romero and the Carlos Brothers on Del-Fi Records who had some local success in Southern California. One of Chan Romero's 1959 songs was 'Hippy Hippy Shake,' a song that was later recorded by The Swinging Blue Jeans and others and went to #2 on the charts in 1964.[67] Through Del-Fi,

---

62   Gioia, *Delta Blues: The Life and Times of the Mississippi Masters Who Revolutionized American Music*, 254.

63   It is important to note that 'Hound Dog' was written by Jerry Leiber and Mike Stoller; for more on the Jewish connections to Latin music, see Billig *Rock 'n' Roll Jews*.

64   Macías, *Mexican American Mojo*, 153.

65   Morales, 'Rock is Dead and Living in Mexico: The Resurrection of *La Nueva Onda*,' 156.

66   Bob Keane has sometimes spelled his name 'Keene'; see Mendheim, *Ritchie Valens: The First Latino Rocker*, 43.

67   Mendheim, *Ritchie Valens*, 125.

Keane also produced records by other artists such as The Fifth Dimension, Barry White and Frank Zappa.[68]

Of course, Zappa's early career had already included stints with multi-ethnic doo wop groups in Southern California that included Latinos, and, without a doubt, the doo wop sounds of the 1950s can be heard throughout his musical career. So, while Zappa's music success only began with 'El Monte,' the music legend remained a fan of doo wop and the music would emerge in his own productions for decades to come. Music fans and scholars have also noted that the 1966 proto-avant-garde-rock album *Freak Out!* (by Frank Zappa and the Mothers of Invention) included a liner notes reference to *pachucos*.[69] The 1968 doo wop tribute *Cruising with Ruben and the Jets* (produced by Zappa and including members of the Mothers of Invention) said something about 'pachuco hop' in the lyrics to the song 'Jelly Roll Gum Drop,' and a now famous and oft-quoted phrase in the liner notes: 'The present day pachuco refuses to die!' Not lost on Zappa fans, of course, is the fact that the first lead singer for the Mothers of Invention was none other than Roy 'Orejón' Estrada (listed in *Freak Out!* liner notes as an 'asthmatic pachuco'), and that *Cruising with Ruben and the Jets* included several other LA Chicanos.

In other early connections that serve as evidence of the strengthening relationship between rock 'n' roll music and Latino/a culture in the early 1960s, the popular vocal group The Platters sang about 'Sleepy Lagoon,' the place associated with LA *pachucos* (zoot suiters) and a controversial murder case. As I noted above, the 'Sleepy Lagoon' murder case provided the backdrop to Luis Valdez' theatrical treatment of the *pachuco* and zoot suit era as it relates to the unlawful and discriminatory treatment of Mexican Americans.

Los Beatles

Also in 1960, Highland Records released another major hit record of the time called 'Angel Baby' by Rosie and the Originals, and Garcia reminds us that 'Angel Baby' was written and sung by Rosalie Mendez Hamlin.[70] The song was a major hit song for Mexican American youth in its time,[71] and given its iconic status as doo wop and a rock 'n' roll 'oldie,' the song remains anthemic for Chicano/a youth to this day.[72] In yet another connection of Latino/as to the mainstream, however, it is known that John Lennon of The Beatles was very familiar with 'Angel Baby' by Rosie and the Originals. He spoke openly about loving the song, and that it had influenced him greatly. Lennon went so far as to say that the voice of 'Angel Baby' was haunting and that he was somewhat obsessed with the song. He eventually recorded it himself around 1975, and the 45-inch single of 'Angel Baby' was even in his private jukebox in his living room, throughout his life and until the day he died.

68   Ibid., 121.
69   Morales, 'Rock is Dead and Living in Mexico,' 156.
70   Rosalie Mendez Hamlin's credit was not given until she won a lawsuit in 1988 to receive royalties for 'Angel Baby'; see Garcia, 'The "Chicano" Dance Hall,' 341.
71   Garcia, 'The "Chicano" Dance Hall: Remapping Public Space in Post-World War II Greater Los Angeles,' 332.
72   For example, see R. Molina, *The Old Barrio Guide to Low Rider Music, 1950–1975*, 126.

Further noting the Latino/a and Chicano/a connections to The Beatles and early rock 'n' roll, Corona and Madrid remind us that,

> The Beatles themselves made occasional use of boleros, Latin instrumentation (e.g., claves and maracas) and rhythms from their earliest recordings, following the precedent of many U.S. musicians who had assimilated Latin rhythms, sounds, musical structures since before World War II.[73]

In 1962, for example, The Beatles recorded a song called 'Three Cool Cats' (a major stage favorite for The Beatles in their early days), a song about three 'hep-cat,' zoot-suiter types of the 1940s. The lyrics of 'Three Cool Cats' allude to the *pachuco* style and subculture by noting the particular behaviors of three Mexican Americans and their girlfriends walking through the *barrio*, hence, the 'three cool chicks' in the song. In one instance toward the end of the song, one can even hear John Lennon's attempt at accented *pachuco* speech through the line, 'Hey, man, save one chick for me!' In addition to The Beatles, the song was covered by Ry Cooder in 2005 as '3 Cool Cats' in his tribute to the lost Mexican American neighborhood 'Chávez Ravine' that was taken over by the city of Los Angeles in the 1950s and wiped out before an eventual land sale to the Los Angeles Dodgers.

Meanwhile, other Beatles connections include more obvious songs such as their stage act favorite 'Bésame Mucho,' a cover of the aforementioned *bolero* sung by Mexican American 'Andy Russell,'[74] as well as other songs, such as 'Twist and Shout' that is connected to 'La Bamba.' While some scholars describe 'Twist and Shout' as a kind of mambo rhythm,[75] Billig notes how the song's Jewish composer synthesized secular gospel tradition and an instrumental break that goes into the 'La Bamba' rhythm perfectly.[76] Meanwhile, scholars have noted other hit songs by The Beatles that had some form of 'Latin' influence, such as their 1964 hit song 'And I Love Her' that is in its essence a *bolero* (a song in the style of love ballads popular throughout Latin America), 'complete with bongó and claves.'[77] The 1966 hit 'Daytripper' has been called 'a typical mambo construction'[78] and a '*mambo* turned into rock 'n' roll,' although as it progresses it sounds like a *cha-cha-chá*.[79]

While mediated productions such as these attest to the extent to which Latin music was highly influential in popular culture in the late 1950s and early 1960s, I contend that it is precisely the extent of Latin influence in mainstream popular music that resulted in a reaction to all things Latin, such as the celebration of the so-called 'British Invasion,' marked by the famous arrival in New York by The Beatles in 1963, a cultural reaction that subsequently stifled the recognition of

---

73 Corona and Madrid, *Postnational Musical Identities: Cultural Production, Distribution, and Consumption in a Globalized Scenario*, 12.
74 Perhaps as a result of the lingering popularity of the *cha-cha-chá* dance craze in years prior, The Beatles' version of 'Besame Mucho' included the closing refrain, 'Cha Cha Boom!'
75 Morales, *Living in Spanglish: The Search for Latino Identity in America*, 1.
76 Billig, *Rock 'n' Roll Jews*, 83.
77 Sublette, 'The Kingsmen and the Cha-Cha-Chá,' 89.
78 Sublette, 'The Centrality of Cuban Music,' no pagination.
79 Sublette, 'The Kingsmen and the Cha-Cha-Chá,' 89.

various Latin/o cultural influences such as those presented here, and that survives in the present.[80]

The Eastside Sound

Moving forward to the 1960s, and the music of the people who were in the process of becoming Chicano/as, Steve Loza offers a rich historiography in *Barrio Rhythm* of what came to be known as the 'Eastside Sound' of Los Angeles that featured the music of East LA bands that took names like The Premiers, The Blendells, The Heartbreakers, The Emeralds, The Romancers, and the most popular group of the East LA scene, Thee Midniters.[81] Remembered as 'the most significant rock and roll band to emanate from the Mexican-American community of Los Angeles' from 1964–1970, Thee Midniters' most famous song was their 1965 hit 'Whittier Boulevard,' a song about cruising in cars that is also remembered as a kind of anthem for young Chicano/as in Southern California and especially in East LA.[82] Also worth noting is the influence of Thee Midniters on hard-rock music. Musicologist Loza notes how Thee Midniters were producing 'exceptional hard rock' in 1967 in an era when hard-rock would have been something new and still revolutionary, while other scholars note how Thee Midniters were even playing 1960s proto-punk as well as other innovative sounds of the day.[83]

Closely connected to Thee Midniters was another popular East LA band known as Cannibal and the Headhunters.[84] Led by Frankie 'Cannibal' Garcia whose nickname 'Cannibal' came from a street gang fight,[85] Cannibal and the Headhunters made the US Top Forty in 1965 with 'Land of a Thousand Dances (Naa, Na, Na, Na, Naa)' and were in fact the opening act for The Beatles during their second tour of the US.[86] Garcia suggests that he got his start as a rock singer only after being a singer in a high school *mariachi* band, doing traditional Mexican songs, and had it not been for his chops as a *mariachi* singer, Frankie Garcia might not have ever received local attention and might not have been recruited to front the early 1960s rock band, The Headhunters.

Scholars like Loza, and Reyes and Waldman have carefully documented the significance of many Latino/Chicano rock bands of this period.[87] Of course, as Chicano/a identity further crystallized in the late 1960s and early 1970s, many other 'Chicano' (or 'Latin Rock') bands emerged, such as Santana, Malo, Sapo, Azteca, Tierra, and the many other bands that followed at the height of the

---

80   Noting this, scholars such as Ned Sublette offer the sudden fall of Havana to communist insurgents in 1959 and the subsequent political, economic, and social/cultural embargo of Cuba as contributing factors to the disappearance of Latino/as in North America's collective memory; See Sublette, 'The Centrality of Cuban Music' and 'The Kingsmen and the Cha-Cha-Chá.'
81   'Thee Midniters' of the East LA scene in the 1960s should not be confused with 'The Midnighters,' a popular R&B vocal group of the 1950s; for more on The Midnighters of the 1950s, see Busnar, *It's Rock 'n' Roll*.
82   Loza, *Barrio Rhythm*, 98–9.
83   Reyes and Waldman in Loza, *Barrio Rhythm*, 100.
84   See Loza, *Barrio Rhythm*, 100–1.
85   Lipsitz, *Time Passages*, 145.
86   Loza, *Barrio Rhythm*, 101.
87   Ibid., 101–2, 145.

Chicano movement. Attesting to the social and cultural shifts related to Latino/a identity, bands like The VIPs changed their name to 'El Chicano,' and 'El Chicano' would become one of the most famous bands of its era. Of course, it is important to note that during this time the meaning of 'Chicano' was still being negotiated and the effects of such emerging identities were elsewhere in other popular music.

The *Tejano* Connection and other Waves

The sentiment of being unsuccessful in a popular music market that was structured by racial factors and the rigid Black/White dichotomy was echoed by the musicians in South Texas who later went on to create *tejano* music. As musicologist Manuel Peña reveals about *conjunto* musicians in the mid 1960s, many musicians who played various forms of *tejano* music were also playing rock 'n' roll.[88] In addition to the diverse repertoires of the musicians that involved complex mixing of the music of Mexican *tríos*, German and Czech polkas, the Colombian *cumbia*, and sophisticated *boleros*, musical groups like the famous Conjunto Bernal played all those and 'even a few rock-and-roll songs.'[89]

From the mid 1960s to the early 1970s, during what Peña calls 'La Onda Chicana' (the Chicano wave) in the history of *tejano* music, other forms of music were emerging in the southwest, such as *orquesta tejana*. Giants of what became the *orquesta tejana* tradition like frontman Sunny Ozuna of Sunny and the Sunglows/Sunny and the Sunliners fame and Joe Hernández from Little Joe and the Latinaires were both in fact caught up in a desire to be rock 'n' roll stars and achieve glory in the US Top Forty during their younger days. Like many youth across the nation, they were influenced by the overwhelming popularity of the new rock 'n' roll style, and, like many Mexican American youth in Texas, they were members of a generation in which Texas-Mexican communities were deeply immersed in processes of Americanization.[90]

One of the historical gems left over from that early era is a rock song called 'Safari' (which has two parts). Recorded around 1958 by the Latinaires, who at that time were dreaming of becoming rock stars like Elvis Presley, Chuck Berry, and other early rock 'n' roll idols, 'Safari' may be the first rock 'n' roll song recorded by a *tejano* group, and songs such as these attest to the fact that many 'Mexicans' in South Texas, like other Latino/as throughout the nation, were identifying with the language of mainstream 'American' popular music.[91] Little Joe Hernández admitted that at that time, their dreams were still about being on the Dick Clark Show and cracking the Top Forty.[92]

Little Joe's rival, Idelfonso 'Sunny' Ozuna, came out of a poor San Antonio neighborhood, and also grew up with a strong desire for American popular music and especially for rock 'n' roll. During his high school days with Sunny and the

---

88 In a telling example, in 1958 Peña himself was part of The Rocking Kings and later The Matadors; see Peña, *Música Tejana: The Cultural Economy of Artistic Transformation*, 182.
89 Ibid., 102–3.
90 Ibid., 151–2.
91 Ibid., 153.
92 Ibid., 154.

Sunglows, his band consciously played mainstream American music in English. Not at all unrelated to his strong liking for American pop music, he disliked Mexican music and especially *tejano* music.

Ironically, just as the Sunglows were breaking up, the song 'Talk to Me' was getting airplay and actually made the Top Forty for fourteen straight weeks between 1962 and 1963. The song later went 'gold,' and Sunny even made a guest appearance on the famous show *American Bandstand* with Dick Clark.[93] However, the Sunglows were never able to duplicate the success of 'Talk to Me,' and years later Sunny Ozuna came to conclusions about differences between the fickle rock 'n' roll market and the newfound *tejano* music market. He eventually concluded that the *tejano* market was different because those audiences were loyal, held on to their 'roots,' and always backed their stars, which was rather different from their experiences in rock 'n' roll.[94] Similarly, because they were unable to compete in the Top Forty, Little Joe and the Latinaires focused their time and attention on the traditional *tejano* market in which they would eventually become superstars.

After the demise of Sunny and the Sunglows, Sunny Ozuna met the three Villanueva brothers from Houston who were originally known as The Rocking Vs. Soon after they became Sunny and the Sunliners, and to this day, Sunny and the Sunliners are *tejano* music legends. They probably remain in the vinyl record collections of many Chicano/as and may still be heard at family parties in many Texas-Mexican American homes. The same can be said of Little Joe and La Familia who came out of Little Joe and the Latinaires of the 1960s. Once again, as evidence of the fact that the relationship between Latino/as and rock 'n' roll music was one of a complex cultural matrix related to ethnic identity, language, socioeconomic class, national identity, and the affiliation with rock 'n' roll by *tejano* musicians and later, their divergence from it, reveals a little more of what Latino/as have come to terms with over several decades. They found their identities in rock 'n' roll music, but when, for a variety of reasons, they were unable to be a part of mainstream rock music in the US, they sometimes reverted to holding on to cultural ties, maintaining Spanish, and playing music more in touch with their local Latino/a communities. Furthermore, although their careers began with aspirations of reaching the mainstream, they eventually returned to 'Chicano/a' and 'Tejano/a' identities. Yet another example of emerging 'Chicano' identity can be seen through Anglo-Texan Doug Sahm, who first became famous as Sir Douglas with the Sir Douglas Quintet. Doug Sahm eventually adopted his own Chicano persona, which is evident through compositions such as 'Chicano,' in which Sahm famously sang, 'Chicano! Soy Chicano!' Given his life story and how he interacted with Tex-Mex culture, Chicano/as, and 'Mexicans,' these lyrics were obviously autobiographical for Doug Sahm (an aspect of his life that I address in the following chapter on 1960s garage-rock). More interesting perhaps, is that one of his signature songs became a rallying cry for Chicano/as in the 1970s and for Chicano/as thereafter.[95]

93 Ibid., 156–7.
94 Ozuna in Peña, *Música Tejana*, 158.
95 Garza, 'Remembering Doug Saldaña,' no pagination.

Conclusion

To conclude this chapter, I offer some other ways in which the *pachuco* era has had enduring effects in rock music and extensions into North American popular culture. Excluding the various artists and songs that I have not yet come across in my research and might some day be able to add to this discussion, there is evidence of other less obvious ways in which *pachucos*, *pachuco* style, and the effects of the *pachuco* era linger in North American popular culture. For example, an aspect of the era that I have not yet covered is the extent to which *pachuco* era politics influenced lowrider car culture, that featured the extreme customization of vehicles and allowed 'Mexicans' and 'Chicano/as' another new way to express their identity. Borrowing from African American zoot suiter's tendencies toward personal stylization, 'Mexicans' in the post-World War II era developed their own personal stylization in music, clothing, slang, and eventually in automobiles as well. Apart from the stylization of cars, driving, cruising, and late-night boulevard street culture were all part of the culture that fostered the new music and new identities.[96] And while car culture was eventually adopted by Whites, Asians, and Blacks in Southern California and other places in the Southwest, its legacy is evident in recent manifestations in popular culture (e.g., MTV's *Pimp My Ride*). In 1990s popular culture, the development of West Coast rap and the gangsta rap genres also resulted in the wide-scale adoption of customized car culture by African Americans and continues in the present as a once-again multicultural youth trend. Furthermore, although doo wop songs such as the ones mentioned above were immensely popular among LA youth, today it is mostly Chicano/as and Mexican Americans who continue their enduring obsession with 'lowrider' cars and the fascination with oldies from the 1950s and 1960s.

Another trend of the *pachuco* era existed in fashion through the use of brown leather jackets. Macías has recently documented the somewhat forgotten fashion trend and its connotations of toughness, masculinity, and rebellion. As Macías notes, 'In snapshots of the [early 1940s], quite a few young Mexican Americans can be seen sporting leather bomber and flight jackets. With their tough, working-class look, Mexican Americans originated the cool postwar "rebel without a cause" style a decade before it became part of mainstream fashion.'[97]

Another rock 'n' roll style and fashion inspiration came through the *pachuco* hairstyle of the time, which was also called a 'Ducktail,' 'Argentine ducktail,' 'Duck's Ass,' 'Duck's Arse' (for Teddy Boys in England), and otherwise, a 'pompadour.'[98] The name 'Argentine ducktail' itself recalls another connection to Latin America since it related to the Argentine tango fad of previous decades in North American popular culture, and perhaps because of the Latin connection, slicked-back hair become part of *pachuco* style. Also significant here is that 'Mexicans' were some-

---

96 Macías, *Mexican American Mojo*, 151–2; For an excellent article that details the meanings of lowriders and car culture, see M. Stone, 'Bajito y Suavecito [Low and Slow]: Low Riding and the "Class" of Class[*].'

97 Macías, *Mexican American Mojo*, 84.

98 On this point, see Rubin and Melnick, *Immigration and American Popular Culture*; and Macías, *Mexican American Mojo*.

times called 'greasers' by Anglo-Texans and other European Americans since the late 1800s.[99] Thus, it is interesting that the term 'greaser' came to signify a subversive and dangerous masculinist posture, that was eventually co-opted by rock 'n' rollers in the 1950s.

Given the Latin/o essence of this style, it is no wonder that Latino punk-rockers of the 1980s such as Robert Lopez (El Vez) saw themselves in early rock 'n' roll aesthetics. As Lopez noted in the documentary *Americanos*, he thought that Elvis Presley dressed like his Chicano uncles and that with his dark hair and looks, could have been a Latino.[100] Moreover, since leather jackets and slick hair became such a major part of the early rock 'n' roll scene through images of James Dean as the 'Rebel Without a Cause' and Elvis Presley's early fashion, the documentation of its origination with working-class Mexican Americans and *pachucos* is remarkable, and demonstrates another way in which 'Mexican' and 'Latino/a' culture profoundly influenced mainstream popular culture and the forthcoming rock 'n' roll style. In fact, the term 'greaser' and the slick hair look were so defining for the rock 'n' roll era that they became emblematic rock 'n' roll fashion trends through movies such as *American Graffiti* (1973) and *Grease* (1978) and television programs like *Happy Days* (1974–1984) and *Sha Na Na* (1977–1981).[101]

Another more controversial example, the use of marijuana in the *pachuco* subculture, has also been mentioned above. While its significance has been documented by others, it is worth mentioning here because of how it remained significant for rock 'n' roll culture from the 1960s and beyond, and perhaps earlier as well. Given that the (still-transgressive) cultural practice was most often associated with 'Mexicans' in the 1930s and 1940s, it is significant that recreational marijuana smoking would become such a major part of the counter-culture of the 1950s, 1960s, and 1970s, and eventually, became such a standard part of the rock aesthetic that its connection to rock music is virtually unremarkable and its origins virtually unknown.

To note recent reverberations on this trend, one can point to a popular song by the southern-rock band the Black Crowes, who released the song 'High Head Blues' in 1995 — at the end of which, a person is heard exhaling a puff of smoke, and then saying in Spanish, '*Esta es la mejor mota . . .*' (This is the best weed). Such examples can also be found in music by Sublime, a popular reggae/punk/alternative-rock band of the 1990s, who became notorious for their numerous references to 'weed' and 'getting high.' Nor is it a coincidence that Sublime's lyrics frequently referenced the multicultural character of Southern California culture, or that singer Bradley Nowell often sang completely in Spanish and sometimes even in 'Spanglish' (e.g, 'Chica Me Tipo,' 'Caress Me Down,' 'Waiting For My Ruca'). Constructing such a genealogy will obviously lead to many other hit songs, such as 'Hotel California' by the Eagles, in which Don Henley sang about the 'warm smell of *colitas*' — Mexican

---

99   On this matter, see Paredes, *With His Pistol in His Hand: A Border Ballad and Its Hero*; Tovares, *Manufacturing the Gang: Mexican American Youth Gangs on Local Television News*.

100   Todd et al., *Americanos: Latino Life in the United States*.

101   Perhaps because of the Latin(o) resonance of this era, Sha Na Na even nicknamed one of the band members 'Chico.'

slang for the tails/ends of marijuana cigarettes, and to various bands and artists through the decades. Given the evidence presented in this chapter, examples such as these cannot be seen as mere coincidence, and can be connected to a long chain in rock 'n' roll in which, in one way or another, Spanish phrases and references to Mexican and Latin/o culture are ever present in spite of the fact that they remain obscure, unknown, and forgotten in the popular imagination.

Moving forward several decades, I offer a final example to conclude this discussion. Macías also discusses the 'cholo' and 'chola' as a post-*pachuco* style, as another form of Mexican American expressive culture, and as hardcore successors to the *pachuco* style.[102] Cholo/as were almost always associated with street gangs, as they continue to be with contemporary youth culture. Yet, in spite of such connotations, the list of people in rock who were influenced by post-*pachuco* style (and the 'Pachuco Boogie' moment) could even include Gwen Stefani, lead singer of No Doubt (the ska/alternative-rock band most popular in the 1990s), for the style that made her a fashion idol and cultural icon — a defining 'chola' look through 1940s hair, heavy face makeup, and *barrio* street-kid clothing — a style she actually took from 'cholas' in high school.

I suspend my analysis here, but I conclude that what should be evident throughout all of these historical examples is that Latino/as influenced — either directly or indirectly — various musical styles that were beginning to flow into the new hybrid expression called 'rock 'n' roll.' Moreover, these histories demonstrate evidence that the development of rock 'n' roll music, as it pertains to 'Mexicans' and other Latino/as, was also marked by complicated issues of identity. From the limited opportunities for being too dark-skinned, to achieving success by passing as White, to returning to (ethnic) roots in music and language, to a difficult US/México trade relationship, to the class position of Blacks, Whites, and Latino/as in LA that led to intercultural exchange and multicultural sensibilities, the early roots of rock 'n' roll are colored Black, White, and 'Brown.' Given such evidence, I suggest that Latino/a identities can also be understood through how they disrupted stable notions of identity as much as they can be read for the way they register cultural shifts with regard to race in US culture. To put it another way, the single greatest contribution by Latino/as to American culture might just be how Latino/as disrupted identity categories and related racial hierarchies — whether through dance-hall spaces, spoken language and slang, youth fashion, counter-cultural trends, or through multicultural music that would eventually be called 'rock 'n' roll.'

---

102 Macías, *Mexican American Mojo*, 169–70.

Interludio 2° (second interlude)

Returning to *pachuco* legacies and moving forward into the late 1970s and 1980s, the Texas music scene produced a new incarnation of Tex-Mex music through Joe 'King' Carrasco and the Crowns, veterans of the Austin scene of the late 70s and early 80s who had achieved some measure of punk and indie credibility.[1] As Joe 'King' Carrasco and the Crowns, they recorded various Mexican and Latin-themed songs about Tex-Mex culture, borders, Mexican food, and revolutionary heroes, and utilized awkward Spanish choruses and other 'Spanglish' lyrics. While one could possibly hear their music as campy, parodic songs in their engagement with Latin/o culture(s), their legacy was cemented through a song titled 'Pachuco Hop'. The song was released in 1987 on the *Bandido Rock* album that also featured other songs such as 'Bandido Rock,' 'Juarez and Zapata,' and 'Chicano Town' (to name just a few). While a relatively obscure record and somewhat forgettable recording, 'Pachuco Hop' achieved greater historical significance as a 'Latin' cultural production when it was covered in 1991 as 'Patchuko Hop' by Mano Negra — a French/Spanish *rock en español* band, who became famous in the 1990s throughout Latin America and the US for their fusions of rock music with Latin American pop and Latin American cultural politics. Thus, when Mano Negra covered 'Pachuco Hop,' in one fell swoop they resignified a forgotten North American Tex-Mex song from the 1980s about 1940s-era *pachucos*, and rearticulated it to France, Spain, and *rock en español* throughout Latin America.

Rock en español's connections to *pachucos* were also evident in the 1990s through music by Mexican giants Maldita Vecindad y Los Hijos del Quinto Patio (or just, 'Maldita Vecindad'), who recorded some of their greatest hits such as 'Pachuco' in 1991 and 'Cocodrilo' in 1998. 'Pachuco,' an up-tempo ska-rock song, tells the tale in Spanish of a young Mexican rocker in dialogue with his disapproving father. The very beginning of the song features the phrase that made the band famous: '¡Carnalitos y Carnalitas, ya llegó su Pachucote!' (Brothas and Sistas, your big *pachuco* is here!). Not coincidentally, the band actually used the voice of the aforementioned Mexican icon 'Tin Tan' for this brief song introduction, and as Solórzano-Thompson declares about this significance, 'the friendly greeting announces the pachuco's entrance into a new generation's social imaginary.'[2]

As the song proceeds, the youth is defending himself against his father's

---

1   For more on Austin's punk scene, see Barry Shank, 'Punk Rock at Raul's,' 91–117.
2   Solórzano-Thompson, 'Performative Masculinities: The *Pachuco* and the *Luchador* in the Songs of Maldita Vecindad and Café Tacuba,' 90.

derisive comments about rock 'n' roll, youth fashion, and generational failures, and the youth counters with realizations such as '*Ey, Pa. Fuiste Pachuco. También te regañaban. Y te bailabas mambo*' ('Hey, Pop. You were a *pachuco*! You got in trouble too. And you also danced mambos'). Through this type of lyrical discourse, Maldita Vecindad provided an anthemic chorus and rallying cry for an entire generation of youth who identified with the new *rock en español* sounds that still connoted counter-culture in México. What's more, Solórzano-Thompson's recent research further comments on the lasting significance of the *pachuco* for Mexican popular culture. In an analysis of Maldita Vecindad's music, lyrics, and themes, she argues that the *pachuco* remains one of the two main performative identities for lower-class men in Mexican popular culture, and that such 'portrayal of lower-class masculinity as positive and epic through the figures of the pachuco and the luchador offers the potential for cultural change and provides a new form of reimagining the nation.'[3] Noting such implications for national identities, Solórzano-Thompson also reminds us that *rock en español* bands such as these have also crossed over into other nations, including the US.

Thus, in addition to US Latino/a articulations to *pachucos*, it is important to point out the other, more obvious and well-known *pachuco* rearticulations that happened north of the border in the mid to late 1990s and the entire retro-swing movement from the 1990s to the present. In this era, various new bands such as Big Bad Voodoo Daddy, Cherry Poppin' Daddies, The Brian Setzer Orchestra, and Squirrel Nut Zippers were at the forefront of a neo-swing movement in popular culture that further recalled zoot suits, *pachucos*, boogie woogie, and swing. While the Cherry Poppin' Daddies scored a hit in 1997 with direct references to the zoot suit riots (see 'Zoot Suit Riot' from the album of the same name), they also dressed in zoot suits and the style of the era and made swing-dancing a part of their performances. Similarly, other bands like Big Bad Voodoo Daddy cut songs like 'Mambo Swing' (from the 1998 *Americana Deluxe* album) and the Royal Crown Revue had songs such as 'Hey Pachuco!' (from the 1995 album *Mugzy's Move*) which continues to be their most popular song and thus, has been re-recorded and re-released on subsequent albums.

Meanwhile, the aforementioned 1998 cut 'Cocodrilo' by Maldita Vecindad begins with the slow-paced feel of a piano jazz tune that builds to saxophone solos, and tells a story through *pachuco* slang lyrics. As Solórzano-Thompson notes on this song, a *pachuco*'s ghost serves as the narrator in lyrical discourse (about a 1950s taxi) that essentially serves as 'a challenge to the official history of the nation.'[4] In the same year Monterrey, México's Plastilina Mosh, an internationally popular alternative-rock/electronica band, released their smash hit 'Mr. P Mosh' (from 1998's *Aquamosh*) which was widely popular and even garnered attention on alternative-rock radio in the US. Interestingly, their huge hit began with a line in English, 'I'm the Pachuco King!' before breaking into Spanish lyrics, thereby providing another example of the resignification of the term 'pachuco' and its

---

3   Ibid., 96.
4   Ibid., 90–1.

Plastilina Mosh. Photo by: Alex Luster

significance for another generation, but also signifying the very dual nature of the identity inherent in the term 'pachuco.'

By 2004, the music came full circle to Latino/a connections through the music of retro-swing band Los Skarnales, a Houston, Texas ska-rock band with their own connections to Latin music and Mexican Americans, who recorded the album *Pachuco Boogie Sound System*. Through this album, Los Skarnales directly referenced 'Pachuco Boogie' music and the era, and, fittingly, made other connections through the album cover, which included an image of the zoot suit style. Not coincidentally, the album included the song 'Juana,' which featured the singer Roco from the aforementioned Mexican rock band Maldita Vecindad.

Selective Discography and Tracks Listed Here and in Chapter Two:

The Beatles. 'Three Cool Cats,' 'Besame Mucho,' *Anthology 1* (Apple Corps, 1995).
The Black Crowes. 'High Head Blues,' *Amorica* (American Recordings, 1994).
The Cherry Poppin' Daddies. 'Zoot Suit Riot,' *Zoot Suit Riot: The Swingin' Hits of The Cherry Poppin' Daddies* (Mojo Records, 1997).
Cuarteto De Ramon Martínez (Don Tosti's Quartet). 'Chicano Boogie,' *Pachuco Boogie, featuring Don Tosti — The Original Historic Recordings* (Arhoolie Productions, 2002).
Cuarteto Don Ramon Sr. (Don Tosti's Pachuco Boogie Boys). 'Pachuco Boogie,' 'Guisa Gacha,' *Pachuco Boogie, featuring Don Tosti — The Original Historic Recordings* (Arhoolie Productions, 2002).
Don Ramon Sr. y Su Orquesta (Don Tosti's Pachuco Boogie Boys). 'Wine-O Boogie,' 'El Tírili,' *Pachuco Boogie, featuring Don Tosti — The Original Historic Recordings* (Arhoolie Productions, 2002).
Handsome Jim Balcom. 'Corrido Rock,' *Art Laboe's Memories of El Monte* (Original Sound Record Co., 1991).

Higgins, Chuck. 'Pachuko Hop,' *Art Laboe's Memories of El Monte* (Original Sound Record Co., 1991).
Joe King Carrasco y Los Coronas. 'Pachuco Hop,' *Bandido Rock* (Rounder Records, 1987).
Lalo Guerrero y Su Orquesta. 'Chicas Patas Boogie,' *Pachuco Boogie, featuring Don Tosti — The Original Historic Recordings* (Arhoolie Productions, 2002).
Lalo Guerrero y Sus Cinco Lobos. 'Muy Sabroso Blues,' 'Los Chucos Suaves,' *Pachuco Boogie, featuring Don Tosti — The Original Historic Recordings* (Arhoolie Productions, 2002).
Maldita Vecindad (y Los Hijos del 5º Patio). 'Pachuco.' *Rock en Español: Lo Mejor de Maldita Vecindad* (BMG Entertainment, 2001).
Mano Negra. 'Patchuko Hop,' *Amerika Perdida* (EMI Latin, 1991).
The Mothers of Invention (with Frank Zappa). 'Jelly Roll Gum Drop,' *Cruising with Ruben and the Jets* (Rykodisc, 1968).
The Penguins. 'Earth Angel,' 'Memories of El Monte,' *Art Laboe's Memories of El Monte* (Original Sound Record Co., 1991).
Rosie and the Originals. 'Angel Baby,' *The Best of Rosie and the Originals* (Ace Records, 1999).
Royal Crown Revue. 'Hey Pachuco!,' *Mugzy's Move* (Warner Bros., 1995).
Sunny and the Sunglows. 'Talk To Me,' *Talk To Me* (Collectable Records, 1991).

3

Latinos in the Garage: Latin/o Presence and Influence in Garage-Rock... and Other Rock and Pop Music

Clearly different from a taste for any other music, liking punk rock seemed to produce momentary experiences for middle-class Anglo-Texans akin to the everyday life of Blacks and Hispanics. Soon Raul's [club] was packed every night with students longing for that identity streaked with power and danger.[1]

Mira la esencia, no las apariencias.[2]

While the previous chapter concluded with notable examples from the early to mid 1990s regarding the Latin/o legacy in popular music such as the *pachuco* era's lasting significance in rock music, marijuana's centrality to rock 'n' roll's rebellion, and *chola* fashion in Gwen Stefani's iconic look, the current chapter begins with a brief consideration of popular music trends in the late 1990s. For example, with regard to popular music, the year 1999 will likely be remembered by many writers, critics, media experts, and fans as 'the year of Ricky Martin,' after his phenomenal success at the Grammy Awards. Some have suggested that it may be more accurate to call it 'the year of the Latino' in recognition of other popular Latino/a artists who enjoyed success in North American mainstream culture. Ricky Martin only led the pack as he was quickly followed by Enrique Iglesias, Marc Anthony, Lou Bega, Christina Aguilera, and Jennifer Lopez, who all achieved unprecedented chart success in the US pop charts all within a matter of a few months to a year.[3]

---

1   Barry Shank, 'Punk Rock at Raul's,' 110.
2   Lyrical excerpt from 'El Estuche' by Aterciopelados; see discography in Third interlude.
3   Ricky Martin rose to the top of the charts in 1999 with 'Livin' La Vida Loca,' and followed with 'Shake your Bon Bon.' Almost on cue, Enrique Iglesias released an album with the hits 'Rhythm Divine' and 'Bailamos,' while Marc Anthony scored with 'I Need To Know' and Lou Bega broke through with 'Mambo No. 5.' Similarly, Jennifer Lopez' 'If You Had My Love' was a major success, while Christina Aguilera's self-titled debut album featured #1 hit songs in addition to acclaim by music critics.

Aterciopelados. Photo by: Aldo Brando

Around the same time, rocker Carlos Santana once again achieved major chart success with the release of *Supernatural* (1999), and was hailed by music critics, winning several Grammy Awards and tying Grammy records previously held by pop culture icon Michael Jackson.[4] While other allusions included the 'Latin explosion,' the 'Latino pop phenomenon,' the 'Latin music craze,' and the 'Latin(o) music boom,'[5] Latino/a artists were a common presence in the popular culture mainstream, and, in fact, the presence of Latino/as in US popular culture seemed to reach significant and perhaps unprecedented proportions.

While this supposed emergence of Latino/as in popular music served as fodder for media, who called it a phenomenon or craze, it is important to note that the growing presence of Latino/as in the US was visible elsewhere. In addition to the many awards won by Latino/as in 1999 and 2000, Latino/a artists performed in the Super Bowl, at the Republican National Convention, and at President Bush's inauguration.[6] *Rock en español* bands appeared on bags of Doritos chips, while

---

4   Granados, 'Latinos, Once So Anxious to Join the American Mainstream, Have Rediscovered a Passion for their Heritage: Born Again Latinos.'
5   Cepeda, '*Mucho Loco* for Ricky Martin; or The Politics of Chronology, Crossover, and Language within the Latin(o) Music "Boom"'; Ehrenreich, 'Confessions of a White Salsa Dancer: Appropriation, Identity and the "Latin Music Craze"'; Roberts, *The Latin Tinge*; Roiz, 'Los Lobos: The Legend Lives On.'
6   Bender, 'Will the Wolf Survive?*: Latino/a Pop Music in the Cultural Mainstream.'

another *rock en español* band's music provided the soundtrack for Coors Light beer commercials during *Monday Night Football* broadcasts, and still others as background music for Levi's jeans commercials aired during the Super Bowl and otherwise regularly on television. In 2001, *The Tonight Show* host Jay Leno hosted Los Aterciopelados,[7] a rock band from Colombia that became wildly popular throughout the world in the 1990s and continues to produce some of the most highly regarded *rock en español* and Latin alternative music in the 2000s. By the early to mid 2000s, Colombian pop-rock star Shakira could be seen in as many Pepsi commercials as MTV music videos, and was being touted by the music industry as 'the next Madonna.' Most recently, the Colombian pop-rock star Juanes was a featured artist at the 2009 NBA All-Star game. As a result of these and other cultural shifts such as 2000 US Census data revealing the emergence of Latinos/ Hispanics[8] as the largest minority group in the US, contemporary Latino/as are opening up new areas increasingly worthy of scholarly investigation.

Worth noting is the fact that although the latest US Census revealed that Latino/as are now the largest minority group, the news came on the heels of a decade of controversy for Latino/as. From legacies of racism and ethnocentrism to controversial proposals in the 1990s like California's Proposition 187 (which sought to eliminate social services for undocumented immigrants based on their undocumented status),[9] from complicated social issues like affirmative action to heated 'English-only' debates, from increasing immigration from Latin America to rampant xenophobia and antiforeigner sentiment after September 11, 2001, and most recently, from increased visibility in popular culture to the increase in hate crimes against Latino/as, the rising tide of the Latino/a demographic in the US must be further contextualized through discussing complex social issues. In other words, a correlate can be proposed here that while scholars recognize that Latino/as are now more visible than ever in mainstream American culture, the supposed emergence of Latino/as in popular music is an issue that provides insight into contemporary issues in politics and relevant societal questions and, as I argue here, provides further insight into questions of cultural identity.

All of this establishes the rationale for this research and the questions that follow: What else can be gleaned from the notable presence of Latino/as in US popular culture? Can Latino/as in popular music aid better understanding of Latino/as, Latino/a identity, or, perhaps, the complications of Latino/a identity discourse(s)? In short, one of the aims of this chapter is to reiterate the fact that popular music should not be dismissed as just popular music but is, in fact, an important cultural site of discourse, debate, and conflict. Thus, a premise of this chapter is that some of the tensions and complications of Latino/a identity are articulated in media and popular culture. At the same time, some further

---

7   Guzmán and Valdivia, 'Brain, Brow, and Booty: Latina Iconicity in U.S. Popular Culture,' 208–9.
8   The 2000 Census uses the category of 'Spanish/Hispanic/Latino.'
9   For more on Proposition 187, see Hasian and Delgado 'The Trials and Tribulations of Racialized Critical Rhetorical Theory: Understanding the Rhetorical Ambiguities of Proposition 187,' and Ono and Sloop, *Shifting Borders: Rhetoric, Immigration, and California's Proposition 187*.

qualifications are warranted regarding the connections between Latino/as, popular music, and identity questions.

Given the range of possibilities available to Latino/as in language use (e.g., speaking Spanish, speaking English, bilingualism, code-switching, etc.), assimilation (e.g., joining the dominant culture, retaining ethnic identities, hybrid identities, etc.) and other identity questions (e.g., arguments related to choosing identity according to government classifications), and with the notable rise in the Latino/a population in the US as well as impossible-to-determine statistics on illegal immigration, Latino/as comprise a significant group for understanding US culture in the present as well as in the near future. As Johnson notes on the significance of such understanding, 'Recognition of [the need to understand Latino/as] by Anglos and Hispanics alike is necessary for informed thinking about multicultural communication in a society of increasing multiethnicity.'[10] How, then, can a study of Latino/as and garage-rock contribute to such an understanding? It is my contention in this chapter that the prominence of British and Anglo-American garage-rock bands in common discourse on garage-rock signifies a limited Anglocentric view of rock history (and popular music history) where Brits, Anglo-Americans, and other European Americans figure most often and most prominently, at the expense of a wider class-based perspective of rock 'n' roll that should include various ethnic strains, such as contributions by US-based Latino/as.

In this chapter, I continue one of the themes of this book by following scholars who have explored some of the identity-related dimensions of popular (rock) music and, specifically, how ethnic identities have influenced the production and consumption of rock music.[11] More specifically, this chapter disrupts common understandings of garage-rock and remaps the history of garage-rock through a cultural lens that has Latino/a artists in its focus. In order to accomplish this task, this chapter follows a 'genealogical' approach, tracing the significance of Latino/Hispanic artists in the pre-garage-rock era.[12] What follows is a discussion of several different Latino/a contributions to the garage-rock phenomenon that place Latino/as and Latino/a issues at the center of some of the most important and memorable garage-rock compositions. Finally, this chapter explores some of the ideological implications of excluding the highly significant contributions of minority groups and maintaining an Anglocentric history of rock 'n' roll. This chapter therefore establishes a 'genealogical' link with Latino/as that extends the understanding of garage-rock with a perspective that illuminates the contributions of Latino/as and Hispanics, problematizes the aforementioned notion of a recent Latin explosion or 'boom,' and, therefore, requires further consideration and analysis of popular music as a mode of intercultural discourse between minority groups and mainstream society in the US.

10 Fern Johnson, *Speaking Culturally*, 196.
11 Lipsitz, *Time Passages*; Reyes and Waldman, *Land of a Thousand Dances*; Billig, *Rock 'n' Roll Jews*; Stratton, 'Jews, Punk and the Holocaust: From The Velvet Underground to the Ramones — the Jewish-American story.'
12 Foucault, *Language, Counter-Memory, Practice: Selected Essays and Interviews*.

Nuggets and Garage-Rock

The recent Rhino Records compact disc box set titled *Nuggets II: Original Artyfacts from the British Empire and Beyond, 1964–1969*, released in 2001, was devoted to the project of uncovering the forgotten, obscure, unknown, and underground history of garage-rock. In what was obviously a monumental project of collecting and documenting obscure garage-rock histories, the producers of this collection were wise enough to the fact that garage-rock was a worldwide phenomenon. As such, the collection includes tracks from various international garage-rock bands of the 1960s. Of salience for this analysis, the multi-CD collection includes some Latino/Hispanic groups and artists such as Los Bravos,[13] a group from Spain that struck gold in 1966 with 'Black Is Black,' which made the Top Five in both England and the US,[14] and who had other minor hits such as 'Bring a Little Lovin'' and 'Going Nowhere';[15] Los Chijuas, a group from northern México that *Nuggets II* calls 'disciplined garage-psych';[16] Los Shakers, a 'towering presence' from Uruguay and Argentina;[17] We All Together, a Peruvian garage band;[18] and the Brazilian band Os Mutantes, known for psychedelic music, controversy and 'risk-taking'[19] as well as their later influence on the alternative-rock scene in the 1990s through artists like Nirvana, Beck, the Beastie Boys, David Byrne, Stereolab, Portastatic, Superchunk, and Yo La Tengo.[20]

Other Latin American or Hispanic garage bands not included in *Nuggets II* include Los Mockers, a band from Uruguay whose records are sought by collectors for being among the best garage groups of the 1960s and Los Cheyenes, another group from Spain who remained unknown perhaps due to their insistence on singing in Spanish. Unfortunately, with regard to their inclusion of a few Spanish, Brazilian, and other Latin American bands in garage-rock history, the *Nuggets II* producers relied on a mostly international view of garage-rock obscurities and forgotten moments. What was overlooked in this collection was the multicultural and intercultural timbre of the forgotten contributions by domestic (i.e., US-based) Latino/Hispanic garage-rock bands and artists that are of great significance for the garage-rock era.

On the contrary, the previous *Nuggets* collection (*Nuggets I*, 1998) actually does mention some US Latino/as in 'garage' and 'proto-punk' bands from the period of 1964 to 1968, although it seems to include these as mere footnotes. Among others from the original *Nuggets* compilation, one might note Dave Aguilar of the

---

13 It is important to provide some context with regard to my decision to include Los Bravos here, despite their being from Spain and not from Latin America. Because with Spanish-language rock music in general, and especially with the *rock en español* genre, Spain is often linked to Latin America by the music industry, I am therefore including them here with Latino/as and Latin Americans.
14 'Black is Black' reached the #4 position in the United States in 1966; see Whitburn, *Billboard Top 1000 Singles, 1955–2000*.
15 *Nuggets II*, 14, 36,
16 Ibid., 17, 63.
17 Ibid., 17–18, 82.
18 Ibid., 38.
19 Ibid., 18, 86–7.
20 Harvey, 'Cannibals, Mutants, and Hipsters: The Tropicalist Revival.'

Chocolate Watchband;[21] Bob Alaniz of the Kim Fowley band;[22] Bob Gonzalez, who was a founding member of the Syndicate of Sound[23] (yet another band from the San Jose, California scene);[24] Bobby Cortez, the drummer for The Groupies;[25] Billy Garcia and Danny Garcia, guitarist and bassist of The Lyrics;[26] and John Lopez, guitarist and vocalist for The Zakary Thaks.[27] Likewise, the original *Nuggets* collection goes beyond individuals and actually includes entire bands that revealed more Latin/o influence than the mere existence of a Spanish surname on the band's roster. In this list one can note bands such as The Premiers, a band that cracked the Top Twenty in 1964 with 'Farmer John';[28] Sam the Sham and the Pharaohs, who had a top hit with the unforgettable garage-rock/frat-rock classic 'Wooly Bully' in 1965;[29] and the Sir Douglas Quintet, who scored a hit in 1965 with 'She's About a Mover.'[30]

My analytic focus in this chapter turns to the last few garage bands mentioned here — as well as one that seems conspicuously absent — in order to develop my argument that, in some contexts, Latin/o music, people, and culture have been central to the development of rock music, and, more specifically, that some of the most important garage-rock songs were related to, inspired by, or composed by Latino/as that faced complex identity questions. Moreover, the Latino/Hispanic presence and influence continues through less obvious connections such as the 'Bo Diddley beat' in 'I Want Candy' by The Strangeloves, the (in)famous 'Louie Louie' by The Kingsmen, and other garage-rock classics. As stated above, this chapter addresses the relatively unknown, the obscure, the forgotten, and the marginalized Latin/o connections to garage-rock moments and, by extension, to rock-music history, and simultaneously sheds light on Latino/a identity issues.

From Early Latin Rock to Ritchie Valens

In addition to his contributions to understanding rock 'n' roll as a profoundly working-class phenomenon, George Lipsitz has also explored some of the Latino/Chicano connections to rock history.[31] As Lipsitz and others note, the intercultural influence among African Americans, Anglo-Americans, Latino/as and others in Los Angeles was clearly visible by 1952. Early Latino/a influence was witnessed when Black saxophonist Chuck Higgins from LA's Eastside recorded a saxophone

---

21 *Nuggets*, 50.
22 Ibid., 53.
23 Ibid., 60.
24 For an analysis of the San Jose scene, see Kauppila, 'The Sound of the Suburbs: A Case Study of Three Garage Bands in San Jose, California during the 1960s.'
25 *Nuggets*, 69.
26 Ibid., 70.
27 Ibid., 89.
28 'Farmer John' reached the #13 position in the United States in 1964; Whitburn, *Billboard Top 1000 Singles, 1955–2000*.
29 'Wooly Bully' reached the #2 position in the United States in 1965; Whitburn, *Billboard Top 1000 Singles, 1955–2000*.
30 'She's About a Mover' reached the #13 position in the United States in 1965; Whitburn, *Billboard Top 1000 Singles, 1955–2000*.
31 Lipsitz, *Time Passages*; Lipsitz, *Dangerous Crossroads*; Lipsitz, *Rainbow at Midnight*.

instrumental called 'Pachuco Hop,'[32] a reference to the *pachuco* (zoot suiter) subculture of the 1940s that remained popular among Latino/as and Hispanics in many big cities, as well among other racial/ethnic groups. Along with Higgins and other White musicians like Big Jay McNeely, there were several other R&B artists and musicians who were able to tour regularly and make a life playing music, primarily by working steady gigs for 'Mexican' audiences in Southern California. As I discussed in the previous chapter, scholars have noted how many of these musicians acknowledge a huge debt to the 'Mexican' audience that helped R&B come into being in Southern California and further helped R&B as it eventually developed into the rock 'n' roll scene in LA.[33]

Broadening the evidence of Latin connections to rock 'n' roll, a direct line of Latin influence on R&B can be identified in the music of Antoine 'Fats' Domino, who himself was influenced by New Orleans pianist 'Professor Longhair' (also known as Roy Byrd). In describing his own particular style, Professor Longhair acknowledged Spanish beats, *calypso* downbeats, *rumba*, and mambo in his music.[34] Through Fats Domino, Roy Byrd's Latinized piano rhythms had become part of mainstream rock 'n' roll during the 1950s.[35] Roberts contends that a 'Latin tinge' was also evident in other early 1950s R&B hits like 'Mambo Baby' by Ruth Brown, 'Tweedle Dee' by Lavern Baker, 'Old Time Shuffle Blues' by Lloyd Glenn, 'Down in Mexico' and 'Loop the Loop Mambo' by The Coasters,[36] and of course, Bo Diddley's hits like 'I'm a Man' and 'Bo Diddley,' which will be discussed further below. In 1954 the flipside of the major hit song 'Earth Angel' was a song called 'Hey, Señorita,' which one scholar believes has a resemblance to the Ritchie Valens song 'Cry, Cry, Cry.'[37] The same song, 'Cry, Cry, Cry,' is also linked to the guitar riff in 'Birthday' by The Beatles, who exploded just a few years later in the early 1960s.[38]

Bill Haley and the Comets, famous for the classic 'Rock Around the Clock,' also had another hit in the pop category called 'Mambo Rock,' which made the Top Twenty in 1955.[39] Furthermore, Sublette notes how 'Rock Around the Clock' by Bill Haley and the Comets was actually based on the *clave*, and other clues exist that indicate the extent to which Latin music was prevalent. For example, the follow-up, 'Mambo Rock,' wasn't actually a mambo, but as Sublette astutely notes about its Latin connections, the song did borrow from 'El Manicero (The Peanut Vendor)' in different places, and even the movie *Rock Around the Clock* featured a Latin band playing music along with Bill Haley and the Comets.[40] Yet, Bill Haley

---

32 Guevara, 'The View from the Sixth Street Bridge: The History of Chicano Rock,' 117; Loza, *Barrio Rhythm*, 81; Reyes and Waldman, *Land of a Thousand Dances*, 12–14.

33 Reyes and Waldman, *Land of a Thousand Dances*; Garcia, 'The "Chicano" Dance Hall: Remapping Public Space in Post-World War II Greater Los Angeles'; Macías, *Mexican American Mojo*).

34 Roberts, *The Latin Tinge*.

35 Roberts, *The Latin Tinge*; Palmer, 'The Cuban Connection.'

36 Roberts, *The Latin Tinge*, 136–7.

37 Mendheim, *Ritchie Valens*.

38 Ibid., 79.

39 'Mambo Rock' reached the #18 position in the United States in 1955: Whitburn, *Billboard Top 1000 Singles, 1955–2000*; Busnar, *It's Rock 'n' Roll: A Musical History of the Fabulous Fifties*.

40 Sublette, 'The Kingsmen and the Cha-Cha-Chá,' 81.

and the Comets had other Latin credentials. After widespread success with 'Rock Around the Clock,' Haley signed a contract with a Mexican record company as 'Bill Haley y Los Cometas' and became a fixture in México's early rock scene. As Bill Haley y Los Cometas and with their own television show, the band capitalized on the dance craze of the era and found success throughout México and Latin America with songs like 'Twist Español' and 'Florida Twist,' and were proclaimed the Kings of the Twist (at least in Latin America). Bill Haley himself eventually recorded several songs in Spanish, and, perhaps mimicking the African American bluesmen that he admired, even moved to México and eventually retired there. Of course, facts such as these help explain why 'Bill Haley y Los Cometas' still appear on greatest hits compilations for México's classic rock 'n' roll.[41]

North of the border, Roberts also describes how the Black–Latin music links grew stronger on the East Coast in the mid 1950s. Several New York R&B groups, such as The Harptones and The Vocaleers, included both Black and Latino members, and were locally successful. Another such quintet called the Teenagers (famously fronted by Frankie Lymon), who had major success in 1956 with the song 'Why Do Fools Fall In Love?,' had two Puerto Rican members who were passing as Black.[42] By 1957, the consolidation of rhythm and blues with Latin influences was also evident in Clyde McPhatter's 'Long Lone Nights,' which revealed *marimba* and *bolero*, and Chuck Willis' 'C. C. Rider,' which was based on *rumba* patterns that were popularized by Fats Domino. Another song featuring Latin rhythms was Ray Charles' song 'What'd I Say,' released in 1959, which, according to Roberts, 'clearly portended the growing Latinization of black music that was to take place throughout the 1960s,'[43] and 'Unchain My Heart,' released in 1961, which the musicologist/historian Sublette argues is, a 'very Latin sounding' song.[44]

On the West Coast, Latinos like Gil Bernal, Bobby Rey, the Armenta brothers, the Rillera brothers (actually Filipinos), and many others associated with East LA 'Mexicans' all contributed to the establishment of R&B in LA throughout the 1950s by playing high school dances, parties, and local dance halls, and by producing local hit songs.[45] Gil Bernal, a Mexican American from Watts, was mostly into jazz music and got his start by playing with Lionel Hampton until 1952.[46] Through music classes, Bernal befriended songwriter Mike Stoller and joined him in his early recordings with The Robins. By 1955, The Robins and both Leiber and Stoller were signed by Atlantic Records and moved to New York. The Robins went to New York without Bernal, became The Coasters, and achieved major success with rock songs like 'Yakety Yak' and several others. As rock historians know very well, Mike Stoller and Jerry Leiber wrote seminal rock songs like 'Hound Dog,' 'Jailhouse Rock,' and 'There Goes My Baby' and became one of the most successful

41   See Bill Haley y Los Cometas in Third interlude.
42   Busnar, *It's Rock 'n' Roll*, 137–8; Lipsitz, *Footsteps in the Dark*, 223.
43   Roberts, *The Latin Tinge*, 138.
44   Sublette, 'The Kingsmen and the Cha-Cha-Chá,' 83.
45   Reyes and Waldman, *Land of a Thousand Dances*.
46   For more on Lionel Hampton's connection to Latin music, see Palmer, 'The Cuban Connection.'

songwriting duos in popular music history.⁴⁷ What is less known is that before the famous duo left LA, they were working with rising young talent like Gil Bernal who had produced some instrumental recordings for Leiber and Stoller. One of those Bernal songs, 'The Whip,' was used for the introduction to 'The Moon-Dog Show' by Cleveland disc jockey Alan Freed.⁴⁸ Thus, the introduction to the radio program that supposedly made rock 'n' roll a household name in the US was therefore the product of Leiber and Stoller, several other musicians, and Gil Bernal, a young Mexican American from LA. That is to say, Alan Freed's groundbreaking rock 'n' roll show began with a theme song that was a White, Black, and 'Brown' (i.e., Latino/a) amalgamation.

Extending this significance, the songwriting team of Leiber and Stoller is relevant on another level entirely. Noted as an important songwriting team for rock 'n' roll history, Leiber and Stoller were, in fact, Jewish. In *Rock 'n' Roll Jews*, Michael Billig has gone to great lengths to describe the Jewish contributions to rock 'n' roll and thus further acknowledges rock's multicultural roots. Yet, Billig also notes how both Leiber and Stoller were influenced by Latin music(s). Upon arriving in California, Mike Stoller lived in a Mexican American neighborhood where he listened to the Latin music of his neighbors. Stoller was even in a *pachuco* club in his youth, and, therefore, Latin music and rhythms were always interacting with the African American, Anglo-American, and, of course, Jewish musical traditions that eventually birthed the music produced by Jerry Leiber and Mike Stoller.⁴⁹

From this same early rock 'n' roll era emerged a band called The Rhythm Rockers. Formed around 1955 by Barry and Rick Rillera, they fused blues, gospel, jazz, R&B, and Latin music.⁵⁰ In addition to their connection to R&B artist and songwriter Richard Berry (discussed further below), The Rhythm Rockers later met up with Bill Medley, who was drawn in by their 'ethnic' sound and played with The Rhythm Rockers in local events like Mexican weddings. Eventually, Bill Medley moved on to form The Righteous Brothers with Bobby Hatfield, and went on to achieve major chart success with such songs as 'You've Lost That Lovin' Feeling' in 1964, 'Unchained Melody' in 1965, and '(You're My) Soul and Inspiration' in 1966.⁵¹ Yet when The Righteous Brothers were formed, Barry and Rick Rillera from The Rhythm Rockers were part of the group and were used as backup musicians on some of their early hits.⁵²

In early 1958 there was the famous hit song 'Tequila' by The Champs — a so-called 'Tex-Mex' band that included musicians who were schooled in western swing — that went to #1 on the national music charts.⁵³ While western swing itself includes Latin influences (as I described in Chapter one), 'Tequila' sounds

---

47 Reyes and Waldman, *Land of a Thousand Dances*; Billig, *Rock 'n' Roll Jews*.
48 Reyes and Waldman, *Land of a Thousand Dances*, 28–9.
49 Billig, *Rock 'n' Roll Jews*, 48–9.
50 Reyes and Waldman, *Land of a Thousand Dances*, 19.
51 Ryan, *American Hit Radio: A History of Popular Hit Singles from 1955 to the Present*.
52 Reyes and Waldman, *Land of a Thousand Dances*, 31–2.
53 Loza, *Barrio Rhythm*, 82.

like several other mambo-rock 'n' roll productions of the era.[54] Meanwhile, there were other Latin-influenced rock songs by Black duos such as Mickey & Sylvia and Billie & Lillie.[55] Of course, 'Ritchie Valens' (Richard Valenzuela before it was anglicized for better marketability in the US) was immensely popular in the late 1950s with pop hits like 'La Bamba,' 'Come On Let's Go,' and 'Donna.' Yet, before Valens made it big in 1958, and after his death in 1959, there was also Baldemar Huerta (whom country music fans might remember as 'Freddy Fender'), who came out of the Texas-Louisiana music scene and recorded 'Wasted Days, Wasted Nights' and other rockers months prior to Valens in 1958 — including some in Spanish. Recognizing this, it is worth noting that Freddy Fender's Tex-Mex music is a candidate for the first *rock en español*, since he was producing rock 'n' roll in Spanish, some of which was popular in México at the time.

California's Bobby Rey, whose musical resumé included a show backing up James Brown on saxophone in 1958, was at one point a member of the Masked Phantom Band. Loza observes how The Masked Phantom Band produced such songs as 'Corrido Rock,' an instrumental with a *norteño*-style riff on a fast rock beat. According to Loza, the 'Corrido Rock' dance was fast and wild and might have been an early form of slam-dancing. The Masked Phantom Band also wore masks on stage and 'outlaw' garb to attract audiences,[56] and therefore The Masked Phantom Band can be seen as a predecessor to various acts in rock 'n' roll history that would don masks, makeup and costumes on stage. After The Masked Phantom Band, Bobby Rey went on to become the leader of the Hollywood Argyles, a band that eventually reached #1 in 1960 with the song 'Alley Oop.'[57]

While R&B/soul singer Sam Cooke sang songs like 'Everybody Likes to Cha-Cha-Cha,'[58] other artists forged a Latin connection with their band names, like The Fiestas,[59] who charted hits like 'So Fine' in 1959.[60] The vocal group The Drifters, whose 'There Goes My Baby' was a smash hit in the category of R&B and a #2 hit on the US charts in 1959,[61] also had another minor hit with 'Down in Mexico.' Worth noting, The Drifters were working with songwriter/producers Jerry Leiber and Mike Stoller, who were experimenting with Latin rhythms and percussion,

---

54 Sublette, 'The Centrality of Cuban Music.'
55 Mendheim, *Ritchie Valens*.
56 Loza, *Barrio Rhythm*, 24.
57 Ibid., 25–6.
58 Busnar, *It's Rock 'n' Roll*, 131.
59 While changing band names to Spanish- or Latin-sounding names seems insignificant, it is important to note that band name changes have been an important part of the Latin/o engagement with rock 'n' roll music (in different national contexts). Moreover, what began with bands like The Fiestas in the 1950s continues to be a part of the rock story as various bands have continued this naming practice in recent decades, especially in punk/alternative/indie-rock (e.g., The Mescaleros, The Latino Rockabilly War, The Del Fuegos, Los Olvidados, Yo La Tengo, Calexico, Gomez, Los Campesinos!).
60 The Fiestas are relevant on another level in that they included the famous Johnny Otis, a Greek American who was often believed to be an African American because of his dark complexion. On his own, Johnny Otis also scored a hit with 'Willie and the Hand Jive,' a song that features the famous *clave* beat that is often called the 'Bo Diddley beat.' Other famous Latinized songs by Johnny Otis include 'Willie Did the Cha Cha' and 'Mambo Boogie.'
61 Busnar, *It's Rock 'n' Roll*, 115.

and other records by The Drifters that followed also used the South American rhythm known as *baion*.[62] Also in 1959, Dave 'Baby' Cortez scored a #1 hit with 'The Happy Organ.'[63]

Of course, Latin musical influences spilled over into the 1960s and are evident in songs such as 'Twist and Shout' by the Isley Brothers in 1962 (later covered by The Beatles), the flip-side of which was 'Spanish Twist.'[64] There was also 'Louie Louie' which was covered by various bands in addition to The Kingsmen (1963), 'Hang On Sloopy' by The McCoys (1965), and 'Get Off of My Cloud' and 'Satisfaction' by the Rolling Stones (1965/66) which were all influenced by *cha-cha-chá* or were simply *cha-cha-chá*-based rock 'n' roll songs.[65]

While speaking of the Rolling Stones, Sublette reminds us that rock classics such as 'Sympathy for the Devil' (1968) were loosely based on mambo, and that 'Not Fade Away' featured a prominent *clave* sound. Early footage even reveals Mick Jagger playing maracas on the song as well as on 'Let's Spend the Night Together,' in which he even said 'cha-cha-cha.'[66] Other mambo-influenced songs include 'Brown-Eyed Girl' by Van Morrison, a Top-Ten hit in 1967, which Sublette argues is derived from Israel López song 'Cachao.'[67] Sublette also calls 'Break On Through (To the Other Side)' by The Doors (1967) a mambo, 'complete with an organ solo imitating typical horn-section figures.'[68]

In addition to the prevalence of mambo, *rumba*, and *cha-cha-chá* in early rock 'n' roll, there was also the up-tempo rhythm called *guarácha*. Notable rock 'n' roll *guaráchas* include 'Good Lovin'' by The Rascals (1966),[69] 'Cherry, Cherry' by Neil Diamond (1966), and another Top-Ten hit 'Cool Jerk' by The Capitols (1966).[70] Other musicological observations note how the *campana*, or cowbell, features prominently in so many rock songs, such as 'Time Has Come Today,' 'Honky Tonk Woman,' 'All Right Now,' 'Mississippi Queen,' 'We're An American Band,' and 'Old Time Rock and Roll,' as well as 'untold numbers of R&B, funk and disco records.' As Sublette argues, 'imagine pop music without maracas, conga[s], bongó[s] and campana [cowbells].'[71]

What all this evidence reveals is that there was a significant Latino/a presence in rock 'n' roll from very early on in its history. Further, the fact that the Latino/a presence in rock 'n' roll history is not part of mainstream accounts of rock history speaks to a particular moment in United States history when, with regard to ethno-racial relations, the dominant cultural paradigm in previous decades was assimilation. With regard to assimilation, however, this version was not necessarily

---

62   Billig, *Rock 'n' Roll Jews*, 55–6.
63   Whitburn, *Billboard Top 1000 Singles, 1955–2000*.
64   Sublette, 'The Kingsmen and the Cha-Cha-Chá,' 88.
65   Ibid., 90.
66   Ibid., 89–90.
67   Ibid., 88.
68   Ibid., 89.
69   Sublette further notes that the 1965 original by The Olympics had a more apparent mambo feel.
70   Ibid., 88–9.
71   Ibid., 79.

that people assimilate to Anglo-European culture, as the term often connoted in recent decades. The previous version of assimilation reflected a 'melting pot' metaphor where many flavors blended with each other. In other words, Whites assimilated Black and Latin styles, Blacks assimilated Latin styles, and Latino/as assimilated Black, White, and other Latin/o styles. Moreover, the history of Latin/o rock also suggests an ambivalent relationship between Latino/as and acculturation processes. While many were able to assimilate into a burgeoning scene that incorporated different musical styles and different races and ethnic groups, a few artists during this period remained openly 'Latin' or 'Chicano.' One such case was the most famous Latino rocker of the 1950s, Ritchie Valens, whose music represents the greatest Latin/o contribution to early rock 'n' roll history.

Hailing from a working-class, agricultural, immigrant-family background in Pacoima and San Fernando, California, Valens arrived on the rock 'n' roll scene while still a teenager in high school. Although his career was cut short by a tragic plane crash in early 1959, he achieved phenomenal success in a short period of time. Only recently has the Valens legacy been examined by scholars and all agree that his influence on rock 'n' roll is immense. Rock journalist Lester Bangs noted how it all goes back to Ritchie Valens' 'La Bamba.' Commenting on the guitar riff that Valens played on 'La Bamba,' Bangs wrote:

> Just consider Valens' three-chord mariachi squawkup . . . There: twenty years of rock & roll history in three chords, played more primitively each time they are recycled.

As Bangs averred, Valens' chord progressions can be directly traced throughout rock 'n' roll history through groups such as the Ramones, The Stooges, The Kinks, and of course, The Kingsmen.[72]

Latinos and the Garage-Rock Moment

The story of 'Louie Louie' by The Kingsmen is yet another story connecting Latino/as to rock 'n' roll history, and, more directly, connects Latino/as to the garage-rock moment of the mid 1960s. 'Louie Louie' has been called the 'world's most famous rock 'n' roll song,'[73] and an entire book was written on the significance of the song for rock music history. Others note how 'Louie Louie' led 'directly' to 'All Day and All of the Night' by The Kinks and 'Wild Thing' by The Troggs, which in turn led directly to heavy metal.[74] 'Louie Louie' can boast anthem-like status through its use in the movie *Animal House*. It is included in numerous greatest hits compilations for the 1960s, and remains somewhat of a classic rock 'n' roll song. Although the song 'Louie Louie' itself is even more (in)famous in its own right for other reasons, such as sparking much controversy and even FBI investigations, historians Reyes and Waldman have written on the significance of the

---

72   Bangs, 'Protopunk: The Garage Bands,' 261.
73   Marsh, *Louie Louie*.
74   Eddy, *The Accidental Evolution of Rock 'n' Roll*, 184.

version by The Kingsmen, a Seattle-based group who made 'Louie Louie' a now classic garage-rock song.

Before the immensely popular version by The Kingsmen,[75] 'Louie Louie' was covered by various other garage-type bands. Prior to that, it was an unknown song written by an R&B singer from Los Angeles named Richard Berry. Berry was a veteran of the Los Angeles R&B scene, having played with The Hollywood Blue Jays, The Flairs, The Crowns, and other vocal groups. According to Reyes and Waldman, Richard Berry wrote 'Louie Louie' when he was in a multicultural rock/blues/Latin music ensemble called The Rhythm Rockers, and the two Filipino members of that band, the aforementioned Rillera brothers of The Rhythm Rockers, had introduced Berry to Latin jazz. The Latin sound that The Rhythm Rockers added to the R&B music scene in LA was the result of their affinity for Latino musicians such as Tito Puente and René Touzet. Little could those musicians have known that they were directly influencing future rock 'n' rollers and R&B artists like Richard Berry, who later wrote 'Louie Louie' based on Touzet's 'El Loco Cha Cha' — a song The Rhythm Rockers even played in their set.

Berry acknowledged in an interview that his 'Louie Louie' song was influenced by René Touzet's 'Loco Cha Cha,' considered an otherwise obscure Cuban *cha-cha* record.[76] Morales further notes on this, 'The five-note vamp that runs through the song is played on an electric organ, resembling the *son* clave (i.e., 1–2–3, 1–2) and the song progresses through *tumbao* figures that are strongly reminiscent of Afro-Cuban music.'[77] Reyes and Waldman further attest to this, 'To those hearing "Loco Cha Cha" for the first time, the similarities between the two songs are remarkable.'[78]

Yet, the story seems more complicated with regard to Latino/a identity issues as Berry revealed that he actually wanted to make 'Louie Louie' a Latin song in the studio, but was prevented from doing so by his record company for fear of putting anything 'too exotic' or 'too ethnic' before a White audience. And so 'Louie Louie' remained, a Latin-influenced song that was pared down to the point where any Latin traces were virtually imperceptible. One can conclude that, whether or not The Kingsmen were directly influenced by Ritchie Valens, or whether it was the pre-Valens, Latin jazz influence by The Rhythm Rockers and René Touzet on Richard Berry (who wrote 'Louie Louie'), the song that is a classic for rock music history can also go down as an important song revealing significant Latin/o influence. Although garage-rock is more commonly discussed in terms of the British influence on rock music that turned back toward the United States, the example of 'Louie Louie' points to a situation in which the continuing US influences on the British rock scene were not just African or Black influences, but included various Latin influences as well.

Another Latin/o garage-rock connection occurred in 1965 when Doug Sahm

---

75 'Louie Louie' by The Kingsmen reached the #2 position in 1963; Whitburn, *Billboard Top 1000 Singles, 1955–2000*.
76 Morales, *Living in Spanglish: The Search for Latino Identity in America*, 153.
77 Ibid., 155.
78 Reyes and Waldman, *Land of a Thousand Dances*, 15.

(or, 'Sir Douglas') and his band, billed as the Sir Douglas Quintet, scored an international hit with the song 'She's About a Mover' that went as high as #13 on the US pop charts in 1965. Although 'She's About a Mover' sounds much like a take-off of 'She's a Woman' by The Beatles,[79] the Sir Douglas rendition took The Beatles sound and blended it with the 'Tex-Mex sound' for which they would become famous.[80] The salience of this point lies in the fact that the Sir Douglas Quintet was actually a Texas band that was created in order to mimic the popular English bands of the time. Producer Huey P. Meaux came up with the idea and 'unlocked the secret formula' for the success of the British sound, and the band's name and image were deliberately concocted in an attempt to appear ethnically English.

The Sir Douglas Quintet, however, was from south-central Texas and included some Latino members. Liner notes inform us how, in order to keep up the charade for as long as possible, the Sir Douglas Quintet even resorted to taking photographs in silhouette in order to disguise the Latino members of the band.[81] Singer/frontman Doug Sahm, a caucasian of German descent, was a native of a primarily Black neighborhood in San Antonio, Texas, who combined the influences of western swing, country, blues, rock, polka, and Tex-Mex. When Sahm hooked up with producer Huey Meaux, he was already a veteran of the Texas music scene for several years. Among his contemporaries and collaborators were Tex-Mex legends like Freddy Fender. Of course, Doug Sahm's Latin/o credentials became more numerous thereafter.

One scholar notes that after a stint on the West Coast during the late 1960s, Sahm returned to Texas to take up 'Chicano' music, and in 1971 recorded an album under the name 'Doug Saldaña' titled *The Return of Doug Saldaña*. As Sahm recalled, 'Saldaña is the name the Mexicans gave me. They said that I had so much Mexican in me that I needed a Mexican name.'[82] As noted previously, Sahm even composed the Chicano/a anthem 'Soy Chicano,' and perhaps fittingly, Sahm was nominated for 'Chicano of the Year' by *Rolling Stone* magazine.[83] Throughout his career, Sahm played, performed, or recorded with many musicians including many different Chicanos. In his later years, Sahm's most successful project was with the Texas Tornados in the 1990s, an all-star band that included other Chicano legends like Augie Meyers, Flaco Jimenez, and Freddy Fender.

To hear Sir Douglas songs like 'She's About a Mover,' 'Mendocino,' and various other songs that reveal the profound influence of country and blues, rhythmic Tex-Mex organ and piano by Augie Meyers, and the 'accordion-influenced melodies'[84] that sound much like *tejano* music, it seems somewhat ridiculous to think that the Sir Douglas Quintet could have ever passed as English or British. As Ward notes, 'In fact, the song "Mendocino" is practically pure Border pop, and with a different

---

79 The author wishes to acknowledge both Rick Sanger and Paul Kauppila (respectively) for their insight regarding this matter and for a factual correction.
80 Mendheim, *Ritchie Valens*; Roberts, *The Latin Tinge*.
81 Nuggets, *Nuggets*, 65.
82 Levy, J. 'Doug Sahm and the Sir Douglas Quintet: A Brief History.'
83 Roberts, *The Latin Tinge*, 195.
84 Ward, Liner notes to *Mendocino*.

vocalist and Mexican Spanish lyrics, it could be something you'd hear drifting out of a cantina somewhere in Brownsville, Texas.'[85] Further noting the ability of the Sir Douglas Quintet to cross cultural borders, McLeese notes:

> *Mendocino* shows the ability of the quintessential Texas garage band to connect the dots geographically as well as stylistically, to straddle very different worlds without suffering any identity confusion.[86]

In spite of this assessment, trying to pass for British is part of the early story for the Sir Douglas Quintet. Interestingly, the Sir Douglas Quintet could never escape their various South Texas influences and the Tex-Mex sound. Since then, 'She's About a Mover' remains another garage-rock classic.

Another Latin/o connection was made with Sam the Sham and the Pharaohs, who were also connected to the Texas music tradition and the Tex-Mex sound in rock 'n' roll, and have been called the quintessential Tex-Mex band of the 1960s. The band became famous for their major hit 'Wooly Bully,' which went as high as #2 in the pop charts in 1965, and other songs like 'Li'l Red Riding Hood'[87] in 1966. Liner notes to the aforementioned *Nuggets* box set attest to the importance of 'Wooly Bully,' stating that, '[the song] is not only one of the all-time great dance stompers, it is also an important link in the American rock 'n' roll chain.'[88] And not only is 'Wooly Bully' called the ultimate 'frat-rock' song, the band members of the Pharaohs were actually college students at the time of, or just before, scoring their major hit.

'Sam the Sham' was actually Domingo Samudio (aka 'Sam'), who was born and raised in Dallas, Texas.[89] While Sam the Sham and the Pharaohs had limited success thereafter, their legacy is evident in the famous introduction to their song 'Wooly Bully.' In the introduction to the song, Samudio brought in the Spanish language with the famous count-off, '*Uno, dos* . . . one two, *tres, cuatro!*' and made popular music history. 'Wooly Bully' itself has been covered by many rock acts through the years like Jimi Hendrix, Canned Heat, Joan Jett and the Blackhearts, Los Lobos, and many others, and the bilingual count-off has been imitated and modified countless times throughout popular music history, noted recently through pop/rock bands like U2 to pop/country acts like Big and Rich.

Aside from the famous count-off in Spanish, an important link to issues of Latino/a identity surfaces with their song '(I'm In With) the Out Crowd,' which, along with 'Wooly Bully,' was one of the few songs included on their greatest hits compilation that was written by Domingo Samudio. In liner notes to their greatest hits, Dahl notes that this song was about Samudio's laments on not fitting in and

---

85 Ibid.
86 Mcleese, 'Sir Douglas Sahm and the Garage as Big as Texas,' 448.
87 Mendheim, *Ritchie Valens*, 129–30; 'Li'l Red Riding Hood' reached the #2 position in 1966: Whitburn, *Billboard Top 1000 Singles, 1955–2000*.
88 Nuggets, *Nuggets*, 77.
89 In addition to Samudio, the original incarnation of the Pharaohs in 1961 included Omar 'Big Man' Lopez as well as Vincent Lopez (no relation), who were also from Dallas, Texas.

being an outsider, which referred (according to Samudio) to his beard and earrings that set him apart from the cultural mainstream. Years later Samudio would claim that he was the first rock 'n' roller to wear an earring, which, if it's true, reveals another lasting contribution by a Latino/a to American popular music fashion. Yet, what matters more, I submit, is that his outsider status could also be related to his presence as the only Latino band member, as a Hispanic minority on the college/university scene, or perhaps as a rare Mexican American in the burgeoning rock 'n' roll music scene in the United States.

Also worth noting is the Arabic/Egyptian aesthetic employed by Samudio in his costume and headdress and by the Pharaohs in their band name. While Samudio and the Pharaohs could have employed his Mexican heritage for a visual gimmick, especially since the original lineup included two other Latino band members, it is interesting that they shied away from his real Tex-Mex identity[90] in favor of another, perhaps more exotic, ethnic aesthetic. The identity politics in examples like this imply profound contradictions: for Sam the Sham, his ethnic heritage was something that came through in his artistic expression at the same time that it needed to be neutralized.

Like the Sir Douglas Quintet and Sam the Sham and the Pharaohs, another garage band that featured a highly charged organ and had a Tex-Mex sound was ? and the Mysterians (or, Question Mark and the Mysterians). The Tex-Mex sound is not surprising, given that liner notes suggest family origins in Texas, although the Mysterians were a group of Mexican Americans that came from Saginaw, Michigan. Their hit song '96 Tears' reached the #1 position on the US charts in 1966, and they also had minor hits with 'I Need Somebody' and 'I Can't Get Enough of You Baby'. While conspicuously absent from the aforementioned *Nuggets* collection, Lester Bangs and many others refer to the Mysterians as a very important garage-rock band. ? and the Mysterians, in fact, blended eccentricity with angst, soul and R&B with the garage-rock sound, and held it all together with the steady cadence of Tex-Mex organ melodies. Their song '96 Tears' has been called the perfect song, and the Mysterians have been called 'the quintessential garage band.'[91] To underscore their impact, Eddy comments that, '"96 Tears"-type organ notes' can be heard in The Velvet Underground's 'White Light/White Heat' and at the end of 'I'm Waiting for the Man.'[92]

It should not be very surprising, therefore, to understand how the same song that has been called the quintessential song for garage-rock, is also remembered for its influence on punk-rock. For example, Ryan has called the '96 Tears' song 'the first garage-punk,'[93] Bangs called it 'Proto-punk,'[94] and Morales refers to it as,

---

90   Years later Samudio tapped into his Tex-Mex heritage, by recording folk ballads (including some in Spanish) and composing music with Ry Cooder for the soundtrack to the 1982 film *The Border*. Decades later, he even performed with other Tex-Mex musicians like Doug Sahm, Freddy Fender, and the Texas Tornados.
91   Linna, Liner notes to *96 Tears: The Very Best of Question Mark & the Mysterians*.
92   Ryan, *American Hit Radio*, 189.
93   Ibid., 240.
94   Bangs, 'Protopunk: The Garage Bands,' 264.

'seminal to the punk aesthetic.'⁹⁵ Moreover, in a recent book focusing on punk-rock in its British character, Jon Savage also cites '96 Tears' as a significant pre-punk song:

> [It] resulted in a purely white, blue-collar style, in which any black rhythmic influence was bleached out in favour of pure noise and texture: fuzz guitar, feedback, drones and whiny vocal. The flatly rhythmic repetition of a song like ? and the Mysterians' '96 Tears' seemed to be the perfect form through which to express a numb nihilism.⁹⁶

To put this quotation in better context, the author is discussing how ? and the Mysterians reflected a supposedly 'Whiter' style of playing rock 'n' roll, unlike other Black currents in rock. What is most interesting for this analysis, however, is that a song by four Tex-Mex, accordion-influenced Latinos has gone down in history as the quintessential garage-rock song as well as key for early punk-rock. Rather than its apparently assumed English, British, or White character, one can only wonder if the song would be held in such high regard if people were more aware of the band's Latin/o essence.

To return to this issue of race and culture, a *VH1* documentary suggests that ? and the Mysterians were probably successful because of the fact that, initially, people were not sure exactly what they were. Ryan notes how the band members never wanted anybody to know their real names and that the lead singer, Rudy Martínez, wore wraparound sunglasses 'all the time,'⁹⁷ and rock critic Lester Bangs recalled how, in his youth, he and his friends were excited about such mystery — for example, the fact that Martínez never took off his sunglasses.⁹⁸

Although Mexican Americans, part of the mystery seems to be in their non-White and non-Black physical features that further contributed to their mystery and mystique. While this may suggest an attempt to hide their ethnicity, ? and the Mysterians seem to have benefited from — as did Samudio and the Sir Douglas Quintet — ambiguous racial features that allowed them to appear to be something else (at least initially).

Like ? and the Mysterians, George Lipsitz observes that Cannibal and the Headhunters were another popular Latino garage band who had a major hit song during this period but who also suffered from their ethno-racial ambiguity.⁹⁹ As lead singer of Cannibal and the Headhunters, Frankie 'Cannibal' Garcia remembers how their success was stymied after 1965 when record companies didn't know how to market a Mexican American or Chicano group to the United States. As Frankie Garcia recalls, rock 'n' roll in the 1960s included a Black/White dichotomy that was unfriendly to anybody who didn't fit those expectations.¹⁰⁰

95   Morales, *Living in Spanglish*, 161.
96   Savage, *England's Dreaming: Anarchy, Sex Pistols, Punk Rock and Beyond*, 81–2.
97   Ryan, *American Hit Radio*, 240.
98   Bangs, 'Protopunk: The Garage Bands,' 264.
99   Lipsitz, *Dangerous Crossroads*.
100 Lipsitz, *Time Passages*, 146.

Yet another piece of the Latino/a garage-rock puzzle appears with the infectious and catchy song 'I Want Candy' by The Strangeloves. It is not difficult to recall the famous 'Bo Diddley beat,' otherwise known as the 'shave and a haircut' beat, the 'hambone' beat, or the 'Willie and the Hand Jive' beat (see previous note on Johnny Otis, frontman for The Fiestas). 'I Want Candy' by The Strangeloves reached the #11 position in 1965,[101] and is another garage-rock gem that is included in the 1998 *Nuggets* box set. This song did not have a Latino/Hispanic composer, nor were any of The Strangeloves of Latino/Hispanic descent. The Latin/o connection, however, comes through the song's hook, the famous 'Bo Diddley beat' — which was actually an Afro-Latino rhythm.

As music scholars note, throughout the 1930s, 1940s, and 1950s, the Afro-Latino jazz connection was growing stronger. Cuban Mario Bauzá went to New York and played with famous jazz bandleaders like Chick Webb, and changed the jazz world when he began to teach Dizzy Gillespie's band 'Afro-Cuban techniques, including composing melodic lines for brass instruments from Yoruban ritual drum patterns and melodies.' Morales further reminds us, 'Bauzá's influence was primarily responsible for the development of most of the transitions American music has gone through since World War II — from swing to modern jazz; rhythm and blues to rock and roll; rhythm and blues to funk.'[102] Gillespie himself has insisted that Latin-influenced bass patterns are the basis for modern-day funk music. Cuban *rumba* patterns have also been credited as the source for early rock 'n' roll songs by Fats Domino, Lloyd Price, and Little Richard.[103] Further adding to the legacy of Mario Bauzá, Morales and Palmer report on the significance of a renewed emphasis on a five-beat *clave* rhythm that has been called the 'Bo Diddley beat' in rock 'n' roll. Although scholars have acknowledged this famous rhythm in rock history, what remains under-acknowledged is that the famous Bo Diddley sound was actually the influence of Afro-Cuban traditions from Mario Bauzá and other Afro-Latinos as well as a Cuban musical tradition connecting the 'Bo Diddley beat' to Spain.[104]

Around the same time, other Latinos emerged who years later had indirect influences on what came to be known as rock 'n' roll. Led by bandleaders such as Don Azpiazú and Xavier Cugat, the *rumba* fed a national fascination with Latin American music and ballroom dancing with songs like 'El Manicero/The Peanut Vendor.' This song also featured the aforementioned *clave* rhythm, known as the source for the 'Bo Diddley beat,'[105] and to hear 'El Manicero/The Peanut Vendor,'

---

101 Whitburn, *Billboard Top 1000 Singles, 1955–2000*.
102 Morales, *Living in Spanglish*, 153.
103 Ibid.; Also see Palmer, 'The Cuban Connection.'
104 Although the contribution of Bo Diddley to rock 'n' roll continues to be acknowledged in recent music magazines like *Rolling Stone* (see Strauss, 'The Indestructible Beat of Bo Diddley') and *MOJO* (see Hurtt, 'Bo Diddley: The In Sound from Way Out!'), these recent articles also continue the debate about the origins of the famous 'Bo Diddley beat.' In one of these recent articles Bo Diddley himself admits that he was not its creator and that he stumbled upon it accidentally. While some authors point to its origin in Chicago and others suggest Texas or New Orleans, others like musicologist Robert Palmer point to its origins in Cuba and Spain.
105 Starr and Waterman, *American Popular Music*, 56.

there is no question about its similarity to the 'Bo Diddley beat.' Thus, 'I Want Candy' further exemplifies the Latin/o influence on early rock 'n' roll music and later, garage-rock and punk-rock.

Like the often forgotten Latin legacy of songs like 'I Want Candy' by The Strangeloves, yet another major Latin/o garage-rock contribution came through The Sonics. The Sonics are another band that might claim the title of quintessential garage-rock band, and, noting their importance, one critic calls The Sonics' 1965 album 'the greatest punk rock album ever made.'[106] Nonetheless, The Sonics are another band included on the 1998 *Nuggets* collection, for songs like 'Psycho,' without any mention of a Latin/o connection. The Sonics did not have any Latino/a members or any other obvious indication of a connection to Latin/o music. However, a brief review of the liner notes to the recent release of their breakthrough album from 1965 indicates yet another possible link.

The Sonics themselves recalled and acknowledged that the famous rock 'n' roll guitarist Jerry Miller was a huge influence on their music. In this story of The Sonics evolution, The Sonics recalled that Jerry Miller happened to be a neighbor, and they came to know him after he had returned from Texas. In Texas, Jerry Miller had played with The Bobby Fuller Four, a band from El Paso, Texas that had scored a hit with the song, 'I Fought the Law' (later covered by The Clash, as a punk-rock song, and others). As one member of The Sonics recalls about Jerry Miller, 'He was down there in Texas listening to that stuff and when he came back with all these new tunes and a new style, well, nobody in the Northwest had ever heard anything like that before.'[107]

So, as before, there is tantalizing evidence to suggest that another significant garage-rock song arose out of the intercultural and cross-cultural influence of musicians in Texas, and perhaps reveals another articulation of rock 'n' roll to US Latino/as. As all of the examples above demonstrate, the Latin/o connections to garage-rock, as well as rock 'n' roll and popular music in general, are extensive and the stories of their origin are worth retelling, most notably, I believe, for what they reveal about the place of Latino/as in mainstream popular music in the US — that the Latin/o contribution has been longstanding, consistent, and, I would argue, quite profound.

Latino/as and Mainstream Society

At the outset of this chapter, I introduced the topic of the supposed emergence of Latino/as in mainstream popular music that parallels recent cultural shifts and points toward a need for greater understanding of Latino/a people in the United States. As I have argued, these recent cultural shifts in the US beg the question of what such trends have to offer in terms of attempting to understand Latino/a identity. Once again, the oft-celebrated 'emergence' of Latino/as in US popular music cannot be free of controversy. Building on a stream in popular music studies that examines popular music as a form of mediated communication, I argue that

---

106 Linna, Liner notes to *The Sonics: Here are The Sonics!!!*
107 Ibid., 5.

popular music should be seen as a discursive space where Latino/a cultural issues can be examined and better understood with regard to the relationship between Latino/as and a larger society, specifically the US mainstream. The logical question that follows here is: what, then, is a Latino/a cultural issue?

One of the more prominent cultural issues related to the place of Latino/as in US society centers around language use, and scholars and journalists have begun to discuss language and identity issues in relation to popular music. For example, Bender recognizes that language issues are significant for discussions of Latino/a music artists and the connection to identity and assimilation and/or hybridization. As Bender notes, 'the current mainstream success of [Latino/a pop] artists is achieved predominantly through English language recordings, as it generally has been for Latino/a artists in the past.'[108] For Latino/as however, the significance of crossover attempts by Latino/a artists from various nations attempting to capitalize on the North American market is that such attempts are often correlated with a loss of identity or 'selling out.' The international superstar Celine Dion, a native French-speaking Canadian, is a relevant example here, given that she was said to have lost her authentic French-speaking identity and was accused of selling out to US audiences and the English language.[109] In other words, singing in English or catering to US audiences can change the perception of some artists in relation to their avowed or ascribed ethnic identity.

In other circumstances, a reverse process has occurred where some US Latino/a artists have produced songs in Spanish to capitalize on Central American and South American markets, or even for Spanish-speaking markets in North America. Christina Aguilera is a recent example for Latina/Hispanic women, but it has happened with other artists like Selena and Linda Ronstadt in previous decades. While Linda Ronstadt's celebrated return-to-roots *mariachi* projects received a great deal of public attention in the 1980s and 1990s (achieving gold-record status, selling millions per year, and winning Grammy Awards),[110] Bender reminds us that these albums were reviled by non-Spanish-speaking people in the US who attended her concerts expecting to hear her sing country and rock.[111] Conversely, her *mariachi* albums were also seen as inauthentic by some Latino/as, since she was a Chicana (not a Mexican national) recording and performing México's revered national music.

However, Loza informs us that such musical productions are significant in other ways. For example, Loza notes the fact that Ronstadt's *mariachi* albums obviously contributed to a 'mariachi renaissance' that ensued throughout the US Southwest, and 'especially among young female adolescents' — suggesting reclamation of Mexican identity for US Mexican Americans. Moreover, as Loza astutely observes, such significance was magnified as Ronstadt's *mariachi* releases proved subversive in how they proved that a US Latina (Mexican American/Chicana) could

---

108 Bender, 'Will the Wolf Survive?*: Latino/a Pop Music in the Cultural Mainstream,' 723.
109 Berger and Carroll, *Global Pop, Local Language*.
110 See Loza, 'Assimilation, Reclamation, and Rejection of the Nation-State by Chicano Musicians' on this point.
111 Bender 'Will the Wolf Survive?*: Latino/a Pop Music in the Cultural Mainstream.'

be successful with Mexican *ranchera* (*mariachi*) music, and how they signified resistance to the music industry and its networks that prevent integration of US Latino/as into 'Latin,' 'Latin American,' and 'Mexican regional' music.[112] I suggest that further significance of these examples lies in the fact that capitalization on a market correlates with changing identity(ies), and often, with differing opinions about what those changes signify. For Latino/as in the US perhaps, it seems success is always questionable with regard to maintaining Latino/a identity.

In other words, just as quickly as Latino/as achieve a certain presence and measure of success in the US mainstream, they are also plagued by identity questions related to language, ethnicity, and nationality. Moreover, Latino/as face apparent paradoxes with respect to living between two (or more) cultures and moving in and out of vastly different ways of being. While assimilation to English or the US mainstream seems ultimately beneficial and positive to some, to others it represents, with respect to identity, the negativity of change, loss, or 'selling out.' For some, 'crossovers' can come to symbolize successful integration of citizens or cultural or ethnic groups into the US mainstream. Yet, for others, it still seems that the US mainstream is not completely ready for such paradoxes. The examples above reveal that rather than a willingness to accept bicultural and multicultural people and their identities, mainstream culture in the United States tends to impose pressures on artists and musicians. The pressure to sing in English is just one form of such pressure; the pressure to assimilate (i.e., to be more 'American') is another. The salience of these facts is that the presence of Latino/as in the North American mainstream further reveals the complications of Latino/a identity(ies). Furthermore, the examples above characterize attempts at assimilation to mainstream culture (through hiding, passing, disguising, masking, forgetting, blending their Latino/a identity). Perhaps this is why the Latin/o legacy in rock 'n' roll has been undervalued and virtually forgotten. And perhaps this explains how many people could believe in a Latin 'explosion' in 1999/2000.

By the same token, the story of garage-rock that is presented here is significant beyond the fact that it debunks the myth of a recent Latino/a explosion or 'boom' in popular music. Rather, the garage-rock story should contribute to our society's often-problematic relationship with ethnic minorities and marginalized groups. Beyond being left out for more White-washed versions of history, this research reveals some of the tensions that Latino/as (like others) face with regard to assimilating, maintaining their heritage, retaining a language, trying to pass as White and not passing as White, fitting in and not fitting in, being victims of exclusion and/or marginalization with regard to organizations and structures because of physical features or cultural barriers, being forgotten and under-appreciated, and, overall, walking the line between the Black and White dichotomy of mainstream US culture.

---

112 Loza, 'Assimilation, Reclamation, and Rejection of the Nation-State by Chicano Musicians,' 145.

Conclusion

In this chapter, I have reviewed several critical garage-rock songs through a Latin/o cultural lens. The significance of the 'genealogical' chain presented in this chapter is, first, that the history of rock 'n' roll is not solely the province of Black and White youth in the United States and, secondly, that the garage-rock phenomenon, as it emerged in the mid 1960s, was not solely the creation of British or Anglo-American youth. Rather, this chapter demonstrates that some of the most important garage-rock songs were related to Latino/as in different ways. As mentioned earlier, the fact that these examples are not a part of the more common history of rock 'n' roll speaks more to the fact of dominant ideologies of binary constructions of ethno-racial relations in the US. This is an issue that has been mentioned by some scholars of popular music,[113] but what is interesting is that these facts have not been addressed in greater depth. With regard to this, one conclusion that I can reiterate here is that the development of rock 'n' roll music (as well as its cultural aesthetic) has been one of intercultural exchange between the United States and US Latino/as (and Latin America) as much as it has been between Blacks and Whites within the United States. I argue that the evidence outlined here requires us to remember that rock 'n' roll music was and is an intercultural, transnational product of many cultures and various ethnic groups, and that the history presented here proves that much of rock 'n' roll can be understood through its Latin American inflections.

Moreover, the story of rock 'n' roll music and what is has gone through, how it developed, and what it has become, has much to do with Cuban, Afro-Cuban, Mexican, Mexican American, Chicano/a and other Latin American cultural contributions in addition to many other ethnic and cultural groups that have taken part in the rock 'n' roll conversation. In other words, it would be foolish to think of rock music and continue to ignore the rich Latin/o history of this era. From the earliest jazz influences through tangos, *rumbas*, *cha-chas*, and mambos, to everlasting guitar riffs by Ritchie Valens; from Black-Latino vocal groups to Black-White-Latino fusions; from the original creator of 'Louie Louie' who wanted to make it a Latin song, to Sam 'the Sham' and counting off in Spanish; from ? and the Mysterians being ambiguously ethnic, to the Sir Douglas Quintet's 'Chicano' identity and trying to pass as English; from the Latin-influenced 'Bo Diddley beat' in 'I Want Candy,' to the numerous Latino/Hispanic individuals in various US garage bands; and from obscure contributions like slam-dancing and wearing costumes and makeup, to the rebellious fashion of wearing an earring, the garage-rock story deserves at least a mention of its Latin/o legacy.

Furthermore, the study of Latin/o rock music reveals tensions that I mentioned at the beginning of this chapter. As I began this discussion with the supposed emergence of Latino/as and the Latin 'boom' of recent years, I further contend that such discourse reveals a dominant US paradigm that sees Latino/as as foreign, exotic, and immigrant. Rather than move beyond the Black/White paradigm of

---

113 Cepeda, 'Columbus Effect(s)': Chronology and Crossover in the Latin(o) Music "Boom."

popular music history, it appears that mainstream accounts (and some scholars) continue to reinforce such stereotypes that discuss US history as White and Black and further displace the significance of various racial, ethnic, and cultural groups within our borders. As Sublette argues:

> it's time to take another look at our popular music mythology, which is focused almost exclusively in terms of the drama of black and white, and missed the Spanish-speaking elephant in the kitchen. It's the other great tradition.[114]

As with this addition to the story of garage-rock, the story of rock 'n' roll in general, deserves the same resolve, and both deserve further exploration of rock music's connections to complex societal issues that link rock music, in various forms, to the politics of identity and culture — be it language, nationality, gender, class, sexual orientation, race, or ethnicity.

As this piece of garage-rock history reveals, the story of popular music is loaded with complex issues related to the politics of language, skin color and race, and avowed or perceived ethnic identity, and these are just a few examples of the many issues that can be raised by critical treatments of popular music history. It is my aim here to shed light on some of these issues as they relate to the garage-rock phenomenon, the larger rock 'n' roll story, and the larger story of ethnic and cultural relations in US society. As this research suggests, further exploration into continuing issues of minority exclusion and the reification of the Black/White dichotomy in US culture, I am hopeful that future scholars in music, history, cultural studies, American studies, and various other areas of research will be willing to take up the call and make the case for discussing phenomena like garage-rock through various cultural lenses in order to fully understand their impact on the lives of individuals past, their continuing impact in the present, and of course, their broader implications for the future.

---

114 Sublette, 'The Centrality of Cuban Music.'

Interludio 3° (third interlude)

The Latin/o legacy can still be heard in much of the popular music that followed the garage-rock period. 'Louie Louie' remains an all-time rock 'n' roll classic, but the *clave* beat can be heard in several different songs by Bo Diddley as well as in 'Not Fade Away' by Buddy Holly, which as also covered by Bobby Fuller and, more famously, by the Rolling Stones, the Grateful Dead, and others. 'I Want Candy' by The Strangeloves was covered in the 1980s by Bow Wow Wow, creating a new-wave/pop classic and introducing the song and the *clave* rhythm to yet another generation of Americans. In 1979, while 'I Fought The Law' was covered by The Clash as a punk-rock song, 'La Bamba' was also covered as a punk-rock song by The Plugz — thereby bringing *clave* and *son jarocho* to the punk generation.

In the 1980s and 1990s the internationally popular band Los Lobos covered both 'La Bamba' and 'Wooly Bully,' bringing both songs to new Chicano/as and Latino/as as well as other American audiences. The song 'Can't Get Enough Of You Baby,' originally by ? and the Mysterians, was a widely popular (cover) song by Smash Mouth in the 1990s. Most recently, 'Have Love Will Travel' by The Sonics was covered in 2003 by alternative-blues-rock duo The Black Keys, and the song has even been featured in recent car commercials. And as I indicated at the outset of Chapter three, Domingo Samudio's famous count-off has been imitated by countless rock acts, most recently by U2 and others.

South of the border, 'I Fought The Law' was covered once again by Ataque 77, an Argentina punk band that made it a *punk en español* song called 'Yo Combatí La Ley' (from their 1993 *Todo Está Al Revés* album). And in yet another interesting turn, in the late 1990s ? and the Mysterians translated '96 Tears' to Spanish, and continue to perform both the English and Spanish versions. It appears that like Domingo Samudio and others, who came around to acknowledge their Latino/a or Chicano/a identity decades after their brush with fame, ? and the Mysterians are another example of Latino/as who no longer try to pass as White. Moreover, examples such as '96 Tears (En Español)' indicate how Latino/as have come around to acknowledging their Latino/a heritage and the significance of the Spanish language for their marginal, bicultural identity(ies).

Not to be forgotten, long hair and earrings eventually became a standard part of rock music culture, and to some extent, continue to be a 'rebellious' fashion for the mainstream. Likewise, makeup, masks, and outrageous costumes have become such a common sight in rock 'n' roll that they have become cliché. Meanwhile, the artist Prince also changed his name to a symbol (perhaps more famously), and 'slam-dancing' at concerts is so ubiquitous with young people at rock shows now that it too has become a rather standard aspect of rock and punk-rock music culture. All told, I offer all of the facts in this genealogical exploration of garage-rock history as evidence of the notable presence and profound influence of Latin/o contributions to popular music over several decades.

Selective Discography and Tracks Listed Here and in Chapter Three:

Ataque 77. 'Yo Combatí La Ley (I Fought The Law),' *Todo Está Al Revés* (RCA International, 1993).

Aterciopelados. 'El Estuche,' *Caribe Atómico* (BMG Music, 1998).

Bill Haley y Los Cometas. 'Al Compas Del Reloj,' *15 Grandes Éxitos Del Rock And Roll* (SonoDis Hollywood Records, 1997).

The Black Keys. 'Have Love, Will Travel,' *Thickfreakness* (Fat Possum, 2003).

The Bobby Fuller Four. 'I Fought The Law,' *I Fought The Law: The Best of The Bobby Fuller Four* (Rhino, 2004).

Bow Wow Wow. 'I Want Candy,' *I Want Candy* (RCA, 1982).

Cannibal and the Headhunters. 'Land of a Thousand Dances,' *Golden Classics* (Collectables, 1996).

The Clash. 'I Fought The Law,' *The Story of the Clash, Vol. 1* (Epic/Legacy, 1988).

The Kingsmen. 'Louie Louie,' *Greatest Hits* (K-Tel, 1998).

Nuggets II. *Nuggets II: Original Artyfacts from the British Empire and Beyond, 1964–1969* (Rhino Records, 2001).

The Plugz. 'La Bamba,' *Electrify Me* (Restless/Plugz, 1978).

? and the Mysterians. '96 Tears,' 'Can't Get Enough Of You Baby,' *The Best of ? & the Mysterians: Cameo Parkway 1966–1967* (ABKCO, 2005).

_____. '96 Tears (En Español),' *Feel It!: The Very Best of Question Mark & the Mysterians* (Varese, 2001).

Sam the Sham and the Pharaohs. 'Wooly Bully,' *20th Century Masters — The Millennium Collection: The Best of Sam the Sham & the Pharaohs* (Mercury, 2003).

The Sir Douglas Quintet. 'She's About a Mover,' *Mendocino* (Smash, 1969).

Smash Mouth. 'Can't Get Enough Of You Baby,' *Astro Lounge* (Interscope, 1999).

The Sonics. 'Have Love, Will Travel,' *Here Are The Sonics!!!* (Norton, 1965).

The Strangeloves. 'I Want Candy,' *I Want Candy: The Best of The Strangeloves* (Legacy/Epic/Associated, 1995).

4

Las Ondas de José Agustín: The Birth of Rock in México and the Latin/o Rock Diaspora (1970–1990)

> *We [Onda kids] were born when the train of the Mexican revolution was on its way out and the dream of modernity was coming in. That's when everything changed. We saw that we were full of contradictions, in a country where the border is everywhere. And in these contradictions is where we found our identity.*[1]
>
> *¡Tenemos punk, tenemos heavy metal, tenemos en español y en inglés, tenemos al Jim Morrison y El Tri!*[2]

While rock 'n' roll exploded in North America in the 1950s, within a few years it was burgeoning further as a worldwide phenomenon and beginning to splinter into its own subgenres, of which garage-rock was one notable example (in the mid 1960s). Yet, as the new form of popular music took the world by storm, México was not an exception. The impact of rock 'n' roll music was so profound that not even Mexican society — with its strict codes of conduct and behavior deeply rooted in Catholicism, as well as its aversion to US cultural imperialism and 'Americano' influence on their youth — could not escape the influence of this new transnational music. México's first wave of rock 'n' roll came to be known as '*La Onda Roquera*' or, more simply, '*La Onda*.' In Spanish, *onda* translates as 'wave' or even 'vibration.' Street slang usage would mean something like 'the vibe,' 'the scene,' or 'the new style,' and can be heard when a person asks the question '*¿Que onda?*' ('What's new?' or, 'What's going on?'). When *La Onda* began in México, one of its greatest proponents would be José Agustín. Agustín, renowned Mexican author and the first Mexican rock journalist, has written numerous books and countless newspaper and magazine articles on the subject of rock music. Interestingly, *La*

---

1   Author's translation of López, 'El Rockondero,' 400.
2   Street vendor in México City's 'El Chopo' flea market; see Martínez, *The Other Side: Fault Lines, Guerilla Saints, and the True Heart of Rock 'n' Roll*, 148.

Onda was not only the subject of much of Agustín's professional journalistic writing, but the rock 'n' roll style would come to manifest itself in Agustín's writing and in the dialogue of his subjects, even when he was writing fiction, that one might assume had nothing at all to do with rock 'n' roll music. With other Mexican authors, Agustín was part of a new literary style that also came to be known as *Onda* (the 'new style' in Mexican literature).

Onda was significant because for the first time in Mexican literature, and likely in other Latin American literature, characters were written in various scenes with seemingly insignificant details like playing '*rocanrol*' (Spanish slang for rock 'n' roll) records in their apartment. Drawn in the complex colors of their youth, they discussed musicians at length and told each other stories of going to Rolling Stones concerts. Some took pleasure in listening to rock music to torment their family. Others would form friendships and relationships in which they would conjure up socialist manifestos, and then declare that 'everybody must get stoned' and, of course, listen to Bob Dylan. While much of Agustín's early writing was inspired by rock 'n' roll music in journalism and chronicling the counter-culture, the connection between *rocanrol* and José Agustín is perhaps better reserved for the literary genre which he helped to create. The rock 'n' roll wave, or *La Onda Roquera*, which Agustín illuminated in his many books, demanded a different style of writing that the Mexican public had never seen before. His mastery of dialogue, street slang, playful rhyme, sarcasm, vulgarity, popular culture allusion, and inclusion of North American English euphemisms pointed to an identification with the 'new style' and on another level suggested a hybridized and transnational identity.

Worth noting anecdotally at this point, is the fact that the literature of José Agustín is not something I was personally familiar with until recently. Aside from my interest in popular music as a mode of communication, and, specifically, in the way popular music mediates identity, my investigations partly came about as a result of the fact that I married a Mexican woman. A US resident before she met me, my wife was born and raised in northern México where, somewhere along they way, she was exposed to the literature of José Agustín. She remembers that it was through her father, a Mexican cowboy and at the same time an intellectual type, who has spent a great deal of his life resisting the hegemony of North American culture. He still lives in the mountains of Chihuahua, México's largest state, and my wife was holding his old books for him when I began to discover his passion for classical music, history, Marxist critique, counter-culture, and *Onda* writers like José Agustín, Parménides García Saldaña, and Gustavo Saínz, who were distinguished (for various reasons) from their more famous and mainstream contemporaries such as Carlos Castañeda, Carlos Fuentes, Carlos Monsivaís, and Elena Poniatowska.

What was striking to me in conversations with my wife was the fact that I, growing up in Texas as a US citizen, had never heard of José Agustín. Nor had I ever been taught anything about the literary movement, *Onda*, with which he is associated. Oftentimes, one can simply attribute such a situation to the fact that José Agustín is a Mexican author. Frankly, people of the US are hardly ever exposed to literature or popular culture from countries other than the US. Likewise, college and university students are often exposed to the wonderful canon of English literature that always includes Shakespeare and other great European men. In advanced classes, it may happen that senior students and graduate students will be exposed to an expanded literary canon that might include a few famous Latin American authors. And while internationally famous Latin American writers like Pablo Neruda, Ruben Darío, and Gabriel García Marquez, are not often part of curriculum for primary education in the US, and are often just as rare in college or university course schedules, some programs at progressive colleges or universities might actually include them, although it seems fair to say that in the US such a thing is surely the exception rather than the rule. My previous ignorance of José Agustín made complete sense to me in that light. Why then should one seemingly obscure Mexican author be known to a North American, or anybody outside of his home country?

The simple answer for this book is that José Agustín remains the foremost journalist who chronicled early rock 'n' roll in México, and provides a knowledge base for rock 'n' roll's development in México. For that reason alone, José Agustín should be more well known and his significance better documented for people who study literature, music, culture, history, politics, media, communication, culture, or rock music history. Of course, another answer is that in addition to his journalistic writing on rock music, Agustín is linked to, and could be called a founding father of, the literary movement in México known as *Onda*. And when combining the two, the development of rock 'n' roll in México and the creation of a literary *Onda*, one can arrive at another perspective on Latin/o connections to rock music that further illuminates the complexities of Mexican and other Latino/a identity(ies) as well as more of rock's connections to Latin America.

So, what exactly was *Onda*? Is there a defining characteristic? Or are there characteristics for this new wave, or movement? Who is/was José Agustín and where did he come from? What was the significance of *Onda* to the social, political, and cultural climate? What, if anything, does this have to do with a conversation about rock 'n' roll, popular music, or Latino/a identity? This chapter will engage these questions through a focus on the connections between music genres and literary genres.

Specifically, this chapter analyzes the relationship of rock 'n' roll music in México with the literary movement known as *Onda*. As an entry point, this chapter takes a biographical road trip with, and examines the life experiences of, José Agustín, whose experiences directly contributed to his literary style that came to be known as *Onda*. His story is particularly telling; a man who seems to have always been on the margins of society, since he came to be so closely associated with counter-cultural currents like *Onda*, and hence, the politics of rock 'n' roll as they unfolded in México. Moving forward chronologically, this chapter also traces the history of Mexican rock waves from the late 1950s to the late 1990s. In the concluding section, I establish the link between the musical genre and the literary genre and make a case for the significance of each one for the other.

Defining *Onda*

Interestingly, the literary wave in México known as *Onda* was significant enough that it actually garnered some attention from a few literary scholars in the US. In an edited collection of articles on José Agustín and *Onda* that was published just over twenty years ago, several scholars contributed to our understanding of what exactly *Onda* was. For example, some defined *La Onda* as a 'youth phenomenon in Mexican literature . . . that alluded both to the sound waves of rock music and to a slang expression meaning something like "cool" or "with it,"'[3] while another referred to *La Onda* simply as the '*chingodélica*' phase of José Agustín's literary career.[4] '*Chingodélica*' is a Mexican Spanish slang word that can mean something like 'fucking-delic' or 'fuck-delic' (from 'psychedelic'). Of salience here is the fact that the word is rather difficult to translate. This is a point about *Onda* that is important enough to warrant further explanation.

In Mexican Spanish, the word '*chingar*' can mean, in its simplest use, to fuck. Like the word 'fuck' in English, the word '*chingar*' can be used far beyond its original usage as a verb. Just as 'fuck' is versatile in English (it can be used as a noun, a verb, an adjective, an adverb, etc.), the Spanish word '*chingar*' can be also deployed in many different ways, and it is especially vulnerable to the language shifts and idiosyncrasies of youth culture. In this way, '*chingar*' can become '*¿Que chingado?*' (What the fuck?), '*¡No chingues!*' (Stop whining!), and '*¡Chingate!*' (Fuck off!). While the linguistic versatility of the words 'fuck' and '*chingar*' are mildly interesting, what is pertinent here is that the very presence of such words was an identifiable aspect of the new literary style. In other words, such profanity and vulgarity in language was a virtual trademark for Agustín, and earned him disgust by many readers in addition to official censorship by the Mexican government. At the same time, the translation difficulties people experienced of such words and phrases has been seen by literary critics as a failure on Agustín's part. His North American critics argued that his works contain too much slang, that his characters are vulgar, that words and phrases are untranslatable, and that his works are particular to time and place and, therefore, not transcendent.

To get back to '*chingodélica*,' the significance of this word is the very multiplicity of ways it can be deployed that makes José Agustín more interesting as an *Onda* writer. The phrase '*chingodélica*,' one would think, should be a word that is simple enough to translate. It seems to be a simple combination of the words '*chingar*' (to fuck) and '*sicodélico*' (psychedelic). Yet the word is just one example of how such odd pairings of words and phrases presented many readers with a certain level of difficulty in making sense of the dialogue and the characters in José Agustín's writing. When one reads the words 'fucking-delic' or 'fuck-delic' in English, it absolutely makes no sense, just as '*chingodélica*' wouldn't make sense in Spanish. These words, or this word, can only make sense if one imagines a goofball conversation between two young hipsters in México City that are into rock music and, most likely, Sartre, Nietzsche, and marijuana. And this is exactly who the character

---

3   Carter and Schmidt, 'Introduction' to *José Agustín: Onda and Beyond*, 1.
4   Kirk, 'The Development of an *Ondero*,' 23.

in a José Agustín story or article would be, and perhaps the person for whom the literature was written. Thus, *Onda* was about playfulness with language, about drug use, about coming into consciousness, about the *jipiteca* (hippie) counter-cultural movement, and, more than anything, about youth identity in rock 'n' roll.[5] Just as much, and maybe even more, it was about Mexican youth speaking in terms that most adults wouldn't, or couldn't, understand. This is what the literary *Onda* (the new wave) was all about, and what it signified.

Perhaps a more complex understanding of *Onda* is offered by another scholar who also noted that *Onda* writers were famous, and infamous, for their use of slang, rock 'n' roll music references and lyrics, foreign languages — North American English in particular — and allusions to popular culture. The same scholar added that the literary movement was supposedly a 'revolutionary, anti-literary discourse' and representative of the authors' 'radical revolutionary spirits,'[6] but also that *Onda* was much more. To a great extent, *Onda* was about parody, specifically about a kind of antiliterary parody. In a similar vein, another scholar referred to *Onda* as a form of 'new criticism,' while yet another wrote that the wave was one that 'reflected the social context of the affluent urban middle class' and could be understood through how it symbolized 'a complete separation between generations.'[7]

The same scholar further argued that *Onda* writers opted for a colloquial language that resulted in a kind of 'intranscendent discourse.' According to this idea, 'Words are meant to mean only what they mean,' and, as another scholar argued, this is what made *Onda* works revolutionary, 'both in content and form.'[8] All the same, other definitions of *Onda* attributed other characteristics like a 'phase of escapism,' reveling in 'surface iconoclasm,' and being 'highly satirical' of one's own generation as well as the generation of the adults.[9] It has also been said that *Onda* was also about 'intertextual links,' 'obvious parodies,' and iconoclasm 'within the tradition of literary parody.'[10] We might add to these definitions, stylistic play on ideological differences, puns, foreign languages, neologisms, and, more salient for this book, references to popular music and especially to rock 'n' roll.[11] Cynical, disillusioned, pathetic parody,[12] and 'hip'[13] could also describe *Onda*. At the same time, it might possibly have been just 'radical novelty' in literature.[14] Other descriptions include *Onda* as 'behavior' and 'life-style,'[15] simple innovation in language and/or youth argot.[16]

5   For more on *jipitecas*, see Agustín, *La Contracultura en México: La Historia y El Significado de Los Rebeldes Sin Causa, Los Jipitecas, Los Punks y Las Bandas.*
6   Bruce-Novoa, 'La *Onda*: Parody and Satire,' 37.
7   Ibid., 39.
8   Ibid., 39.
9   Ibid., 40.
10   Ibid., 42.
11   Ibid., 43.
12   Ibid., 47.
13   Ibid., 49.
14   Ibid., 51.
15   Ibid., 53.
16   Ibid., 54–5.

Nevertheless, the supposed radical, revolutionary, and rebellious character of *Onda* is not something that has been completely accepted, nor has it remained unproblematic or unchallenged. As mentioned earlier, literary critics investigated the literary works of José Agustín and found that Agustín's literary *Onda* can be placed squarely within the tradition of Western European literature and the category of modern literature. Such critics argued that Agustín's style was not so much rebellious or revolutionary of anything as much as it was parody of itself, which would include the youth movement and a younger generation's hypocrisy. Carter and Schmidt, for example, have also surmised on the significance of a problematic class subject position,

> The writers of La Onda represented a constituency — specifically, middle-class adolescents from Mexico City — not previously established within Mexican literature whose behavioral and aesthetic values contrasted strikingly with those of the previous generation. For the first time, adolescents were not being portrayed from a reminiscent adult point of view but rather from their own.[17]

This is a point that has been labored in previous analyses of Agustín, but what is striking here is that by the late 1980s, an apparent judgment was handed down about Agustín's literature. After the publication of at least one book and several articles devoted only to the *Onda* and José Agustín, the interest in Agustín began to wane. Add to this the fact that by the 1980s Agustín had traveled extensively in the US, lectured at various universities, and declined offers to stay in departments of Spanish, departments of English, and departments of literature, and eventually returned to his home country of México. For most of us outside of México, the life and work of José Agustín might otherwise be left to the dustbins of history. It is almost no wonder that the work of José Agustín seems to be presently forgotten in North American and Anglocentric scholarship.

My contention, however, is that the literary, societal, and cultural significance of Agustín and *Onda* is worth re-examining by scholars of today in various disciplines. To advance this position a little further, this chapter will now turn to brief biographical highlights and a description of the contributing factors that provide more insight into José Agustín. This is followed by an analysis of how the literature of José Agustín and other *Onda* writers are deserving of more critical attention in terms of intersections and inter-relations with rock 'n' roll in México.

José Agustín and *La Onda Roquera*

José Agustín was born in 1944 in Huautla, México, in the southern state of Oaxaca, although he has been known to shun his hometown in favor of Acapulco, México and what has been called the 'bustling, rather sleazy atmosphere of Acapulco, where he spent most of his early life.' As the same scholar added, 'That city, with its decadent, international flavor, its beaches, and its eccentrics, is perhaps the city that has most influenced Agustín, who spent many formative years there, both as a

---

17   Carter and Schmidt, 'Introduction,' 1.

child and as an adolescent.'[18] After the Agustín family moved to México City, where José began his formal education, he was rebellious and it seems, in constant trouble with teachers. When his father, who was a pilot, began to make regular trips to the US, it represented growing cultural connections between the US and México that many Mexicans resented and that Agustín would come to write about, and write into, and write from. Like others in México, there were surely times when Agustín resented the cultural imperialism of the US and the hegemony of popular culture emanating from North America. Yet, it was the apparent inevitability of transnational cultural processes that provided the exposure to rock 'n' roll music, and like many of his generation, José Agustín was not immune. The conspicuous relationship and the sharp contrasts between México and the US — English versus Spanish, Anglo versus Latin, Protestantism versus Catholicism, puritan versus *mestizo*, first world versus third world — became the background for one of Agustín's most famous novels, *Ciudades Desiertas*,[19] that overtly dealt with the contradictions of living in the US as a Mexican.

His literary proclivities, however, actually date from before the age of ten, and he had spent much of his early life writing and painting in México. Through the creative influences of his family (acting, writing, painting, composing) he wrote plays with his brother while in his teens, and first published his own short play in 1960 which would eventually lead to a few other prize-winning plays in the 1960s and 1970s. By the early 1960s, Agustín had already completed his first novel, *La Tumba*, at the age of seventeen, and it topped México's best-seller lists.

For a while he lived in Cuba, and was associated with Marxist movements. As one scholar noted, 'the year 1961 was extremely important for Agustín, since it marks the emergence of his political awareness and his affiliation with the anti-imperialist group Movimiento América Latina.'[20] He eloped to Cuba with Margarita Dalton, a writer and sister of a guerilla leader, Roque Dalton, from El Salvador. After making their way from Veracruz to Havana, Agustín was involved with a literacy campaign, teaching peasants to read and write. He also formed a theater group, studied political economy, taught English, gave speeches at cultural and political meetings, and traveled throughout Cuba. John Kirk reminds us that even in the 1980s, José Agustín remained an outspoken defender of the Cuban Revolution.[21]

Around 1962, Agustín returned to México for family reasons. The significant events related to his return would include the death of his mother, the annulment of his marriage to Margarita Dalton, his new relationship with Margarita Bermúdez, the completion of his secondary education, and further experimentation with his own writing. By the mid 1960s different novels by Agustín were at the top of best-seller lists simultaneously. As one scholar noted, 'Not since the advent of Carlos Fuentes had there been a more spectacular launching of a writer

---

18   Kirk, 'The Development of an *Ondero*,' 10.
19   Agustín, *Ciudades Desiertas*.
20   Kirk in Carter and Schmidt, 'Introduction,' 13.
21   Ibid., 14.

in Mexico.'[22] José Agustín would later be troubled by meteoric success, controversy, and 'outrageous comments and behavior' that had much to do with his outspoken criticism of the old guard in Mexican literature.

For several months in the late 1960s he did time in a Mexican prison, for carrying a small bag of marijuana, and was imprisoned for seven months without a trial. As with other experiences in his life, he continued writing and made literary use of his prison experiences producing a few novels and a play, one of which took place in a prison. However, once again his books were protested and censored by the Mexican government for slang, vulgarity, and obscenities in the language of his characters. Nonetheless, it has been noted that his marginalization probably had more to do with his speaking out about the Mexican penal system and the denunciation of Mexican society as a whole.[23]

In addition to José Agustín's problematic place in the public spotlight and on the margins of Mexican society, John Kirk's biographical analysis of José Agustín also tells that in addition to his literary production, Agustín spent much of the 1960s and early 1970s writing articles and reviews about rock music and conducting interviews with rock stars. In 1967, Agustín even wrote the screenplay for a popular 'semi-underground' cult film of the time that featured the early Mexican rock band Los Dug Dug's.[24] Thus, not only was Agustín a part of *Onda*, helping to create it through his characters, stories, plays, and novels, but he was also documenting the *Onda* generation through rock journalism. His first book-length treatment of rock 'n' roll, *La Nueva Música Clásica* was first published in 1968. Thus, it is fitting that the story of 'La Onda Roquera,' or the rock 'n' roll wave in México, should begin with none other than José Agustín.

La Onda Roquera (The Rock Wave)

As José Agustín became (in)famous as part of the *Onda* in Mexican literature, he was also becoming more and more famous as a rock 'n' roll writer in the 1960s and 1970s. As for the rock 'n' roll part of the new wave, Agustín was perfectly positioned to emerge as its proponent and chronicler. Rock 'n' roll had exploded and was being quickly transported to other nations such as England, Canada, and, of course, México. Agustín himself tells us in *Contra la Corriente* (1990) that since childhood he was just so fascinated with the new music that out of pure fascination, he took copious notes, made lists, and tracked bands with the hits they had and the albums they released. It was a fascination that paid off when he was promoted time and time again as a journalist for his knowledge of the rock 'n' roll *Onda* in México. As Agustín recalled, rock 'n' roll could be heard in México as early as 1956,[25] and it was in those years that Mexican youth began to copy the sounds they heard coming from North America. Yet, as he astutely observed in 1990, the early absorption of rock 'n' roll in México should not be a surprise given

---

22 Ibid., 16.
23 Ibid., 21–2.
24 Zolov, 'Armando Nava and Los Dug Dug's,' 216.
25 Agustín, *Contra La Corriente*, 75.

the proximity of Los Estados Unidos Mexicanos ('The United Mexican States') to the United States of America.

Meanwhile, another iconic figure in Mexican rock lore is Javier Bátiz (from Tijuana, México), a pioneer and legend who supposedly taught Carlos Santana how to play guitar and whose career speaks to significant and long-standing connections that México has had with US rock music and therefore serves as an axle for multiple connections between rock music and México. According to Bátiz, he first heard North American blues, R&B, and rock 'n' roll as a child in Tijuana, due to US entrepreneurs who were broadcasting from Tijuana because they couldn't play 'race music'[26] on US radio. As historians well know, there was segregation of Blacks and Whites in Southern California as in the rest of the US. With regard to music, Lipsitz notes, 'Discrimination prevented whites and blacks from living and working together freely, and the sheet music, phonograph, and radio industries deliberately isolated white audiences from black music,'[27] and, put more simply, radio station managers were not allowed to air Black 'race music' in the US. Bátiz recalls that a San Diego record store owner named Ray Robinson went to Tijuana, bought air time on a Tijuana station, and broadcasted rock 'n' roll music on Mexican radio (another X station story?). Of course, this was a promotional scheme for his own record store, but such a fact belies the impact of this move: youth beyond Tijuana and into San Diego and Southern California were able to hear blues, R&B, and later, rock 'n' roll because of Ray Robinson's business move. In other words, if Javier Bátiz' memories prove correct, it could be argued that some of the earliest rock 'n' roll music heard in Southern California was, at least in part, a result of the vision of Ray Robinson who was playing it on Mexican radio, through another border radio station, due to the limitations of racial politics in the US.

Moreover, as Lipsitz locates the fermentation of rock 'n' roll music in the South, Southwest, and West Coast's inter-ethnic and intercultural working-class locales of the 1940s and 1950s, it is important to recognize that in addition to growing out of such intercultural scenes, rock 'n' roll music also helped to intensify the interactions among those diverse ethnic groups[28] (a fact to which I alluded in a previous chapter on border radio and X stations). Of lasting significance is the fact that for several decades Southern California remained a center for innovations in rock music. Thus, if Javier Bátiz is correct, the rise of rock 'n' roll in California was likely aided by Tijuana, México — at least in terms of the broadcasting and dissemination of rock 'n' roll music to the US, and not from it.

Indeed, it was under these intercultural and international circumstances that rock 'n' roll was born in México, but Bátiz's recollections are helpful in other ways. Bátiz reports that he taught himself to play guitar (although he also reports being influenced by an American expatriate, Gene Ross, who performed in Tijuana),

---

26   'Race music' was an early moniker for the African American blues and rhythm and blues music that, in combination with southern white hillbilly and western music, would later came to be known as rock 'n' roll music. For more on this, see Lipsitz, *Rainbow at Midnight*, and Garofalo, *Rockin' Out*.

27   Lipsitz, *Rainbow at Midnight*, 309.

28   Ibid., 323.

and that he started his own band by 1957 called Los TJ's.[29] Carlos Santana has said that he used to go and see this band as a teenager around 1959, and he eventually joined as a bass guitarist. This, of course, is why Bátiz claims that he taught the young Santana how to play guitar.

Nevertheless, Javier Bátiz can also be connected to other Mexican rock figures such as 'Baby Bátiz' (his little sister who was described as 'Etta James doing Janis Joplin' and has been discussed as an important female in early Mexican rock 'n' roll)[30] as well as to Abraham Laboriel (who also learned to play bass guitar from Bátiz and went on to play with Los Profetas in México — becoming a rock 'n' roll legend in his own right — and became an internationally known bassist and session musician).[31] Among these significant Mexican rock connections, Bátiz is also linked to other rockers who left México for the US and became successful in US rock bands of the 1960s and 1970s. One such person was Adolfo 'Fito' de la Parra (drummer for the famous band Canned Heat), and another is Carlos Santana. On the question of why people call him a Mexican rock legend, Bátiz says that because Carlos Santana came to the US, he became a huge commercial success, but because he (Bátiz) remained in México, his own legacy will always be that of 'legend.'[32]

While the story of Bátiz and the TJ's provides the backdrop for local rock 'n' roll in Tijuana, José Agustín claims that it was Los Locos del Ritmo that was 'the first or one of the first' bands to start playing rock 'n' roll music in México City.[33] According to Agustín's chronicles, not too long after, bands followed like Los Teen Tops, Los Black Jeans, Los Hooligans, and Los Rebeldes del Rock. Agustín notes, however, that it was not a very culturally inflected type of rock 'n' roll music. Like many other aspects of North America's cultural influence, most of the early rock 'n' roll music in México was, in fact, simply a matter of Mexicans covering popular North American and British pop songs and singing in English, but with a Mexican face and a Spanish surname. Agustín recalls that for every Doris Day there was a 'Julissa' in México, for every Paul Anka there was a César Costa, for every duo like The Everly Brothers there were Los Hermanos Carrión, for every Elvis Presley there was an Enrique Guzmán, and for every band like The Beatles or the Stones there were Mexican acts like Los Sleepers, Los Dug Dug's, and Los Yaki. In all but their names, rock 'n' roll musicians in México only followed and copied the trends that were happening in the US during this time.[34]

However, Agustín recognized early on that an exception to Mexicans copying North Americans came with The Beatles. According to Agustín, The Beatles by that time were already copying the 1950s Chicano rocker Ritchie Valens. As

---

29 Furthering the intercultural connections, Bátiz recalls that his first electric guitar was purchased at a Sears store in the US; See Bátiz, 'Javier Batiz: Biografía.'
30 See Estrada, *Sirenas al Ataque: Historia de las Mujeres Rockeras Mexicanas (1956–2000)*; Palacios and Estrada, "'A Contra Corriente'': A History of Women Rockers in Mexico.'
31 It is important to note that Abraham Laboriel is a Black Mexican. Because knowledge about African peoples in México is rather sparse, musicians such as Laboriel point to potentially rich areas in scholarship on Mexican music and cultural history.
32 Bátiz, 'Javier Batiz: Biografía,' no pagination.
33 Agustín, *Contra La Corriente*, 52.
34 Ibid., 54.

Agustín contends, the music and rhythm of 'Twist and Shout' by The Beatles shows that it was really just a pirated 'La Bamba,'[35] and Agustín is not alone in this opinion (see notes on 'La Bamba' in previous chapters). *Village Voice* writer Ed Morales also noted recently how there had always been a Latin sound in rock 'n' roll, and that he also always heard 'Twist and Shout' as a kind of mambo rhythm.[36] What this historical digression actually signifies is Agustín's recognition that the processes of transnationalism were in motion, as well as the possibility of cross-cultural influences through popular music between the US and other nations. Nonetheless, cross-cultural influences were heavily in favor of US influence on other continents, nations, and cultures.

Of course, North American (and English) rock's influence on Mexican culture was a rather significant factor in that all of the influence of North American culture on Mexican culture was beginning to be seen as a social problem in México, and youth singing pop songs in English were seen as a transgression. As Agustín reminds us, Mexicans especially disliked rock music because they viewed it as 'cultural colonization, imperialism, and infiltration.'[37] Moreover, as Solórzano-Thompson also notes on this matter,

> *La Onda*'s utilization of musical forms from the United States caused critics to regard its music as a form of cultural imperialism that threatened Mexican national integrity ... It was part of a symbolic battle between the 'national and native' (the corrido, mariachi music, etc.) and threatening foreign products (Coca-Cola, Hollywood films, etc.).[38]

Without a doubt, transnational, commercial interests dominated the rock music situation in the 1960s. It was one in which, according to Agustín, The Beatles appeared everywhere you looked, in México just like in the US — '... *hasta en la sopa!*' ('... even in your food!').[39]

In terms of Mexicans singing in their own language, however, Agustín recalls that the first groups to start singing in Spanish and 'composing in Mexican' were Three Souls in My Mind and Los Dos. Other bands such as La Revolución de Emiliano Zapata and La Máquina del Sonido also played original rock 'n' roll music in Spanish, but, according to Agustín, not very well. Others like Los Sleepers were playing regular gigs and had a following, but most of the bands of the time were still doing cover songs in English. It was not until the late 1960s that the baby of Mexican *rocanrol* had begun to crawl with the music of Rodrigo González (known as Rock-drigo). José Agustín claims that he was blown away when he saw González. Known as México's Bob Dylan, Agustín notes that by the time he finally saw him live, Rodrigo González was playing cover songs of his Mexican

---

35 Ibid., 81.
36 Morales, *Living in Spanglish*; Morales, 'Rock is Dead and Living in Mexico.'
37 Agustín, *Contra La Corriente*, 82.
38 Solórzano-Thompson, 'Performative Masculinities: The *Pachuco* and the *Luchador* in the Songs of Maldita Vecindad and Café Tacuba,' 83.
39 Ibid., 84.

predecessors Three Souls in My Mind,[40] which signified how Mexicans were finally covering other Mexicans. Thus, Agustín argues, it was in Rodrigo González that 'we finally have, an entry, a rock that is more complex, critical, intelligent and very Mexican.'[41]

Las Dos Ondas: Connecting the Rock *Onda* and the Literary *Onda*

The fact that Rodrigo González was playing covers of songs by Three Souls in My Mind, points to the fact that Mexican rock was beginning to have its own history and becoming self-referential. Second, Rodrigo González covering Three Souls in My Mind also highlights the national significance of that particular band. Three Souls in My Mind was born around 1968, claims Agustín, in the wake of student rioters that were killed by national police in México City and the culmination of *La Onda*, a reference to the apex of the counter-cultural movements in México. As Agustín recalls, while the repression of rock music and culture was 'intense' during the López Mateos presidency from 1958 to 1964, it was simply 'characteristic' of the Díaz Ordaz administration from 1964 to 1970.[42] By this time, the Mexican government was publicly and officially against rock 'n' roll music.

In the face of such repression, musical groups like Three Souls in My Mind and other *Onderos* (*Onda* kids, or new-wave kids) would find a cause and unite around the repression of the counter-culture. As Agustín recalls in his analysis of *Onda*, by 1968 people were talking about '*la onda*,' and precisely because of the ambiguity of the term, it was accepted as a generic label for all of the artistic, political, and social changes that united youth, who opted for rock music as a point of convergence.[43]

The connection between the counter-culture in literary form and counter-culture in music form is exemplified in one particular song by Three Souls in My Mind, who later became El TRI. In a song titled 'Chavo de Onda' (*Onda* kid), the hard-driving electric guitar plays a distinctively 1950s rock 'n' roll rhythm, sounding much like the guitar riffs of 'Johnny B. Goode' by Chuck Berry, while the lyrics can be heard as in the style of 'Jailhouse Rock' by Elvis Presley. In 'Chavo de Onda' singer Alex Lora expresses exactly what it was like to be caught up in the rock 'n' roll counter-culture. Any reader will easily recognize the references to long hair, blue jeans, rock shows, and the fact that parents and elders just can't understand. The lyrics are my translation into English:

> I like to let my hair down when I'm hanging out.
> I know the words to the songs of the Rolling Stones.
> I'm always wearing blue jeans, when I go to shows.
> I am an *Onda* kid, and I like the rock 'n' roll.

---

40 Agustín, *Contra La Corriente*, 61.
41 Ibid., 62.
42 Ibid., 224.
43 Original quotation: '*Ya durante 1968, en nuestro país, se hablaba de 'la onda.' Y ese término, precisamente por su vaguedad, fue aceptado por todos para 'etiquetar' un fenómeno artístico, político, social y económico que reunió a una gran cantidad de jóvenes y que optó por el rock como punto de convergencia*' (Agustín, 'Cuál Es La Onda,' 11).

> Poor old people, they just can't understand it.
> I am an *Onda* kid, and I like the rock 'n' roll.⁴⁴

What is most significant here, I contend, is the fact that El TRI's lyrical discourse actually refers to the name of the movement, *La Onda*, and proclaims a conscious identification as part of *Onda*. Given the public sentiment against rock music and counter-culture, the official Mexican government position against rock, and the harassment and massacre of people associated with the counter-culture, the significance of such a public statement cannot be overstated. As another famous Mexican writer Carlos Monsiváis attests, 'Around those times, everything that [singer Alex] Lora was saying is whatever everybody else knew, but no one dared to say.'⁴⁵ In other words, rock music became a discursive mode for *Onda*.

Furthermore, the song illustrates how the literary wave and the rock 'n' roll wave were not exactly distinguishable from each other. The band El TRI, like many others, such as José Agustín, were part of *Onda* as a counter-cultural movement and used their music as a medium for its expression, perhaps also creating *Onda* or, at least, advancing the cause by attaching the movement's name to their own cultural and identity politics. Moreover, *Onda*'s brief success and its 'desire to delegitimize state authority by creating alternative social imaginaries would eventually inspire and foretell the 1980s [Mexican rock] movement.'⁴⁶

As several scholars have noted, shortly after the 1968 student riots and the literal massacres that followed,⁴⁷ the middle-class youth interest in rock 'n' roll had dwindled, and Mexican society became repressive.⁴⁸ After the student riots at the 1968 Mexico City Olympics, and subsequent massacre of the rioters, rock music in México was embraced by students and intellectuals who had resisted it previously as cultural imperialism. Although a minor resurgence occurred after 1968 in what was being called 'La Onda Chicana' (the Chicano wave) in México, it eventually went too far for Mexican society.⁴⁹ The Mexican government of President Diaz Ordaz was publicly against rock music, and as the 1970s began, rock music in México entered its dark ages. Subject to disapproval and repression for many years, the situation worsened and rock music in México virtually disappeared a few years later after the 1971 Avándaro Music Festival.⁵⁰

'Avándaro' (or, the *Rock y Ruedas* festival) was a Woodstock-like event at a racetrack on the outskirts of Mexico City,⁵¹ in the resort site of Avándaro, and the

---

44 Excerpt from 'Chavo de Onda' by El TRI.
45 Original quotation: '*Desde aquellos tiempos, todo le que Lora decía todos lo sabían, pero nadie se atrevía decirlo.*'; See Monsiváis, 'El TRI y Alejandro Lora.'
46 Solórzano-Thompson, 'Performative Masculinities: The *Pachuco* and the *Luchador* in the Songs of Maldita Vecindad and Café Tacuba,' 83.
47 For more on the 1968 massacre, see Carey, *Plaza of Sacrfices: Gender, Power, and Terror in 1968 Mexico*.
48 Agustín, *Contra La Corriente*; Morales, 'Rock is Dead and Living in Mexico'; Zolov, *Refried Elvis*.
49 Zolov, 'Armando Nava and Los Dug Dug's.'
50 For a thorough analysis of the 1968 student massacre see Carey, *Plaza of Sacrifices*; and for more on the politics of the 1971 Avándaro Music Festival see Zolov, *Refried Elvis*.
51 Morales, 'Rock is Dead and Living in Mexico.'

festival was the culmination of student protests and the counter-cultural youth movement known as *La Onda*. The huge festival proved to Mexican society what it had suspected for a long time. Some youth cavorted nude, while others only offended through their long hair and hippie dress. Some touted Mexican flags with the peace sign replacing the national symbols of eagles and serpents, while others represented the 'national crisis' through their open use of drugs.[52] Others subverted the hegemony of Mexican nationalism by sporting US flags.

News of the events that transpired fed conservatives, who decried the generation's lack of morality and the collapse of Mexican values, but it also fed leftists and intellectuals who again argued against rock music, concluding that the generation was being colonized by a foreign culture. The cultural trauma that ensued virtually wiped out rock 'n' roll music in México, at least for middle-class youth. After the Avándaro festival, the government cracked down on bars and clubs, closing many of those in which people were nurturing rock 'n' roll music. Rock 'n' roll concerts were shut down, and according to José Agustín, some rock musicians and fans were rounded up and 'only' had their heads shaved, while others were harassed or jailed for being associated with rock 'n' roll.[53] Zolov writes,

> Rock concerts were cancelled, record contracts were severed (or left to languish), and repression set in as native rock was eliminated from the airwaves and literally pushed into the barrios on the outskirts of the city, where it remained isolated from mainstream society for more than a decade.[54]

For Mexican rock there wasn't very much going on after that, and the answer to '*¿Que onda?*' ('What's going on?') was simply, *nada*. According to scholars, these were the dark ages for Mexican rock, and yet, out of those dark ages came a kind of 'Guaca-rock' (Mexican rock) renaissance.[55]

What resulted was a Mexican rock that, instead of dying and going away, went entirely underground and then got better. Ed Morales writes of what happened after the 1971 Avándaro festival,

> If rock became, for the most part, mass-marketed corporatized product and trivialized fashion in the U.S., in Mexico it was marginalized, creating a small, devoted community with strong, supportive bonds and a fierce resistance to cooptation.[56]

Thus, from the early 1970s through the early 1980s, Mexican rock was the activity of the poor and working-class youth in México. In places called *hoyos funquis* (funky holes), Mexican rock survived and thrived. As Agustín recalls, the funky

---

52   Zolov, 'Armando Nava and Los Dug Dug's,' 221.
53   Agustín, *Contra La Corriente*, 93.
54   Zolov, 'Armando Nava and Los Dug Dug's,' 221–2.
55   I use the term 'Guaca-rock' here simply because José Agustín here starts to use the term 'Guaca-rock.' Other journalists sometimes use the term as well.
56   Morales, 'Rock is Dead and Living in Mexico.'

holes were the places where only poor people would dare go.⁵⁷ They were dives, ghettos, and nasty places where only the toughest of México City youth could survive. According to Agustín, the Mexican bands that were making music during those times were La Revolución de Emiliano Zapata, El Epílogo, La División del Norte, Peace and Love, El Ritual, Sombrero Verde, Hangar Ambulante, Nuevo México, and Chac Mool. Other rock veterans included Javier Bátiz, Armando Nava and Los Dug Dug's, Ricardo Ochoa with Kenny and the Electrics, Federico Arana with Naftalina, Jorge Reyes, and Guillermo Briseño, and Alejandro Lora with Three Souls in My Mind/El TRI.⁵⁸ Agustín also remembers that although there were many bands that came out of the *hoyos funquis* in the 1970s, the problem remained that a great deal of it still wasn't very good, and when it was, it was only copying what was going on in North America and Europe. Agustín notes one exception, the progressive-rock band Manchuria, as his only example of a 'good band' in spite of merely imitating what was going on outside of México. However, after several years of fermentation in the so-called funky holes, 'Guaca-rock' was starting to get good, and the end product was a thing Agustín calls the '*rock rupestre*' (proletariat, lowlife, trash rock).⁵⁹

This association of rock music and lower-class 'trash' culture, vulgarity, obscenity, and all things offensive can be compared to the association of rock 'n' roll with the concept of '*desmadre*.' In *Refried Elvis*, Eric Zolov has written an excellent contribution to the history of Mexican rock and how its development resulted from transnational cultural processes, political economic imperatives, and (of all things) the legacy of México's hyper-nationalism. Zolov writes:

> ... in Mexico what came to matter in public discourse was the association of rock 'n' roll (and later rock) with desmadre. An offensive, lower-class slang word, desmadre expresses a notion of social chaos introduced by the literal 'unmothering' of a person or situation. This stands in antithesis to that other Mexican phrase, buenas costumbres, which encapsulates all that is proper and correct – 'family values,' as we might say in the United States.⁶⁰

The emergence of *rock rupestre*, and the shift in association of rock 'n' roll with the middle class to the association of rock 'n' roll with the working class, would come to signify, for Agustín, a critical point in history when Mexican rock music was coming into its own. Adding to the history, Agustín claims that although it began with Three Souls in My Mind, it reached its maturity through Rodrigo González. According to Agustín, the *rock rupestre* that was the best rock music México had ever produced eventually gave birth in the early 1980s to new Mexican rockers like Botellita de Jerez, Jaime Lopez, and Cecilia Toussaint. Cecilia Toussaint was so

---

57 Agustín, *Contra La Corriente*.
58 Ibid., 111.
59 Ibid., 111–12.
60 Zolov, *Refried Elvis*, 27.

good and so original, according to José Agustín, that he calls her the best example of México's *'rock nacional'* (national, native rock).[61]

To the Other Side (USA, 1960s–1970s)

The end of the 1960s brought major changes to societies, and, just as it was in other parts of the world, popular music in the US was still at the center of controversy, and, just like elsewhere, rock 'n' roll in North America was forging new Latin/o connections. During this time of emerging social movements, war protest, and a rising tide of counter-culture, the song 'The Night They Drove Old Dixie Down' by Joan Baez was a major hit and served as an antiwar protest anthem. Known as the 'Queen of Folk'[62] and remembered as 'Bob Dylan's counterpart in folk protest,'[63] Baez is still remembered as one of the most important folk artists of the 1960s. According to an official biography, 'In 1966, Joan Baez stood in the fields alongside César Chávez and migrant farm workers striking for fair wages, and opposed capital punishment at San Quentin during a Christmas vigil.' Aside from Chicano/a rights issues, Baez had other connections to Latino/as and Latin Americans. Having become famous for civil rights and anti-Vietnam War protests, Baez also shed light on suffering of people living in Chile under Augusto Pinochet:

> To those people she dedicated her first album sung entirely in Spanish, a record that inspired Linda Ronstadt, later in the '80s, to begin recording the Spanish songs of her heritage. One of the songs Joan sang on that album, 'No Nos Moverán' (We Shall Not Be Moved), had been banned from public singing in Spain for more than forty years under Generalissimo Franco's rule, and was excised from copies of the album sold there. Joan became the first major artist to sing the song publicly when she performed it on a controversial television appearance in Madrid in 1977, three years after the dictator's death.[64]

What is also not commonly known is that Baez is the daughter of a Mexican physicist and a Scots-Irish mother, and how Baez recalled discrimination during her youth in New York and Boston for being dark-skinned, where she was called a 'nigger.'[65] This explains Baez' motivation to pursue a career of making music in the name of civil rights, social protest, social justice, taking political stances, and marching — for example, in the famous marches in Washington and Birmingham for desegregation in the early sixties.[66] As much as she became a voice for civil rights causes and an icon for protest, she was also singing for Chicano/as and other Latin Americans. Likewise, while Baez was a major symbol of folk music and counter-culture in the US, it was (at least in part) related to her own identity

---

61   Agustín, *Contra La Corriente*, 111–12.
62   Novas, *Everything You Need to Know about Latino History.*
63   Szatmary, *Rockin' in Time: A Social History of Rock-and-Roll.*
64   A. Levy, 'Official Bio: Joan Baez.'
65   Szatmary, *Rockin' in Time*, 90.
66   Ibid., 90.

politics, or the confrontations with discrimination and racism and her experiences of being a 'dark-skinned' Latina in the US.

Aside from the political and social causes that Baez championed, the Baez legacy in rock 'n' roll cannot be overstated. Some of her early songs were covered by famous rockers such as The Animals, The Byrds, The Searchers, Led Zeppelin, the Grateful Dead, The Band, and many others. One artist who was highly influenced by Joan Baez was Grateful Dead frontman Jerry Garcia. Garcia was of Spanish descent, and came into his own in San Francisco's rock scene. In addition to his bloodlines and heritage, Jerry Garcia connects in other ways to the Latin influence on rock 'n' roll music. One easy connection is the *clave* beat, or 'Bo Diddley' rhythm, that can be heard on the Grateful Dead's famous version of 'Not Fade Away' (originally a Buddy Holly song), that also became a signature song for the Grateful Dead,[67] and one scholar proposes a clear connection between the Grateful Dead's trademark imagery — colorful skulls, skeletons, and brightly colored images — and Mexican *Day of the Dead* iconography.[68] If this observation is true, then such histories and imagery further underscore the evidence connecting rock music with popular culture in México (and Spain), that remains under-acknowledged in most mainstream treatments of rock 'n' roll and rock history. Moreover, examples such as these also reject simplistic notions of US cultural imperialism, or a one-way flow of US culture to other nations. Rather, connection between rock music and Latino/a culture(s) such as these illuminate rock 'n' roll history as a site of identity-based music, intercultural exchange, significant influence by US Latino/as, and various other Latin/o inflections.

Another Latina folk singer who connected to US rock music was Linda Ronstadt, a member of a folk group called The Stone Poneys who came out of the LA folk scene. Born and raised in Tucson, Arizona, Linda Ronstadt (of German and Mexican descent) is the daughter of Gilbert Ronstadt — another musician and an Arizona contemporary of Lalo Guerrero in the 1930s. Although Linda Ronstadt's music career began in the 1960s with The Stone Poneys, who scored a hit in 1967 with 'Different Drum,' it was the LA folk-rock music scene that proved to be far more relevant for Ronstadt's rock music connections as a solo artist. Her own band would eventually break off and become known as the Eagles, although Ronstadt had further success as a solo artist and many hits throughout the 1970s. She became one of the most famous artists of the decade — through country and rock.

By the late 1960s The Doors had also achieved major success. In addition to their origins in the Southern California rock scene that in many ways owed its very existence to early rockers and the 'Eastside Sound' of the early to mid 1960s, lead singer Jim Morrison and The Doors can also be connected to Mexican rock in other ways. In yet another connection to the aforementioned artist Javier Bátiz, the Tijuana rock legend recalls his early memories of the Tijuana rock scene, and that

---

67 Morales, *Living in Spanglish*, 161.
68 Ibid., 177.

they often included the frequent sightings of Jim Morrison in Tijuana nightclubs.[69] As Bátiz used to play many of the local Tijuana clubs throughout the 1950s and 1960s, he claims frequent sightings of Morrison, and in Bátiz's reminiscences, Morrison would sit in a corner by himself and drink a few beers as he listened to the band. According to Bátiz, in those days it was not only Jim Morrison, but a lot of other 'Americano' rockers that were frequent visitors to Tijuana to drink and listen to music. While anecdotal evidence, this is an intriguing connection, given some of The Doors' music with Latin resonance.

One scholar has noted the mambo-like rhythm of 'Break On Through (To the Other Side)'[70] while rock critic Ed Morales notes that the 1967 hit song by The Doors contained an odd structure, 'a weird overlapping of bossa nova and clave rhythm.'[71] In a nod to 'Spanglish,' a term employed by Morales to denote intercultural dialogue and cultural hybridity, he also suggests that 'Break On Through (To the Other Side)' may be a veiled reference to the politics of the border or at least, a conflation of sex and the border. If this proposition is true, one can only wonder whether Jim Morrison's musings on the border were about the penetration of Mexican culture by US culture, or the penetration of US culture by Mexican culture. Perhaps we'll never know. As such stories reveal, however, at the same time that Mexicans were listening to and learning the wonderful new music called rock 'n' roll (and later, 'rock') and absorbing it into their own cultural lexicon, more and more US rock was being influenced by Mexican and Latin/o culture.

Such intercultural exchange and cross-assimilation was evident in other places as well. For example, Latino/as were highly sought after in the Hollywood movie industry in the late 1960s (e.g., Anthony Quinn, Raquel Welch, etc.). One recent documentary, *The Bronze Screen*, reminds us of the contributions to US popular culture by Argentina-born composer Lalo Schifrin. Among Schifrin's most memorable credits are the unforgettable *Mission: Impossible* theme songs, music for the Paul Newman film *Cool Hand Luke* in 1967, and the theme song for the 1968 Steve McQueen movie *Bullitt*. As Lalo Schifrin recalls of his *Bullitt* composition, 'It was a strange Latin rhythm in 5/4 . . . the orchestra is doing a *guajira*.'[72]

In other connections, historians recall how The Spencer Davis Group's Top Ten-hit in 1967, 'I'm a Man,' had 'the most devastating extended Latin-American conga beat in guitar-rock history.'[73] Also around 1967, Mitch Ryder and the Detroit Wheels had a Top-Forty hit with 'Little Latin Lupe Lu.'[74] The work of Eric Zolov on Mexican history, youth culture, and rock music also reveals more Latino/a articulations to rock 'n' roll and music history. As Zolov comments on the popularity of Mexico as a site for North American and British youth to converge, explore,

---

69   Bátiz, 'Javier Batiz: Biografía,' no pagination.
70   Sublette, 'The Kingsmen and the Cha-Cha-Chá,' 89.
71   Morales, *Living in Spanglish*, 160.
72   Racho et al., *The Bronze Screen: 100 Years of the Latino Image in Hollywood* [documentary film].
73   Eddy, *The Accidental Evolution of Rock 'n' Roll: A Misguided Tour Through Popular Music*, 190.
74   Ibid., 204.

and experiment with drugs since the early 1960s, it is remarkable that hippie trends such as the use of leather sandals, hair beads, and even the use of drugs like marijuana and mushrooms for recreation and experimentation, probably had their roots in México and were a by-product of North American youth's experiences and contacts across the border.[75]

Beyond more obvious Latin/o connections there was the band Love, who were known for their mellow country-rock sound that often included horns (trumpets) in the style of *mariachi*-influenced songs of previous decades, and released obscure songs like '*¡Que Vida!*' (from 1967's *Da Capo* album). Two years later, the folk-rock classic 'Suite — Judy Blue Eyes' by Crosby, Stills & Nash revealed more Latin connections when the song reached its crescendo via Caribbean rhythms, Spanish singing, and garbled words about Cuba. In 1970, US folk singers Simon and Garfunkel released 'El Condor Pasa (If I Could),' a cover song derived from a Peruvian folk melody ('El Cóndor Pasa') and that featured Paul Simon's lyrics on top of an instrumental track by a group called Los Incas.[76] Also around this time, in the early 1970s, Uriah Heep were using Latin percussion in 'Look at Yourself'[77] while Steely Dan were singing of the plight of 'Nuyoricans' in Manhattan.[78] In another the nod to bilingual musicality and code-switching, Morales' concept of 'Spanglish,' reminds us how other US artists like Stevie Wonder can be heard singing the Spanish word *chevere* (meaning 'cool' or 'groovy') in songs like 1973's 'Don't You Worry 'Bout a Thing.'[79]

Yet another major hit (and now classic rock song), the psychedelic/acid-rock song 'White Rabbit' by the Jefferson Airplane (1969), was based on Spanish-guitar compositions and *boleros*, and, thus, is yet another all-time rock classic with Spanish or Latin/o influence. Without a doubt, many of the most significant, memorable, and defining rock songs of the 1960s should be reconsidered for their Latin/Hispanic articulations, but also for how they demonstrate intercultural communication between Latino/as and others as well as the intercultural dialogues between Latino/as themselves.

Furthermore, at the same 1969 Woodstock concert where rock music became famous for its connections to counter-culture, social protest, and generational shifts, Jimi Hendrix left lasting images and sounds of an electrified, rock 'n' roll guitar virtuoso's version of 'The Star Spangled Banner.' Yet journalist/critic Morales reminds us that the blind Puerto Rican singer José Feliciano was actually 'the first musician, well before Jimi Hendrix,' to do an alternative version of 'The Star Spangled Banner' and that when Hendrix performed it so famously at Woodstock, it was already 'a very '60s phenomenon.'[80] Adding to the Woodstock layers, the very band that backed Hendrix in his defining Woodstock performance included

75 See Zolov, *Refried Elvis*; Zolov, 'Armando Nava and Los Dug Dug's'; Zolov, '*La Onda Chicana*: Mexico's Forgotten Rock Counterculture.'
76 Starr and Waterman, *American Popular Music: From Minstrelsy to MTV*, 389–90.
77 Eddy, *The Accidental Evolution of Rock 'n' Roll*, 190.
78 Morales, *Living in Spanglish*, 161.
79 Ibid., 161.
80 Ibid., 160.

Puerto Rican drummer/percussionist Gerardo Velez. In the same moment, the iconic hippie band Canned Heat included the Mexico City-born Fito de la Parra on drums, and in a recent band biography of Canned Heat, de la Parra tells the tale of running into Carlos Santana backstage and how both were excited that Mexicans were also part of Woodstock.[81]

Of course, Woodstock was the place where Carlos Santana more famously articulated rock music to Latin American rhythms and music. Santana emerged out of Tijuana, México and later from the San Francisco, California rock scene with an Afro-Latino hard-rock sound. A Mexican by birth, who grew up in Tijuana and was later transplanted to San Francisco in 1966, Carlos Santana came into the mainstream rock music scene through Woodstock where he and his band famously performed their unique, eclectic mix of rock, blues, jazz, Mexican, Latin and Afro-Cuban beats, rhythms, and influences. Aided and influenced by promoter Bill Graham, the Santana band appeared just in time to play at the famous Woodstock concert in August of 1969, and went on to achieve Top-Five success in the US charts with their debut album, which featured such memorable songs as 'Evil Ways' and remained in the charts for an incredible two years. The 1970 release of their second album featured classic hits, such as 'Black Magic Woman' and 'Oye Como Va,' a song that eventually became a Top-Ten single in the US charts, while the album reached the #1 spot.

The song 'Oye Como Va' is interesting in itself because Santana's popular version was actually a cover of an original song by famous New York salsa percussionist Tito Puente who wrote it in the 1930s. Interestingly, before 'Oye Como Va' was part of US rock history, it was a Cuban mambo done by a Puerto Rican from New York,[82] which was itself a 'rewrite' of another song by Cuban Cachao López.[83] One scholar notes that Santana was turned on to 'Latin' music by promoter Bill Graham, who was a mambo fanatic in the late 1950s and early 1960s.[84] In other words, 'Oye Como Va' wasn't just a Latin/o rock song or even just a Latin song, it was a Latin/o cultural production with different layers of Latin/o connections (from Cubans to Puerto Ricans to Mexicans). Nevertheless, Carlos Santana, through all his successes in the 1960s and 1970s as well as his most recent hits, remains one of the most important and influential Latino/a musicians in popular music to this day, having sold millions of albums and achieving popularity all over the world. As Morales observes, with his recent reemergence in popular culture, Carlos Santana has 'solidified his place as an immortal in pop music history.'[85]

Yet another interesting connection takes the conversation back to Texas Mexicans. As scholars note, the years 1965 to 1969 are often remembered as

---

81   See Fito de La Parra et al., *Living The Blues: Canned Heat's Story of Music, Drugs, Death, Sex, and Survival*.
82   Further noting the multiculturalist history of rock 'n' roll music, Morales reminds us that the mambo was actually developed in México City by the Cuban Pérez Prado, who was mixing North American swing and bebop with Cuban traditional music (see Morales, *Living in Spanglish*); Again, for more on rock and multiculturalism, see Billig *Rock 'n' Roll Jews* and Lipsitz, *Rainbow at Midnight*.
83   Sublette, 'The Kingsmen and the Cha-Cha-Chá,' 89.
84   Ibid., 88–9.
85   Morales, *Living in Spanglish*, 162.

'heydays of Chicano activism,'[86] and Chicano/as were just beginning to move toward recognition in North American political consciousness. Although not explicitly aligned with the Chicano movement, it is fitting that in popular music consciousness, the Santana band came around to electrify crowds with their Latin sound and to energize Latino/a and Chicano/a communities, who noticed their lack of representation in mainstream popular culture and must have been thirsting for superstars. One such community was the *tejano* music community of Little Joe Hernández.

In South Texas, Little Joe and the Latinaires had fluctuated between rock 'n' roll songs and *rancheras* until 1967. At this point, Little Joe Hernández was gravitating toward a new Chicano aesthetic. After traveling to San Francisco and seeing Santana and others, Little Joe and the Latinaires dropped their matching suits, grew their hair long, engaged a counter-cultural lifestyle, and even moved toward the politics of the Chicano movement. At the heart of such a transformation was a name change from the English name 'The Latinaires' to a name in Spanish, 'La Familia' (the family), and the end result was a new 'Spanglish' band name, *Little Joe y La Familia*, that symbolized the new cultural nationalism of the Chicano/a movement. Little Joe attributed his newfound ideology to a growing *Latinismo* of the time. With Santana reaching unprecedented levels of success in the rock world and other bands from the San Francisco Bay Area being Latinized, Little Joe remembers it as a time when things were happening and 'speaking Spanish was hip.'[87] Fittingly, the cultural nationalism of the Chicano movement would have its influence on music as artists like *Little Joe y la Familia* began to identify with the movement more strongly. Another interesting result was that with the success of people like Santana, 'Little Joe' increasingly identified with rock music.

In anticipation of getting back into the rock music market, Little Joe upgraded his band in 1971. As they launched with full force into *La Onda Chicana* (The Chicano Wave) in *tejano* music, they still entertained the possibility of breaking into the rock market. Their first album in 1972 was an LP titled *Para La Gente* that ethnomusicologist/historian Manuel Peña calls the first *tejano* exploitation of 'compound bimusicality.'[88] Just as code-switching in language happens between English and Spanish, the music alternated between Mexican *ranchera* and North American swing-jazz oriented sounds. Roberts touches on *Little Joe y La Familia* and adds that when they did venture back into rock music later on, as in the song 'La Tuna,' they were as heavily salsa-oriented as other groups that followed Santana's lead in California and other New York-based ensembles that, coincidentally, were combining salsa with heavy metal guitar solos.[89]

As Peña astutely points out, the significance of such hybridity and fusion was such that it went beyond the assimilation/resistance dialectic of Chicano ideology or other mainstream discourses. This 'compound bimusicality' foreshadowed new

---

86   Gutierrez, 'Community, Patriarchy and Individualism: The Politics of Chicano History and the Dream of Equality,' 47.
87   Peña, *Música Tejana*, 163–6.
88   Ibid., 168.
89   Roberts, *The Latin Tinge*, 99.

ways of intercultural accommodation and assimilation, therefore transforming difference into a new identity.[90] Peña furthers this point by acknowledging the debt that *tejano* music has to *La Onda Chicana* and artists like Little Joe and Sunny Ozuna who were predisposed to cultural fusion and musical diversity. As Peña declares, 'Unconsciously they may have perceived the style-switching peculiar to La Onda as an extension of the speech they used in their most intimate circles.'[91] In other words, like speech, rock music had become a mode of Chicano/a discourse.

With regard to Puerto Ricans and rock, Roberts notes in *The Latin Tinge* the emergence of salsa-rock fusions that developed on the East Coast of the US and how New York groups like Toro, Changó, Seguida might have been called rock-tinged salsa or Latin-tinged rock, while Puerto Rican and Miami-based Latin rock bands also emerged. As Roberts notes, 'Puerto Rico was in fact something of a Latin rock center in the mid-1970s'; exemplars included Tempo 70, who mixed rock with salsa, and Raices, who had strong Brazilian influences. In Miami, Wild Wind and Opus articulated rock to salsa in different ways.[92] Following this trend, Roberts includes others groups like Nebula, Sabor, and Caldera but concludes that while the various salsa-rock combinations may have been more interesting, none of them were able to have the success of more famous Caribbean-influenced, Latin rock combinations like Santana.[93] Eventually, East Coast Latin rock bands moved away from rock and toward disco-oriented music.[94]

Meanwhile, on the other side of the continent, Santana's influences were more evident and perhaps stronger. Several bands from east LA followed the lead of Santana and created Latin rock fusions through their music. Two of those bands were actually offshoots of Santana's success with Afro-Latino-Anglo, hard-rock-salsa-blues-jazz fusion. The popular 'Chicano' group Malo was actually founded by Carlos Santana's younger brother Jorge. Azteca, another popular east LA band, was started by musicians from Santana's band who were more jazz oriented and wanted to move in a different musical direction. Other popular east LA bands like El Chicano and Tierra were not necessarily linked to Santana, but they were nonetheless connected to the Latin rock fusion and part of the newfound cultural nationalism among Chicano/as in the US.[95]

Noting how in the years prior to 1970 many Mexican Americans in the US had just begun to identify as 'Chicano' instead of 'Mexican American,' 'Mexican,' and especially, 'Hispanic,' one example in Latin/o rock was the popular band Thee Midniters (who had previous success in the mid 1960s with 'Whittier Boulevard') who chose to record songs about Chicano empowerment. In 1970 they recorded

---

90   Peña, *Música Tejana*, 169.
91   Ibid., 175.
92   Roberts, *The Latin Tinge*, 193.
93   Ibid., 194–5.
94   For more on the rock versus disco tensions in the 1970s, see Garofalo, *Rockin' Out*; For more on the Puerto Rican engagement with rock 'n' roll, and differences between Puerto Ricans and Mexican Americans in their dialogues with rock music, see Pacini Hernández, 'A Tale of Two Cities: A Comparative Analysis of Los Angeles Chicano and Nuyorican Engagement with Rock and Roll,' 71–92.
95   Roberts, *The Latin Tinge*, 192.

a song called 'Chicano Power' and another called 'The Ballad of Cesar Chavez.' In similar fashion, another group known as The VIP's changed their name to 'El Chicano,' 'a name that openly proclaimed the members' solidarity with the new-found cultural identity politics of east L.A.' and the Chicano/a movement.[96] It was around this time that East LA musicians first began to feature Latin musical forms and Spanish-language lyrics more prominently — foreshadowing identity expressions that would later happen with rock music in México in the 1980s. Emerging from tight community-based music scenes, the East LA Chicano/a bands performed at outdoor festivals called 'Chicano Woodstocks' by some.[97] Of particular relevance for shifting identities, these festivals and communities displayed Mexican flags and celebrated images of Mexican history and thus, Chicano identity. Reyes and Waldman remark that,

> What made many of the Chicano bands different from others in rock was that they put their ethnicity front and center. Groups with Irish-American members did not take Gaelic names, African-American groups did not record music in Swahili. But for many Chicano musicians from this period, Spanish (or Indian) names, Mexican songs, and Latin rhythms were a statement of how they saw themselves and, more important, how they wished to be seen by their community.[98]

As Lipsitz notes of this period, the band Tierra emerged as a favorite for Chicano car customizers with their lowriders, but it also marked the emergence of another Chicano rock band, Los Lobos, who began their careers in this period and even recorded their first album through a project with César Chávez and the United Farm Worker's Union.

Moreover, pointing to the music that would define the 1970s and much of the popular music that followed in the next decades, Led Zeppelin released 'Babe I'm Gonna Leave You' on their self-titled debut album on 1969, considered a groundbreaking release and one of the first 'heavy metal' records. Lost on most Zeppelin fans, however, was the significance of the song's acoustic-folk-guitar introduction. 'Babe, I'm Gonna Leave You' was originally by folk artist Joan Baez, who recorded it herself (in 1962) years prior to Led Zeppelin. Meanwhile, another Zeppelin connection to US Latino/as came with their 1975 song 'Boogie With Stu,' a boogie-woogie piano rocker that borrowed from 'Ooh, My Head' by Ritchie Valens, although the connection was denied by Led Zeppelin. Not only did their version sound a lot like 'Ooh, My Head' by Valens, but the Led Zeppelin version actually contains a line in the middle of a break where famous frontman Robert Plant wails, 'Ooh . . . my head!' Scholars have noted how the similarity was so great that Led Zeppelin was eventually sued for copyright infringement by the Valens estate. The Valens camp won the lawsuit, and Led Zeppelin were ordered to pay a

---

96   Ibid., 119.
97   Lipsitz, *Time Passages*, 148.
98   Reyes and Waldman, *Land of a Thousand Dances*, 112.

sum of money and future royalties to Valens' heir, his mother, Mrs. Valenzuela.[99] To this day, the liner notes for 1975's *Physical Graffiti* indicate that 'Boogie With Stu' was written by Led Zeppelin's John Bonham, John Paul Jones, Jimmy Page, Robert Plant, Ian Stewart, and a certain 'Mrs. Valens.'[100]

The early 1970s saw other releases with possible Latin/Hispanic traces, such as two songs by Black Sabbath, who, along with Led Zeppelin, were creating the sound that was becoming known as heavy metal music. In 1972 and 1973, for example, Black Sabbath recorded numerous songs in Los Angeles, California, and eventually released songs such as 'Laguna Sunrise' and 'Fluff,' which are considered two of their greatest hits. Both songs are probably best described as simple acoustic-guitar instrumentals, but given the band's proclivities for harder, louder, electric-guitar sounds, the context for these songs (i.e., the band's location in Los Angeles) suggests inspiration by Spanish-guitar sounds, *boleros*, or similar sounds that can be heard in Mexican folk music.

Meanwhile, other 1970s Latin-inspired rock can include some music by the band War (or, 'Eric Burdon and War'), a multicultural jazz and funk ensemble who are most famous for the song 'Lowrider.' War was known for the multi-racial and multi-ethnic character of the band members, but their music further symbolized the cultural crossings, racial disruptions, and intercultural communication within the band. As Lipsitz attests, the significance of 'Lowrider' lies in the fact that it expressed the band's own experiences playing for Mexican Americans and Chicano/as in the East LA and Southern California rock music scene,[101] but the song's significance also lies in the fact that it indexed the growing intercultural dialogue between Blacks and Chicano/as. In the words of Lipsitz, 'The clear Latin influence on the subject and style of "Lowrider" testifies to the importance of Chicano music to American popular music, even when Chicano artists themselves might not enjoy access to a mass audience.'[102]

Furthermore, while 'Lowrider' was released in 1975 and made the band popular with Latino/as, and especially with those invested in customized car clubs, War had other Latin/o credentials. The original 1962 lineup was brought together as the brainchild of producer Jerry Goldstein who can be connected to other Latin-influenced songs in the rock 'n' roll era such as 'Hang On Sloopy' and 'I Want Candy' (both mentioned in previous chapters), but the original War release in 1969 included the track 'Spill The Wine,' which was a major hit in rock that reached the #3 position in 1970 and a song that was known to have Latin influence. By 1972, War had released another song titled 'The Cisco Kid' that drew on Tex-Mex western lore and that essentially cemented their popularity with Latino/as — most likely because of its lyrics. Even after their split from famous frontman Eric Burdon, War continued into the 1980s and released the minor hit 'Cinco De Mayo'

---

99 Mendheim, *Ritchie Valens*.
100 Led Zeppelin, Liner notes to *Physical Graffiti*, 1975.
101 Lipsitz, *Time Pasages*, 148.
102 Ibid., 148.

in 1982, while 'Lowrider' remained an anthem for many Chicano/as and lowrider subculture into the 1980s and beyond.

'¡Que Ondas!' (What Waves!)

Some points of clarification are necessary here with regard to the significance of José Agustín's literary *Onda*, as well as with the connections between the literary *Onda* and the rock *Onda*. With regard to the first issue, it is important to return to the issue of *Onda*'s critics. While the significance of Agustín's rock *Onda* of which he wrote and the literary *Onda* which he helped to create with his writing have both been documented by many Latin American writers and remain somewhat common knowledge among younger generations in México, it is interesting that the literature of José Agustín seems lost and almost forgotten to North America, at least after the scholarly critiques of his writing that surfaced in the 1980s.

As mentioned above, Agustín was critiqued by US literary scholars and was found to be a modernist, or, at least, well within the modernist paradigm. One critic wrote that Agustín's first novel, *La Tumba*, is 'consciously linked to high-culture texts, both musical and literary' and 'that he is a cynical, disillusioned, and finally pathetic parody of the romantic hero makes him none the less a consciously literary creation well within modern tradition.'[103] Likewise, comparisons between Agustín and European literature found his works to be so similar to Western European classics that they simply could not be considered new, fresh, innovative, revolutionary, or counter-cultural at all. A feminist critique, furthermore, reminds us that one must not ignore the gendered implications of José Agustín's life, his writing, and injection of such gender-loaded phrases such as the aforementioned *chingar* (to fuck) in the way it implies a male-centered use of language and discourse.[104] Correspondingly, one cannot ignore his personal life and the numerous affairs and relationships that also made José Agustín famous throughout México, and of course, there is always the issue of a male-dominated history of early Mexican rock. While Agustín's histories have presented us with a wealth of information about male rockers in México, a recent publication has turned the focus toward the female contribution to Mexican rock music that presumably, writers like Agustín, so sexistly ignored previously.[105]

While it may be true that *Onda*, manifested in either José Agustín's literature or in his chronicles of Mexican rock, is deserving of such critiques, my position is that neither is enough to warrant its dismissal by scholars of literature or popular music history. The aforementioned contradictions of a modernist literary tradition that manifested itself in a supposedly postmodern time and place, and the paradox of a supposedly rebellious and revolutionary wave that failed to recognize its own masculinist and sexist nature are exactly what writers like José Agustín were attempting to extort. In other words *Onda*, and especially *La Onda de José*

---

103 Bruce-Novoa, '*La Onda*: Parody and Satire,' 43–7.
104 The author wishes to thank Professor Michelle Habell-Pallán for her comments and insight on this issue.
105 See Estrada, *Sirenas al Ataque*.

Agustín (in literature), was in its essence all about self-parody and contradictions. As one scholar concluded,

> ... his works are highly satirical of his own generation as well as the generation of the adults. With respect to literary discourse, Agustín has never been a naïve writer or a nonliterary one. Not only did he know traditional literature, but his first works openly establish intertextual links and obvious parodies that make the metaphorical reading essential to the understanding of his literary project.[106]

It is worth mentioning here my contention that *Onda* was exactly about such 'failures,' that Mexican society (if not others as well) was full of such failures and could be critiqued from many different perspectives, or that society was 'bullshit' and nothing was truly revolutionary. These insights about the hypocrisy of his own generation's politics, perpetuated classism as well as sexism, are characteristic of *Onda*'s aesthetic. That Agustín was doing so when it wasn't acceptable to do so, like Alex Lora of El TRI, is what makes such a history worthy of scholarly attention.

Moreover, these responses are not mentioned here to detract from the previous insight and critique but, rather, because those critiques should not negate the significance of either *Onda* literature or *La Onda de José Agustín* in particular. It could be said that *Onda* matters because people thought it mattered. Whether the *Onda* ethos was all in vain or temporary fad in retrospect (as North American literary scholars claimed) should not deny the importance of what *Onda* was all about at that time — rebellion, resistance, revolution, counter-culture, vulgarity, obscenity, offensive language, local slang, common people, low-life, proletariat, *rupestre, desmadre,* and, one cannot forget, about rock 'n' roll. It is in the context of the time and place where *Onda* existed, in the hearts, souls, and minds of individuals, perhaps, and in the context of México in the late 1960s that *Onda* can best be understood.

Finally, my second point of clarification returns to the ambiguity of the relationship between the two waves, between the literary *Onda* and the rock *Onda*, as there has been some recent debate concerning the unstable relationship between the two. The connection is, in fact, not an easy one. On one hand, insight on the topic would suggest that the connection is very problematic and related to early rock in México. Eric Zolov's historical work on rock music in México is telling in that connecting rock music to the counter-culture was contrary at first.[107] Because early rock 'n' roll music in México was associated with the privileged youth of the middle class, there was no easy connection to the counter-cultural *Onda*. In fact, the leftists, progressives, and intellectuals (as well as parents and official government policies) regarded early rock 'n' roll music in México as simple, uncritical absorption of the influences of US popular culture. As Zolov contends, 'there was no merging of Mexican rock bands and the student movement itself.'[108] Another

---

106   Bruce-Novoa, '*La Onda*: Parody and Satire,' 41–2.
107   Zolov, *Refried Elvis*; Zolov, 'Armando Nava and Los Dug Dug's.'
108   Zolov, 'Armando Nava and Los Dug Dug's,' 218.

recent return to *Onda* by Jaime López, who muses on the topic of *el rockerondero* (the rocker-waver) as a Mexican cultural myth, also notes differences between the rock *Onda* and the literary *Onda*.

However, other scholars have noted some connectivity between the rock *Onda* and the literary *Onda*. Solórzano-Thompson, for example, concludes that while some insist *rock en español* was separate from *Onda* counter-culture, she believes that some of *Onda*'s counter-culture elements are integral parts of *rock en español*.[109] As López puts it, 'the acetate grooves became waves on paper, and LP records led to the new literature.'[110] This recognition suggests, perhaps, that the rock wave came first and led to what was later the literary wave.

On the other hand, the changes that occurred after the 1968 student massacre and other significant events in México's rock history place the two more squarely together and see *onderos* identifying with rock more than ever before. Zolov writes, 'La Onda had evolved from a fashion statement into a vehicle of direct social protest.'[111] Further, while rock bands like El TRI declared that they were *Onda* kids, as Carlos Monsiváis recalls, saying what everybody else wanted to say, other connections between the literary and the musical included band names that, like the literary *onderos*, employed playful rhyme (e.g., El TRI versus El PRI) and through other discursive expressions seemed to suggest identifications with the US and English (e.g., Los Dug Dug's using an apostrophe and English-spellings).[112] And if they didn't necessarily identify with the US, English, and rock 'n' roll, they were at least disrupting Mexican nationalism.

Moreover, it cannot be left unsaid that much of the early history of Mexican rock music exists because of the work of José Agustín. Well before the rock *Onda* had fully merged with the literary *Onda*, Agustín was documenting rock music for Mexicans through his journalistic endeavors and several books and continued to do so for several decades — *La Nueva Música Clásica* (1968), *El Rock de La Cárcel* (1986), *Contra La Corriente* (1990a), *Tragicomedia Mexicana 1* (1990b), *La Contracultura en México* (1996), *El Hotel de Los Corazones Solitarios* (1999). While the connection between the rock *Onda* and the literary *Onda* is contextual and debatable in some ways,[113] José Agustín's place in both of them remains unquestionable. He was directly connected to both of them and remains an important link for both the rock *Onda* and the literary *Onda*. One might conclude that the significance lies in the way he simultaneously chronicled *Onda* and (re)created it through his own literary production. Perhaps because of the solid connection of writers like Agustín, musicians like Alex Lora proclaimed that they were '*chavos*

---

109 Solórzano-Thompson, 'Performative Masculinities,' 83–4.

110 Original quotation: '*Y los surcos en el acetato hicieron olas en el papel. Los fonogramas, en masiva explosion de consumo, generaron una novedosa perspective en la literatura*' (López, 'El Rockondero,' 396).

111 Zolov, *Refried Elvis*, 219.

112 Eric Zolov also notes how bands like Los Dug Dug's used the apostrophe in their name knowing that the apostrophe does not exist in the Spanish language. Similarly, others bands like Los Yaki anglicized the spelling of their name (Yaki instead of Yaqui); see Zolov, 'Armando Nava and Los Dug Dug's.'

113 See for example, Agustín's recent discourse on *Onda*, 'La Onda Que Nunca Existió.'

de onda' (*Onda* kids) and further solidified the connection between the music genre and the literary genre.

What this analysis reveals is, first, that the literature of José Agustín is significant in its connections to *Onda*. This chapter has also shown how the life experiences of José Agustín contributed to his development as an *Onda* writer. Through Agustín, the literary genre of *Onda* and the rock genre of *Onda* became a part of each other. *Las Ondas*, the two Ondas, were in fact intersected, interconnected, and interrelated, at least by José Agustín and others such as El TRI. Finally, this chapter lays out a history of Mexican rock music that articulates it to other counter-cultural movements and significant social changes in México throughout the past thirty to forty years. In conclusion, I offer a final point about the contemporary significance of *Las Ondas de José Agustín*.

Concluding Remarks: Beyond *Onda*

Throughout this chapter, I have chronicled the birth of rock music in México based on the story told by José Agustín (and others) about the rock *Onda* and existing literature about the literary *Onda*, with which he was associated. However, a final point about *Onda* remains. In a recent reflection on *Onda* and rock music, Jamie López revealed something more about what exactly *Onda* was. As López astutely observed,

> We [*Onda* kids] were born when the train of the Mexican revolution was on its way out and the dream of modernity was coming in. That's when everything changed. We saw that we were full of contradictions in a country where the border is everywhere. And in these contradictions is where we found our identity.[114]

Such discourse and sentiment seems to echo that of José Agustín in an early analysis of *Onda*. As Agustín asserted, waves are about energy and motion. They are circular movements that permit communication.[115] And it is *Onda* as a form of discourse that I wish to expound upon here. As Agustín wrote,

> At its core, La Onda represents change, the common inalterable spirit that leads to transformation. Only on the surface is Onda all of the other waves and manifestations of transformation: the argot, the clothes, the marijuana, the long hair, etc.[116]

For José Agustín, *La Onda* provided a language, a means, a medium of communication for youth in an era of strict adherence to a romanticized and nostalgic

---

114   Original quotation: '*Nacimos cuando el tren de la Revolución se iba y el sueño (de la modernidad) empezaba. Ahí cambió el siglo. Y vimos que estábamos hechos de contradicciones en un país que es todo frontera Y aquí encontramos nuestra afirmación*' (López, 'El Rockondero,' 400).

115   Original quotation: '*Así pues, una onda 'ondera' es energía, movimiento circular que propicia la comunicación*' (Agustín, 'Cuál Es La Onda,' 12).

116   Original quotation: '*Lo profundo, la onda, es, entonces, el cambio: lo inalterable, el espíritu común que permite la transformación. Y lo superficial son las demás ondas: las manifestaciones de la transformación, lo transitorio; en este caso, el caló, la ropa, la mariguana, el pelo, etcetera*' (Agustín, 'Cuál Es La Onda,' 12–13).

Mexican nationalism and serious oppression of rock 'n' roll and youth culture by parents, Mexican politicians, and government policies. In this sense, *Onda* was a mode of intercultural communication for youth that found themselves in an ambiguous relationship between the traditions of México, and the future that pointed north toward the US. This is to say, Agustín's perspective speaks to the reality of cultural convergence and cultural influence. It was through the discourse of cultural convergence that *Onda* acquires its significance. And it is this manifestation of youth culture that registers a national dialogue between generations (thus, between the past and the present), and a larger, inter-ethnic, intercultural dialogue across nations (thus, between the present and the future). Interestingly, the defining characteristics of *Onda* are still being contested in Mexican society as well as in the neo-conservative politics in the US. The culture and society that gave birth to *Onda* politics, in other words, are still ever-present.

I offer these thoughts in response to discourse about Latino/as in the US such as that which surfaced in scholarly fora like *Foreign Policy*, where Harvard University political scientist Samuel Huntington argued that Latino/a peoples in the United States threaten to divide the United States. Framing his arguments through metaphors of war, Huntington employs 'invasion,' 'beach-heads,' 'entrenchment,' and 'turf wars' to make the claim that Latino/a people's refusal to assimilate is a major threat to life and culture in the US.[117] Similarly, others in the US are very vocal about their intercultural fears. Before the presidential election day in November of 2004, one Valley Center, Kansas woman was quoted as saying, 'It's pathetic that the United States wants to cater and appease these illegal aliens because they want cheap labor,' adding, 'Illegals try to force us to adapt to their language and values — the very culture which they are trying to escape.'[118]

Given such disdain for immigrants and vitriol for Latino/as in media as well as 'academic' discourse, questions related to the relationship between Latino/as and US culture loom larger and are perhaps more relevant than ever. If Latino/as appear threatening to anybody because of the presumption that they will not, do not, or cannot assimilate to English and mainstream US culture, I argue that it follows that Latino/a culture warrants further attention and investigation. Beyond that, I contend that the history of *Onda* reveals a much longer 'battle' between 'Mexicans' and 'Americans,' although one that puts the advantage, if one can call it that, with the US and North American cultural hegemony over others. However, fearing that I too have fallen prey to the discourse of war and invasion, I would like to move away from such language and offer an alternative perspective that cultural expressions like music and literature are evidence that in relation to the US, cultural influence is overwhelmingly in favor of other nations having to engage and contest the hegemony of US culture.

Furthermore, the history of *Las Ondas de José Agustín* that is presented here reveals a much more hopeful view of the relationship between the US and México. Literature and music, as modes of intercultural discourse, beg for

---

117 Huntington, 'The Hispanic Challenge.'
118 Woods, 'Immigration Divides Voters, Issues Could Drive Local House Races,' 1A.

further investigation because of how they help individuals assuage the tensions of assimilation and acculturation but also of globalization, transnationalization, and other culture shifts. With respect to the supposed Latin 'explosion,' 'invasion,' and 'booms' in recent years,[119] such discourse evidences how music scholars and journalists sometimes also participate in ethnocentric discourse such as Huntington's, the Kansas woman, and the many others in the US who hold similar opinions. Finally, I must reiterate how such articulations of music and culture have been around for a rather long time, and it is rather unfortunate for most of us that we have been missing out on its rich contribution to rock 'n' roll history, popular music history, literary studies, and of course, media and communication studies.

---

119 Cepeda, '*Mucho Loco* for Ricky Martin; or The Politics of Chronology, Crossover, and Language within the Latin(o) Music "Boom"'; Cepeda, '"Columbus Effect(s)": Chronology and Crossover in the Latin(o) Music "Boom"'; Ehrenreich, 'Confessions of a White Salsa Dancer: Appropriation, Identity and the "Latin Music Craze"'; Roberts, *The Latin Tinge*; Roiz, 'Los Lobos: The Legend Lives On.'

Interludio 4° (fourth interlude)

Chroniclers note that in the early 1980s, rockers in México, for the most part, were still singing in English and still copying whatever was going on in other countries. Around this time, however, singing in English was not just uncritical imitation of North American rock 'n' roll. Morales notes,

> Singing in English was a wannabe desire of Mexicans to emulate North Americans or Europeans, as well as an unconscious rebellion against the official national culture, which discouraged La Malinche, or outside influence, and was imposed by the PRI (Partido Revolucionario Institucional), the institutional party ultimately responsible for the '68 student massacre.[1]

It was not until sometime around the mid 1980s that the situation changed again. Morales cites a groundbreaking article by Rubén Martínez in the *L.A. Weekly* that calls the 1985 México City earthquake as a central event in birthing new Mexican rock bands.

Other scholars have also noted this detail. For example, Hernández writes that,

> On September 19, 1985, Mexico City suffered a devastating earthquake, and more than 10,000 lost their lives. In light of the government's ineffective response to the tragedy, numerous rock groups brought attention to the plight of the most marginalized sectors of life in Mexico City.[2]

While the 1985 earthquake in México City was a major factor in the growth of Mexican rock, others say that there were many factors and other changes in Mexican society were already under way. Zolov notes,

> If rock went from being a metaphor for modernity in the early 1960's, to a symbol of its excesses at the end of the decade, in the 1980s los chavos banda — lumpenproletariat punk rockers in the capital — embodied the utter collapse of revolutionary promise altogether. A stark sociological emblem of la crisis (Mexico's 'Lost Decade' of the 1980's), these punk rockers were now embraced by intellectuals as an authentic representation of popular culture.[3]

---

1   Morales, 'Rock is Dead and Living in Mexico.'
2   Hernández, 'Remaking the *Corrido* for the 1990s: Maldita Vecindad's "El Barzón,"' 108.
3   Zolov, *Refried Elvis*, 13.

According to scholars, the collapse of the Mexican oil business in the 1980s had ended the aspirations that the middle class had about achieving equality with the US and of being like North Americans.[4]

For Mexican youth, the result was a full swing in the other direction, where it became desirable to be Mexican and to show pride in Mexican identity. In striking similarity to US Latino rockers from Texas (e.g., Little Joe and the Latinaires) and many 'Eastside Sound' Chicano/as from California (e.g., The VIPs) of the 1970s who changed their names to reflect their developing cultural nationalism, veteran Mexican rockers like Three Souls in My Mind changed their name to El TRI,[5] while Dangerous Rhythms changed their name to 'Ritmo Peligroso.' Shortly thereafter a compilation of music by El TRI, Ritmo Peligroso, Kenny y Los Eléctricos, and Mask had even reached teenagers in the suburbs of México City, and the baby of Mexican rock was no longer crawling. Now it was standing and getting ready to move forward. The decades-old rockers El TRI signed a contract with the WEA Latina record label, and others followed. According to one account, Botellita de Jerez 'single-handedly revolutionized Mexican rock' as they jumped in the scene with a hybrid kind of rock 'n' roll music that many others followed.[6]

Around the same time, Spanish and Argentine groups like Radio Futura, Charly García, and Soda Stereo were gaining popularity around Latin America. They were being marketed by Mexican media giant Televisa as *'rock en tu idioma'* (rock in your own language), a slogan created by the Ariola International record company that essentially referred to the rock music coming from Spain, Argentina, and México.[7] José Agustín remembers other Mexican rockers in and around México City like Real de Catorce, Caifanes (who came out of an earlier ensemble called Las Insolitas Imagenes de Aurora), Santa Sabina, Tex Tex,[8] Mamá Z, Maldita Vecindad y Los Hijos del 5° Patio (otherwise known as just 'Maldita Vecindad'), Luzbel, Ritmo Peligroso, La Camerata Rupestre, Iconoclasta, Trolebús, Follaje, Los Blues Boys, and Mara y Delirium.[9] Along with the *rock en tu idioma* music, Botellita de Jerez, El TRI, others like Caifanes and the ska-punk-funk combination of Maldita Vecindad were turning the whole scene into a larger cultural phenomenon.[10] Morales writes,

---

4   Morales, 'Rock is Dead and Living in Mexico.'
5   While frontman Alex Lora has stated that the name change resulted from fans who referred to Three Souls in My Mind as 'El Three,' Zolov notes that changing their name to 'El TRI' was a very conscious and bold move by the band in that in the Spanish language 'El TRI' sounds a lot like 'El PRI,' and PRI in México stands for *Partido Revolucionario Institucional*, México's dominant ruling party for over seventy years. It could be argued that by parodying the political, El TRI were invoking the political and making an explicit statement about their music and message as a form of politics, or counter-cultural identity. Interestingly, the name El TRI also carries other nationalist associations with the number three as in the 'tri-color' of the Mexican flag; See Zolov, 'Armando Nava and Los Dug Dug's.'
6   Morales, 'Rock is Dead and Living in Mexico.'
7   Esterrich and Murillo, 'Rock with Punk with Pop with Folklore: Transformations and Renewal in Aterciopelados and Café Tacuba.'
8   For more on Tex Tex and Mexican masculinity, see Hernández, 'Breaking the Mold of Contemporary Working-Class Mexican Masculinity: The *Rock Urbano* Music of Tex Tex.'
9   Agustín, *Contra La Corriente*, 112.
10 For more on Maldita Vecindad, see Hernández, 'Remaking the *Corrido* for the 1990s'; as well

Café Tacuba. Photo by: Alex Luster

As the 80's ended, there was an explosion: Café Tacuba, a less jokey variant of Botellita; Santa Sabina, a goth, prog-rock quintet; Fobia, jangly alternative; La Lupita, La Cuca, La Castañeda, Maná, and a growing array of pop, thrash metal, punk, and the still energetic rock urbano (prole rock) have turned Mexico City, with its integrated network of support and homegrown dynamism, into the Seattle that few outside the Latin world know.[11]

These new musicians and groups can be seen as what has since the 1990s been called *La Nueva Onda* (the new wave) in Mexican rock. The larger point of all of this historical contextualization is, of course, that the development of rock music in México was, from the very beginning and on through several decades now, a particular music genre that developed in a specific relational context.

Rock music in México has emerged and continues to emerge in light of an unstable relationship between the US and México, or, rather, North American cultural imperialism and Mexican youth. From the influence of North American icons like Elvis and early blues and rock 'n' roll influence, to the counter-influence of Mexican American/Chicano rocker Ritchie Valens on The Beatles and many other rock 'n' rollers,[12] to the use of songs in English and North American culture as the antithesis to a dominant culture and powerful political regime in México, to the resistance to English as a hegemonic force and the reclamation of the Spanish

as Solórzano-Thompson, 'Performative Masculinities.'
11   Morales, 'Rock is Dead and Living in Mexico.'
12   Eddy, *The Accidental Evolution of Rock 'n' Roll*; Mendheim, *Ritchie Valens*.

language and pride in Mexican culture, to the constantly changing perceptions of Mexicans themselves in relation to the US. and to heightened nationalism, rock music in México had always had a specific relationship with the US. What cannot go unnoticed is the fact that the various factors of identity and identification that were going on with Mexican youth and the development of rock 'n' roll music in México were, in large part, yielded as a product of transnational commercial processes and recorded popular music as a primary mode of discourse.

Selective Discography and Tracks Listed Here and in Chapter Four:

Baez, Joan. 'Babe, I'm Gonna Leave You,' *Joan Baez in Concert, Part 1* (Vanguard, 1962).
Batiz, Javier. 'Hard Life,' *The USA Sessions* (Canned Heat Records, 2003).
Café Tacvba. 'Chilanga Banda,' *Avalancha de Exitos* (Warner Music Mexico, 1996).
La Cuca. 'La Balada,' *La Racha* (BMG/Ariola, 1995).
The Doors. 'Break On Through (To the Other Side),' *The Doors* (Electra, 1967).
El TRI. 'Chavo de Onda,' *!!Que Viva El Rock and Roll!!* (Fonovisa, Inc., 2000).
Los Fabulosos Cadillacs. 'Calaveras y Diablitos,' *Fabulosos Calavera* (BMG Music, 1997).
Fobia. 'Descontrol,' *Amor Chiquito* (BMG Music, 1995).
García, Charly. 'El Fantasma De Canterville,' *Idolos Del Rock Argentino: Charly García* (Orfeon Videovox, 2001).
Gonzalez, Rodrigo. 'Estación Del Metro Balderas,' *Hurbanistorias* (Spartacus Disco, 1995).
Guzmán, Enrique. 'Tu Cabeza En Mi Hombro,' *Lo Esencial: Enrique Guzmán* (Sony Discos, 1990).
Led Zeppelin. 'Boogie With Stu,' *Physical Graffiti* (Swan Song, Inc./Atlantic Recording, 1975).
_____. 'Babe, I'm Gonna Leave You,' *Led Zeppelin* (Atlantic, 1969).
La Lupita. 'Contrabando y Traición,' *Pa' Servir a Ud.* (BMG México, 1992).
La Revolución de Emiliano Zapata. 'Nasty Sex,' *La Revolución de Emiliano Zapata* (Dynamic, 2006).
Soda Stereo. 'Entre Caníbales,' *Soda Stereo Unplugged* (BMG Music, 1996).
The Stone Poneys [feat. Linda Ronstadt]. 'Different Drum,' *Evergreen, Vol. 2* (Capitol, 1967).
Tijuana No! 'Pobre De Ti,' *Lo Mejor De: Tijuana No!* (BMG Entertainment México, 2001).
Valens, Ritchie. 'Ooh My Head,' *Ritchie Valens* (Rhino, 1959).
Various artists. *15 Grandes Exitos Del Rock And Roll* (SonoDis Records, 1997).

5

Transnational Punk(s): On the Transnational Character of the Latin/o Rock Diaspora

The creation of important parts of national culture in the homeland of the colonizer and in other nations that have been similarly exploited even though independent reveals the surprisingly transnational nature of nationalism and the distinctly national inflections of transnationalism.[1]

Pelos parados como un penacho, bailes como ritos a Xipe-Totec, su piel morena chichimeca, pero en el punk ella aún cree.[2]

While in the previous chapter I analyzed the literature of Mexican author José Agustín for its connections to the literary genre known as *Onda* and for Agustín's contributions to the story of rock's development in México, this final chapter also begins with a connection to literature, although this time with a significantly more noticeable literary illustration. In 2008, Junot Díaz dropped a bomb on the literary world with *The Brief Wondrous Life of Oscar Wao* and was awarded the Pulitzer Prize for the fictional novel, a landmark event that flagged Díaz as a must-read contemporary writer and signaled the increasing significance of Latino/a cultural productions in the mainstream consciousness of North America. Interestingly, the Dominican American Díaz garnered widespread appreciation for his novel in spite of the difficulty that some readers have expressed about his complex writing style (e.g., employing pseudo-historical footnotes for a novel), about his streetwise bilingual writing (including slang words and profanity), and about other Latino/a cultural nuances that can make his writing seem difficult to comprehend. Perhaps because of the complexity and non-mainstream orientation, Díaz has won numerous awards for his literature in recent years and has subsequently become recognized worldwide for his literary brilliance and as one of the best writers of the new century.

To this I would add that part of Díaz' literary brilliance relates to the complex bicultural characters in his novels and to the ways in which Díaz' characters cross

---

1 Lipsitz, *Footsteps in the Dark*, 231.
2 Lyrical excerpt from Café Tacuba's 'La Chica Banda'; see discography in Fifth interlude.

borders (literally) and social circles. One such person in *The Brief Wondrous Life of Oscar Wao* is the character of Jenni Muñóz, a girl whom the main character befriends in college, who is actually a Puerto Rican 'goth' chick and who loves the English goth/punk band Joy Division. As Díaz writes of 'Jenni Muñóz,'

> She was this boricua chick from East Brick City who lived up in the Spanish section. First hardcore goth I'd ever met — in 1990 us niggers were having trouble wrapping our heads around goths, period — but a Puerto Rican goth, that was as strange to us as a black Nazi. Jenni was her real name . . .[3]

While the unusual sight of a Puerto Rican goth is exactly the point of this vignette, I submit that the significance is greater. In my assessment, the presence of a Latina goth in such a profoundly 'Latino' novel — complete with racial identity politics, transnational identities, immigration narratives, and bilingualism rampant — actually speaks volumes of the ways in which articulations of Latino/as to rock subcultures were becoming more prevalent by the 1990s, to how rock music was becoming more and more relevant to Latino/as living within US borders as well as beyond, and to how various Latino/a groups were absorbing characteristics of US popular culture (thereby assimilating to mainstream US culture).

In this chapter, I employ the term 'punk' as an anchoring concept for an investigation of the ways in which various Latino/as, from various Latin American nations (including the US), have engaged rock music and how those Latino/as have used rock music to express complex transnational identities. First, 'punk' signifies a literal connection between punk-rock music and Latino/as, and demonstrates the ways that Latino/as have constructed identities through punk-rock discourse (music, lyrics, style, ethos, etc.). Second, 'punk' — as something marginalized, looked down upon, or deemed worthless and unimportant — is an apt metaphor for the ways in which Latino/as have used rock music to communicate their own particular notions of identity and community in the context of national narratives, but also illuminates the ways in which local Latino/a groups discursively link themselves to other Latino/as by using rock music as a mode of discourse through which they communicate an inherently intercultural and increasingly transnational 'Latino/a' sensibility. This chapter's analysis opens by tracing academic literature on the beginnings of *rock nacional* in Argentina, moves forward to discuss significant Latino/a articulations to punk-rock's 'first wave' (in the 1970s), and further maps the intercultural, international, and transnational nature of *rock en español* and 'Latin alternative' music in the 1990s and 2000s.

Rock Nacional in Argentina

To understand the cultural significance of the emergence of rock music in Argentina, one needs only imagine a soccer-stadium concert with over 250,000 people, holding hands in solidarity, and drawn together by the symbolic value of

---

3   Díaz, *The Brief Wondrous Life of Oscar Wao*, 181–2.

rock music.[4] Scholarship reveals that in Argentina, the significance of rock music has traditionally been in its symbolic value and its use as a medium for political expression. Because rock music was so intricately connected to political issues and resistance to a military dictatorship throughout most of its early existence in Argentina, *rock nacional* (Argentina's homemade/native rock) has been extremely important to the lives of young people and their political identity. Pablo Vila is careful to note that *rock nacional* was only one part of the youth movement in Argentina, but makes sure to mention that *rock nacional* was more than just popular music. In Argentina, rock music was connected to identity, politics, social practice, ideology, and democratic ideals. As one youth noted, '*rock nacional* is a movement that goes beyond music. It's a philosophy, a way of life.'[5]

Although North American pop and rock music had previously made their way into the lives of the younger generations in Argentina, rock music in early years was seen as simple youth culture and, to some extent, was synonymous with the label *música progresiva nacional*, or 'national progressive music.'[6] Argentina had seen national rock through native bands like Manal, Almendra, Moris, Los Gatos, Tanguito, Vox Dei, El Reloj, Pescado Rabioso, and Riff, but it was not until the late 1960s and early 1970s when rock music began to take on greater significance for Argentine youth as '*rock nacional*.' As scholars note, tension was evident early on when bands like Manal and Almendra, 'the two most important Argentine groups of the late 1960s,' found themselves polarized in relation to what was and was not rock. A band like Manal played blues in Spanish 'with the typical vocal inflection of Black musicians, and their lyrics were protests.' Contrastingly, the band Almendra fused rock, Argentine folklore, tango, and jazz in more of a pop music vein (i.e., love songs and ballads).[7] At this time, the importance of rock music as ideology and protest music was so profound and inflexible that by the mid 1970s, Almendra eventually began to reconcile their place in Argentina's rock scene and reverted to what they saw as the true and authentic rock music ideology. By this time, the connection between rock music and the youth counter-culture was so significant that rock music acquired its new moniker, *rock nacional*, that made the music explicitly about national politics and social protest as much as a label for new youth music. Another tension occurred in the early 1970s between *eléctricos*, or 'electric rockers,' who emphasized electric guitars (e.g., La Pesada del Rock and Roll, Pappo's Blues, etc.), and the *acústicos*, who offered acoustic-guitar music in the style of folk rock á la Bob Dylan (e.g., Raúl Porchetto, León Gieco, Sui Generis). According to Vila, the tension was a simple one. The former claimed legitimacy through the 'true' rock ideology, while the latter represented commercialism in rock music and appealed more to the middle class.[8]

Throughout this time Argentina had been ruled by a series of military governments, but by 1972 Juan Domingo Perón, who was immensely popular among the

4   Cuccioletta and Cuccioletta, *Soda Stereo: La Historia*.
5   Vila, 'Argentina's *Rock Nacional*: The Struggle for Meaning,' 7.
6   Ibid., 10.
7   Ibid., 12.
8   Ibid., 13.

masses in previous decades, was allowed to return to power. However, after his death in 1974 Perón was succeeded in his presidency by his second wife, Maria Estela Isabel Martinez (de Perón). In an interesting turn of events, Argentina had become a refuge for other Latin American bands like Los Jaivas from Chile, who were forced to take exile in Argentina as a result of a military coup in Chile in 1973 (which was backed by the US) that resulted in the installment of Army General Augusto Pinochet as President of Chile. As political turmoil increased in Argentina, however, Los Jaivas took exile in France just a few years later.

As another result of such turmoil in the period from 1974 to 1975, youth in Argentina were becoming suspect and the youth movement was beginning to be seen as a threat within national politics. Paralleling such political shifts, by the mid 1970s the two sides of rock in Argentina had reached a stalemate, and to some extent, they found middle ground. When bands like Sui Generis validated the *acústicos* of their side by being more 'electric' through sound and through a return to protest lyrics, they brought the middle class with them into the *rock nacional* fold. Yet as a result of the changing times, in 1975 Charly García dissolved his band, Sui Generis, 'the most important band of the 1970s,' because, according to Vila, *rock nacional* groups and artists were bored with making protest songs. The down period did not last very long, however, because by 1976 Marxist revolutionaries took control through violent military campaigns and a new military regime was in power.

In the period of *rock nacional* that Vila marks, between 1976 and 1983, youth in Argentina unified against a crude military dictatorship (1976–1983) and in their belief in the need for democratic changes. Some scholars explain it as through the communicative power of rock music that youth came together.[9] As Vila maintains, 'when normal channels of political participation were blocked and collective action was in the main banned, young people found a sense of community and a potential mode of resistance in rock music.'[10] In sum, during the harshest years of the dictatorship, musicians functioned as leaders of political consciousness and effect,[11] and it was *rock nacional* that created the 'means of communication.'[12] Fittingly, it was during the early period of the new military regime that *rock nacional* flourished.

Vila comments on the social importance of Alas, a band that did 'tango rock'; Litto Nebia, who mixed jazz in a trio and later experimented with Brazilian music and Argentine folklore; Charly García (one of the major figures in the entire history of *rock nacional*),[13] who returned with La Máquina de Hacer Pájaros and directly engaged societal issues about the military; Invisible, a group that also fused tango and addressed urban themes; Crucis and Espíritu, bands that copied English rock groups; Polifemo, a band that attempted 'traditional rock 'n' roll'; the return of blues-based rock by Pappo; León Gieco, who fused with Los Jaivas and

9   See Jelin et al. *Los Movimientos Sociales Ante La Crisis.*
10 Vila, '*Rock Nacional* and Dictatorship in Argentina,' (1987) 131.
11 Ibid., 146.
12 Ibid., 134.
13 Semán and Vila, 'Rock Chabón: The Contemporary National Rock of Argentina,' 78.

Chilean folklore; Raúl Porchetto, famous for ballads; Soluna, who performed folk songs; Bubu, with its 'theatrical-musical' bent; and Pastoral and Nito Mester, who engaged music in the style of earlier *rock nacional* bands.[14] The political significance of all of these, according to Vila, lies in the fact that youth in Argentina, and *rock nacional* as a social movement, continued to respond to changes in the political climate. More and more, the name *rock nacional* replaced *música progresiva nacional*, and, likewise, the youth movement became a target in the political scene.

During the years of the dictatorship, many people disappeared, and most of the people that disappeared were in their teens and twenties;[15] thus, it is not surprising that rock music (i.e., youth music) came to symbolize protest and to express feelings of solidarity as well as resistance to hegemonic Argentine nationalism and the military dictatorship. Just as youth became the victims of death, torture, violence, and disappearance, the status of *rock nacional* also grew. As Vila declares, *rock nacional* allowed the young 'to construct an identity of life in a world surrounded by death.'[16] Another scholar notes how rock concerts symbolized an open space, offering 'harmony, community, and a sense of identity.'[17] From 1976–1977 it was through rock music that youth were able to separate themselves as 'we' and 'us,' and differentiate themselves from the 'they' and 'them' of the adults, the military, brutality, and corruption.[18] However, the period from 1978–1979 marked a different era for rock in Argentina, one in which rock music went into hiding. Rock concerts, perceived as threats, were banned; musicians went into exile. Disco music had taken over popular music in Argentina, as in many parts of the world, and rock music was less visible in the political discourse. As popular music was more commercialized, the political value of rock was minimized. Moreover, the influence of popular music in English was so great at this time, Vila quips, that in Argentina, 'English replaced Spanish.'[19]

Moreover, by mid 1979 the political sting of rock music had diminished, and rock music was less of a threat. Exiled musicians and rock groups had returned and staged concerts. The rockers of the early 1970s had returned from exile and entered into a period of jubilation, rediscovery, and reconnection to what the band Almendra proclaimed as 'our identity.'[20] The dictatorship's response was again repression, but government policies against rock music only galvanized *rock nacional* as a social movement. As 1979 turned into 1980, university students and intellectuals came to *rock nacional* for the first time. More changes occurred in 1981 when a new military administration 'adopted a strategy of dialogue with the movement.'[21] As the second wave of rock music in Argentina was nearing its peak

---

14   Ibid., 15–16.
15   Jelin, *Los Movimientos Sociales Ante La Crisis*, 34.
16   Vila, 'Argentina's *Rock Nacional*: The Struggle for Meaning,' 16.
17   King, 'Review Essay on "Rock Nacional: Crónicas de la Resistencia Juvenil" by Pablo Vila,' 252.
18   Ibid., 251.
19   Vila, '*Rock Nacional* and Dictatorship in Argentina,' (1987) 136.
20   Ibid., 138.
21   Ibid., 139.

in 1982, youth culture and rock music were once again less of a threat and the Malvinas/Falkland Islands war kept the military regime preoccupied.

Interestingly, wartime politics included the banning of British music in Argentina, which actually led to the fermentation of the native Argentine rock community. Because British music was banned, local artists were forced to develop music that was more their own, and to communicate their perspectives through their local culture. Where English had previously replaced Spanish, English was now a forbidden tongue and rock bands and musicians once again found cultural nationalism in the Spanish language. Moreover, as Vila explains, 'rock concerts became one of the many rallying points against government and the music and lyrics spoke openly of the need to return to democracy.'[22] Argentina's rock leaders like Serú Girán (fronted by Charly García), Fito Páez, León Gieco, and Pedro y Pablo, all led the social movement against youth disappearance and against the military dictatorship. As Vila notes, it is for this reason that the first mass setting in which slogans were chanted against the government and the military regime (or 'dictatorship') was a *rock nacional* concert.[23]

Furthermore, the significance of Argentina's relationship with rock 'n' roll was more straightforward than it was for Latino/a youth in the US or even México. While in the US Latino/as faced complicated questions of identity that centered around skin color, language, and the assimilation-versus-differentiation dialectic, youth in Argentina were caught in a more overtly political web. For their associations with rock 'n' roll they faced repression, violence, exile, and even death. While youth in México faced the disapproval of rock 'n' roll by parents, government officials, and a dominant culture that saw rock 'n' roll music as North American cultural imperialism, youth in Argentina were repeatedly caught in the political web of international politics, and thus, the gravitation toward rock 'n' roll came to signify much more. In Argentina the rise of rock 'n' roll (as *rock nacional*) symbolized generational identifications as well as a profound social movement against military dictatorship and for democracy. As Vila's work demonstrates, many attributed the democratic changes that came in the 1980s to the growing phenomenon of youth identification with rock 'n' roll music and their related political efforts.

One of the political refugees from this period in Argentina's history is Gustavo Santaolalla, who began recording at an early age and became famous with the band Arco Iris. As the military regime cracked down on rock 'n' rollers and other young people, however, many musicians were forced to leave. As Santaolalla recalled recently,

> I never got hurt, thank God, but they knew who I was . . . I do have lots of friends who disappeared. I was blacklisted and couldn't get airplay. It became very dangerous to express your thoughts or even have long hair.[24]

---

22   King, 'Review Essay on "Rock Nacional: Crónicas de la Resistencia Juvenil" by Pablo Vila,' 251.
23   Vila, '*Rock Nacional* and Dictatorship in Argentina,' (1987) 144.
24   Gilbert, 'For Bajofondo, It Takes Eight to Tango,' no pagination.

Naturally, it wasn't long before Santaolalla became a rock 'n' roll refugee, and he eventually settled in the US, landing in Los Angeles.

Punk-Rock and Identity Politics in 'El Lay'

While *rock nacional* in Argentina was increasingly politicized throughout the late 1970s and early 1980s, rock music in other parts of Latin America was increasingly becoming 'punk-rock.' Of course, scholars have already commented that the roots of punk-rock indicate at least some Latin/o heritage. Ritchie Valens' chord progressions became a staple for the punk music that the Ramones are said to have invented, while '96 Tears' by ? and the Mysterians reveals deeper significance as 1960s 'proto-punk.' Yet, Latino/as were more fully articulated to punk-rock than most accounts of punk's 'first wave' have acknowledged. For example, one recent account reminds us that, '. . . the "artistic director" of the Ramones, the man who designed their famous pseudo-military logo, was Chihuahua, Mexico-born Arturo Vega.' Taking note of punk music's fashion aesthetic from the mid 1970s, the same scholar astutely observes that, 'The invention of the scissor-cut holes in T-shirts, a London and New York punk staple, was attributed to a Puerto Rican tailor named Frenchy who accompanied the New York Dolls on a European tour.' And to extend the point of under-acknowledged Latin/o articulations to punk-rock, another account of forgotten punk influences notes, 'The lead guitarist of Roxy Music, one of London's seminal post-glam, modern rock bands, was Phil Manzanera.'[25] It is widely known that Manzanera is of Colombian descent, but was raised English. What is less known is that he spent much of his childhood in Cuba, Venezuela, Colombia, and Hawaii, and that it was in Cuba that Manzanera first became interested in the Spanish guitar that belonged to his mother. It was also in Cuba where he learned Cuban folk songs and began to play other Latin American music like *boleros* (from México), *cumbia*, and *merengue*.[26]

Moreover, it is worth remembering how bands such as The Clash, one of the most famous punk-rock bands of all time, were also inspired by Latin America. One might note the Spanish lyrics in some of the most famous Clash songs of the late 1970s and early 1980s, such as 'Should I Stay or Should I Go?' and 'Spanish Bombs,' where the choruses featured the band singing in awkward, somewhat incomprehensible Spanish, which left generations of both English and Spanish speakers wondering what they were singing about, but also left Latin Americans and US Latino/as with an important and tangible connection between Latin/o America and rock music. Of course, such transnational influences and bilingual recordings were elsewhere. In 1980, for example, Deborah Harry had recorded Blondie's major hit 'Call Me' in Spanish for its release in the Mexican market, indicating existing links between rock music and Latin/o America from decades prior to the rise of *rock en español* and 'Latin alternative' in the 1990s.

---

25   Morales, *Living in Spanglish*, 161.
26   Interestingly, Phil Manzanera has recently produced *rock en español* acts such as Héroes del Silencio from Spain, and has collaborated on other *rock en español* projects, such as 1998's Outlandos D'Americas, a tribute to The Police by various *rock en español* artists.

Yet another Latin connection by The Clash came with the 1980 release of their fourth album, *Sandinista!*, which took its name from the *sandinistas* (as opposed to *contras*) in Nicaragua and was their first album to make it into the Top Thirty in the US charts. Interestingly, The Clash were known to identify with third-world struggles, or at least, to express ideological solidarity with third-world revolutions.[27] As Chang notes, however, such connections to Latin America by The Clash were not necessarily understood in the US or elsewhere. Rather, the result was that the members of The Clash were actually treated to lessons in the workings of US racial logic that prevented White youth from identifying with the third world. The Clash learned that in the way race/ethnicity categories operated in the US, music genres such as disco and hip-hop were connoted Black, while punk-rock was connoted White.[28]

Related to the complications of transnational punk music, the emergence of punk-rock music is most often situated in working-class communities of London, New York, and Detroit. However, other locales were just as much a part of the rise of punk-rock music, and East Los Angeles was one of those places. Interestingly, the Chicano/a community in 'East Los' picked up on the punk-rock aesthetic, and in tune with punk's ethos, Chicano/a punk-rockers communicated the same feelings of anger, distress, marginalization, alienation, and class-consciousness. Such an ideological connection fostered the relationship between Latino/as and punk-rock music in LA, and, interestingly, another stream of Chicano nationalism was communicated through Chicano/a punk-rock. Thus, it was through punk-rock that Southern California Chicano/as made another direct link with rock music. As one scholar notes, punk music may have been the most direct way to map Chicano and Latino rock music's transition from the 1970s to the 1980s.[29]

As Reyes and Waldman contend, 'Punk — and new wave — became a vehicle for Chicano groups to mix rock with social commentary.'[30] While in the early 1970s Southern California Chicano/a bands like Tierra and El Chicano were seen as somewhat political, it was not until the late 1970s and the punk-rock explosion that bands like Los Illegals consciously articulated a form of Latino/a politics to rock music. Whereas in 'La Bamba' Ritchie Valens had sung the famous lines, '*¡Yo no soy marinero, yo no soy marinero, soy capitán . . .*,' the Chicano punk-rockers The Plugz preferred a rendition of 'La Bamba' with the punk dissonance of '*¡No soy capitalista, No soy fascista, soy anarquista!*' [I'm not a capitalist, I'm not a fascist, I'm an anarchist!][31]

Bands such as Ruben Guevara/Ruben and the Jets, The Zeros, The Brat, The Odd Squad, The Bags, The Plugz, and Los Illegals were the exemplars of a

---

27 Chang, *Can't Stop Won't Stop: A History of the Hip-Hop Generation*; Beyond the known connections, Joe Strummer is known to have spent time in México as a child and, after The Clash, he formed bands called The Mescaleros, and The Latino Rockabilly War.
28 Ibid., 154–5.
29 Morales, *Living in Spanglish*, 161.
30 Reyes and Waldman, *Land of a Thousand Dances*, 135.
31 For more on the Chicano/a punk-rock scene, see Sorrondeguy, *Beyond the Screams/Mas Alla De Los Gritos: A U.S. Latino/Chicano Hardcore Punk Documentary*.

Chicano/a rock scene that represented another wave of Latino/as in rock music, further extended the influence of Latino/as on rock music, and strengthened the articulation of Chicano/a identity politics to rock music.[32] Emphasizing self-awareness, bands like Ruben and the Jets (in the early 1970s), and Los Illegals and The Brat (in the late 1970s and early 1980s), all demonstrated a knack for 'political and social commentary' by using wit, irony, humor, multiple meanings, and, often, bilingualism. In making social statements, some used slide shows, on-stage costumes, and masks during their performances. Like other punk-rockers of the time, their performances were angry, mocking, 'harsh' and 'unsparing.'[33] Unlike other punk-rock music of the time, they expressed the politics of ethnic pride, sang about gangs, street life in LA, and run-ins with the INS, and sometimes featured all-Spanish lyrics.

The Brat, however, was an exception to the typically male punk-rock music scene; they featured Teresa Covarrubias as lead singer. Articulating feminist politics to ethnic politics, Covarrubias was known for her angry lyrics.[34]

In an example of communicating gender politics, one account notes,

> The band the Brat brought the protest from the streets into the heart of Chicano home life, and it gave a voice to women beyond the romantic lyrics of oldies ballads, confronting issues of domestic violence, personal freedom, and the complexities of Chicano identity.[35]

With regard to ethnic politics, Covarrubias commented on The Brat's limited success, recalling how The Brat was actually limited by an industry that wanted them to be more 'Latino,' as in Carmen Miranda or 'Teresa... with a bowl of fruit on her head.'[36] In a glaring contradiction to previous Chicano politics (which celebrated Mexican and Latin heritage and emphasized Spanish words, phrases, and names), artists like Teresa Covarrubias of The Brat expressed themselves through a lighter emphasis on Chicano roots and through their zeal to become successful on mainstream radio. In other words, while many Chicano/as at the time differentiated themselves from the US mainstream, artists like Covarrubias were trying to become a part of it.[37] Historians Reyes and Waldman further attest to the significance of this fact, observing that other LA bands of the 1970s like Tierra and El Chicano have rarely if ever drawn more than a handful of Whites to their shows, while The Brat and Los Illegals actually had more Anglo-American than Chicano fans.[38]

Another East LA punk band, The Odd Squad, was 'closer to new wave and pop'

---

32 Reyes and Waldman, *Land of a Thousand Dances*, 133.
33 Ibid., 136–40.
34 For more on Teresa Covarrubias and The Brat, see Loza, *Barrio Rhythm*, or Lipsitz, *Dangerous Crossroads*.
35 Narrator Edward James Olmos in Wilkman, *Chicano Rock!: The Sounds of East Los Angeles* [documentary film].
36 Reyes and Waldman, *Land of a Thousand Dances*, 141.
37 Lipsitz, *Dangerous Crossroads*, 88.
38 Reyes and Waldman, *Land of a Thousand Dances*, 144.

and also featured women in the band, while another punk band that featured a female singer was The Bags, featuring Alice Armendariz who was known as Alice Bag.[39] In a significant statement about an element of the Chicano/a punk scene that placed a lesser emphasis on the 'Chicano' aspect of their identity and emphasized an identification with various misfits and marginalized people (of different races and ethnic groups), Armendariz recalls, 'I felt like I was part of, not a Chicano community, but I was part of a weirdo community, I was part of the outcasts. I was a part of the people that didn't fit in with anybody else.'[40] Teresa Covarrubias of The Brat expresses this sentiment more explicitly,

> When we were in the Brat, that wasn't something that we kind of put on ourselves ... that we were a Chicano band. It was sort of like, people came to see us: 'Hey, they're brown, they're Chicano ... it's a Chicano band.' Automatically there was this expectation that, because we were a Chicano band, that somehow we had to carry our culture on our sleeve. You know? And that's fine. Some people do it really well, but that wasn't where we were coming from.[41]

As Alice Bag further notes on how some Chicano/a punkers were assimilating, 'The [LA] punk scene was really like, a melting pot. We never went to see the Zeros thinking it's a Latino band ... they were just the Zeros.'[42]

Speaking of which, yet another Chicano rocker who began his career with the punk band called The Zeros and became visible in the same LA scene was Robert Lopez. A punk-rocker turned comedian/performance artist, Lopez has recently garnered acclaim and scholarly attention for his performances as 'El Vez.'[43] Habell-Pallán notes that through recent popular music parody and Elvis impersonation, Lopez (as El Vez) enables both critique of the status quo and dialogue concerning progressive social transformation in relation to Chicano/as and Latino/as in the US.[44] While also not explicitly expressing Latino/Chicano politics during the punk era, Lopez and his career reveal striking similarities to different Latin/o rock predecessors (e.g., Question Mark, Sam the Sham, and Linda Ronstadt), expressing Chicano (or Latino) identity politics decades after emerging in popular culture.

Interestingly, The Zeros also included Javier Escovedo, brother of yet another first-wave punk musician, Alejandro Escovedo. Alejandro Escovedo played with The Nuns, who are often considered the very first punk band from California and opened for the Sex Pistols at their final show. In addition to coming from a rock family (with a *mariachi*-singer father who took the family from San Antonio to

---

39   Lipsitz, *Dangerous Crossroads*, 88–90.
40   Alice Armendariz, quoted in Wilkman, *Chicano Rock!: The Sounds of East Los Angeles* [documentary film].
41   Teresa Covarrubias, quoted in Wilkman, *Chicano Rock!: The Sounds of East Los Angeles* [documentary film].
42   Alice Armendariz, quoted in Sorrondeguy, *Beyond the Screams/Mas Alla De Los Gritos* [documentary film].
43   Habell-Pallán, 'El Vez Is "Taking Care of Business": The Inter/National Appeal of Chicano Popular Music'; Saldívar, *Border Matters*.
44   Habell-Pallán, 'El Vez Is "Taking Care of Business," 195.

Southern California, and two brothers who played with Santana and went on to form Azteca in the 1970s),[45] Alejandro was also a member of the band Rank & File, a so-called 'cow-punk' band that is said to have influenced the alt-country movement of recent decades. However, Alejandro Escovedo is now more famous for his contemporary rock, roots-rock, alt-country, and indie music, as well as his connections to the Austin, Texas scene. Recently, he was listed as one of the 100 greatest songwriters of all time, and legendary rock critic Dave Marsh called Escovedo's 2008 album, *Real Animal*, the 'Album of the Year.'

In all of these examples, it is interesting that not only were Chicano/as highly visible in LA's punk-rock scene, but Chicano/as were once again situated somewhere between assimilation and resistance to dominant US culture, reflected in their subject positions and expressed in their identities through the idiom of rock music. Yet, while all of these Chicano/a punk bands grew out of the burgeoning LA punk scene, there were other Latin/o connections to rock music during this period. By 1981, The Plugz had recorded and released *Better Luck*, which actually included various other guests like Argentinos, and future *rock en español* stars, such as the aforementioned Gustavo Santaolalla (from Argentina's rock movement who had moved to LA and become a 'punk new waver')[46] and Anibal Kerpel, as well as Steve Berlin (future member of Los Lobos). At the same time, the famous Chicano rockers Los Lobos themselves had begun to influence Chicano/a punkers such as Los Illegals when they began to write songs about Latino/a issues, culture, and identity.

The significance of Los Lobos is well documented in scholarly literature,[47] but a minor theme in the existing literature relates how Los Lobos were another band that was indirectly aligned with the LA punk-rock scene. As one scholar avers, 'More than others, Los Lobos reflect the musical diversity and processes of change, maintenance, and adaptation among the Mexican/Chicano peoples of Los Angeles.'[48] In the late 1960s, singer/guitarist Cesar Rosas' first group, The Young Sounds, played rock 'n' roll and R&B. His next band, Fast Company, exclusively played funk music covers. Bassist Conrad Lozano's first band was The Royal Checkmates, who played soul/R&B, while his next band, Euphoria, was a hard-rock band. Other Lozano stints included 'playing soul music and funk to all-black audiences,' 'heavy metal to long-haired white kids,' and a stint with the previously mentioned Tierra.[49] As evidence of fluctuations in Latino/a identity politics, when Lozano got together with Los Lobos, who sought inspiration from traditional Mexican music, he didn't understand the Spanish words. However, listening to Mexican, South American, and Latin music became an obsession thereafter.

Although all the band members had early stints with rock 'n' roll groups in the

---

45   Other relatives include Mario Escovedo (of The Dragons) and percussionist Sheila E. who found fame with Prince and later as a solo artist.
46   Gilbert, 'For Bajofondo, It Takes Eight to Tango,' no pagination.
47   Cullen, *The Art of Democracy: A Concise History of Popular Culture in the U.S.*; Lipsitz, *Dangerous Crossroads*; Loza, *Barrio Rhythm*; Reyes and Waldman, *Land of a Thousand Dances*.
48   Loza, *Barrio Rhythm*, 233.
49   Ibid., 148.

1960s (and different rock subgenres), by the early 1970s Los Lobos were making a name for themselves playing traditional Mexican music. They first came together around 1973 and jump-started their career working with activist César Chávez and the United Farm Workers Union on an album titled *Sí Se Puede*.[50] To some extent, the music of Los Lobos was related to the political symbolism of the Chicano movement.[51] However, irrespective of their place in the local Chicano/a community, and in spite of the fact that they had taken their name from a Mexican *norteño* band called Los Lobos del Norte,[52] they refused to speak Spanish. They were also very conscious of their hippie-like hair and dress, and were unwilling to change in order to have to come across as 'Mexican' musicians. In spite of the fact that they were aligned with the Chicano movement and performed Mexican music, Los Lobos recall that they were mostly listening to punk-rock music by the end of the 1970s. Even on their drive to gigs where they were hired to play Mexican music, they would be listening to the Sex Pistols and the Ramones. By 1980, Los Lobos were ready to return to rock music. As scholars note, they were 'taking a leap forward by taking a leap backward' as they were returning to their rock roots.[53]

Given their varied musical interests that included blues, R&B, 1960s rock 'n' roll, funk, punk-rock, heavy metal, classical, jazz, and several Mexican folk styles, Los Lobos played Mexican music at community weddings and also played rock and blues at local clubs throughout the early 1980s. By the mid 1980s Los Lobos were contracted to record the soundtrack to the 1986 film *La Bamba*, at the request of Ritchie Valens' mother.[54] The soundtrack and the title single were #1 simultaneously, and as scholars observe, the song was more successful for Los Lobos than it was for Ritchie Valens since the version by Valens never made it to #1.[55] The movie and soundtrack propelled Los Lobos to a level of popularity and mainstream success in the US that they had never known. Yet, at a time when Los Lobos were fully into rock 'n' roll and blues, and had achieved skyrocketing success with the *La Bamba* tribute to early rock 'n' roll history, they turned their interests in what seemed like the opposite direction. Their following release, 1988's *La Pistola y el Corazón*, featured original music in the form of all-Spanish songs and acoustic Mexican folk sounds — an effort for which Los Lobos eventually won another Grammy.[56]

As Los Lobos moved into the 1990s, their further successes were even greater, and they have grown in popularity around the world, in stature as musicians and performers, and in significance for their contributions to popular music. What is pertinent for this analysis in the example of Los Lobos is how they managed to negotiate their Latino/a identities through musical expression as 'Mexicans,'

50   Torres, 'Siendo la Verdadera Historia de Los Lobos del Este de Los Angeles,' 15.
51   Loza, *Barrio Rhythm*, 238.
52   Torres, 'Siendo la Verdadera Historia de Los Lobos del Este de Los Angeles,' 5.
53   Reyes and Waldman, *Land of a Thousand Dances*, 146.
54   Mendheim, *Ritchie Valens: The First Latino Rocker*.
55   Reyes and Waldman, *Land of a Thousand Dances*, 151.
56   Los Lobos won a Grammy Award in 1983 for their version of the Spanish-language/traditional Mexican song 'Anselma.'

'Mexican Americans,' and 'Chicanos' doing Mexican-inspired music and as 'Americans' doing rock (through different subgenres). Their career moves symbolize processes of acculturation. Like other Latino/a wannabe rock 'n' rollers of the 1960s, they never reached any measurable success in their early years. Also like other Latino/as in rock 'n' roll, they were able to return to their own ethnic music and their collective heritage for inspiration. However, unlike others, they would eventually find success in the rock and pop music markets, and, paralleling the moves of others artists like Linda Ronstadt, they used their success to leverage projects that eventually aligned them with Latino/as and Latin Americans beyond the US.

Loza provides further critical insight on Los Lobos, noting how they were part of the pursuit of raising Chicano/a consciousness. As Loza puts it, 'Los Lobos, in effect, reversed the standard process and began to enculturate their audience, making the socialization process reciprocal.'[57] In other words, if previous generations of Mexican Americans were assimilated to US culture through rock 'n' roll, Los Lobos used rock music to introduce their audiences to Mexican and Latino/a culture(s). The case of Los Lobos represents the identity questions at the heart of this research project. If, indeed, the use of identity signifiers or labels is difficult to grasp, Los Lobos embody this difficulty.

For example, Los Lobos were known to have confused rock promoters and journalists in Europe who labeled them as 'Mexican' rock and as a Mexican band 'from East LA.'[58] Similarly, Los Lobos might commonly be known as 'Mexican American,' 'Chicano,' and, as in a recent article, simply 'American.'[59] At the same time, Los Lobos have expressed feelings of being left out of recent Latin Grammy Awards and the larger 'Latin music' community.[60] Lipsitz argues that the fact that Los Lobos performs jazz, rock 'n' roll, and other musical styles is not a way of denying their Mexican heritage, but rather, as one part of the Chicano/a experience and 'a way of claiming citizenship in a larger artistic and political world.'[61] As another assessment suggests, 'The legacy of Los Lobos points in two directions — one a continued exploration and reinvention of Mexican traditions, the other an embrace of America's multi-cultural future.'[62]

Moving beyond Los Lobos, other major punk bands such as Black Flag, the Misfits, the Descendents, Bad Religion, Danzig, and possibly others also demonstrate links between Latino/as and punk (and other subgenres), and the increasing relevance of punk-rock for Latino/as.[63] Of course, by the mid 1980s punk-rock had

---

57 Loza, *Barrio Rhythm*, 266.
58 Reyes and Waldman, *Land of a Thousand Dances*, 158.
59 Nailen, 'Summer at Red Butte: Concert Series Offers a Bumper Crop of Great Acts,' D1–D12.
60 For example, see Roiz 'Los Lobos: The Legend Lives On,' 6–24.
61 Lipsitz, *Dangerous Crossroads*, 90.
62 Narrator Edwards James Olmos in Wilkman, *Chicano Rock!: The Sounds of East Los Angeles* [documentary film].
63 For example, Puerto Rican Ron Reyes was at one time a member of Black Flag, Manny Martínez played with the Misfits, Karl Alvarez with the Descendents, Tim Gallegos with Bad Religion, Joey Castillo with Danzig; and there are likely very many other Latino/as in punk throughout the Southwest and throughout California, although likely with less well-known bands.

become post-punk and new-wave, while some bands and artists left punk-rock behind to move into industrial-rock and goth-rock (or, just 'goth'). Punk-rock was also blending with heavy metal to produce other subgenres such as hardcore punk (or, just 'hardcore'), speed metal, thrash metal, and eventually, the so-called grunge sound. Scholars note that by the late 1980s, heavy metal had already integrated some more obvious elements of Latin music (e.g., Santana), and other symbolic aspects further contributed to its articulation to Latino/as. For example, Weinstein notes that heavy metal's reliance on the symbolism of death would easily resonate with Latino/a youth, and also that by the late 1980s, the Latino/a audience for heavy metal was rapidly growing and the metal subculture was taking root with Latino/as.[64]

Moreover, given how rock subgenres such as goth and heavy metal were becoming increasingly relevant in the late 1980s and early 1990s for Latino/a youth — goth for both young Latinas (likely because of its subversion of traditional and conservative sex norms, and how it voiced alternative romanticism, emotionality, expressiveness, and femininity) and for gay/lesbian/bisexual/transgender (GLBT) youth (due its proximity to the gender-bending new-wave community and sense of alienation and marginalization), and heavy metal for young Latino men (because of its working-class masculinist codes that resonated across race and ethnicity)[65] — there are many significant aspects of heavy metal that were responsible for its resonance with Latino/as in the US and elsewhere throughout the 1980s (e.g., masculinity rooted in working-class codes, symbolism of death, prevalence of Catholic-religious imagery, primacy of the guitar, and musicological similarities to Spanish/classical-guitar playing). Nonetheless, while punk and hardcore punk can boast of various Latino/as, heavy metal can also speak to a 'Latin' legacy. For example, the widely popular thrash metal band Slayer had bassist/vocalist Tom Araya (born Tomás Enrique Araya), who was born in Chile but grew up near Los Angeles, and now resides in Texas. Otherwise, Brazilian thrash metal/death metal band Sepultura further demonstrated heavy metal's reverberations throughout Latin America. Besides symbolizing Brazil's engagement with heavy metal since the 1980s, Sepultura were widely popular in the 1990s and considered a major force in heavy metal worldwide.

The significance of heavy metal for Latino/as is further symbolized by Metallica's Rob Trujillo (born Roberto Agustín Trujillo), who has roots in Guanajuato, México but was also raised in Los Angeles. Trujillo has played with Ozzy Osbourne, Suicidal Tendencies, and more famously with Metallica — having been inducted into the Rock and Roll Hall of Fame with Metallica in 2009.[66] Trujillo has recently been noted for bringing flamenco-style guitar playing to Metallica, and, perhaps fittingly, he has recently played with contemporary Mexican duo Rodrigo y Gabriela — famous worldwide for their unique flamenco/

---

64   Weinstein, *Heavy Metal: A Cultural Sociology*, 112–13.
65   On heavy metal's masculinity and working-class codes, see Weinstein, *Heavy Metal: A Cultural Sociology*, 111–14.
66   See http://www.rockhall.com

Spanish-guitar interpretations of heavy metal music, and who are often connected to contemporary Latin alternative music.

The Rise of *Rock en Español* and Latin Alternative

In order to begin this next section of analysis, it is important to note first how the term *rock en español* (rock in Spanish) followed and replaced other marketing terms like *rock en tu idioma* (Rock in Your Own Language) that had been used to describe the new wave of rock and pop music throughout Latin America in the late 1980s,[67] and how the term *rock en español* became the new moniker in the early 1990s to refer to popular rock music from Spanish-speaking countries like México, Argentina, and Spain and, later, to popular rock music from various other Latin American nations such as Chile, Colombia, Puerto Rico, and Venezuela. However, as with previous designations like the *rock en tu idioma* marketing slogan of the 1980s, *rock en español* began to lose favor as well. Perhaps because of the specific connotation as a marketing slogan, artists and producers have resisted the label since the late 1990s and began to use the term *rock Latino* instead. Moreover, recognizing that 'rock' was somewhat limiting in its attempt to describe a subgenre of popular music that is informed by many other genres, such as hip-hop, reggae, ska, and electronica as well as *ranchera*, salsa, mambo, *nueva canción*, and various other musical traditions, artists and producers began referring to their music as 'Latin alternative' music.

Of course, alternative-rock was the prevalent term used in the 1990s to categorize music outside of the cultural mainstream; it was often used to connote independently produced music or non-corporate authenticity. While it is a problematic term in that 'alternative' music began to move over into the mainstream through heavy rotation of videos on MTV or through airtime on corporate radio (as 'modern rock' or 'adult contemporary' radio formats), alternative-rock music's cultural cachet remained in its origins with artists and scenes committed to independent production or indifference to commercial success. It is worth noting that as a result of the shift in the 1990s of alternative-rock into the pop category, as well as debates about what constituted alternative music and criticism of alternative music,[68] the term 'alternative' has also lost currency in contemporary popular culture while terms like 'indie' (independent) and 'underground' (non-mainstream) are more commonly used at present. The 'alternative' label, however, has returned to the lexicon of popular music fans, scholars, and business executives through its Latin/o connections. The term 'Latin alternative' has gained currency as a result of the increasing profile of artists and musicians who came from the *rock en español* scene, Latino rock (or *rock Latino*) and other popular music subgenres. In fact, a recent National Public Radio series defines the significance of the subgenre of 'Latin alternative,' noting how the music relates to contemporary issues of

---

67   Hernández, 'Remaking the *Corrido* for the 1990s: Maldita Vecindad's "El Barzón."'
68   For example, see Frank, *Alternative to What?: Sounding Off! — Music as Subversion / Resistance / Revolution*.

identity and nationality.⁶⁹ Thus 'Latin alternative,' although sometimes replaced by synonymous Spanish terms such as 'Latino Alternativo' and even 'Alter-Latino,' has emerged as the most commonly used term in recent years and at present. Interestingly, the careers of some bands, such as Café Tacuba, have paralleled the changing genre signifiers, since the band emerged out of the México City rock scene in the late 1980s on the *rock en tu idioma* wave, rose to international prominence as *rock en español* by the early to mid 1990s, and remain an international heavyweight in what is now being called Rock Latino or Latin alternative.

While US bands such as Los Lobos were creating their own transnational, hybrid music productions in the early to mid 1990s, many *rock en español* bands such as Café Tacuba were doing the same. By the 1990s rock 'n' roll music in México, Spain, Argentina, Brazil, and other Latin American countries, was burgeoning after several decades worth of fermentation.⁷⁰ Likewise, a growing awareness of *rock en español* was so prevalent in such unexpected places as the English-dominant United States, so that in the early 1990s, the *rock en español* scene seemed ready to explode. While decades of fermentation in various Latin American countries provided rock a wider fan base, other social forces like modernization and the Latin music industry's notice of rock in Spanish also contributed. Many artists and fans were hopeful about its potential impact throughout the world.

There were also, however, other events that led to the growth of *rock en español* in the US. Scholars note how in places like California, where there were often cultural differences between US Latino/as and more recent arrivals from México and other countries, political controversies such as Proposition 187, the North American Free Trade Agreement (NAFTA), and events in Chiapas that resulted from NAFTA had made US Latino/as more aware of racism and discrimination toward 'Mexicans.' As one scholar observes, by the mid 1990s Latino/a immigrants and US Chicano/as had more in common than ever before, and increasingly identified with each other.⁷¹ In other words, instead of being against each other, by the 1990s Latino/a immigrants and US Chicano/as now shared feelings of alienation from mainstream society, and rock became culturally relevant for

---

69   For more recent perspectives on 'Latin alternative' music, see Contreras 'Defining Latin Alternative Music'; Contreras, 'Monterrey, Mexico: Latin Alternative Central'; Ulaby, 'U.S. Cross-Over Hits Elude Latin Alternative'; del Barco, 'Latin Alternative's Big Cheese: Gustavo Santaolalla.'

70   Aparicio and Jáquez, *Musical Migrations: Transnationalism and Cultural Hybridity in Latin/o America, Volume I*; Avelar, 'Defeated Rallies, Mournful Anthems, and the Origins of Brazilian Heavy Metal'; Esterrich and Murillo, 'Rock with Punk with Pop with Folklore'; Harvey, 'Cannibals, Mutants, and Hipsters'; Hernández, 'Remaking the *Corrido* for the 1990s'; Kun, 'The Aural Border'; Kun, 'The Sun Never Sets on MTV: Tijuana NO! and the Border of Music Video'; Kun, 'Rock's *Reconquista*'; Morales, 'Rock is Dead and Living in Mexico'; Pacini Hernández et al., *Rockin' Las Américas: The Global Politics of Rock in Latin/o America*; Perrone, 'Changing of the Guard'; Rodríguez Marino, 'MTV Latino: Identidad, Nación, y Rock'; Saldívar, *Border Matters: Remapping American Cultural Studies*; Semán and Vila, 'Rock Chabón: The Contemporary National Rock of Argentina'; Stigberg, 'Foreign Currents during the 60s and 70s in Mexican Popular Music'; Vila, '*Rock Nacional* and Dictatorship in Argentina' (1987); Zolov, *Refried Elvis*; Zolov, 'Armando Nava and Los Dug Dug's.'

71   Leal, lecture/conference presentation at EMP's annual POP conference in Seattle, WA. (2008).

Triple. Photo by: Alex Luster

them and allowed them to express feelings of discrimination, marginalization, and alienation.

In other local scenes, such as in Houston, Texas, US Latino/as also increasingly identified with the *rock en español* music of México and other Spanish-speaking nations such as Spain and Argentina in the 1990s.[72] In this case it was Tex-Mex Latino/as, and as Houston scenesters note, it began with the arrival of Mexican rock bands such as Caifanes to Houston, but it also resulted from tours, such as Watcha Tour, and other music festivals featuring Spanish-language rock music that brought various *rock en español* and Latin alternative bands/artists from throughout Latin America (and Spain) to places like Houston and were attracting 'a new wave of Hispanics, the ones that didn't like *tejano* or other typical music that was being played at other clubs.'[73] As Edson Sanchez notes about such developments and the increasing significance of Latin/o rock and the eventual creation of a dedicated internet site for Latin/o rock music in Houston, there was a need to provide a common space for artists, bands, fans, producers, and promoters within the growing Latin/o rock music scene in Houston, Texas, and through the creation of an internet site (*RockenHouston.com*), 'the community found a voice and a way for like-minded people to communicate.'[74]

By 1997, of course, journalists across the US were more aware of the burgeoning *rock en español* movement and its growth around the world. According to

---

72 Sanchez, 'A Brief History of Latin Alternative Music in Houston, Part 1,' no pagination.
73 Ibid., no pagination.
74 Ibid., no pagination.

Señor Flavio. Photo by: Vito Rivelli

one account, the growing fan base of the *rock en español* genre was made up of 'bilingual Hispanic youth who dismissed *salsa, tejano,* and other traditional styles as out of date.'[75] The same article cited the existence of many US-based *rock en español* bands, domestic record labels in LA and San Francisco dedicated to Spanish-language rock, and *La Banda Elástica* (a new publication dedicated to *rock en español*) as evidence that *rock en español* was finally being embraced by 'the US Hispanic community'. Moreover, by the 1990s famous producers like David Byrne were getting behind bands like King Changó, as well as other bands and artists.

However, while festivals in LA featured increasingly popular bands like Los Olvidados from LA, Los Skarnales from Houston, and King Changó from New York, reports noted that *rock en español* continued to suffer from a lack of radio airplay.[76] According to many industry insiders, the lack of radio airplay had hampered the movement of *rock en español* into the mainstream, but nonetheless, they still predicted and anticipated the growth in the US, especially among US Latino/a youth. Eventually, what constantly had industry insiders raising eyebrows in the late 1990s was the fact that *rock en español* was growing consistently, despite the lack of radio and MTV airtime.

Along with the growth of *rock en español*, and its steady growth in the US and with US Latino/as, another important trend that emerged in the 1990s came in the form of tribute songs and albums. While many US rockers were honoring their

75 Holston, '*Rock en Español*: A Youth Market Comes of Age, but Record Executives Turn a Blind Eye,' 50.
76 Ibid., 52.

Los Fabulosos Cadillacs. Photo by: Claudio Divella

rock predecessors in various compilations that were produced in the 1990s, rock 'n' roll's dialogue with Latino/as perhaps came full circle when *rock en español* artists began to acknowledge their own influences from the US and England. In the 1990s, the Argentine ska-rockers Los Fabulosos Cadillacs, another *rock en español* heavyweight, recorded cover versions of 'Strawberry Fields Forever' by The Beatles and 'Revolution Rock' by The Clash. The former tribute featured the vocals in Spanish by punk-rocker Deborah Harry of Blondie (who had recorded her own rock songs in Spanish in previous decades), while the latter actually included Mick Jones of The Clash. Clash members also made guest appearances on the Cadillacs' popular release *Rey Azucar* in 1995, as did producers Tina Weymouth and Chris Frantz of Talking Heads.

Given such significant articulations of rock music to Latin America that go back decades, it is easy to understand how, in the 1990s, Los Fabulosos Cadillacs were paying tribute to their punk-rock inspirations in The Clash. As Chuck Eddy notes, 'it's not hard to *comprende* why the Clash are such a popular influence on '90s Latin American *Rock en Español* bands.'[77] Further noting the intercultural influence, cross-cultural fertilization, and transnational exchange related to The Clash and their music, Tijuana, México's *ska/rock en español* band Tijuana NO! also paid tribute to The Clash in 1995 when they recorded their own cover version of 'Spanish Bombs,' for the album *Transgresores de la Ley*. Singer Ceci Bastida, however, sang more naturally in Spanish than The Clash, which, when combined

---

77 Eddy, *The Accidental Evolution of Rock 'n' Roll: A Misguided Tour Through Popular Music*.

with The Clash's pro-revolutionary or pro-third-world politics, has probably contributed to why the song is widely considered one of the best Tijuana NO! songs and a favorite with fans, as well as having something to do with The Clash's lasting popularity throughout Latin/o America as well as with Latin/o rock fans elsewhere around the world.

Yet another transnational tribute came from México's Cuca, who released their breakthrough album, *La Racha*, in 1995, which featured a cover of 'Break On Through (To the Other Side),' the famous 1967 song by The Doors. While the new Cuca version was still in English, the song was transformed into a Mexican hard-rock song that demonstrated the familiarity of Mexicans with the North American rock canon, and further connected *rock en español* to mainstream rock music in the US. Because the original 'Break On Through' itself signified a dialogue between Latin America and rock music through its origins as a mambo construction,[78] the new version by Cuca was significant; La Cuca's version was not just a connection, but a re-articulation of the song to Mexicans and Latin America.

From an analytical perspective, such musical productions can be understood as recontextualization(s), which, in discourse analytic terms, refers to semiotic practices in which social actors produce representations of other practices and incorporate them into their own practice.[79] In other words, rather than seeing these tribute efforts and collaborations by *rock en español* artists and others as mere imitation or cheap copy, an alternative reading suggests that these artists are recontextualizing rock music, and the implications of such recontextualization point toward larger social factors like globalization and transnationalization of culture. Recontextualization, in other words, is useful for understanding the growth of *rock en español* among US Latino/as as well as how rock music in general is being recontextualized by *rock en español*, but the examples of tribute efforts also illustrate a sort of double recontextualization, or a reclamation of rock music that had previously been recontextualized with Latin/o music by others.

During the second half of the 1990s, some of the most popular music in *rock en español* circles came from a series of tribute albums through which various *rock en español* artists more overtly tipped their hats to their North American and English influences in popular music. For example, in 1996 and 1997 artists came together for the album *Tributo a Queen: Los Grandes del Rock en Español*, a tribute to Queen that was one of the most talked about *rock en español* releases of the year in 1997 and one of the most popular in the years that followed. In 1998, artists fashioned a similar tribute to the reggae-rock influences of The Police in *Outlandos D'Americas: A Rock en Español Tribute to The Police*. The project featured artists from Argentina, Brazil, Colombia, Spain, México, Puerto Rico, Chile, Venezuela, and the United States. Yet another popular release in that year was *Tributo a The Cure (Por Que No Puedo Ser Tú)*, a tribute to new-wave/alternative-rock band The Cure that also featured Cure songs translated into Spanish and reinterpreted by various *rock en español* bands from different Latin American nations. Of further

---

78 Sublette, 'The Kingsmen and the Cha-Cha-Chá,' 89.
79 Fairclough, 'The Discourse of New Labour: Critical Discourse Analysis,' 234–5.

interest to this discussion is the fact that these Latin American tribute albums began to include US Latino/a artists, representing a kind of collocation in which artists from various Latin American nations were discursively linked to US Latino/as and further illuminating intercultural, international, and transnational 'Latino' identities.

Furthermore, while such tribute projects enabled Latin/o rock music to cement its place in Latin America, the expansion of Latin/o rock's presence in the US was also well under way. In a 1997 *Newsweek* article on *rock en español*, journalists noted how *rock en español* music was being featured in Hollywood 'hipster'[80] film soundtracks such as Quentin Tarantino's 1996 film *Curdled* and in the 1997 soundtrack for *Grosse Pointe Blank*.[81] Worth noting, the *Curdled* soundtrack featured established *rock en español* artists as well as LA Chicano rockers like The Blazers, further connecting Latin music acts to Latino/as in the US. The 1997 soundtrack to the feature film *Star Maps* also included various *rock en español* artists as well as US 'Chicano underground' artists like Lysa Flores as well as other Anglo-rockers.[82] As Kun reminds us about the significance of such mediated productions,

> What the soundtrack to *Star Maps* ends up suggesting is that the music of contemporary Chicano identity is an increasingly transnational formation, both *de aqui* and *de alla*, both de Los Angeles and de Mexico City, and both the bilingual hip-hop and rock fusions of Mexico City's Molotov and the English-language L.A. folk-rock of Flores.[83]

Further revealing such connections between Latin/o rock with US rock formations, a 1997 AIDS charity release titled *Silencio = Muerte* (Silence Equals Death) featured various *rock en español* artists in conjunction with well-established US artists, such as David Byrne and Melissa Etheridge.

Also in 1997, Los Angeles alt-rockers Concrete Blonde teamed up with Chicano punkers Los Illegals and released the album *Concrete Blonde y Los Illegals*. Such an alliance made perfect sense, because they were all longtime friends and came out of the same LA music scene. Described as 'razor sharp' with political wit, music reviewers conceded that the political nature of this effort would obviously block it from mainstream radio. The disc contains songs that address such topics as the harsh realities of living in the *barrio*, the lack of Latino/a representation in media, bilingualism, esoteric quotations from Mexican muralist José Clemente Orozco, and a song ('Another Hundred Years of Solitude') based on a critical view

---

80   For more on the 'hipster' and alternative-rock music's movement toward Latin/o rock, see discussion on Brazilian rock by Harvey, 'Cannibals, Mutants, and Hipsters,' 117–20; An interesting parallel can be drawn with 'cool honkies' and the Anglo-American embracing of lowriders in Southern California car culture (see Stone, 'Bajito y Suavecito [Low and Slow]: Low Riding and the "Class" of Class[*]').

81   Hayden and Schoemer, 'Se Habla Rock and Roll? You Will Soon,' 70.

82   Not coincidentally, this soundtrack was supervised and produced by the aforementioned producer Gustavo Santaolalla along with artist Lysa Flores.

83   Kun, *Audiotopia*, 196.

of the mythic notion of the American dream and that plays on Gabriel García Marquez's famous book *One Hundred Years of Solitude*. This 1997 collaboration between Concrete Blonde and Los Illegals also features an acoustic rendition of a traditional Mexican song 'La Llorona.' In the examples of 'La Llorona' and *One Hundred Years of Solitude*, one gets a sense of the discursive intertextuality at play, the borrowing or referencing of cultural productions from other Latin American nations and countries other than the US. The significance of this, of course, lies with the collaboration of established US artists with Chicano/a musicians, music, themes, and artists. At the same time, further significance lies in the fact of US-based Chicano/a cultural productions that simultaneously allude to Latin American culture.

Nonetheless, it is worth remembering that the LA band Concrete Blonde began their dialogue with Latino/a culture much earlier; in 1993 their *Mexican Moon* album was released, which featured the title track and another song called 'Bajo La Luna Mexicana.' Also significant was their use of dancing skeletons and bright flowers on the album cover — another possible connection to Mexican Day of the Dead imagery — following other US alt-rockers like The Pixies, Red Hot Chili Peppers, and Jane's Addiction in the early 1990s, and bands like the Grateful Dead in previous decades who deployed a Mexican/Latin/Spanish aesthetic for album cover artwork.

Following such trends, the Southern California connections between Latino/as and mainstream US rock music, and between Southern California Chicano/as and *rock en español* became more numerous and more noticeable in the late 1990s. In 1996, for example, the LA-based punk-rock band Voodoo Glow Skulls released their album *Firme* in both English and Spanish. Not only were the song titles in both languages, but so were all of the lyrics. In other words, the release was 100 per cent bilingual. A year later, the internationally famous group known as the Gipsy Kings covered 'Hotel California' (the famous classic-rock song by the Eagles), and translated it to Spanish. They gave it their trademark *flamenco*/Spanish-guitar sound, called it 'Spanish Hotel California,' and further demonstrated how American popular music productions are also part of the lexicon of people outside of the US as well as how famous rock songs are sometimes reclaimed by Latinos/Hispanics for their 'Latin' essences.

In 1999, Southern California's rap/rock group Cypress Hill re-released their greatest hits, but this time in Spanish. Interestingly, the Afro-Latino rap group (including a New York Italian, a Mexican Cuban, and a Cuban) had achieved fame and notoriety in alternative-rock circles and through Lollapalooza concert festivals throughout the 1990s, breaking down barriers between rock, hip-hop, alternative, metal, reggae, ska, and Latin music. However, their all-Spanish compilation, titled *Los Grandes Éxitos en Español*, specifically emphasized their Latino/a identity, and it even featured collaborations with *rock en español* heavyweights — México's immensely popular rap/rock combo Control Machete. Within the next few years, rap/rock music by Control Machete would be featured in soundtracks to feature films, in Levi's jeans commercials, and even in *Monday Night Football* broadcasts.

By 1999, famous US producers, such as the New York-based Phil Ramone, were also getting into the Latin/o rock action. Having worked previously with the likes of Frank Sinatra, Quincy Jones, Luciano Pavarotti, James Taylor, Jon Secada, and many others, the multi-Grammy-Award-winning producer collaborated with Argentine rocker Fito Páez on his 1999/2000 Latin Grammy-winning *Abre*, and on his 2001 follow-up project, *Rey Sol*.[84] Not to be left out, of course, other music producers like David Byrne, former frontman for the popular 1980s group Talking Heads, furthered his own Latin/o rock connections by re-releasing (through his own Luaka Bop label) music by Os Mutantes, a Brazilian psychedelic-rock band from the early Brazilian rock era of the 1960s and 1970s. Most recently, the musician producer Byrne is also responsible for the production and dissemination of other Latino/a artists such as Los Amigos Invisibles, Los de Abajo, Clinton, Moreno, Susana Baca, and Tom Zé that increasingly blur the lines between 'world beat,' rock music and Latin alternative.

Of course, by the late 1990s, just as non-Latino/a producers and promoters were increasingly interested in Latin/o rock music and in attracting more and more sponsors for tours as well as increasing numbers of fans, Latin/o rock tours made their way through Los Angeles, San Diego, San Francisco, Texas, Denver, Chicago, Detroit, Atlanta, Miami, New York, and Massachusetts. Describing the slow, steady growth, one talent-buyer for a famous LA music club argued that while it might be expensive for the short term, in the long term they would gain more and more customers and cross cultural lines like never before.[85]

Another late 1990s and early 2000s trend indicated the movement of female rockers to the *rock en español* vanguard. As *Billboard* articles noted, Latina rockers had finally moved to the forefront of *rock en español* and occupied an important place in the 1990s. Although rock in any language has traditionally been the realm of men,[86] journalists noticed how artists like Andrea Echeverri of Colombia's Aterciopelados were moving to the front in what was now being called 'Latin alternative,' and some noted that female band members and soloists are no longer regarded as a novelty. From performers like México's Alejandra Guzmán and Colombia's Shakira, whose pop leanings and multi-million-dollar sales have led to virtual dismissal by *rock en español* circles, to other Mexican '*rockeras*' (girl rockers) like Ely Guerra and Julieta Venegas, who emerged as immensely popular solo artists and even graced the cover of *Time* magazine in 1999 as leaders of 'the era of *la roquera*' (the era of women rockers), Latina rockers appeared to be influencing Latin/o rock music than ever before. From Argentina's Erica García, who recorded an album in 2000 with Beck Hansen's band, to emerging US singer/songwriters like the Chicana Lysa Flores,[87] Latina women became prominent in Latin alternative music, which is not something that can be said of other rock subgenres or of other mainstream popular music genres. And from other singer/songwriters, like Claudia Brant who recorded her first album for release in the US, to Argentine

---

84   Cobo et al., 'Argentine Folk Rock, L.A. Labels, and a Brazilian Festival.'
85   Wadell, '*Rock en Español* Takes Off on Tour.'
86   Cobo, 'Women Who Rock,' para. 7.
87   Doss, 'Choosing Chicano in the 1990s: The Underground Music Scene of Los(t) Angeles.'

pop veterans like María Gabriela Epumer who moved on to her second and third solo releases, Latina 'rockeras' in the 1990s were more commercially successful than ever, being recognized by music critics for their excellence, nominated for Grammy Awards, and headlining rock tours like the aforementioned 'Revolución Tour' and the 'Watcha Tour.'

Of relevance for the issue of the Latin/o rock diaspora's discontinuities and necessary contextualizations, Latina rockers demonstrated an ambiguity with regard to their feminism. As one put it,

> Latin *roqueras* [female rockers] agonize about gender far less than their English-speaking counterparts. Lyrically, they are also less self-centered and self-absorbed; many of their songs talk about the more distressing reality around them. And even when they sing about love, they do so in different terms.[88]

Furthermore, artists like Andrea Echeverri (of Aterciopelados) were said to be the symbol of South American feminism as a result of their tattoos, piercings, and plainspoken attitude,[89] as well as their antisexist quips and their presence as 'sexy, uniquely stylish and singularly intent on having neither looks nor gender override their message and music.'[90] These observations are significant because of how US Latinas and non-US Latinas demonstrate differences in their gender politics, and such differences are likely to be related to important class differences as well.

In addition to the appearance of Latina and Chicana women at the forefront of Latin/o rock music, the decade of the 1990s revealed many other changes. More changes occurred in Latino/a communities in the US where hardcore 'Latino/Chicano' punk-rock and the 'Chicano underground' music scenes provided voice for the fragmented identities of US Latino/as that were aware of both their differences and similarities to US rock music and the growing *rock en español* music.[91] Mirroring the strengthening connections between Latin Americans and US Latino/as, Gustavo Santaolalla — first famous throughout Latin America as a folk-rock musician from Argentina — was heavily involved as a *rock en español* music producer, and was single-handedly responsible for a majority of the music called '*rock en tu idioma*,' '*rock En español*,' and then 'Latin alternative' music that was coming out of Latin America (and the US) in the 1990s. One could argue that Gustavo Santaolalla emerged as the single most important contemporary figure (as an artist/musician/producer) in Latin/o rock, since he has been instrumental in the success of industry giants like Café Tacuba, Molotov, Juanes, and many other groups, solo artists, and projects, winning several Grammy Awards in the process.

Another trend in the late 1990s highlighted the continuing legacy of Latino/a influences in mainstream US rock music. In 1999, for example, Sugar Ray scored a major hit with the song 'Every Morning' which was based on a sample from the

---

88   Cobo, 'Women Who Rock,' para. 12.
89   Farley, 'Sounds of Magic Realism: Aterciopelados Updates South American Traditions,' para. 3.
90   Cobo, 'Women Who Rock,' paras. 1–3.
91   Sorrondeguy, *Beyond the Screams*.

1972 song by Malo called 'Suavecito' — which is still popular with Chicano/as in the US and remains an emblem of Chicano/a identity. In the same year, the fledgling indie-rock band At the Drive-In released songs like 'Rascuache' from their 1999 EP *Vaya*. The band eventually broke up, but would give birth to Sparta, Sleepercar, and The Mars Volta (as well as the solo career of Omar Rodríguez-López), which would all go on to different levels of success in indie-rock, alternative-rock, hard-rock, prog-rock, and alt-country in the following decade. Meanwhile, Santana's immensely popular *Supernatural* album included collaborations with Mexican pop-rock band Maná, and spawned major hits such as 'Corazón Espinado.' In other examples, Los Lobos fashioned another Latin American connection through the cut 'Cumbia Raza' on 1999's *This Time*, while Argentina's Los Enanitos Verdes released the song 'Tequila' on the *Nectar* album. Although this 'Tequila' was not a cover of the late 1950s rock 'n' roll classic, it provides evidence of further connections between Argentina and México and of the intercultural tones heard within the Latin/o rock diaspora.

The Latin/o Rock Diaspora (Y2K and Beyond)

Just as the Latin/o rock diaspora in the 1990s seemed to have reached a certain level of cultural significance for the music industry and for what it suggests about shifting Latin/o identity(ies), there is evidence that such significance is intensifying. *Billboard* magazine recalls how, in August 2000, the first-ever Latin Alternative Music Conference was held in New York City to concentrate on alternative music, rock, and hip-hop in Spanish.[92] Not coincidentally, the city of Los Angeles declared a 'Watcha *rock en español* day' just a few days prior to that conference, noting how 'Los Angeles is, in fact, the cradle for *rock en español*,' due to how many bands are nurtured there.[93] Since then, Los Angeles has been called 'the mecca of Latin alternative music,'[94] while yearly tours like the 'Watcha/Latin Warped' tour are providing more outlets for Latin alternative groups and artists throughout North America.

Furthermore, other reports note how 'Latin Alternative music has made it to major record labels' for global distribution.[95] Among the many signals of Latin rock's coming of age throughout the world, Cobo cites radio shows like *The Red Zone* in the US, a twenty-four-hour *rock nacional* radio station in Argentina,[96] three radio stations with 'Latin alternative' formats throughout México,[97] another twenty-four-hour *rock en español* radio station in Puerto Rico as well as its own burgeoning scene,[98] and growing internet sites that allow listeners to hear their favorite Latin alternative artists or to listen to new ones. Furthering the *rock en*

---

92   Unsigned article, 'Confab showcases *rock en español*,' 2000.
93   Ibid., para. 7.
94   Cobo, 'Growing Up and Looking for an Audience.'
95   Cobo, 'Latin Crossover's New Twist.'
96   Cobo, 'Not Yet Rockin' the Radio: Hugely Popular in Argentina, Latin Rock Needs to Find its Audience in the U.S.'
97   Padilla, 'Rocking in Mexico: Bands Continue to Struggle with Radio's and Labels' Attitudes.'
98   Cobo, 'Puya: Rocking Harder Than Ever,' para. 4.

español and Latin alternative connections to the US, one of MTV's spin-off projects in 2001 was a one-hour, bilingual television program airing *rock en español* and Latin alternative videos.[99] Moreover, Latin alternative bands like Puerto Rican hard-rockers Puya have been playing on tours like Sno-Core and Ozzfest, and opened up for famous groups like the Red Hot Chili Peppers,[100] and by the early 2000s *rock en español* superstars Café Tacuba were touring the US with alternative-rocker Beck.

Nonetheless, although Latin alternative is finally emerging in pop music markets, that does not necessarily mean that it is losing its political edge. As Cobo relates about rock music in Puerto Rico,

> While Puerto Rican rock is as hard to pinpoint as *rock en español* everywhere else — with influences ranging from reggae to hip-hop — the common threads ... are the lyrics, which constantly deal with Puerto Rico's social and political context, and the inclusion of salsa beats.[101]

In 2001, *Billboard* took further notice of landmark events in Latin/o rock as with Brazil's 'Rock in Rio Festival,' the third in fifteen years. Billed as 'the largest rock festival in the world,' the massive festival featured a hundred and fifty US and other international rockers as well as various Brazilian rock acts.[102] Two other such events had occurred in México in the fall of 2000: the 'Encuentro De Titanes' at the massive Azteca Stadium with a capacity for 120,000, and the 'Vive Latino 2000' concert that included various *rock en español* bands.[103]

Another concert series called 'Rock en Ñ' uses the letter 'ñ' from the Spanish alphabet as a symbol of identity and cultural pride. The festival might have been called 'Rock en España' as it tends to feature rock music from Spain. Featuring Latin alternative acts from Spain and playing in the US and México, the tour represents another example of the possibility of Latin/o rock music to communicate socio-political issues related to language, culture, and identity. While Mexican artists in the 1960s emphasized the 'modernity' of their time and place by using English-language apostrophes in their band names — Los Dug Dug's is one example[104] — Spaniards in the new century have come full circle, using the Spanish alphabet's letter ñ as a symbol of their cultural pride and foregrounding it in the title of rock and alternative music shows.

Journalists are further noting how Latin/o rock music is aiding Spaniards in embracing their identity in relation to the rest of Europe. As one journalist explains about the fermentation of rock in Spain, 'Spaniards are losing their fear of rock, which is still seen as mainly Anglo-Saxon, and their shame of being Hispanic in

---

99   Aguilera et al., 'Latin Music 6-Pack: Programming,' para. 6.
100 Cobo, 'Puya: Rocking Harder Than Ever,' para. 5.
101 Ibid., para. 12.
102 Farley, 'Rock and Redemption in Rio'; Farley, 'Rock in Rio, Part 2.'
103 Cobo et al., 'Argentine Folk Rock, L.A. Labels, and a Brazilian Festival.'
104 See Zolov, '*La Onda Chicana*: Mexico's Forgotten Rock Counterculture.'

Europe.'[105] Not only does Latin rock music in Spain include the standard Latin/o rock characteristic of genre blurring and category busting, but Spain's own *mestizaje* (mixture) includes international rock and pop, flamenco, Spanish Celtic influences, Arab/North African sounds, and Mediterranean music. To put it another way, the development of Latin/o rock in the US is not the only example of the radical hybridity of Latino/a culture or Latino/Hispanic identity(ies). Of course, the question of identity is increasingly significant in the context of US Latino/as.

In 2000, one *Billboard* journalist noted the growing number of Latino/a artists releasing music in English, aiming for mainstream markets.[106] Using Latin rhythm and instrumentation with injections of Spanish, this trend is evident in several US Latino/a teen artists partial to making room in the pop mainstream, but it also became part of various *rock en español* songs such as those on Manu Chao's 2001 release, *Proxima Estación: Esperanza*. Similarly, in 2001, Argentine rocker Dante Spinetta Salazar, better known as part of Illya Kuryaki and the Valderramas, was taking English classes and working on a solo effort that mixes Spanish with English.[107] Many more recent releases like Mexican group Kinky's 2003 release, *Atlas*, which contains songs in English like the widely popular 'Airport Feelings' and 'The Headphonist,' reflect this trend in the Latin alternative scene.

One conclusion is that the mixing of English and Spanish is appealing to US Latino/a youth, of second- or third-generation status, because it allows them to merge their heritage with their present place.[108] Among the discovery of US Latino/a teenagers for new markets, other Latin/o rock articulations include lesser-known US rock acts like Vallejo and Calexico. Vallejo come out of the Austin, Texas music scene and include diverse rock influences as well as Tito Puente, Herb Alpert, Santana, and other Latin music,[109] while Calexico's music comes from Tucson, Arizona and combines the aesthetic of western lore with a revision of the Herb Alpert-style of so-called 'amer-iachi' and mixes it with Portuguese *fado*, 'gypsy' music, 1960s surf-rock, American country, Argentine tango, and various Latin American musical influences.[110] One important issue is that US Latino/a artists can actually choose to sing in English or Spanish because labels are finally viewing both as marketable. While popular music is certainly aiding in the maintenance of identity for some US Latino/s, the overall trend appears to be that US Latino/a artists are learning Spanish because they see it as a marketing tool, while Spanish-speaking Latino/as are learning English, probably because they see it as a marketing tool as well. While US pop and rock are still being Latinized in recent years (perhaps just more obviously), music forms like Latin alternative are simultaneously becoming more 'Americanized,' and including more English than ever before.

---

105 Llewellyn, 'Rockers Develop Cultural Confidence.'
106 Cobo, 'Puya: Rocking Harder Than Ever.'
107 Anthony, 'Latin Music 6-Pack,' para. 1.
108 Cobo, 'Latin Crossover's New Twist,' para. 5.
109 From http://www.vallejomusic.com
110 From http://www.casadecalexico.com

In 2001, the *rock en español* tribute phenomenon of previous years took another turn when various groups aligned in homage to *norteño* music stars, Los Tigres del Norte.[111] Billing the compilation as 'the greatest homage to Los Tigres del Norte,' this release featured several *rock en español*/Latin alternative artists like Café Tacuba in addition to Chicano rockers Los Lobos. What is particularly significant about this multigroup tribute to the internationally popular music of Los Tigres del Norte is that two super-bands, one from México (Café Tacuba) and the other from the US (Los Lobos), were paying tribute to a *norteña* group from Sinaloa, México that sings about living in California and the issues concerning Mexicans living in the US as immigrants. As I've mentioned in other research,[112] it is significant that although one group has won Grammy Awards for Mexican American rock and the other has won Latin Grammy Awards for Latin rock/alternative, they can be heard on the same compilation. Seemingly in spite of industry constructs like 'Latin' rock and 'Mexican American' rock as separate categories, Café Tacuba and Los Lobos were paying tribute to an enormously popular band known for its transnational *norteña* music. This is significant, I contend, in that the producers or the musicians themselves appear to be rejecting the differences separating categories such as 'Latin' and 'Mexican American' within marketing constructs of the music industry and other media messages.

Noting the cultural significance and 'symbolic capital' of Los Tigres del Norte, Saldívar writes:

> Los Tigres del Norte's border music is simultaneously national and transnational in that it affects everyday life in the local (Silicon Valley) region and thematizes the limits of the national perspective in American studies. In the story of Los Tigres del Norte's discrepant crossings, we can discover the shifting pattern of un/documented circulations, resistances, and negotiations.[113]

Perhaps more importantly, such collaborations by Los Lobos, Café Tacuba, and others can be understood in terms of the subject matter and references to borders, migration, assimilation patterns by US Latino/as, the hegemony of English, and a segregated society, to name just a few.[114] Given that Los Tigres del Norte are well known in the US Latino/a communities in the West, Southwest, and Midwest, as well as in México, Cuba, and other places in Latin America, it should not be surprising that various groups and musicians of the Latin rock diaspora came together on such a tribute. Aside from its reverence for Los Tigres del Norte, one song, 'Jefe de Jefes,' plays on the range of early rock 'n' roll through brief musical allusions to Cannibal and the Headhunters (LA Chicano rockers from the 1960s) as well as The Beatles ('British invasion' rockers) — demonstrating their own awareness

---

111 For more on the significance of Los Tigres del Norte for Latino/a communities in the US, see Saldívar's *Border Matters*.
112 Avant-Mier, 'Of Rocks and Nations: *Voces Rockeras* (Popular Music Voices) and the Discourse of Nationality.'
113 Saldívar, *Border Matters*, 3.
114 Ibid., 1–8.

of rock music's dialogue with Latino/as and revealing further connections within the Latin/o rock diaspora. Interestingly, CD liner notes invoke the Spanish phrase 'el pueblo' (the people) and 'rock latino.' Thus, this tribute serves as yet another example of broader Latino/a identities being imagined and communicated, rather than being limited by genre labels like *rock en español*, Chicano rock, Mexican American rock, and 'Latin music.'

Furthermore, the discursive articulation of Los Lobos to other contemporary Latin alternative bands and artists is highly significant given that Los Lobos are otherwise connected to other Chicano rock bands from the 1970s, such as Little Joe y La Familia, El Chicano, Tierra, and other East LA bands.[115] Just as Los Lobos are often connected to those 1970s-era bands, their association with contemporary *rock en español* and Latin alternative bands marks another rupture in the mainstream narrative of rock music that separates US Latino/as from other Latin Americans, and registers another reconnection between US Latino/as and other Latin Americans, and such an association provides another discursive link in which contemporary Latin alternative music is connected to the cultural issues and identity politics that US Chicano/as and Latino/as faced in decades prior as well as in the present.

Conclusion

This chapter has traced various elements of the Latin/o rock diaspora, such as the growth of rock music in Argentina and its related politics and cultural significance, and the various Latin/o articulations to punk-rock's 'first wave' which includes various Latino/a connections, influences, and even significant bands/artists that were part of the original punk-rock moment and even went on to have success as they moved beyond punk and came into Chicano and/or Latino consciousness. In another section of this chapter, I discussed how other popular artists of the 1990s such as various alternative rock bands like Jane's Addiction, Concrete Blonde, Nirvana, Beck, Red Hot Chili Peppers, Cypress Hill, and The Pixies revealed their own dialogues with Latino/a culture(s) (in addition to others like the Beastie Boys, Nirvana, Sublime, and Rage Against the Machine, which I discussed in previous chapters). Meanwhile, Hollywood films had also picked up on this fashion and used many *rock en español* groups in their film soundtracks. Likewise, many *rock en español* groups continued their own dialogues with mainstream rock and US culture through various individual tributes and tribute compilations, and these examples demonstrate reversals of sort in which *rock en español* was being recontextualized by mainstream US artists.

By the mid 1990s, the '*rock en tu idioma*' marketing campaign that featured the predominance of Mexican rock bands had yielded to the term *rock en español*, and for the first time began to include rock bands produced in places like Chile and Colombia. By the late 1990s, changes occurred and Mexican bands once again dominated *rock en español* scenes, although rock's place in Mexican culture was

---

115　See for example, Loza, 'Assimilation, Reclamation, and Rejection of the Nation-State by Chicano Musicians,' 140–3.

solidified enough that local scenes were developing, and bands were coming from locales outside of the Mexico City metropolis as they had been previously.[116] By the end of the 1990s, various *rock en español* groups were included in CD compilations alongside Chicano/a rockers and many other non-Latino/a musicians and artists, in what can be seen as the breaking-down of ethnic, cultural, national, linguistic, and even ideological barriers. Another important event saw the rise of Latina women in the Latin/o rock diaspora. The result was an intricate network of articulations providing insights into identity and cultural politics.

In sum, what came about in the 1990s was a growing self-awareness of the larger Latin/o rock diaspora, an awareness that, perhaps paradoxically, communicated politics of unity as much as it communicated politics of difference. In other words, what the Latin/o rock diaspora signaled was that although Latino/a people are marked by differences and discontinuities, there were instances of continuities and contexts in popular music that register and reveal some similarities and suggest new possibilities for emerging and future Latino/a identities — identities that are increasingly based on rampant bilingualism or multilingualism (and thus, multiculturalism), an internationalist orientation, inherent transnationalism, and intercultural communication.

Finally, it is helpful to close this chapter with a brief return to the driving theme in this book. Since the worldwide rise of nation-states reached its apex in the 1800s and early 1900s, it is no wonder that such numerous transnational productions such as those presented here (and the identities they evidence and register) are still viewed as coincidental, unimportant, marginal, and insignificant. Like punk(s), intercultural expressions in the Latin/o rock diaspora are ever-present, in spite of the fact that they remain ignored and seen as worthless by monolingual and ethnocentric journalists and cultural analysts in the mainstream. In other words, Latin/o rock productions are also significant because they symbolize and emblematize the inherently transnational 'punks' that Latino/as represent in their respective national contexts.

---

116 Padilla, 'Rocking in Mexico: Bands Continue to Struggle with Radio's and Labels' Attitudes,' paras. 8–9; See also Kun, 'File Under: Post-Mexico,' 275.

Interludio 5° (fifth interlude)

In another transnational, cross-cultural tribute, in 2001, México's El Gran Silencio released *Chuntaros Radio Poder* that included a track titled 'La Chicana,' a song about a Mexico City guy who wishes to go back to 'Califas' (California) to see his 'Chicana' (Mexican American girlfriend). Meanwhile, a bonus track on the album was 'Dejenme Si Estoy Llorando,' a cover of a 1970s hit by a pop-ballad group from Chile called Los Angeles Negros.[1] Yet another transnational homage occurred in the 2003 *Tributo a José Alfredo Jiménez* compilation, which was dedicated to the internationally famous Mexican *ranchera* songwriter. This release followed the release of *Volcán: Tributo a José José* in 1998. The significance of all of these recent releases is that they refashioned the previous trend of paying tribute to British and North American rockers. By the late 1990s and into the new millennium, various Latin/o rock artists were also acknowledging their own national heroes and other artists, singers, bands, and influences from other Latin American nations.

Continuing such dialogues between Latin/o rock dialogue and Anglo-American rock, musician/producer David Byrne augmented his own connections to the Latin/o rock diaspora. Byrne's *Look Into The Eyeball* album (2001) had Byrne singing in Spanish on an all-Spanish song, 'Desconocido Soy,' along with the lead singer of Café Tacuba. Noting all of these trends in the Latin/o rock diaspora, a 2001 *Billboard* article astutely declared that 'eclecticism is the name of the game' in Latin rock music.[2]

Also in 2001, singer/artist Manu Chao, who became famous throughout many parts of the world in the 1990s through his pop/reggae/rock/folkloric fusions, released a landmark album with *Próxima Estación: Esperanza*. With roots in France and Spain, it is not surprising that songs like 'Me Gustas Tú' had bilingual lyrics in Spanish and French, but the song lyrics also referenced Cuba, El Salvador, Nicaragua, and Guatemala, and included jargonistic words and phrases from various Latin American Spanish dialects, some of which translate across cultures and some that don't. Another song on the album, titled 'Chinita,' spoke of '*chinitas*' (Asian girls/women) and '*negritas*' (Black girls/women), signifying the intercultural and interracial aspects of Latin/o experiences. As Lipsitz has noted about 'Chinito Chinito,' which was written by the great *pachuco* icon Don Tosti in the 1940s and covered decades later by Ry Cooder in 2005, references such as

---

1   Padilla, 'Rocking in Mexico: Bands Continue to Struggle with Radio's and Labels' Attitudes,' para. 14.
2   Aguilera et al., 'Latin Music 6-Pack,' para. 11.

these evidence the proximity of cultures and how 'proximity permeates' cultural productions such as song and popular music.[3]

Characteristic eclecticism and intercultural influence were further proven true when another 2001 soundtrack to the Hollywood film *Crazy/Beautiful* featured various Anglo-American artists, several *rock en español* artists, and the Chicano rappers Delinquent Habits with Cuban American rapper Mellow Man Ace.[4] The soundtrack to the widely acclaimed Mexican film of the same name, *Y Tu Mamá También* (2002) was another significant release. This soundtrack included various Latin alternative artists and musicians, signaling the growing relevance of Latin alternative artists in popular culture, but it also included other non-Latin artists and musicians such as Brian Eno, Frank Zappa, and others. The compilation also featured 'La Tumba Será El Final' by Flaco Jiménez (a Tex-Mex/*tejano* music accordionist) in addition to various other North American artists, Mexican bands, and rapper La Mala Rodríguez from Spain. One particularly significant connection was a song by La Revolución De Emiliano Zapata, one of México's classic rock bands from the 1970s, potentially reviving interest in Mexican rock bands of previous decades, but more importantly, discursively linking Mexican rock's past to Mexican rock's present as well to a diasporic Latino/a present and future.

Like that film's musical score, the soundtrack to *Once Upon a Time in Mexico* (2003) featured Manu Chao and US Chicano Tito Larriva as well as other Anglo-Americans, Chicano/as and Latino/as. Another contributor was Brian Setzer, frontman of The Stray Cats as well as The Brian Setzer Orchestra, who covered the Spanish-guitar flamenco classic 'Malagueña' (which has been covered by various others throughout rock history), thereby making the *Once Upon a Time in Mexico* soundtrack a French/Spanish/US Chicano/Mexican/Latino/Anglo-American cultural production. Another new millennium example, and significant Latin alternative release, came from México's Café Tacvba (also known as Café Tacuba, with the interchangeable letters 'u' and 'v') when they released *Valle Callampa* (EP) that featured cover versions of famous songs by Chilean band Los Tres. Josh Kun observes the importance of this tribute effort that articulates Café Tacvba to Los Tres and thus, México to Chile (and elsewhere in Latin America), noting that Café Tacvba redefines what it means to be Mexican — voicing a transnational musical identity — by suggesting new meanings for *rock en español* and Latin alternative music that articulate a transnational present and simultaneously recognizing an already transnational past.

Selective Discography and Tracks Listed Here and in Chapter Five

At the Drive-In. 'Rascuache,' *Vaya* (Fearless Records, 1999).
Aterciopelados. 'Baracunátana,' *La Pipa de La Paz* (BMG Music, 1996).
Bersuit (Vergarabat). 'Yo Tomo,' *Libertinaje* (Universal Latino, 1999).
Café Tacuba. 'Esa Noche,' *Re* (WEA Latina, 1994).
_____. 'La Chica Banda,' *Café Tacuba* (Warner Music, 1992).

---

3 Lipsitz, *Foosteps in the Dark*, 51.
4 For an excellent analysis of the intersection of Chicano/as, *Chicanismo*, and rap music, see Delgado, 'Chicano Ideology Revisited: Rap Music and the (Re)Articulation of Chicanismo.'

Concrete Blonde y Los Illegals. *Concrete Blonde y Los Illegals* (Ark 21, 1997).
Cypress Hill. *Los Grandes Éxitos en Español* (Sony, 1999).
Los Enanitos Verdes. 'Tequila,' *Nectar* (Polygram, 1999).
Los Fabulosos Cadillacs. 'Mal Bicho,' 'Strawberry Fields Forever,' *Rey Azucar* (Sony International, 1995).
El Gran Silencio. 'La Chicana,' *Chuntaros Radio Poder* (EMI International, 2001).
Jane's Addiction. 'Stop,' *Ritual de lo Habitual* (Warner Bros. Records, 1990).
Los Lobos. 'Cumbia Raza,' *This Time* (Hollywood Records, 1999).
Malo. 'Suavecito,' *Malo* (Warner Bros. Records, 1972).
Manu Chao. 'Me Gustas Tú,' *Próxima Estación: Esperanza* (Virgin, 2001).
Os Mutantes. 'Baby,' *Everything is Possible!* (Luaka Bop, 1999).
The Pixies. 'Vamos,' *Surfer Rosa* (4AD, 1988).
Tijuana NO! 'Spanish Bombs,' *Transgresores de la Ley* (RCA International, 1995).
Vallejo. 'Rock Americano,' *Stereo* (VMG Records, 2002).
Various artists. *Crazy/Beautiful* [motion picture soundtrack] (Hollywood Records, 2001).
_____. *El Mas Grande Homenaje a Los Tigres del Norte* (Fonovisa, 2001).
_____. *Once Upon A Time In Mexico* [motion picture soundtrack] (Milan, 2003).
_____. *Outlandos D'Americas: A Rock en Español Tribute to The Police* (ARK 21, 1998).
_____. *Red Hot + Latin: Silencio = Muerte* (Hola, 1997).
_____. *Star Maps* [motion picture soundtrack] (Geffen Records, 1997).
_____. *Tributo a The Cure (por que no puedo ser tú)* (WEA International/Warner Music Latina, 1999).
_____. *Tributo a José Alfredo Jiménez* (RCA International, 2003).
_____. *Tributo a Queen: Los Grandes del Rock en Español* (Hollywood Records, 1997).
_____. *Y Tu Mamá También* [motion picture soundtrack] (Volcano, 2002).
Voodoo Glow Skulls. *Firme* (Epitaph, 1995).

Conclusion

Alter-Latino: The Latin/o Rock Diaspora and New *Latinidades*

In many cases, the original references to third-world scenarios by first-world musicians are playfully inverted or alluded to as an implicit ideological contestation of certain identitarian constructions ... [and] the adoption and deconstruction of musical genres and styles imported from modern metropolises often amounts to 'cannibalization' of cultural hierarchies, as these serve as the medium for the expression of political resistance and cultural difference.[1]

Nuestras diferencias somos. Nuestras diferencias somos ... No hay pureza ... No hay pureza.[2]

In late 2007, an all-female punk-rock band from San Antonio, Texas called Girl In A Coma released their debut album which included the song 'Clumsy Sky,' a song that became a major hit in its own right but also benefited from exposure from the accompanying video for the song. Directed by Jim Mendiola, the brilliant video places the all-female punk band in their hometown of San Antonio in what seems like a divey, old-timer's *tejano*-music bar where Tejano, Chicano, and Mexican American men are most likely to go. As the video begins, the camera focuses on old black-and-white photos of singers/performers with accordions and other *tejano* music artists, as if to suggest the nature of the place and the culture that it nurtures. Also notable in the camera shots are prominent male figures such as the tough-looking male bartender and another man with forearm tattoos who sits at a table, waiting to watch the show that is about to begin.

As the video's narrative progresses, the emphasis shifts to the performance of the song, and the videographic shots of the old-timers become interspersed with images of younger people wearing obviously different clothes, one of whom has a high-standing Mohawk haircut, at which an old-timer cannot help from staring. The video includes a typical objectification of a young woman, in a revealing, short green dress, who is dancing alone and seems to be performing solely for

---

1   Corona and Madrid, *Postnational Musical Identities: Cultural Production, Distribution, and Consumption in a Globalized Scenario*, 16.
2   Lyrical excerpt from Maldita Vecindad's 'Salta Pa' Tras'; see chapter's discography.

the viewer's gaze. However, a narrative disruption occurs when another camera shot reveals the same woman affectionately holding another woman, suggesting a lesbian relationship and, thus, homosexual, erotic desire. Given that the band includes the publicly 'out' lesbian Jenn Alva, the video's narrative suggests a strong statement about the sexual politics of a new generation of Tejanos, Mexican Americans, and young Latino/as who no longer remain suppressed and oppressed by the sexual mores of either mainstream American culture or other conservative Mexican values. Moreover, the all-female band's presence in the *tejano* bar also makes a feminist statement in which the female punks conduct a literal takeover of the (predominantly male) *tejano* music club, as well as a metaphorical takeover of what it means to make Tex-Mex music.

A sort of resolution occurs toward the video's conclusion on two levels. On one hand, the camera shots of the two females holding hands are interspersed with shots of other youth, including heterosexual couples, who are dancing wildly to the hard, loud, and fast rock music. Following these scenes, the video concludes as a black-and-white snapshot of Girl In A Coma gets tacked onto the wall, alongside the other (much older) *tejano* artists, resolving a generational difference and placing Girl In A Coma among other musicians, bands, and artists who have played in that club. The brilliance of such a video lies in the fact that the identity disruptions are working on different levels — ethnic, generational, gender, and sexual orientation.

As I further demonstrate in the rest of this final discussion, mediated productions such as these are important discursive registers given that music (and videos) by bands such as Girl In A Coma signify the cultural politics of a new generation of Tejano/Chicano/Mexican American/Latino youth, who more than ever include rock music in their musical expressions, and, in this case, include the punk-rock ethos in their personal identity politics, without suffering any identity confusion. Moreover, such statements are more significant when considering the sexual, gender, generational, and other identity disruptions that are being announced through popular music discourse(s), as well as the changing nature of Latino/a identity signifiers that are being represented in such examples.

In the following sections of this conclusion, I will briefly describe some internet sites related to Latin/o rock music, where shifts in Latino/a identities can also be monitored. The following section describes some more of the dialogue(s) that characterize the Latin/o rock diaspora, and, in the final discussion, I revisit some of the main arguments within this book project and address some necessary caveats and qualifications in order to conclude this study of Latin/o rock music and Latino/a identity(ies).

Latin/o Rock On-line

In a final layer of analysis, this investigation turns to how some internet sites, specifically music-content websites, are demonstrating the shifts in Latin/o cultural productions with regard to Latino/a identity(ies). One such music-content website is www.batanga.com (henceforth, '*Batanga*'), which, along with its accompanying music magazine that features music news and information on new releases, has

Conclusion

been a major promoter for various Latin music genres in the 2000s. With the ability to click on any of several choices of 'Latin' music to stream over the internet, it also allows users to click on a music 'station.' While this option is telling enough in that *rock en español* and *rock alternativo* are actually choices among various Latin music options, the significance of *Batanga* goes further. In my own experimentations with *Batanga* and what the website offers, I discovered that on the *rock alternativo* station, one is just as likely to hear music by US Latino/as (e.g., Austin, Texas band Vallejo) in addition to established *rock en español* stars from México, Argentina, and other Latin American nations (e.g., México's Café Tacuba and Argentina's Enanitos Verdes). While such a realization might have been surprising and perhaps not even possible in previous decades, I contend that such trends are the result of the increasing conflation of *lo Latino* (Latino/a cultural productions) with *lo Latinoamericano* (other Latin American cultural productions).

Another music-related website, www.ritmolatino.com (henceforth, *Ritmo Latino*), was essentially a mere web presence, a supplementary tool, for a semi-weekly radio program featuring 'Latino' music hits. Although the *Ritmo Latino* program did exist in the form of an actual radio program, its greatest utility was perhaps in the form of a recurring podcast (portable broadcast), which users could set to automatically download from the internet to their personal computer and then to their portable mp3 player. Through receiving the (free) *Ritmo Latino* podcasts, one could both appreciate classic Latin American music that ranged from México to virtually every country throughout Latin America, but also keep abreast of recent hits in Latin/o pop music (which often included *rock en español* and Latin alternative hit songs) from the 1990s and even current hits and trends in the 2000s. As with other sites like *Batanga*, the *Ritmo Latino* program would often include US Latino/a artists alongside their Latin American counterparts, and, thus, further demonstrates the implicit association of US Latino/as with other Latin Americans.

Yet another significant music-related production that emerged in recent years was 'Rock en Rebelión' (Rock in Rebellion), a weekly radio program from Berkeley, California's KPFA with two accompanying websites — www.kpfa.org/rock-en-rebelion and www.myspace.com/rockenrebelión. In this program, we see once again the articulation of US Latino/a rock music to Latin American rock music. Moreover, various examples reveal more about the flexibility and alterability of Latino/a identity(ies). For example, in the program broadcast on 30 October 2008, *Rock en Rebelión* discussed and played music by bands and artists from México but also included music from Cordero, a New York City-based band that fuses rock music with Spanish lyrics and traditional Latin music sounds, as well as Rupa and the April Fishes, a band from San Fransisco's Mission District. In the same broadcast they included music by A Polka Madre, a band of México City musicians and various other European musicians. The *Rock en Rebelión* broadcast also included a song by Kumbia Queers, a tribute to Robert Smith of The Cure that springs from the goth subculture in México City and elsewhere throughout México. Including bands like Kumbia Queers is significant, on one hand because they are made up of musicians from both México and Argentina, demonstrating

Rock en Rebelión radio program

intercultural and transnational collaboration, but on the other hand, including Kumbia Queers illuminates changes in Mexican youth culture that is more accepting of GLBT people and identities than previous generations. In this sense, Latin alternative music can be seen as a potentially liberating cultural force for GLBT people and issues that might otherwise remain repressed in different Latin American cultures, and it signifies emerging Latin American identities that are being influenced by US Latino/as and other cultures and nations.

In another broadcast on 4 January 2009, the *Rock en Rebelión* radio program included more rock and Latin alternative bands from México, such as the popular group Zoé, but also included a song by Monte Negro (an LA-based, US Latino band with an Asian American guitarist) who perform bilingual songs such as their 2008 hit song 'Me Duele No Estar Junto a Ti.' The same broadcast also included other songs by Los Fabulosos Cadillacs (from Argentina) and Manu

Chao (from France), lyrical 'shout-outs' to Panama, Guatemala, and Paraguay, and another song by Salvador y Los Leones (with origins in Spain). In further discursive twists, the same program highlighted a new release titled *Chicha Libre*, a compilation that historicizes the 1960s/1970s mix of psychedelic-rock influences with traditional Peruvian music (known as *chicha*) throughout Peru and other parts, calling it the 'Amazon sound.'[3] In more pronounced interculturalism and internationalism, the broadcast included songs by Cambodian rock band Dengue Fever and a new release by 'Las Rayas Blancas' (otherwise known as The White Stripes in the English-speaking world) in which singer Jack White sings the 2007 hit song 'Conquest' in Spanish (to which I alluded in a previous chapter). Re-titled 'Conquista,' the 2008 version in Spanish provided Latin alternative music fans with another link between North American rock music and Latin America's popular rock music.

Another new website, www.rockenhouston.com (hereafter, *Rock en Houston*), began as 'a forum to discuss events and shows,' and serves as an organizing space for the increasing numbers of Houston-area youth who identify with *rock en español* music and the Latin alternative movement. Moreover, such internet spaces like *Rock en Houston* further indicate how on-line communities are being formed around Latin/o rock music and how such expressions are springing from, as well as contributing to, the corresponding identities of youth with altered perceptions of themselves as well as their musical identities and expressions.

From on-line discursive space(s) — internet websites, radio programs, and podcasts — one can logically conclude that the boundaries between genres such as Latin rock (or, *rock en español*) and other, virtually indescribable, US-based Latin/o rock subgenres are increasingly untenable. Moreover, current trends and new bands and artists, as well as their cultural productions, demonstrate an ardent multiculturalist orientation and transnationalist bent, and through allowing space for differentiation in gender and sexual orientations, is always open to re-signification and alters the way we can conceive of contemporary Latino/a identity(ies). In other words, discursive spaces such as these can be understood as registers of the changes and transformations in culture and in contemporary (and future) Latino/a identity(ies). In the following section, I return to musical productions (songs, albums, lyrics, and bands/artists) in order to further illustrate such changes and the transformations in Latino/a identity(ies) that are happening in the 2000s.

The Latin/o Rock Dialogue(s) Continued

Moving forward from where I left off in the previous chapter, 2003 brought the release of Tommy Guerrero's third album, *Soul Food Taqueria*. Guerrero became famous in the 1980s through skateboarding fame, although, like many other Latino/as, he turned his attention toward punk-rock music. By the late 1990s, however, Tommy Guerrero had resurfaced in popular culture with his unique style

---

3 For more on *chicha* music and its rock music elements, see Bullen, '*Chicha* in the Shanty Towns of Arequipa, Peru,' 232.

of smooth, surf-rock/soul-jazz instrumental music, and his *Soul Food Taqueria* album was ranked #2 by *Rolling Stone* in the best albums of 2003.

Meanwhile, another important 2003 release came from Los Lonely Boys who achieved considerable commercial and critical success with their self-titled album through songs like 'Heaven' and 'Nobody Else,' which have been called some of the most memorable songs of that year and of the decade, and still benefit from consistent radio airplay. Interestingly, the three brothers from San Angelo, Texas were aided in their quest to become musicians by their father, a native Texan 'Chicano' who himself had tried to break into mainstream popular music decades earlier, although to no avail. Thus, when the Garza brothers (i.e., Los Lonely Boys) reached international fame in 2003 and 2004, they were continuing a family's decades-long commitment to popular music, and specifically to country and rock 'n' roll. Moreover, their 2003 *Los Lonely Boys* debut included English/Spanish code-switching songs like 'Señorita' and 'Dime Mi Amor' as well as all-Spanish ballads like 'La Contestación,' which, except for the slight Texas lilt of the Garza brothers, sounds like it could have come from anywhere in Latin America.

Meanwhile, the same album also included other Spanish songs such 'Heaven (en Español),' an all-Spanish translation of what is arguably their biggest hit, almost as if the Garza brothers always knew how famous they would become and as if they just assumed that the popularity of 'Heaven' would reach across oceans and continents. Another track on their debut album, titled 'Onda,' seems to be a tribute to the 1970s Latin rock of Carlos Santana and other West Coast rock bands but picks up on the very word, '*Onda*' (the wave), that at once signifies the growth of rock 'n' roll in México,[4] the literary movement that I alluded to in Chapter four that connects México's youth counter-culture to rock music,[5] as well as the late 1960s/early 1970s wave in *tejano* music that was influenced by the politics of the US Chicano movement.[6] Exactly which 'wave' Los Lonely Boys is referencing in this song is unclear; given the evidence provided in this book, it could be more than one! However, given such bilingual, bicultural, and transnational propensities, it should be no wonder that Los Lonely Boys are responsible for such significant musical expressions. As other examples, Los Brothers Garza also cut a cover of the Johnny Cash classic 'I Walk the Line' in 2004 (translating some of the final lines into Spanish); a cover of John Lennon's 'Whatever Gets You Through the Night' on a Lennon-inspired political/humanitarian effort in 2007; and a cover of the José Feliciano classic 'Feliz Navidad' in 2008. The Garza brothers, in other words, single-handedly seem to be referencing different aspects of Latin-inspired or Latin-connected songs from decades earlier — all of which symbolize prior articulations of rock music to Latino/as.

Another Latin/o rock link exists with the band Calexico, an indie-rock/

---

4 In *Refried Elvis*, for example, Zolov refers to *Onda* simply as the new wave of Mexican rock, although resisting the connection to *Onda* as a literary and counter-cultural movement.
5 See my Chapter four on the connection between *La Onda* in Mexican literature and *La Onda* in rock 'n' roll music by México's El TRI.
6 In *Música Tejana*, for example, Peña is only referring to the Texas 'Chicano' wave of the late 1960s/early 1970s.

alternative/country-rock act out of Tuscon, Arizona, and a band that has had its own dialogue with traditional Mexican and Latin American music since the 1990s and emerged in the 2000s as an immensely popular indie-rock band. With the release of 'Corona,' from 2004's *Convict Pool*, Calexico connected themselves to the Minutemen, another famous 'indie-rock' and 'indie-punk' band from the 1980s that are said to have influenced many of the grunge-rockers, indie-rockers, and alterna-rockers of the 1990s. For example, the original 'Corona,' by the Minutemen, is an otherwise forgotten punk-rock song from 1984's *Double Nickels on the Dime* that suggests a North American's reflections on poverty in México and Latin America and perhaps even sympathy for a poor Mexican woman. However, the song is actually famous for the opening ten seconds of guitar strumming, which became the opening music for MTV's comedy-stunt show *Jackass* and the movies that followed. When Calexico covered 'Corona' in 2004, however, they transformed the famous opening riffs into an acoustic strum that resonated like Spanish guitar, and followed with loud fiddles and blaring trumpets instantly recognizable as *ranchera* (or, *mariachi*) music. Thus, in their cover of the classic 1980s song by the revered and influential Minutemen, Calexico provides a more tangible Latin/o connection but also displays 'ruptures' and simultaneous 'recombinations'[7] that are layered with meaning and laden with significance for rock music's ongoing dialogue with Latino/as and Latin/o cultures.

In addition to their own Spanish songs and Latin-inflected musical productions throughout the 1990s and 2000s, Calexico have even participated in the *Heard it on the X* (the tribute to the heydays of 'border radio') with Los Super Seven in 2005, and contributed to the Gotan Project through collaborations with musicians from Argentina and others on songs such as the all-Spanish 'Amor Porteño' from the album *Lunático* in 2006. The Gotan Project (whose name is a variation on 'tango') is a contemporary indie music project that may be single-handedly reviving tango music with North American and other youth through their indie-rock, electronica, folk, and tango amalgamations. Otherwise, Calexico furthers their Latin/o rock connections through various other recent recordings such as 'Roka,' sometimes called 'Roka (Danza de la Muerte),' with Spanish singer Amparo Sanchez from Calexico's *Garden Ruin* (2006) album. Perhaps beloved for their ability to turn their indie-rock, country-rock sounds into an excellent *mariachi*-rock composition, Calexico is also forging its dialogue with Latin/o music through songs like 'Victor Jara's Hands' and 'El Gatillo (Trigger Revisited)' from *Carried To Dust* in 2008, contemporary music from Spain (e.g., 2009's *DePedro*), and the many other Latin-inflected or Latin-influenced songs in their repertoire.

Aside from the many Anglo-Americans, like the Minutemen, Calexico, and Jack White (among many others), who are creating their own Latin/o rock music, there are many more Latino/a musicians who are pushing ahead with the union of Latin music and rock. For example, in 2004 the band Cordero, led by Ani Cordero, released their debut album, *Somos Cordero*, which fused indie-rock/alternative-rock in English to Latin American songs and rhythms and several

---

7   Ibid., 77.

Cordero. Photo by: Cody Ranaldo

songs in Spanish. With connections to Georgia, *Somos Cordero* revealed collaborations with Latino musicians as well as with the Antibalas Afrobeat Orchestra. Cordero has since become part of the New York indie-rock scene and continue to produce innovative indie-rock/Latin fusions, although their most recent effort, *De Donde Eres* in 2008, was all in Spanish. Through such musical expressions, bands like Cordero subvert the very notions of genres at the same time that they disrupt traditional (and fixed) notions of Latino/a identity.[8]

Another example came when The Mars Volta burst onto the indie-rock scene in 2003. The band's two primary members are Puerto Rican Omar Rodríguez-Lopez and Chicano Cedric Bixler-Zavála, who were both part of the lauded band At the Drive-In that was being touted in the 1990s as the next Nirvana. As The Mars Volta (which includes some African American band members) the two set out to make music that was closer to their Latino roots, and released *De-Loused in the Comatorium* in 2003 which included the instrumental song 'Tírame A Las Arañas' and signaled the Spanish/English and jazz/acid-rock/Latin sounds that would make the band famous. With their 2005 follow-up release *Frances the Mute*, The Mars Volta exemplified their Latin rock fusion(s) through songs like 'L'Via L'Viaquez' (a collaboration with famed salsa musician Larry Harlow) and through occasional Spanish songs. Other subsequent releases, however, have nearly indistinguishable Latin elements and no songs in Spanish. Through musical expression that sometimes emphasizes their bilingual and bicultural Latino roots and sometimes does not, The Mars Volta have achieved widespread fame and

---

8   In an interesting connection, the current lineup of Cordero also includes the nephew of Frankie Lymon, who became famous in the 1960s with The Teenagers, revealing yet another layer of (generational) Latin rock articulations.

a cult-status so rare that they retain indie-rock credibility in spite of benefiting from signing with a major label and garnering worldwide attention as a significant indie-rock/alternative/prog-rock band.

Another significant 2005 production came from Los Lobos, who released a live recording, *Acoustic En Vivo*, which listed 'Mexico Americano' among it's other popular greatest-hits tracks. While the bilingual title itself signifies the extent of Los Lobos' bicultural, hybrid productions, the song 'Mexico Americano' features (Spanish) lyrics that describe the experience of being both 'Mexican' and 'American' and suggest a new identity marker ('Mexico Americano' or, Mexico American in English) that makes explicit the contradictions of being bilingual, bicultural, and binational. Interestingly, the album also includes a version of the traditional Mexican *ranchera* song 'Volver, Volver' (which has been covered by various artists for many decades, including Los Lobos themselves prior to this). This latest version of 'Volver, Volver' by Los Lobos, however, moves away from the sounds of typical Mexican *ranchera* music and blends it with a honking saxophone and oldies/doo wop resonance, suggesting a significantly hybrid, oldies-*ranchera*-doo-wop sound — and a quintessential 'Chicano' production with various 'Latino' layers.

Another significant statement came from Pistolera, another New York-based indie-rock band bent on singing in Spanish and combining traditional Mexican music with rock attitude. The band is led by Sandra Velasquez (born in San Diego), who states that her intentions with the band's music is to recreate a sense of Mexican culture and identity in New York,[9] and also names classic-rock and alternative-rock influences such as Led Zeppelin, Pink Floyd, The Smiths, Mudhoney, and Nirvana.[10] Noting how many songs have a political edge, the band's 2006 release, *Siempre Hay Salida*, featured 'Cazador,' addressing 'hunters' such as Arizona's 'minutemen' vigilante group who patrols the border and searches for undocumented travelers and immigrants. The song 'Cazador' tells them to go home, while 'Extranjero,' from *En Este Camino* (2008), is a statement of frustration about being asked about where they are from or why they always sing in Spanish, as well as a reminder that all Americans are immigrants.[11] In recent years Pistolera has played in various parts of the world and in significant venues such as the Latin Alternative Music Conference as well as Austin's South By Southwest music festival, which increasingly features Latin/o rock, Latin alternative, and other bands and artists in another era would have been called *rock en español*.

Another release in 2006 came from Rodrigo y Gabriela, who released their self-titled album to worldwide acclaim, international fame, and a story that could only be described as a pop culture phenomenon. The Mexican duo performs a style of instrumental, acoustic-guitar rock music that one might call flamenco or Spanish-guitar. However, Rodrigo and Gabriela have instead called their music 'heavy metal,' and even nod toward their heavy metal influences through cover

---

9   Pistolera also includes the aforementioned Ani Cordero of Cordero fame.
10   See Smith, 'Banda Meets Ska Meets The Smiths in the Sound of Pistolera.'
11   See Capistrano, '9 to 5'ers by Day, Rock Stars By Night.'

Pistolera. Photo by: Hector Vasquez

songs, such as 'Stairway To Heaven' covering the Led Zeppelin classic, and their cover of 'Orion,' originally by the quintessential heavy metal band Metallica. More notable than the fact this Mexican duo that performs Spanish-guitar, flamenco-rock instrumentals claims heavy metal as a genre, is the fact that the band is based in Ireland. In other words, while *Gitano* culture gave the world the Gipsy Kings, and Texas gave the rock world Del Castillo, México and the rest of the Latin rock diaspora (and even Ireland) can now also claim Rodrigo y Gabriela. Interestingly, all of these articulate Latino/as to rock music through an acoustic-guitar sound that often conjures Spanish flamenco music.

Conclusion

Meanwhile, another 2006 production was a promotional compact disc release for the 'Brotherhood Tour' called *The Brotherhood Compilation*. This compilation featured music by Los Lonely Boys (the brothers performing Texas-Chicano rock/pop/country), Ozomátli (the internationally famous, multicultural ensemble from LA), Calexico (Arizona-based alternative/indie-rock), Del Castillo (another set of Texas brothers with a prominent Spanish flamenco-guitar sound), Vallejo (yet another set of Texas brothers from the Austin, Texas scene), Kinky (*rock en español*/Latin alternative from Monterrey, México), and other artists. The Vallejo contribution to *The Brotherhood Compilation* was the song 'Rock Americano' with lyrics that described being 'half American' and 'half Chicano.' Interestingly, the Vallejo brothers have roots in Guatemala and México, thus signifying a 'Chicano' identity that could also be considered 'Latino.' Moreover, while the tour/compilation's moniker 'Brotherhood' obviously stemmed from the different sets of brothers that were included, the double entendre was such that various Latinos, from different Latin American backgrounds, were discursively linked to symbolic 'brothers' from México and music from México, Latin America, and Spain, as well as to other non-Latino 'brothers' who are famous for their musical articulations of Latin American music and culture,[12] and even other multi-ethnic and multicultural sensibilities.

The same Vallejo brothers had covered 'Mexican Radio' as a bonus track on their 2002 *Stereo* album, a somewhat forgotten song (with memorable lines about being 'south of the border' in Tijuana, 'eating barbecued iguana') that was originally made famous in the 1980s by Wall of Voodoo through heavy rotation on MTV, giving the song another level of significance since the new version was done by 'Chicanos' from Texas. By 2007, however, the band Kinky (from the exploding music scene in Monterrey, México)[13] released *Sassy* (EP), which included their own cover of 'Mexican Radio.' In the 2007 version, however, Kinky added more than just an obscure lyrical reference to Mexican radio — they translated the English lyrics to Spanish and added Spanish verses to re-signify 'Mexican Radio' as a *rock en español* or Latin alternative expression. Without knowledge of the song's historical significance, Kinky's version must have come off as a fresh, new Latin alternative production. However, given the song's origins in US popular music, Kinky demonstrated the familiarity that *rock en español* and Latin alternative bands/artists have with North American popular music as well as a shared, decades-long popular music history between México and the United States.

Also in 2007, indie-rock and 'freak-folk' sensation Devendra Banhart, a Texas-born American who grew up in Venezuela and is bilingual, released *Smokey Rolls Down Thunder Canyon*, and has since gone on to achieve widespread popularity and international fame as an indie-rock and 'freak-folk' star. While his 2007 issue included the popular song 'Carmensita' — with Spanish lyrics, prominent congas,

---

12   It is worth noting that the non-Latino 'brothers' were Calexico, a band that I discussed in a previous chapter, and Shawn Sahm (of Shawn Sahm and the Tex Mex Experience), the son of 'Sir' Doug Sahm whom I discussed in a previous chapter — bringing the Latin/o rock connections back to the Sahm family through another generation.
13   See Kun, 'File Under: Post-Mexico.'

and *cha-cha-chá* rhythm that could be more accurately described as freak-Latin-folk — the accompanying video for the song had Banhart in an Indian-Bollywood aesthetic and 'performing' another type of ethnic identity. While Banhart is visibly European American, he openly acknowledges his Latino (Venezuelan) roots. Meanwhile, the video for 'Carmensita' suggests a cultural performance jarringly similar to Sam the Sham of 1960s fame with the Pharaohs — masking an ethnic identity with another, more exotic, one.

However, while Sam the Sham and other Latino/a artists of previous decades displayed ambiguities and anxieties about their Latino/a identity(ies), current artists like Banhart demonstrate the ways Latino/a identity connections can be celebrated or deployed at will or by choice. Of course, it is important to note that although he sometimes identifies as 'Latino' or with Latino/as, Banhart's White privilege is important to consider for how and when his Latino-ness is to be celebrated or expressed. Ambiguity on the other hand, if it is present at all, might more often be the result of conscious expressions to disrupt facile notions of race/ethnicity, as well as the result of both conscious and unconscious nods to bilingualism, biculturalism, multi-cultural sensibilities, and other intercultural and international proclivities.

Yet another such generational marker came with the song 'Clumsy Sky' by the all-female band Girl In A Coma, who lean toward punk-rock but also reveal new-wave/alternative-rock influences by Morrissey and The Smiths. 'Clumsy Sky,' from *Both Before I'm Gone* in 2007, was a noteworthy hit, propelling Girl In A Coma into mainstream popular music and to international fame, but as I mentioned at the outset of this chapter, the song's video has special significance and also deserves mention. Furthermore, as Girl In A Coma released their sophomore record in the summer of 2009 which is a tribute to their grandfather and his beloved *tejano* music and includes an all-Spanish cover of a song by a Mexican band Los Spitfires, one can only wonder at the possibilities that exist within the Latin/o rock diaspora for young Chicano/as and other Latino/as as they continue to take rock music, and its various subgenres, to places it has never been before as well as *back* to the places it has already been.

Another 2007 release came from a band called Los Straitjackets who since the 1990s have produced many songs and albums, mostly surf-rock instrumentals, that connect them to Latino/as and Latino/a culture(s). While their songs seem to ride the fence between parody or camp and genuine engagements of Latin music and influences, the band members (who don Mexican wrestling masks and sometimes sing in Spanish) perform with no hint of sarcasm, and the band seems legitimized by recordings with Latino artists such as El Vez and Raul Malo.[14] Interestingly, on the 2001 track 'Black Is Black' with Raul Malo (from the album *Sing Along With Los Straitjackets*), Los Straitjackets covered the 1960s garage-rock hit that was originally performed by Spanish band Los Bravos, marking this song

---

14 Raul Malo is mentioned in Chapter four for his connections to Los Super Seven and the tribute to 'border radio,' although he is more famous as the singer/frontman of The Mavericks, who were phenomenally popular in mainstream country music in the 1990s.

as an articulation between Los Straitjackets, a Cuban American/Latino band mostly famous for country music, and a forgotten Spanish-rock 'n' roll band from the 1960s — thereby exemplifying the very intercultural and transnational expressions evident throughout the Latin/o rock diaspora.

The 2007 Los Straitjackets release, titled *Rock en Español Vol. One*, featured various surf-rock songs that were essentially contemporary translations of previous rock 'n' roll classics. For example, the rock 'n' roll classic 'Hang on Sloopy' becomes 'Hey Lupe,' 'All Day and All of the Night' is translated as 'De Dia y de Noche,' 'Gimme Little Sign' is now 'Dame Una Seña,' and 'Lonely Teardrops' is 'Lagrimas Solitarias.' In their contemporary translations, Los Straitjackets even covered the Chicano/a anthem 'Whittier Boulevard' (made famous in the 1960s by Thee Midniters) and recorded songs with famous Chicanos such as Cesar Rosas of Los Lobos and Chicano legend Little Willie G. of Thee Midniters, thus making the *Rock en Español Vol. One* a significant production through its (re-)articulations of Anglo-Americans (from Tennessee) to Chicano/as, other Latino/as, and even to the 'knock-off' English-to-Spanish translations produced in Spain, México, Argentina, and other countries in Latin America throughout the late 1950s and 1960s. In a telling statement, the album's liner notes include the quip 'Border? What Border?' by Louie Perez (from Los Lobos) who tells the short tale of growing up in East LA and listening to US rock 'n' roll and Eastside Chicano/a rock, but also to Mexican bands doing rock 'n' roll in Spanish. As Perez puts it, 'It was as if these rock groups had taken an enormous Pink Pearl eraser and rubbed out the border that separated the USA and Mexico.'[15]

Speaking of erasing borders, another significant 2007 release came from José González, a singer/songwriter who became famous in the US through his indie-rock productions such as 2003's *Veneer*. Born to Argentine parents, José González was raised in Sweden, but sings in English and performs an acoustic-guitar rock style that could be compared to other Latin Rock Diaspora artists such as Rodrigo y Gabriela. When his new efforts, such as 2007's *In Our Nature*, reach levels of popularity in indie-rock circles that rival the best of all other indie-rock and US American rock bands/artists, one can't help but wonder if this is the future of popular music, in spite of the fact that it signifies the present as well as the past of the Latin rock diaspora.

In 2008, artist/musician Lila Downs, who has roots in México and Minnesota and is known mostly for Mexican traditional/folk music and 'soft pop' music, released a new album that includes a song with Rubén Albarrán,[16] the lead singer of Café Tacvba, and another song, 'Black Magic Woman' (with Raul Midón), which is a cover of the classic rock song by Carlos Santana. In this version, however, Lila Downs sings in the first person: 'They call me black magic woman,' and thus reconnects the song to the Latin rock diaspora through Latina women performing in the rock idiom. The *Shake Away* release by Lila Downs also includes songs such

---

15   Louie Perez, in liner notes to *Rock en Español Vol. One*, by Los Straitjackets.
16   Rubén Albarrán has used various other names throughout the years, and in this song with Lila Downs he uses the name Ixaya Mazatzin Tleytól.

as 'Ojo de Culebra' with La Mari de Chambao (from Spain), 'Justica' with Enrique Bunbury (from Spain), 'Los Pollos' with Gilberto Guitierrez of Mono Blanco (from México), and 'Tierra de Luz' with Mercedes Sosa (the internationally famous folk singer from Argentina). Interestingly, just as Lila Downs continues to garner publicity and worldwide acclaim, this important release seems to create its own version of the Latin/o rock diaspora in a single-album release.

In 2008 the LA rock band Monte Negro was launched into the rock stratosphere, powered by songs like 'Me Duele No Estar Junto a Ti' (from the album *Cicatrix*) that became a huge hit for the band and landed them in such important venues as the South By Southwest music festival in Austin, Texas. Interestingly, the song is bilingual (sung in both English and Spanish), but more important is the fact that Monte Negro includes a Chinese American (guitarist Jason Li Shing) and that the band personifies the racial crossing and intercultural expressions that are communicated through their music.

Yet another noteworthy release was *Cold Fact* by Rodriguez (otherwise known as Sixto Rodriguez). In an unusual twist, the forgotten music by another Mexican American from Detroit, Michigan's 1960s music scene (recalling ? and the Mysterians) was revered in South Africa throughout the 1970s and gave Rodriguez a new life as it remained so popular with South Africans that it prompted its recent worldwide release in 2008, making Rodriguez's *Cold Fact* and his psychedelic-folk-rock music another trendy choice for hipsters, indie-rock aficionados, and others interested in rock music history. The reissue was called a 'masterpiece' and a 'buried treasure' by *MOJO* magazine, and has been so successful that another Rodriguez album reissue is in the works for release in 2009. Meanwhile, a similar example exists with the recent re-release of *Louie and the Lovers*, a forgotten 1970s band from Southern California that bridges the southern-rock style of Creedence Clearwater Revival and the 'Chicano' feeling of Doug Sahm, Los Lobos, and Ritchie Valens, and was lauded by *Rolling Stone* critics as a lost gem of the 1970s, prompting its recent re-release in 2009.

Moreover, the example of the reissues of Rodriguez's *Cold Fact* and *Louie and the Lovers* demonstrates the contemporary transnational circulations that are prevalent in contemporary popular music as well as the possibilities that result from current industry practices. In this example, Rodriguez music might have otherwise been forgotten to rock historians and popular music fans in the US had it not been for his popularity in South Africa, and his music and his legacy are now secured because of it. Otherwise, his music, legacy, and contributions to rock music represent another example of significant contributions to rock music by Mexican Americans and other Latino/as, and, like much of the data that I provided throughout this book, are another example of Latino/a rock connections that are only now being discovered, uncovered, and recovered.

As I complete this manuscript, I find myself listening to a 2009 soundtrack production for the recently released feature film *Rudo y Cursi* that includes songs such as 'El Dolor De Micaela' by Los Kumbia Queers. Noting the recent recovery of *chicha* music from Peru that I addressed above, one can listen to songs from the *Rudo y Cursi* soundtrack such as 'El Dolor De Micaela' and understand how

Los Kumbia Queers are paying homage to the historical Latin/o rock connections throughout Latin America and perhaps even demonstrating familiarity with the Latin/o rock canon through Latin/o-rock self-referentiality.

The main track from the *Rudo y Cursi* soundtrack, however, is a song 'Quiero Que Me Quieras,' which is a cover of a popular 1980s hit song by Cheap Trick, 'I Want You To Want Me,' translated to Spanish. The same soundtrack also included another English version of 'I Want You To Want Me' by Latin rock band Juan Son y Los Odio. In addition to various Latin and Latin alternative bands and artists, the soundtrack included another song by none other than the Venezuelan American Devendra Banhart. Of salience here is that, while most US Americans are not knowledgeable of Mexican popular culture, examples such as these illustrate the ways that Mexicans (and other Latin Americans) are often very familiar with North American popular culture. Likewise, such clues reveal that not only is mainstream US rock music (and the film industry) continuing to engage Latin/o rock from 'south of the border,' but also involved are US Latino/a and Chicano/a artists. No longer confined to rigid constructions of 'Latino' and 'Chicano' the trend of eclecticism is demonstrating something closer to a wider and more encompassing label of 'Latin alternative' that also has a place for non-Latino/as. As Loza puts it, these contemporary musical allusions are significant and 'political,' because they 'suggest a movement across national, transnational, and international concerns.'[17]

In sum, Latin alternative (or, *Latino alternativo* as it is also called by some)[18] connotes a negation of the limitations of labels for previous rock subgenres like *rock en español, rock nacional,* and Chicano rock that include some just as they exclude others. Thus, a term like Latin alternative stands to assuage the tensions of nationalism, linguistic nationalism, regionalism, and localism in a way that supports the notion of a diasporic Latino/a perspective, the Latin rock diaspora. Moreover, the analysis presented in this concluding discussion further illuminates this point by demonstrating how other popular music discourses reveal a larger diasporic Latino/a community in which lines between Chicano/as, Latino/as, and others are not so visible.

A Last Word

Throughout this conclusion, I pointed to music videos, on-line magazine articles, internet website discourse, and songs in dialogue within Latin/o rock formations that all illuminate recent and current trends throughout the Latin/o rock diaspora in which US Latino/as are not as easily separated from Latin Americans as they have been in the past. As I demonstrated above, identity markers such as 'Chicano' are sometimes used synonymously with 'Latino' just as 'Latin American' (or more specific national identity categories) are connotatively similar to other identity signifiers such as 'Latino/a.' I also analyzed other internet websites, internet radio

17   Loza, 'Assimilation, Reclamation, and Rejection of the Nation-State by Chicano Musicians,' 147.
18   In the past year, I have noticed that iTunes music now lists some songs as 'Latino Alternativo and Rock Latino.' Much like the collapsing categories of the 2000 US Census, Latin/o rock music categories are also going through redefinition.

programs, and podcasts that signify new meanings, re-definitions, and shifting meanings related to Latin/o music and related Latino/a identity categories. In the previous section within this book's Conclusion, I provided a sketch of 'musical' evidence (songs, song titles, song lyrics, album titles, videos, etc.) of various intercultural, international, transnational, international, and post-national collaborations throughout the Latin rock diaspora.

All of this discursive evidence is indicative of at least some of the changes that occurred and are now occurring within the Latin rock diaspora and of the recent contextualizations required for such an academic discussion of Latin music, 'Latin rock' music, and Latino/a identity categories.

Moreover, throughout this book, I demonstrated some of the nuances, complexities, and problems related to Latino/a identities. In the book's Introduction, for example, I discussed the problems that Latino/a identities posed in the 2000 Census, in recent elections in California, in questions about immigration and the place of Latino/as in North American culture, and in difficult situations where categorizing 'Latin' and 'Latino/a' bands and artists becomes a problem for record stores, music buyers, and even for artists themselves who sometimes resist 'Latin' and sometimes conform to 'Latin.'

In Chapter one, my analysis (re-)introduced 'border radio' and outlaw X stations, specifically noting the extent to which the radio industry and popular music in 1930s, 40s and 50s were highly influenced by the relationship between México and the US — either through the literal transmissions from Mexico the US or through the radio industry practices that developed as a result of border radio and X stations. Another significant theme in this chapter is the level to which Latino/a influence is evident through musical expressions, song lyrics and themes, or the actual bands/artists that contributed to the 'new' sounds transmitted through border radio. With regard to questions of Latino/a identity, I documented how Latin/o musical influence is evident through several decades and even continues into the present, which, I believe, requires us to re-think how we conceptualize the meaning of blues, country, and 'rock 'n' roll' music and how those Latino/a cultural influences in music fostered (through border radio), participated in, and contributed to the developing desegregated expressive space, that itself foreshadowed integrated social spaces and a multicultural music and culture in the US that would follow decades later. More specifically, I contend that such musical influences present a challenge in how we conceptualize the meaning of 'American' and how 'Spanish,' 'Hispanic,' and 'Latino/a' people fit into the national narrative of 'America' and 'American' culture.

In Chapter two, I demonstrated some of the complexities related to Latino/a identities such as the meaning of *pachucos* and how they articulated a countercultural aesthetic associated with African Americans at the same time that they fostered a significant bicultural, bilingual, and binational expression through clothing, slang, and music. That chapter also recognized how the 'Pachuco Boogie' music communicated with other developing music forms (e.g., jazz, swing, boogie woogie, jump blues, and R&B) that would, in turn, develop into ultra-hybrid music that would eventually become known as rock 'n' roll. Moreover, Chapter two documented how the cultural ethos related to the *pachuco* era and 'Pachuco Boogie' music contributed to counter-cultural ethos that would become a central part of rock 'n' roll, and later, rock music. For example, that chapter noted everything from the mixture of different musical forms, in-group slang, clothing/fashion expressions (e.g., outrageous/non-mainstream style, slicked hair, leather jackets, cuffed pants, etc.), smoking marijuana, and more than anything, the notion of being or appearing low, down, violent, dangerous, criminal, and otherwise against the mainstream, which would all become central to mainstream popular culture constructions of masculinity and especially central to rock 'n' roll music scenes, cultures, and subcultures in the following decades.

With regard to identity, however, Chapter two indicated some of the ways that Latino/as assimilated both Black and White culture into their own, already-hybrid cultural sensibilities. Once again, this chapter focused on the influence that Latino/as and Latin/o music had on the still-developing 'American' popular music and the extent to which Latino/a cultural influences are evident in recent popular music expression and in contemporary rock music (in different rock music 'formations'). This chapter therefore extends my proposition that Latin/o music expressions challenge us to reconsider what it means to be 'American' (i.e., forcing us to confront the reality of significant Latin/o influence in 'American' popular culture) as well as challenging us to reconsider how/how much Latino/as fit into narratives about 'America' and/or North American culture. A final note on identity points toward how *pachucos* were part of a growing subculture that increasingly identified with Latin/o music, instead of just Mexican or Mexican American music and culture, which speaks to the fomentation of broader 'Latino' cultural sensibilities. Likewise, another Latino identity category that became evident in the *pachuco* era is 'Chicano,' and we glean that Chicano/a identity was becoming increasingly useful in the late 1940s and how the marker 'Chicano/a' was losing its social stigma or being redeployed because of its stigma.

In Chapter three, I transitioned into the Latin/o musical influences in R&B, blues, and rock 'n' roll in the 1950s and 1960s. More specifically, I turned my attention toward the garage-rock period of the mid 1960s in order to assess the extent to which the original garage-rock moment was highly influenced by Latino/as and Latin/o music, and might be considered a significant Latino/a cultural moment in which Latinos, in spite of showing evidence of assimilatory practices and masking Latino/a identity(ies), were simultaneously making waves in popular music and 'American' popular culture. It is worth noting that the entire garage-rock phenomenon, with its basis in the notion that unskilled and untrained musicians of any color or creed could start their own rock 'n' roll bands that would be formed in a literal garage (and might become rock stars), must have blended easily with the cultural sensibilities of lower- and working-class Latino/as, African, Asian, and European Americans. In this context, it is no wonder that Latino/as and Latin/o cultural influences were so prominent in the initial garage-rock moment, and my analysis only confirms what must have been a natural inclination toward garage-rock by various Latino/as and other Americans connected to the Latino/a cultural influences in garage-rock and rock 'n' roll in general.

Related to this, important considerations that result from this chapter are the fact that a DIY, or Do It Yourself, aesthetic (from your own garage!) was emerging in rock 'n' roll circles and would later contribute to the formation of punk-rock music and its corresponding philosophy, identities, and culture. Moreover, as other historians/scholars noted the significance of songs like '96 Tears' and other garage-rock classics for the culture shifts that would result in the formation of punk-rock — thereby demonstrating another manner (and another rock 'formation') in which Latino/as and Latin/o culture would be influential in/on the rock music and other popular music that followed — contemporary popular music continues to reveal Latin/o inflections. Another prominent theme in this chapter was the fact that Latin/o music can be understood in terms of long-standing, continuous influences on mainstream 'American' popular music and thus, debunks myths about a Latino music 'boom' or 'explosion' in 1999 and early 2000. Meanwhile, other streams of thought in this chapter related to how contemporary popular culture reflects trends in which Latino/as or Latin/o culture are becoming increasingly visible in mainstream North American culture and how Latino/a garage-rock (and punk-rock) expressions and influences further challenge the dichotomy of Black/White music history, as well as dominant narratives in history and popular culture that, more often than not, focus solely on Black and White people in North American cultural history.

By Chapter four, my analysis shifted to the birth of Mexican rock music and the ways in which México engaged rock music and specifically, how rock music signified a mode of communication in which Mexicans (as examples of other 'Latinos' and/or Latin Americans) were able to negotiate their increasingly hybrid, transnational, and globalized identities and to contest both the hegemonic nationalism of México (and by extension, other nations) as well as the cultural hegemony of North American popular culture and its related social trends. In this chapter, my focus moved away from contemporary political issues, compilation CDs and box sets, historical data, and a general focus on popular music discourse(s), and concentrated on literature, or more specifically, the importance of the convergence of an emerging literary genre with an emerging popular music genre that altogether signified the significance of rock music for México, Mexican cultural history, as well as for other Latin American nations and their cultural histories.

It is important to note that this chapter further supports an underlying premise of this book, the challenge to notions of 'nation,' although in this chapter, my observations indicate how México was tied up with promoting acceptable, safe rock 'n' roll music with nationalistic timbres in order to confront the challenge of US cultural imperialism, and with the fact that Mexicans redefined the meaning of rock music by switching from Spanish to English lyrics and then back to Spanish, as well as through a symbolic negotiation of Mexican nationalism through experimentation with new sounds, instruments, song lyrics and themes, and by adopting band names with either pro-national or antinational tones. Further significance in this chapter lies in the fact that México is just one Latin American country in which rock music was used in either supporting or challenging hegemonic nationalisms, and begs for further analysis of the significance of rock music in other Latin American nations. While I introduced some studies that address rock in other Latin American countries, this chapter only hints at what could be a series of more specific investigations on this theme.

Moving forward, this chapter analyzed North American trends in rock music that further signified the articulation of rock music to Latino/as, Latin American, or Latin/o musical influences, and further justified the analysis of rock music, and/or rock formations, from Latin/o perspectives. Moreover, this chapter's significance also lies with the fact that Latin/o rock music can no longer remain tied to US Latino/a articulations and can and should be analyzed in terms of other Latin American cultures and connections. Of course, the conclusion of this chapter focused on contemporary implications such as the fact that US Americans continue to undervalue the influence and presence that Mexicans and other Latino/as have had in US popular culture, in addition to the fact that Mexicans also demonstrate ambivalence about the nature of North American influence on 'their own' popular culture, and that chronicles related to rock music suggest an alternative perspective of Mexican nationalism that goes further beyond the mainstream characterizations of Mexican identity and history, and essentially acknowledges the influence(s) of North American rock music culture. Without a doubt, such recognitions can be applied to contemporary rock formations and the emergence of new forms of Latino/a rock music and Mexican rock music.

Finally, using 'punk' as a thematic concept as well as a starting point for a conversation about more recent Latino/a rock articulations, Chapter five indexed rock music in Argentina, various punk-rock connections to Latino/as, the rise of *rock en español* in the 1990s, and the growth of Latin alternative music and other Latin/o rock music in the US and throughout other parts of Latin America after 'Y2K.' What I believe is revealed is the extent to which rock music formations from North America are increasingly connected to rock music formations from Latin America.

Furthermore, with regard to identity constructions and politics, the brief analysis in this chapter illuminated the ways in which US Latino/as increasingly identified with their Latin American (i.e., non-'American') counterparts and more importantly, how rock music emerged as a primary mode of communication through which emerging Latino/a identities were formulated, expressed, and articulated in the 1990s. Furthermore, this chapter also suggested some of the ways that Latin/o rock music remains influential in other mainstream rock music, and exposes other links to contemporary popular music.

In this book, an underlying theme throughout all chapters is that Latino/a people and Latin/o cultural influence are significant, numerous, and far-reaching, so much so that one should hardly speak of 'American' popular music or even rock music without at least mentioning some aspect of its Latin/o legacy. Through instruments, music, rhythms, language, lyrics, themes, fashions, styles, cultural practices, scenes, subcultures, and through the race/ethnicity of individuals who practice it, Latino/as and Latino/a culture(s) are prominent throughout the history of 'American' popular music as well as the history of rock 'n' roll (and rock) music. My hope, like musicologist/historian Sublette, is that forthcoming analyses and treatments of either rock music or popular music in general will at least mention the significance of what Sublette calls the 'Spanish-speaking elephant in the kitchen' and the 'other great tradition.'[19] While Sublette argues for recognition of Cuban music specifically, this evaluation calls for recognition of other Latino/o music and cultural influences.

As a Latino, my personal hope is also that this analysis of Latino/a identity and the engagement of rock music by 'Hispanics' and 'Latino/as' provides new ways to conceptualize the history of, as well as present and future formulations of, Latino/a identity(ies) — one that moves beyond facile associations of Latino/a people and culture only with salsa and other 'tropical' music, or with Mexican folk and Mexican regional music, or through tired metaphors that associate Latino/as with passion, spice, *sabor*, and *calor* (or the words *sabroso* and *caliente*), etc., or with ideological discourse(s) of exoticism, foreign-ness, alien nature, and invasion (metaphorical, cultural, or literal).

On an academic level, I contend that this book supports recent theorizations of post-nationality and a post-national condition. For example, my analysis is privileged by my intentional emphasis on cross-border cultural practices and notions of a 'Greater Mexico' and a 'Latin diaspora.' However, my discoveries indicate that interculturalism, internationalism, and transnationalism have been much more prevalent in popular music history, and history in general, than many or most accounts are willing to acknowledge. Likewise, the analysis in Chapter five (and part of this Conclusion) provided a perspective that increasingly links US Latino/as to other Latin American (as much as it increasingly links US popular culture to Latino/as and Latin(o) American popular culture).

From a communication studies perspective, this investigation began with a mass-communication-oriented focus on the implications of mass media for culture and identity throughout Latin America and with a focus on how popular music became involved with various propagandistic uses for the purpose of inculcating people with a sense of nationalism, and hence, citizenship. Moving forward, Chapter one operated from the premise that radio and popular music can also be seen as 'public discourse' in which communicative effects are not necessarily evident or immediately quantifiable, and that communication can reach into years and even decades beyond. Such a notion of 'public discourse' begins with the assumption that mass media can take years and decades to acquire significance, that radio and popular music history reveals how cultures can be interactive with each other, and how cultures and individuals respond to existing stimuli over time. Moreover, this notion of 'public discourse' emphasizes that such communication reveals larger cultural expressions to be dialogic, as well as that mediated communication can be connected to the personal and inter-personal forms of communication and can influence group-communication or what might be more accurately called 'cultural' communication in contemporary communication and media studies. Yet another level of communication in this investigation is that of communication as discourse, which is somewhat related to speech

---

19   Sublette, 'The Centrality of Cuban Music.'

communication and rhetoric, and thus moves into other important areas of communication studies. Moreover, the reliance of this study on 'discourse' provides links to cultural-studies-based projects and avenues that are relevant for Latino/a communication studies, ethnic studies, Latin American and Latino/a studies, and American studies research. In this sense, the contribution of this project points toward several areas that represent the present and future of communication studies and the interdisciplinarity that will be required for it.

At the same time, in order to conclude this study, some clarifications are worth considering and revisiting. For example, while my premise throughout this book has been that of a Latin 'diaspora,' it is important to question the very premise of diaspora as it relates to Latino/as. For example, critical scholars might wonder where the homeland lies for the supposed 'Latin diaspora,' since homelands are key aspects of diasporic peoples and cultures. For this question, my best answer is that I follow the suggestion of George Lipsitz who, through his own analysis of popular music, notes that people can be 'doubly diasporic.' In other words, in contemporary (globalized) cultural formations, it may not be enough to talk about people and culture as part of only one diaspora. Like many other people and cultural groups that Lipsitz studies, my current analysis is based on the notion that Latino/as might claim two or even three homelands, marking them as doubly and possibly triply diasporic.[20] Latino/as, for example, might lay claim to both Europe and Africa as important cultural 'homelands,' they might claim both Spain and a region in Africa, or even claim both Spain and some Caribbean nation/culture as a launching point for their own cultural history, family history, or notions of origin. Moreover, some Latino/as (e.g., Chicano/as, Mexican Americans, Central Americans, South Americans, and some Caribbean Latino/as) might claim both indigenous ancestry at the same time as they can claim Spanish (i.e., European) descent. In such cases, none of these is necessarily right or wrong, better or worse, or more legitimate than another. From this perspective, viewing people as doubly-diasporic or triply-diasporic only makes sense for the nature of the times in which we live, and refuses to fall into the traps of singular identities, racial dichotomies, and purist fantasies. Furthermore, if one can claim that Latino/as are no more a single diasporic entity than any other 'racial' group, that is precisely the point. And yet, 'Latinos,' 'Hispanics,' and 'Spanish' people continue to fall between the cracks of US social constructions that can only understand Latino/as as non-White and non-Black.

Another significant question/problem that should arise from conscious, critical scholars is that this analysis has privileged a diasporic view of Latino/a people, and that this may come at the expense of more (locally) focused preoccupations with gender, sexual orientation, race, ethnicity, age/generation, ability, and socio-economic (class) status. My only response to this issue is that such critiques are absolutely correct in such an assessment. While I have tried to contextualize some differences between race and ethnicity, the significance of gender issues, the prominence of class issues in Latin American rock music, and even the recent

---

20 Lipsitz, *Footsteps in the Dark*, 45–6.

salience of GLBT issues in Latin/o rock music formations (as suggested above), I do recognize that my suggestions are ultimately not enough. I therefore suggest that this book is viewed as part of a place from which other, more locally focused analyses and investigations of Latin/o rock can be launched, especially those with a focus on any and all of the above contextualizations.

To put it another way, my 'diasporic view' of Latino/as and Latin/o rock music is, admittedly, an essentializing theoretical formulation, or as I suggested in the Introduction to this book, it is a research heuristic through which one can demonstrate the issues, complexities, and nuances related to Latino/a identities. However, my essentializing premise — a flattening out of ethnicity, nationality, class, gender, sexuality, etc. — should be viewed as a flattening out for the sake of the rough and rugged, a simplification for the sake of the complex. In other words, my heuristic use of Latino/a identity, Latin/o diaspora, and a 'Latin/o rock diaspora' should be understood as only temporary formulations that are utilized to challenge the stubborn Black/White dichotomy that persists in so many academic studies, historical assessments, and mainstream constructions of 'American' nationalism, 'American' popular culture, and rock 'n' roll lore.

Therefore, a specific aspect that I wish to reiterate here and that has motivated this project from the very beginning is that diasporas present challenges to the nation-state as a philosophical construction. Just as there are many examples of national identities that are constructed through music, and of national identities that are based on concepts of race or races (such as the aforementioned Black/White dichotomy), the notion of a Latin diaspora is presented here for the purpose of de-privileging the nation-state as the best way for analyzing people and culture, as the most appropriate way for studying music and popular culture, or as the only logical way of organizing people and societies. Moreover, the notion of a Latin rock diaspora emphasizes 'Latin' people as a racial discourse — a strategic essentialism — that, when put alongside Black (i.e., African American) and White (i.e., European American) racial constructs, disrupts the very notion of race and therefore challenges racial categories and serves as an antiracist discourse. In other words, the essentialism that I am guilty of here, this flattening out, is purposefully put forth as an antiracist notion that I hope will challenge correlations between 'nations' and 'races,' as well as the very meanings of both in the first place.

To put it another way, another important consideration here, related to the problems of the Latin diaspora as an analytical category, is that Latino/as are sometimes also Blacks, or African Americans. And with regard to music, a great deal of Latin/o influence that I documented throughout this book is, in fact, Afro-Latin music influence. Additionally, many musicians who were responsible for Latinizing R&B, blues, and rock 'n' roll were, in fact, African Americans, and some of those musicians are credited on recordings with Latino/as or that have significances as Latino/a cultural productions. For some, such facts might suggest a de-privileging of African music and African American influences on my part. For the record, it is also worth noting the examples where Jewish American composers/songwriters were responsible for 'Black' music and even some of the Latinized 'Black' music (e.g., Leiber and Stoller writing 'Hound Dog' for Big Mama

Thornton), and likewise, that Jewish people themselves symbolize the problematic nature of concepts like 'nation' and 'race.'

However, my point here is that such challenges to my research should not negate the point or the spirit of this endeavor. Rather, my point has been that such intercultural communication, inter-ethnic influence, and interracial collaboration actually point to the ways in which racial constructions are disrupted through popular music expressions. Thus, if anything, noting prominent African American influence in Latinized popular music, or Jewish composers writing Black and Latin/o music, should only further disrupt the persistent Black/White binary that characterizes so much of popular music history as well as mainstream narratives about 'America' and 'Americanness.'

Moreover, I wish to reiterate that if Latino/as do not make sense as a unified, essentializable racial category, it is because all racial categories are false. In other words, all racial categories and racializations should be subject to questioning and challenging. This examination, however, is based on the premise that constructing a pan-Latin racial category can be useful, specifically for raising questions about and challenging other (accepted and customary) racial categories. Another hope, therefore, is that future scholars will pick up where I leave off and both utilize the notion of Latin diaspora in other popular culture productions, as well as other cultural expressions, in order to purse the antiracist agenda that I have followed here. Moreover, I hope that future scholars will focus on the gendered, sexualized, racial, ethnic, and class aspects of Latin/o rock music, and that future scholarship will contribute to the project of deconstructing racial categories and assumptions about national identity categories. From my perspective, the potential of such scholarship will have wide-reaching implications from history and political science, to music and popular culture studies, to Latin American and Latino/as studies, to ethnic studies and American studies, and of course, for media and communication studies, and illuminates a new avenue into which various forms of scholarship can grow.

Finally, I should add a qualification that this research makes no claims at being an exhaustive view of Latin/o rock music or Latin/o music influences in rock or other popular music (how could it be?), and otherwise questions whether an exhaustive view is even possible, especially given the information presented throughout this book that only points to beginnings and entry points into what is certainly a great deal of potential for future scholarship of various disciplines. Noting this, I am mindful that there are many other stories out there to be told about the Latin/o engagement of rock music; that there are countless Spanish, Hispanic, and Latino/as in rock music throughout the decades that I have not been able to touch upon here (those who remain obscure or forgotten, or whose life and details I have just not come across yet); that there are too many bands from México, Argentina, Spain, and the rest of Latin America to mention in a single book (in fact, each nation might deserve its own book-length treatment with regard to its engagement with rock music); that there are potentially thousands of contemporary Latino/a bands and artists that I am not mentioning here; that further investigations are necessary with regard to gender, class, sexual orientation

New England's annual *Rock en Español* conference. Photo by: Michelle Zapata

(and other identities); that the *Latin Alternative Music Conference* just celebrated its tenth year in existence; that Ciudad Juárez/El Paso shares the annual *Rock en el Río* festival which will be in its fifth year in 2010; and that Boston/New England now has its own *Rock en Español* conference that is now in its third year. Finally, I am mindful that there are many other interesting stories related to the Latin/o engagement with rock music that all say something about Latino/a identity(ies) and about how rock music mirrors Latino/a identities. Rock music itself deserves better treatment regarding the true story of its Latin/o influences, Latino/a connections, and individual stories of how Latino/as throughout the US, Latin America, and elsewhere have utilized rock music to mark their cultural differences, to claim their identities, and to mediate their relationships with others. Interestingly, Latino/as continue to do this and, by doing so, Latino/as stand on the precipice of further disrupting music genres, racial discourses, and national categories — in North America and beyond.

Selective Discography and Tracks Listed in This Conclusion

Banhart, Devendra. 'Carmensita,' *Smokey Rolls Down Thunder Canyon* (XL Records, 2007).
Café Tacuba. 'Déjate Caer,' *Valle Callampa* (MCA, 2002).
Calexico. 'Roka,' *Garden Ruin* (Quarterstick Records, 2006).
Cordero. 'Soltera,' *Somos Cordero* (Daemon, 2004).
DJ Bitman. 'Tropilove (featuring Julian Peña & Tea Time),' *Latin Bitman* (Nacional Records, 2007).
Girl In A Coma. 'Clumsy Sky,' *Both Before I'm Gone* (BlackheartRecords, 2007); see music video, available on YouTube.com.
González, José. 'How Low,' *In Our Nature* (Peacefrog, 2007).
Gotan Project. 'Amor Porteño,' *Lunático* (XL Recordings, 2006).
Guerrero, Tommy. 'Organism,' *Soul Food Taqueria* (Mo' Wax Records, 2003).
Kinky. 'Mexican Radio,' *Sassy* (Corner Stone Cues, 2008).
Los Lobos. 'Mexico Americano,' *Acoustic En Vivo* (Los Lobos, 2005).
Los Lonely Boys. 'Heaven,' *Los Lonely Boys* (Epic, 2004).
Louie and the Lovers. 'Rise,' *Louie and the Lovers: The Complete Recordings* (Bear Family Records, 2009).
Maldita Vecindad (y Los Hijos del 5° Patio). 'Salta Pa' Tras,' *Rock en Español: Lo Mejor de Maldita Vecindad* (BMG Entertainment, 2001).
The Mars Volta. 'L'Via L'Viaquez,' *Frances the Mute* (Universal, 2005).
Minutemen. 'Corona,' *Double Nickels on the Dime* (SST, 1984).
Monte Negro. 'Me Duele No Estar Junto a Ti,' *Cicatrix* (Epic/RedRecords, 2008).
Pistolera. 'Cazador,' *Siempre Hay Salida* (Pistolera, 2006).
Plastilina Mosh. 'Viva Las Vegas,' *Tasty + b sides* (EMI Music México, 2006).
Rodriguez. 'Sugar Man,' *Cold Fact* (Light In The Attic, 2008).
Vallejo. 'Rock Americano,' *Stereo* (VMG Records, 2002).
Various artists. *The Roots of Chicha: Psychedelic Cumbias from Peru* (Barbes, 2007).

Bibliography

Aguilera, T., Ross, K., Fernandez Bitar, M., Fortuno, S., and Padilla, X. 'Latin Music 6-Pack: Programming.' *Billboard* 113 (16 June 2001): pLM-12.

Agustín, J. 'La Onda Que Nunca Existió. *Revista De Critica Literaria Latinoamericana* 59 (2004): 9–17.

———. *El Hotel de Los Corazones Solitarios* (México, DF: Nueva Imagen, 1999).

———. *La Contracultura en México: La Historia y El Significado de Los Rebeldes Sin Causa, Los Jipitecas, Los Punks y Las Bandas* (México, DF: Editorial Grijalbo, 1996).

———. *Contra La Corriente* (México, DF: Editorial Diana, 1990a).

———. *Tragicomedia Mexicana 1* (México, DF: Editorial Planeta, 1990b).

———. *El Rock de La Cárcel* (México, DF: Ed. Mexicanos Unidos, 1986).

———. *Ciudades Desiertas* (México, DF: Edivision, 1982).

———. 'Cuál Es La Onda.' *Diálogos* 10 (1974): 11–13.

———. *La Nueva Música Clásica* (México, DF: Instituto Nacional de la Juventud Mexicana, 1968).

Albrecht, R. *Mediating the Muse: A Communication Approach to Music, Media and Culture Change* (Cresskill, NJ: Hampton Press, 2004).

Alvarez, L. 'From Zoot Suits to Hip Hop: Towards a Relational Chicana/o Studies.' *Latino Studies* 5 (2007): 53–75.

Anazagasty-Rodríguez, J. 'Colonial Capitalism, Hegemony, and Youth Praxis in Puerto Rico: Fiel a la Vega's Rock en Español.' *Latin American Music Review* 23 (2002): 80–105.

Anderson, B. *Imagined Communities: Reflections on the Origin and Spread of Nationalism* (New York: Verso, 2006).

Anthony, M. 'Latin Music 6-Pack: Artists ... Music.' *Billboard* 113 (16 June 2001): pLM-6.

Aparicio, F. R., and Jáquez, C. F. *Musical Migrations: Transnationalism and Cultural Hybridity in Latin/o America, Volume I* (New York: Palgrave McMillan, 2003).

Appell, G., and Hemphill, D. *American Popular Music: A Multicultural History* (Belmont, CA: Thompson & Wadsworth, 2006).

Arellano, G. 'Their Charming Man: Dispatches From the Latino Morrissey Love-In.' *OC Weekly* (19 September 2002): no pagination. http://www.ocweekly.com/2002-09-19/features/their-charming-man

Avant-Mier, R. 'Of Rocks and Nations: *Voces Rockeras* (Popular Music Voices) and the Discourse of Nationality.' In *Somos de Una Voz? New Directions in Latin@ Communication* (xx–xx), eds. M. A. Holling and B. M. Calafell (Lanham, MD: Lexington Press, forthcoming).

———. 'Latinos in the Garage: A Genealogical Examination of the Latino/a Presence and Influence in Garage Rock, Rock and Pop Music.' *Popular Music and Society* 31, no. 5 (2008): 555–74.

———. 'Of Rocks and Nations: A Critical Study of Latino/a Identity through Latino/a Rock Discourse,' Ph.D. diss., University of Utah, 2007.

Avelar, I. 'Defeated Rallies, Mournful Anthems, and the Origins of Brazilian Heavy Metal.' In *Brazilian Popular Music and Globalization*, eds. C. A. Perrone and C. Dunn (Gainesville, FL: University Press of Florida, 2001), 123–35.

Bangs, L. 'Protopunk: The Garage Bands.' In *The Rolling Stone Illustrated History of Rock and Roll*, ed. J. Miller (New York: Random House/*Rolling Stone* Press, 1980), 261–4.
Bannister, M. '"Loaded": Indie Guitar Rock, Canonism and White Masculinities.' *Popular Music* 25, no. 1 (2006): 77–95.
Barker, G. C. 'Pachuco: An American-Spanish Argot and Its Social Function in Tucson, Arizona.' *The Mexican Experience in Arizona* (New York: Arno Press, 1976).
Bátiz, J. 'Javier Batiz: Biografía.' [On-line article, no date]. http://www.javierbatiz.com
Bender, S. W. 'Will the Wolf Survive?*: Latino/a Pop Music in the Cultural Mainstream.' *Denver University Law Review* 78 (2001): 719–51.
Bentley, B. Liner notes to *Heard it on the X* [compact disc], (Cleveland, OH: TELARC International Corporation, 2005).
Berger, H. M., and Carroll, M. T. *Global Pop, Local Language* (Jackson, MS: University Press of Mississippi, 2003).
Billig, M. *Rock 'n' Roll Jews* (Syracuse, NY: Syracuse University Press, 2000).
Bruce-Novoa, J. '*La Onda*: Parody and Satire.' In *José Agustín: Onda and Beyond*, eds. Carter and Schmidt (Columbia, MO: University of Missouri Press, 1986), 37–55.
Bullen, M. '*Chicha* in the Shanty Towns of Arequipa, Peru.' *Popular Music* 12, no. 3 (1993): 229–44.
Busnar, G. *It's Rock 'n' Roll: A Musical History of the Fabulous Fifties* (New York: Julian Messner, 1979).
Café Tacuba (unsigned article from NPR). 'Café Tacuba' [On-line document]. *All Songs Considered: NPR's Online Music Show* (2002). http://www.npr.org/programs/asc/archives/asc16/index.html#tacuba
———. (unsigned article from Miami City Search). 'Café Tacuba' [On-line document], (2000). http://miami.citysearch.com/feature/22792/
———. (unsigned article from *tntla*). 'Café Tacuba' [On-line document], (2000). http://www.tntla.com/english/music/cafe_tacuba/
Cameron, D. *Working with Spoken Discourse* (Thousand Oaks, CA; Sage, 2001).
Capetillo-Ponce, J. 'From "A Clash of Civilizations" to "Internal Colonialism": Reactions to the Theoretical Bases of Samuel Huntington's "The Hispanic Challenge."' *Ethnicities* 7, no. 1 (2007): 116–34.
Capistrano, D. '9 to 5'ers by Day, Rock Stars By Night.' *Urban Latino* 177 (2007). http://www.urbanlatino.com/mag/2007/issue77/features/pistolera.php
Carey, E. *Plaza of Sacrifices: Gender, Power, and Terror in 1968 Mexico* (Albuquerque, NM: University of New Mexico Press, 2005).
Carey, J. W. 'A Cultural Approach to Communication.' In *Sources: Notable Selections in Mass Media*, eds. J. Hanson and D. J. Maxcy (Guilford, CT: Dushkin/McGraw-Hill, 1999), 237–46.
Carter, J. C. D., and Schmidt, D. L. *José Agustín: Onda and Beyond* (Columbia, MO: University of Missouri Press, 1986).
Census. *The United States Census 2000* (Washington DC; US Census Bureau, 2000). http://www.census.gov
Cepeda M. E. '*Mucho Loco* for Ricky Martin; or The Politics of Chronology, Crossover, and Language within the Latin(o) Music "Boom."' In *Global Pop, Local Language*, eds. H. M. Berger and M. T. Carroll (Jackson, MS: University Press of Mississippi, 2003a), 113–29.
———. 'Shakira as the Idealized, Transnational Citizen: A Case Study of *Colombianidad* in Transition.' *Latino Studies* 1 (2003b): 211–32.
———. '"Columbus Effect(s)": Chronology and Crossover in the Latin(o) Music "Boom."' *Discourse* 23 (2001): 63–81.
Chang, J. *Can't Stop Won't Stop: A History of the Hip-Hop Generation* (New York: Picador, 2005).

Clifford, J., and Marcus, G. E. *Writing Culture: The Poetics and Politics of Ethnography* (Berkeley, CA: University of California Press, 1986).
Cobb, W. J. *To The Break of Dawn: A Freestyle on the Hip Hop Aesthetic* (New York: New York University Press, 2007).
Cobo, L. 'Growing Up and Looking for an Audience.' *Billboard* 113 (16 June 16 2001a): pLM-1/1–2.
_____. 'Puya: Rocking Harder Than Ever.' *Billboard* 113 (16 June 16 2001b): pLM-1/1–2.
_____. 'Women Who Rock.' *Billboard* 112 (9 December 2000a): pLM-1/1–2.
_____. 'Latin Crossover's New Twist.' *Billboard* 112 (9 December 2000b): 3–4.
_____. 'Not Yet Rockin' the Radio: Hugely Popular in Argentina, Latin Rock Needs to Find its Audience in the U.S.' *Billboard* 112 (9 December 2000c): pLM-6/6–7.
_____., Fernández Bitar, M., Ross, K., and Lopetegui, E. 'Argentine Folk Rock, L.A. Labels, and a Brazilian Festival.' *Billboard* 112 (9 December 2000d): pLM-4/4–5.
'Confab showcases *rock en español*' (unsigned article). In 'Latin Notas' section of *Billboard* 112 (12 August 2000): 46–7.
Contreras, F. 'Monterrey, Mexico: Latin Alternative Central.' On *All Things Considered* [National Public Radio daily series], (10 March 2006). http://www.npr.org/templates/story/story.php?storyId=5256890.
_____. 'Defining Latin Alternative Music.' On *All Things Considered* [National Public Radio daily series], (7 March 2006). http://www.npr.org/templates/story/story.php?storyId=5244351
Cooper, B. L. and Haney, W. S. *Rock Music in American Popular Culture II: More Rock 'n' Roll Resources* (New York: Harrington Park Press, 1997).
Corona, I., and Madrid, A. L. (eds.). *Postnational Musical Identities: Cultural Production, Distribution, and Consumption in a Globalized Scenario* (Lahnam, MD: Lexington Books, 2008).
Cortés, D. *El Otro Rock Mexicano: Experiencias Progresivas, Sicodélicas, de Fusión y Experimentales* (México, DF: Times Editores, 1999).
Cuccioletta, G., and Cuccioletta, M. *Soda Stereo: La Historia* (Buenos Aires: Editorial Galerna, 1997).
Cullen, J. *The Art of Democracy: A Concise History of Popular Culture in the U.S.* (New York: Monthly Review Press, 1996).
Dahl, B. Liner notes to *20th Century Masters — The Millenium Collection: The Best of Sam the Sham & the Pharaohs* (Universal Music, 2003).
Davis, F. *The History of the Blues* (New York: Hyperion, 1995).
de La Parra, F., McGarry, T. W., and McGarry, M. *Living the Blues: Canned Heat's Story of Music, Drugs, Death, Sex, and Survival* (Canned Heat Music, 2000).
del Barco, M. 'Latin Alternative's Big Cheese: Gustavo Santaolalla.' On *All Things Considered* [National Public Radio daily series], (9 March 2006). http://www.npr.org/templates/story/story.php?storyId=5253997
Delgado, F. P. 'Chicano Ideology Revisited: Rap Music and the (Re)Articulation of Chicanismo.' *Western Journal of Speech Communication* 62 (1998a): 95–113.
_____. 'When the Silenced Speak: The Textualization and Complications of Latina/o Identity.' *Western Journal of Communication* 62 (1998b): 420–39.
Dempsey, J. M. 'The Light Crust Doughboys Are on the Air!' *Journal of Radio Studies* 9, no. 1 (2002): 107–25.
Díaz, J. *The Brief Wondrous Life of Oscar Wao* (New York: Riverhead Books, 2007).
Doss, Y. C. 'Choosing Chicano in the 1990s: The Underground Music Scene of Los(t) Angeles.' *Aztlán* 23 (1998):191–202.
Dunaway, D. K. 'Music as Political Communication in the U.S.' In *Popular Music and Communication*, ed. J. Lull (Newbury Park, CA: Sage, 1987), 36–52.

Durán, T., and Barrios, F. *El Grito del Rock Mexicano: Hablan los Roqueros* (México, DF: Ediciones del Milenio, 1995).

Eddy, C. *The Accidental Evolution of Rock 'n' Roll: A Misguided Tour Through Popular Music* (New York: Da Capo Press, 1987).

Ehrenreich, B. 'Confessions of a White Salsa Dancer: Appropriation, Identity and the "Latin Music Craze." *Denver University Law Review* 78 (2001): 795–815.

Esterrich, C., and Murillo, J. H. 'Rock with Punk with Pop with Folklore: Transformations and Renewal in Aterciopelados and Café Tacuba.' *Latin American Music Review* 21 (2000): 31–44.

Estrada, T. *Sirenas al Ataque: Historia de las Mujeres Rockeras Mexicanas (1956-2000)* (México, DF: Pentagrama, 2001).

Fairclough, N. 'The Discourse of New Labour: Critical Discourse Analysis.' In *Discourse as Data: A Guide for Analysis*, eds. Wetherell, Taylor, and Yates (Thousand Oaks, CA: Sage, 2001), 229–66.

_____. *Critical Discourse Analysis: The Critical Study of Language*, (1995). New York: Longman.

_____. 1993. 'Critical Discourse Analysis and the Marketization of Public Discourse: The Universities.' *Discourse and Society* 4(2), (1993): 133–68.

_____. *Language and Power*. (1989). New York; Longman.

Fairclough, N., and Wodak, R. 'Critical Discourse Analysis.' In *Discourse as Social Interaction: Discourse Studies — A Multidisciplinary Introduction, Vol. 2*, ed. T. A. van Dijk, (Thousand Oaks, CA: Sage, 1997), 258–84.

Farley, C. J. 'Sounds of Magic Realism: Aterciopelados Updates South American Traditions.' *Time* 157 (14 May 2001): 72.

_____. 'Rock and Redemption in Rio.' In *Time* [On-line], (January 11 2001a). http://www.time.com/time/sampler/article/0,8599,94786,00.html

_____. 'Rock in Rio, Part 2.' In *Time* [On-line], (January 12 2001b). http://www.time.com/time/sampler/article/0,8599,94971,00.html

Fein, S. 'Myths of Cultural Imperialism and Nationalism in the Golden Age of Mexican Cinema.' In *Fragments of a Golden Age*, eds. Joseph, Rubenstein, and Zolov (Durham, NC: Duke University Press, 2001), 159–98.

Firme, F. 'Spotlight on the Brown: Rampart Records' Hector Gonzalez.' *LatinoLA* [On-line magazine], (21 September 2005). http://www.latinola.com/story.php?story=2849

Flores, L. A. 'Constructing Rhetorical Borders: Peons, Illegal Aliens, and Competing Narratives of Immigration.' *Critical Studies in Media Communication* 20 (2003): 362–87.

Foucault, M. *Language, Counter-Memory, Practice: Selected Essays and Interviews* (Ithaca, NY: Cornell University Press, 1977).

Fowler, G., and Crawford, B. Liner notes to *Heard it on the X* [compact disc] (Cleveland, OH: TELARC International Corporation, 2005).

_____. *Border Radio: Quacks, Yodelers, Pitchmen Psychics, and Other Amazing Broadcasters of the American Airwaves* (Austin, TX: Texas Monthly Press, 2002).

Frank, T. *Alternative to What?: Sounding Off! — Music as Subversion / Resistance / Revolution* (Brooklyn, NY: Autonomedia, 1995).

Garcia, M. 'The "Chicano" Dance Hall: Remapping Public Space in Post-World War II Greater Los Angeles.' In *Sound Identities: Popular Music and the Cultural Politics of Education*, eds. C. McCarthy, G. Hudak, S. Miklaucic, and P. Saukko (New York: Peter Lang, 1999), 317–41.

García Canclini, N. *Hybrid Cultures: Strategies for Entering and Leaving Modernity* (Minneapolis, MN: University of Minnesota Press, 1995).

Garofalo, R. *Rockin' Out: Popular Music in the U.S.A.* (Boston: Allyn and Bacon, 1997).

_____. *Rockin' the Boat: Mass Music and Mass Movements* (Boston, MA: South End Press, 1992).
Garza, O. 'Remembering Doug Saldaña' (On-line document). In . . . to the Sublime (no date). http://tothesublime.typepad.com/to_the_sublime/2009/11
Geijerstam, C. A. *Popular Music in Mexico* (Albuquerque, NM: University of New Mexico Press, 1976).
Gilbert, A. 'For Bajofondo, It Takes Eight to Tango.' *Boston Globe* (29 September 2009).
Gilroy, P. *The Black Atlantic: Modernity and Double-Consciousness* (Cambridge, MA: Harvard University Press, 1993).
Gioia, T. *Delta Blues: The Life and Times of the Mississippi Masters Who Revolutionized American Music* (New York: W. W. Norton & Company, 2008).
Goldrosen, J., and Beecher, J. *Remembering Buddy: The Definitive Biography* (New York: Viking/Penguin, 1987).
Gómez-Peña, G. *The New World Border: Prophecies, Poems & Loqueras for the End of the Century* (San Francisco: City Lights Books, 1996).
Grammy.com. 'The Grammy Awards' [On-line]. *Official Website for The National Recording Academy*. http://www.grammy.com
Granados, C. 'Latinos, Once So Anxious to Join the American Mainstream, Have Rediscovered a Passion for their Heritage: Born Again Latinos.' *Hispanic* 34 (31 May 2000).
Grieco, E. M., and Cassidy, R. C. 'Census 2000 Brief: Overview of Race and Hispanic Origin.' *The United States Census 2000* (Washington DC: US Census Bureau, March 2001). http://www.census.gov
Grossberg, L. *We Gotta Get Out Of This Place: Popular Conservatism and Postmodern Culture* (New York: Routledge, 1992).
Grossberg, L., Wartella, E. A., Whitney, D. C., and Wise, J. M. *Mediamaking: Mass Media in Popular Culture* (Thousand Oaks, CA: Sage, 1998).
Guerrero, D. and De los Santos, N. *Lalo Guerrero: The Original Chicano* [video documentary] (Produced by Guerrero and De los Santos: Original Chicano Productions, 2006).
Guerrero, L., and Mentes, S. M. *Lalo: My Life and Music* (Tucson, AZ: University of Arizona Press, 2002).
Guevara, R. 'The View from the Sixth Street Bridge: The History of Chicano Rock.' In *The First Rock & Roll Confidential Report*, ed. D. Marsh (New York: Pantheon Books, 1985), 113–25.
Gutierrez, R. A. 'Community, Patriarchy and Individualism: The Politics of Chicano History and the Dream of Equality.' *American Quarterly* 45 (1993): 44–72.
Guzmán, B. 'Census 2000 Brief: The Hispanic Population.' *The United States Census 2000* (Washington DC: US Census Bureau, May 2001). http://www.census.gov
Guzmán, I., and Valdivia, A. 'Brain, Brow, and Booty: Latina Iconicity in U.S. Popular Culture.' *The Communication Review* 7 (2004): 205–21.
Habell-Pallán, M. *Loca Motion: The Travels of Chicana and Latina Popular Culture* (New York: New York University Press, 2005).
_____. 'El Vez Is "Taking Care of Business": The Inter/National Appeal of Chicano Popular Music.' *Cultural Studies* 13, no. 2 (1999): 195–210.
Hall, S. 'Cultural Identity and Diaspora.' In *Colonial Discourse and Post-Colonial Theory: A Reader*, eds. P. Williams and L. Chrisman (New York: Columbia University Press, 1994), 392–403.
Hanke, R. (1998). 'Yo Quiero Mi MTV!': Making Music Television for Latin America.' In *Mapping the Beat: Popular Music and Contemporary America*, eds. T. Swiss, J. Sloop, and A. Herman (Malden, MA: Blackwell Publishers, 1998), 219–45.
Harvey, J. J. 'Cannibals, Mutants, and Hipsters: The Tropicalist Revival.' In *Brazilian Popular*

Music and Globalization, eds. C. A. Perrone and C. Dunn (Gainesville, FL: University Press of Florida, 2001), 106–22.

Hasian, M. A., Jr., and Delgado, F. P. 'The Trials and Tribulations of Racialized Critical Rhetorical Theory: Understanding the Rhetorical Ambiguities of Proposition 187.' *Communication Theory* 8 (1998): 245–70.

Hayden, T., and Schoemer, K. 'Se Habla Rock and Roll? You Will Soon: A Musical Invasion from South of the Border.' *Newsweek* 130 (8 September 1997), 70–1.

Hayes, J. E. *Radio Nation: Communication, Popular Culture, and Nationalism in Mexico, 1920–1950* (Tucson, AZ: University of Arizona Press, 2000).

Hernández, M. A. 'Chronicles of Mexico City Life: The Music of Rockdrigo González.' *Studies in Latin American Popular Culture* 26 (2007), 64–78.

———. 'Remaking the *Corrido* for the 1990s: Maldita Vecindad's "El Barzón."' *Studies in Latin American Popular Culture* 20 (2001): 101–16.

———. 'Breaking the Mold of Contemporary Working-Class Mexican Masculinity: The *Rock Urbano* Music of Tex Tex.' *Journal of Popular Music Studies* 20, no. 1 (1998): 3–25.

Herrera-Sobek, M. *The Mexican Corrido: A Feminist Analysis* (Bloomington and Indianapolis: Indiana University Press, 1990).

Hickey, D. *Air Guitar: Essays on Art & Democracy* (Los Angeles: Art Issues Press, 1997).

Holguin, R. S. 'Los Lobos Give La Bamba a Rest' [On-line document], (23 September 1996). http://jam.canoe.ca/Music/Artists/L/Los_Lobos/1996/09/23/747064.html

Holston, M. '*Rock en Español*: A Youth Market Comes of Age, but Record Executives Turn a Blind Eye.' *Hispanic Magazine* 10 (January/February 1997): 46–52.

Huckin, T. 'Critical Discourse Analysis and the Discourse of Condescension.' In *Discourse Studies in Composition*, eds. E. L. Barton and G. Stygall (Cresskill, NJ: Hampton Press, 2002), 155–76.

———. 'Critical Discourse Analysis.' *Journal of TESOL-France* 2(2) (1995): 95–112.

Huntington, S. P. 'The Hispanic Challenge.' *Foreign Policy* (March/April 2004): 30–45.

Hurtt, M. 'Bo Diddley: The In Sound from Way Out!' *MOJO* 141 (August 2005): 64–9.

Jeffords, S. *Hard Bodies: Hollywood Masculinity in the Reagan Era* (New Brunswick, NJ: Rutgers University Press, 1994).

Jelin, E., Dos Santos, T., Filgueira, C., Laserna, R., Verdesoto, L., Ballón, E., Rojas, F., Gómez, L., Campero, G., Rivarola, D., and Calderón Guitiérrez, F. *Los Movimientos Sociales Ante La Crisis* (Buenos Aires: Universidad de las Naciones Unidas, 1986).

Jensen, R. J., and Hammerback, J. C. 'Radical Nationalism among Chicanos: The Rhetoric of José Angel Gutiérrez.' *Western Journal of Speech Communication* 44 (1980): 191–202.

Johnson, F. L. *Speaking Culturally: Language Diversity in the United States* (Thousand Oaks, CA: Sage, 2000.

Kahn, E. 'The Carter Family on Border Radio.' *American Music* 14 (1996): 205–17.

Kauppila, P. 'The Sound of the Suburbs: A Case Study of Three Garage Bands in San Jose, California during the 1960s.' *Popular Music and Society* 28 (2005): 391–405.

Keith, M. C. 'The Long Road to Radio Studies.' *Journal of Broadcasting and Electronic Media* 51, no. 3 (2007): 1–7.

King, J. 'Review Essay on "Rock Nacional: Crónicas de la Resistencia Juvenil" by Pablo Vila.' *Popular Music* 6 (1987): 250–2.

Kirby, D. *Little Richard: The Birth of Rock 'n' Roll* (New York: Continuum Books, 2009).

Kirk, J. 'The Development of an *Ondero*.' In *José Agustín: Onda and Beyond*, eds. Carter and Schmidt (Columbia, MO: University of Missouri Press, 1986), 9–23.

Klosterman, C. '1,400 Mexican Moz Fans Can't Be (Totally) Wrong.' In *Chuck Klosterman IV: A Decade of Curious People and Dangerous Ideas* (New York: Scribner, 2007) 47–56.

Kohl, P. R. 'Reading Between the Lines: Music and Noise in Hegemony and Resistance.' *Popular Music and Society* 21 (1997): 3–17.

Kun, J. D. *Audiotopia: Music, Race and America* (Berkeley, CA: University of California Press, 2005).
_____. 'File Under: Post-Mexico.' *Aztlán* 29, no. 1 (2004): 271–7.
_____. 'Rock's *Reconquista*.' In *Rock Over the Edge: Transformations in Popular Music Culture*, eds. Beebe et al. (Durham, NC: Duke University Press, 2002a), 255–88.
_____. 'The Sun Never Sets on MTV: Tijuana NO! and the Border of Music Video.' In *Latino/a Popular Culture*, eds. M. Habell-Pallán and M. Romero (New York: New York University Press, 2002b), 102–16.
_____. 'The Aural Border.' *Theatre Journal* 52 (2000): 1–21.
_____. 'Against Easy Listening: Audiotopic Readings and Transnational Soundings.' In *Everynight Life: Culture and Dance in Latin/o America*, eds. C. F. Delgado and J. E. Muñoz (Durham, NC: Duke University Press, 1997), 288–309.
Leal, J. '*Yo vivo así*, It's My Reality: How *Rock en Español* Started a Conversation between U.S. Latino Youth and Their Latin American Counterparts.' [lecture/presentation] *Experience Music Project POP Conference* (Seattle, WA: MEP, 2008).
Levy, A. 'Official Bio: Joan Baez' [On-line document]. In Joan Baez Official Website (June 2003). http://baez.woz.org/officialbio.html
Levy, J. 'Doug Sahm and the Sir Douglas Quintet: A Brief History' (On-line document). In *The Vinyl Tourist* (no date). http://www.laventure.net/tourist/sdq_hist.htm
Lewis, G. H. 'La Pistola y El Corazón: Protest and Passion in Mexican-American Popular Music.' *Journal of Popular Culture* 26 (1992): 51–67.
Limón, J. E. *American Encounters: Greater Mexico, the United States, and the Erotics of Culture* (Boston: Beacon Press, 1998).
Linna, M. Liner notes to *96 Tears: The Very Best of Question Mark & the Mysterians* (Cavestomp! Records/Varese Sarabande Records/Universal Music, 2001).
_____. Liner notes to *The Sonics: Here are the Sonics!!!* [compact disc] (Norton Records, 1999).
Lipsitz, G. *Footsteps in the Dark* (Minneapolis, MN: University of Minnesota Press, 2007).
_____. '"Home is Where the Hatred Is": Work, Music, and the Transnational Economy.' In *Home, Exile, Homeland: Film, Media and the Politics of Place*, ed. H. Naficy (New York: Routledge, 1999), 193–212.
_____. *Dangerous Crossroads* (New York: Verso, 1994a).
_____. *Rainbow at Midnight: Labor and Culture in the 1940s* (Urbana and Chicago: University of Illinois Press, 1994b).
_____. 'Chicano Rock: Cruising Around the Historical Bloc.' *Rockin' the Boat*, ed. R. Garofalo (Boston, MA: South End Press, 1992), 267–79.
_____. *Time Passages: Collective Memory and American Popular Culture* (Minneapolis, MN: University of Minnesota Press, 1990).
_____. 'Cruising Around the Historical Bloc: Postmodernism and Popular Music in East Los Angeles.' *Cultural Critique* 5 (1986): 157–77.
Llewellyn, H. 'Rockers Develop Cultural Confidence.' *Billboard* 113 (16 June 2001): pLM-6, 6–7.
Lopetegui, E. 'The Coming of Age of Café Tacuba.' *Billboard* 112 (9 December 2000): pLM-3.
López, J. 'El Rockondero.' In *Mitos Mexicanos*, ed. E. Florescano (México, DF: Taurus, 2001), 393–400.
Loza, S. 'Assimilation, Reclamation, and Rejection of the Nation-State by Chicano Musicians.' In *Postnational Musical Identities: Cultural Production, Distribution, and Consumption in a Globalized Scenario*, eds. Corona and Madrid (Lahnam, MD: Lexington Books, 2008), 137–50.
_____. 'Identity, Nationalism, and Aesthetics among Chicano/Mexicano Musicians in Los Angeles.' *Selected Reports in Ethnomusicology* 10 (1994): 51–8.

———. *Barrio Rhythm: Mexican American Music in Los Angeles* (Urbana and Chicago: University of Illinois Press, 1993).
Macías, A. *Mexican American Mojo: Popular Music, Dance, and Urban Culture in Los Angeles, 1935–1968* (Durham, NC: Duke University Press, 2008).
———. 'Rock con Raza, Raza con Jazz: Latinos/as and Post-World War II Popular American Music.' In *Musical Migrations*, eds. Aparicio and Jáquez (New York: Palgrave Macmillan, 2003), 183–97.
Marcus, G. *Mystery Train: Images of America in Rock 'n' Roll Music* (New York: Plume/Penguin Books USA, 1987).
Márez, C. 'Brown: The Politics of Working-Class Chicano Style.' *Social Text* 48 (1996): 109–32.
Marsh, D. *Louie Louie* (New York: Hyperion, 1993).
———. (ed.). *The First Rock & Roll Confidential Report* (New York: Pantheon Books, 1985).
Martín-Barbero, J. 'The Processes: From Nationalisms to Transnationals.' In *Sources: Notable Selections in Mass Media*, eds. J. Hanson and D. J. Maxcy (Guilford, CT: Dushkin/McGraw-Hill, 1999), 345–53.
Martínez, R. *The Other Side: Fault Lines, Guerilla Saints, and the True Heart of Rock 'n' Roll* (New York: Verso).
McCarthy, J., and Sansoe, R. *Voices of Latin Rock: The People and Events that Created this Sound* (Milwaukee, WI: Hal Leonard Corporation, 2004).
McLeese, D. 'Sir Douglas Sahm and the Garage as Big as Texas.' *Popular Music and Society* 29 (2006): 441–50.
Mehr, 'In the Beginning was the Word . . .,' *MOJO* 163 (August 2008): 92.
Mendheim, B. *Ritchie Valens: The First Latino Rocker*. (Tempe, AZ: Bilingual Press, 1987).
Mitchell, R. 'West Coast Roots: "Raza Rock" Features Major Chicano Voices of the '70s, '80s.' *Houston Chronicle* (11 January 1998).
Molina, R. *The Old Barrio Guide to Low Rider Music, 1950–1975*, 3rd Ed. (La Puente, CA: Mictlan Publishing, 2002).
Molina Guzmán, I., and Valdivia, A. N. 'Brain, Brow, and Booty: Latina Iconicity in U.S. Popular Culture.' *Communication Review* 7 (2004): 205–21.
Monsiváis, C. 'El TRI y Alejandro Lora.' Liner notes to *Los Número Uno: Exitos 1968/2003* [compact disc] by El TRI (Miami Beach, FL: Warner Music Latina, 2003).
———. *Mexican Postcards* (New York: Verso, 1997).
Morales, E. *Living in Spanglish: The Search for Latino Identity in America* (New York: St. Martin's Press, 2002a).
———. 'Rock is Dead and Living in Mexico: The Resurrection of *La Nueva Onda*.' *Village Voice* (2002b). http://www.rockeros.com/tidbit/rockmex.htm
Nailen, D. 'Summer at Red Butte: Concert Series Offers a Bumper Crop of Great Acts.' *The Salt Lake Tribune* (25 April 2003).
Novas, H. *Everything You Need to Know about Latino History* (New York: Plume/Penguin Group).
NPR. 'Mariachi Punk: At Home in L.A.' *National Public Radio* (19 September 2009). http://www.npr.org/templates/story/story.php?storyId=112966664
Nuggets [compact disc box set]. Liner notes to *Nuggets: Original Artyfacts from the First Psychedelic Era, 1965–1968* (Rhino Entertainment Company, 1998).
Nuggets II [compact disc box set]. Liner notes to *Nuggets II: Original Artyfacts from the British Empire and Beyond, 1964–1969* (Rhino Entertainment Company, 2001).
Ono, K. A., and Sloop, J. M. *Shifting Borders: Rhetoric, Immigration, and California's Proposition 187* (Philadelphia, PA: Temple University Press, 2002).
Ostermann, A. C., and Keller-Cohen, D. 'Good Girls Go to Heaven; Bad Girls . . . Learn to be

Good: Quizzes in American and Brazilian Teenage Girls' Magazines.' *Discourse & Society* 9 (1998): 531–58.
Otfinoski, S. *The Golden Age of Rock Instrumentals* (New York: Billboard Books, 1997).
Pachuco Boogie. (2002). *Pachuco Boogie, featuring Don Tosti (Historic Mexican-American Music: Volume 10)* [compact disc release]. (El Cerrito, CA: Arhoolie Productions, Inc).
Pacini Hernández, D. 'The Name Game: Locating Latinas/os, Latins, and Latin Americans in the US Popular Music Landscape.' In *A Companion to Latina/o Studies*, eds. J. Flores and R. Rosaldo (New York: Blackwell Publishing, 2007), 49–59.
_____. 'Amalgamating Musics: Popular music and Cultural Hybridity in the Americas.' In *Musical Migrations*, eds. Aparicio and Jáquez (New York: Palgrave Macmillan, 2003), 13–32.
_____. 'A Tale of Two Cities: A Comparative Analysis of Los Angeles Chicano and Nuyorican Engagement with Rock and Roll.' *CENTRO Journal 11* (2000): 71–92.
Pacini Hernández, D., Fernández L'Hoeste, H., and Zolov, E. *Rockin' Las Américas: The Global Politics of Rock in Latin/o America* (Pittsburgh, PA: Pittsburgh University Press, 2004).
Padilla, X. 'Rocking in Mexico: Bands Continue to Struggle with Radio's and Labels' Attitudes.' *Billboard* 113 (16 June 2001): pLM-4.
Palacios, J., and Estrada, T. '"A Contra Corriente": A History of Women Rockers in Mexico.' In *Rockin' Las Américas: The Global Politics of Rock in Latin/o America*, eds. Pacini Hernadez, et al. (Pittsburgh, PA: Pittsburgh University Press, 2004), 142–59.
Palmer, R. 'The Cuban Connection.' *Spin* (November 1988): 26–103.
Paredes, A. *With His Pistol in His Hand: A Border Ballad and Its Hero* (Austin, TX: University of Texas Press, 1958).
Peña, M. *Música Tejana: The Cultural Economy of Artistic Transformation* (College Station, TX: Texas A&M University Press, 1999).
Perez, L., Liner notes to *Rock en Español Vol. One*, by Los Straitjackets (Chapel Hill, NC: Yep Roc Records, 2007).
Perrone, C. A. 'Changing of the Guard: Questions and Contrasts of Brazilian Rock Phenomena.' *Studies in Latin American Popular Culture* 9 (1990): 65–84.
Peters, J. D. *Speaking into the Air: A History of the Idea of Communication* (Chicago; University of Chicago Press, 2000).
Pineda, R. D. 'Will They See Me Coming? Do They Know I'm Running?: Los Lobos and the Performance of *Mestizaje* Identity through Journey.' *Text and Performance Quarterly* 29, no. 2 (2009): 183–200.
_____. 'Book review of R. O. de la Garza and L. DeSipio, "Muted Voices: Latinos and the 2000 Elections."' *Argumentation and Advocacy* 42, no. 1 (2005): 52–4.
Portales, M. *Crowding Out Latinos: Mexican Americans in the Public Consciousness* (Philadelphia: Temple University Press, 2000).
Racho, S., De Los Santos, N., De Jesus, W., Evans, T., and Zapata, J. *The Bronze Screen: 100 Years of the Latino Image in Hollywood* [documentary film] (Chicago: Questar, 2002).
Reyes, D., and Waldman, T. *Land of a Thousand Dances: Chicano Rock 'n' Roll from Southern California* (Albuquerque, NM: University of New Mexico Press, 1998).
Rhodes, J. 'The Visibility of Race in Media History.' In *Gender, Race, and Class in Media*, eds. G. Dines and J. Humez (Thousand Oaks, CA: Sage, 1995), 33–9.
Richardson, C. *Batos, Bolillos, Pochos, and Pelados: Class and Culture on the South Texas Border* (Austin, TX: University of Texas Press, 1999).
Richardson, E. 'She Was Workin Like Foreal: Critical Literacy and Discourse Practices of African American Females in the Age of Hip Hop.' *Discourse and Society* 18(6), (2007): 789–809.
Rinderle, S. 'The Mexican Diaspora: A Critical Examination of Signifiers.' *Journal of Communication Inquiry* 29 (2005): 294–316.

Roberts, J. S. *The Latin Tinge: The Impact of Latin American Music on the United States* (New York: Oxford University Press, 1999).

Rodríguez Marino, P. 'MTV Latino: Identidad, Nación, y Rock.' *Studies in Latin American Popular Culture* 21 (2002): 120–73.

Roiz, C. T. 'Los Lobos: The Legend Lives On.' *Vista: The Magazine for All Hispanics* (July 2001), 6–24.

Rotella, C. *Good With Their Hands: Boxers, Bluesmen, and other Characters from the Rust Belt* (Berkeley: University of California Press, 2002).

Rothenbuhler, E. W. 'For-the-Record Aesthetics and Robert Johnson's Blues Style as a Product of Recorded Culture.' *Popular Music* 26 (2007): 65–81.

Rothenbuhler, E. W., and McCourt, T. 'Radio Redefines Itself, 1947–1962.' In *Radio Reader: Essays in the Cultural History of Radio*, eds. M. Hilmes and J. Loviglio (New York: Routledge, 2002), 367–87.

Rubin, R., and Melnick, J. *Immigration and American Popular Culture: An Introduction* (New York: New York University Press, 2007).

Ryan, T. *American Hit Radio: A History of Popular Singles from 1955 to the Present* (Rocklin, CA: Prima Publishing, 1996).

Said, E. W. 'The Clash of Ignorance.' *The Nation* 273, no. 12 (22 October 2001): 11.

Saldívar, J. D. *Border Matters: Remapping American Cultural Studies* (Berkeley, CA: University of California Press, 1997).

_____. *The Dialectics of Our America: Genealogy, Cultural Critique, and Literary History* (Durham, NC: Duke University Press, 1991).

Sanchez, E. 'A Brief History of Latin Alternative Music in Houston, Part 1' [unpublished document] (Personal communication, 2009).

Savage, J. *England's Dreaming: Anarchy, Sex Pistols, Punk Rock and Beyond* (New York: St. Martin's Griffin, 2001).

Schelonka, G. 'RockIn' la Frontera: Mexican Rock, Globalization, and National Identity.' In *Postnational Musical Identities: Cultural Production, Distribution, and Consumption in a Globalized Scenario*, eds. Corona and Madrid (Lahnam, MD: Lexington Books, 2008), 151–70.

_____. 'Mexican Rock and the Border Under Globalization.' *Peace Review: A Journal of Social Justice* 18 (2006): 101–8.

Semán, P., and Vila, P. 'Rock Chabón: The Contemporary National Rock of Argentina.' In *From Tejano to Tango: Latin American Popular Music*, ed. W. A. Clark (New York: Routledge, 2002), 70–94.

Shank, B. 'Punk Rock at Raul's.' *Dissonant Identities: The Rock 'n' Roll Scene in Austin, Texas* (Hanover: University Press of New England, 1994).

Simmons, M. 'The Origins of Twelve-String Power.' *Acoustic Guitar* (November 1997). http://www.frets.com/FRETSPages/History/12string/12stOrigins.html

Singh, A., and Schmidt, P. 'On the Borders Between U.S. Studies and Postcolonial Theory.' In *Postcolonial Theory in the United States*, eds. Singh and Schmidt (Jackson, MS: University Press of Mississippi, 2000), 3–69.

Smith, W. M. 'Banda Meets Ska Meets The Smiths in the Sound of Pistolera.' *Houston Press* (29 May 2008). http://www.houstonpress.com/content/printVersion/802945

Solórzano-Thompson, N. 'Performative Masculinities: The *Pachuco* and the *Luchador* in the Songs of Maldita Vecindad and Café Tacuba.' *Studies in Latin American Popular Culture* 26 (2007): 79–96.

Sorrondeguy, M. *Beyond the Screams/Mas Alla De Los Gritos: A U.S. Latino/Chicano Hardcore Punk Documentary* [documentary film], (Chicago: Lengua Armada, 1999).

Spitulnik, D. 'Anthropology and Mass Media.' *Annual Review of Anthropology* 22 (1993): 293–315.

Starr, L., and Waterman, C. *American Popular Music: From Minstrelsy to MTV* (New York: Oxford University Press, 2003).

Stavans, I. [host/producer]. 'Conversations with Ilan Stavans: Gustavo Santaolalla.' *La Plaza* [weekly public television series produced by WGBH Boston] (2006). http://www.wgbh.org/pages/laplaza/index?feature_id=2052748

Stigberg, D. K. 'Foreign Currents during the 60s and 70s in Mexican Popular Music: Rock and Roll, the Romantic Ballad and the Cumbia.' *Studies in Latin American Popular Culture* 4 (1985): 170–84.

Stone, M. 'Bajito y Suavecito [Low and Slow]: Low Riding and the "Class" of Class[*].' *Studies in Latin American Popular Culture* 9 (1990).

Stratton, J. 'Jews, Punk and the Holocaust: From The Velvet Underground to the Ramones — the Jewish-American Story.' *Popular Music* 24, no. 1 (2005): 79–105.

Strauss, N. 'The Indestructible Beat of Bo Diddley.' *Rolling Stone* 25 (August 2005): 56–70.

Sublette, N. 'The Kingsmen and the Cha-Cha-Chá.' In *Listen Again: A Momentary History of Pop Music*, ed. E. Weisbard (Durham, NC: Duke University Press, 2007), 69–94.

———. 'The Centrality of Cuban Music' [lecture/presentation]. *Experience Music Project POP Conference* (Seattle, WA: EMP, 2005). http://www.kexp.org/learn/popcon_sublette.asp

Szatmary, D. P. *Rockin' in Time: A Social History of Rock-and-Roll* (Upper Saddle River, NJ: Prentice Hall, 2000).

Taylor, P. S. *An American-Mexican Frontier: Nueces County, Texas* (Chapel Hill, NC: University of North Carolina Press, 1934).

Todd, S., Young, A., and Olmos, E. J. *Americanos: Latino Life in the United States.* [documentary film] (Burbank, CA: Olmos Productions, 2000).

Torres, L. 'Siendo la Verdadera Historia de Los Lobos del Este de Los Angeles.' Supplemental booklet to *El Cancionero: Mas y Mas* [4-compact disc set] (Los Angeles: Warner Bros./Rhino, 2000).

Tovares, R. D. *Manufacturing the Gang: Mexican American Youth Gangs on Local Television News* (Westport, CT: Greenwood Press, 2002).

Ulaby, N. 'U.S. Cross-Over Hits Elude Latin Alternative.' On *All Things Considered* [National Public Radio daily series], (8 March 2006). http://www.npr.org/templates/story/story.php?storyId=5251735

Valdivia, A. N. 'Is My Butt Your Island? The Myth of Discovery and Contemporary Latina/o Communication Studies.' In *Latina/o Communication Studies Today*, ed. A. N. Valdivia (New York: Peter Lang, 2008), 3–25.

Valenzuela, J. M. *¡A La Brava Ése!* (Tijuana, MX: El Colegio de la Frontera Norte, 1988).

Valenzuela, J. M., and González, G. *Oye Cómo Va: Recuento del Rock Tijuanense* (Tijuana, MX: Centro Cultural Tijuana — Instituto Mexicano de la Juventud, 1999).

van Dijk, T. A. 'Principles of Critical Discourse Analysis.' *Discourse and Society* 4, (1993): 249–83.

Varela, C. Liner notes to *Pachuco Boogie, featuring Don Tosti* (*Historic Mexican-American Music: Volume 10*) [compact disc] (El Cerrito, CA: Arhoolie Productions, 2001).

Viesca, V. H. 'Straight Out The Barrio: Ozomatli and the Importance of Place in the Formation of Chicano/a Popular Culture in Los Angeles.' *Cultural Values* 4, no. 4 (2000): 445–73.

Vila, P. *Crossing Borders, Reinforcing Borders: Social Categories, Metaphors and Narrative Identities on the U.S.-Mexico Frontier* (Austin, TX: University of Texas Press, 2000).

———. 'Rock Nacional and Dictatorship in Argentina.' In *Rockin' the Boat*, ed. R. Garofalo (Boston, MA: South End Press, 1992), 208–29.

———. 'Argentina's *Rock Nacional*: The Struggle for Meaning.' *Latin American Music Review* 10 (1989): 1–28.

———. 'Rock Nacional and Dictatorship in Argentina.' *Popular Music* 6 (1987): 129–48.

Waddell, R. 'Rock en Español Takes Off on Tour.' Billboard 112 (9 December 2000): pLM-1/1–2.
Ward, E. 'SWSX Records: Los Super 7 — Heard it on the X' [music review]. Austin Chronicle (18 March 2005) (Austin, TX: Austin Chronicle Corporation).
_____. Liner notes to Mendocino [compact disc] by Sir Douglas Quintet (Universal Music, 2002).
Weinstein, D. Heavy Metal: A Cultural Sociology (New York: Lexington Books, 1991).
Whitburn, J. Billboard Top 1000 Singles, 1955–2000 (Milwaukee, WI: Hal Leonard Corporation, 2001).
_____. The Billboard Book of Top 40 Hits (New York: Watson-Guptil Publications, 1992).
Wilkman, J. Chicano Rock!: The Sounds of East Los Angeles [documentary film], Produced, written, directed, and edited by J. Wilkman (Wilkman Productions, 2008).
Willis-Rivera, J. L. '"Latino Night": Performances of Latino/a Culture in Northwest Ohio.' Communication Quarterly 45, no. 3 (1997): 335–54.
Wodak, R. Disorders of Discourse (New York: Longman, 1996).
Woods, C. M. 'Immigration Divides Voters, Issues Could Drive Local House Races.' Wichita Eagle (22 October 2004): 1A.
Zolov, E. 'La Onda Chicana: Mexico's Forgotten Rock Counterculture.' In Rockin' Las Américas: The Global Politics of Rock in Latin/o America, eds. Pacini Hernadez et al. (Pittsburgh, PA: Pittsburgh University Press, 2004), 22–42.
_____. 'Armando Nava and Los Dug Dug's.' In The Human Tradition in Mexico, ed. J. M. Pilcher (Wilmington, DE: Scholarly Resources, 2003), 211–24.
_____. Refried Elvis: The Rise of the Mexican Counter-Culture (Berkeley and Los Angeles: University of California Press, 1999).

Resources and Suggestions for Further Research

Alice Bag (website of Alice Bag). http://www.alicebag.com
American Sabor: Latino Innovators In US Pop Music (10-part documentary series by University of Washington School of Music, Experience Music Project, and KEXP Documentaries). http://www.kexp.org/learn/docu_american_sabor.asp
Diccionario del Rock Latino. Coordinado por Zona de Obras (Sociedad General de Autores y Editores, 2000).
East LA Revue. (Internet jukebox featuring Chicano rock music). http://www.eastlarevue.com
Estrada, T. Sirenas al Ataque: Historia de las Mujeres Rockeras Mexicanas [New edition], (México, DF: Editorial Oceano de Mexico, 2008).
Latin Music USA. (Four-part documentary series by PBS, 2009).
Miccio, L., de la Parra, F., Schechter, J., Turner, M., and Koenig, A. Rock 'n' Roll Made In Mexico: From Evolution to Revolution [documentary film], (Happy Trailers HD LLC/Heat Drum Productions, 2008).
Mictlan. (Mictlan Publishing: Compilations/Archives/Images/History of 'Chicano soul' music). http://www.mictlan.com
Pacini Hernández, D. Oye Cómo Va: Hybridity and Identity in Latino Popular Music (Philadelphia: Temple University Press, forthcoming in 2009).
Valenzuela, J. M. ¡A La Brava Ése! (Tijuana, MX: El Colegio de la Frontera Norte, 1988).
Valenzuela, J. M., and González, G. Oye Cómo Va: Recuento del Rock Tijuanense (Tijuana, MX: Centro Cultural Tijuana — Instituto Mexicano de la Juventud, 1999).

Permissions

Chapter two was published previously as: Avant-Mier, R. '*Heard It On The X*: Border Radio as Public Discourse and the Latino Legacy in Popular Music.' In *Radio Cultures: The Sound Medium in American Life*, ed. M. C. Keith (New York: Peter Lang Publishing, 2008), 47–64.

Chapter three was published previously as: Avant-Mier, R. 'Latinos in the Garage: A Genealogical Examination of the Latino/a Presence and Influence in Garage Rock (and Rock and Pop Music).' *Popular Music and Society* 31, no. 5 (2008): 555–74. http://www.informaworld.com

Chapter four was published previously as: Avant-Mier, R. '*Las Ondas de José Agustín*: Remembering *La Onda* through the Literature of José Agustín and *La Onda Roquera* (Rock 'n Roll in México).' *Chapter & Verse* 3, no. 1 (2005): 1–25.

Index

'96 Tears' song 102–3, 110–1, 152, 196,
1968 Mexico City Olympics 124
1985 Mexico City earthquake 142–3

African Americans (*or*, Blacks) 1, 35, 48, 57, 80, 92, 186, 194–5, 202
    Black Mexicans 121
    proximity with Mexicans 35–6, 37–8, 40, 49, 57, 65–6, 73, 82, 94, 96, 127, 135, 176, 194
Aguilar, Dave 91–2
Aguilera, Christina 87
Agustín, José 27, 112–27, 136–40
Alaniz, Bob 91
Alpert, Herb (and the Tijuana Brass) 43–4, 172
alternative music 160–1
Amazing Rhythm Aces, The 43
'Angel Baby' song 75 *see also* Mendez Hamlin, Rosalie
Anglo Americans 4, 14, 34, 59, 68, 79, 81, 87, 90, 92, 95, 98, 108, 118, 133, 154, 166, 171, 176–7, 185, 191 *see also* European Americans
anglocentricism 90, 117 *see also* ethnocentrism
Animals, The 128 *see also* Burdon, Eric
answer songs 20–1
Anthony, Marc 87
Araya, Tom 159
Argentina (*or*, Argentine) 12–13, 27, 72, 91, 110, 129, 143, 147–52, 156, 160–2, 164–5, 168–72, 174, 181–2, 185, 191–2, 197, 201
Argentine ducktail *see* ducktail haircut
Armenta Brothers, The 94
Asian (*or*, Asian American) 57, 80, 176, 182, 195
assimilation (*or*, acculturation process) 4, 49, 89–90, 97–8, 106–7, 129, 132, 140, 147, 151, 155–6, 158, 172–3, 195
At The Drive-In 170, 177, 186
Ataque 77 110
Aterciopelados 87–9, 111, 143, 168–9, 177
Atkins, Chet 40
Audioslave 33
Austin, Texas music scene 83, 156, 172, 181, 187, 189, 192
Avándaro festival 125–6

Axton, Hoyt 43
Azpiazú, Don 104
Azteca 77, 133, 156 *see also* Eastside Sound

Baca, Susana 34, 168
Bad Company 33
Bad Religion 158
Baez, Joan 127–8, 134
bajo sexto *see* twelve-string guitar
Balcom, Handsome Jim 74
Baker, Lavern 93
Band, The 128
Bangs, Lester 98, 103
Banhart, Devendra 189–90, 192
Bátiz, Javier 27, 120–1, 126, 128–9
Bauzá, Mario 104
Beastie Boys, The 91
Beatles, The 39, 59, 75–6, 93, 97, 100, 121–2, 144, 164, 173
Beck (*or*, Beck Hansen) 53–4, 91, 168, 171, 174
Beck, Jeff 40
Bega, Lou 87
Beltrán, Lola 67
Berlanga, Andrés 37
Bernal, Gil 94
Berry, Chuck 46, 78, 123
Berry, Richard 99
Big and Rich 101
Big Bad Voodoo Daddy 84
Big Bopper, The *see* Richardson, J. P.
Bill Haley & the Comets 40, 93–4
Billboard magazine 6, 168, 170–2, 176
Billie & Lillie 96
Black Crowes, The 81
Black Flag 158
Black Keys, The 110
Black Sabbath 40, 135
Blendells, The 77 *see also* Eastside Sound
Blind Faith 33
Blondie 152, 164
blues 34–5, 37–8, 45, 49, 144, 157, 194–5
bluesmen 35–6, 38–9, 45, 94
'Bo Diddley Beat' 47, 104, 108

219

Bob Wills and His Texas Playboys 41, 43–4, 46
boogie woogie 58, 60, 84, 134 see also jump blues
border theory (or, border studies paradigm) 17–18, 26
Boston music scene 127, 168, 202
Brant, Claudia 168–9
Brazil (or, Brazilian) 133, 149, 159, 161, 165, 168, 171
Brian Setzer Orchestra, The see Setzer, Brian
British Invasion 44, 76, 173
Broonzy, Big Bill 38
Brown, Clarence 'Gatemouth' 34–5, 40
Brown, Ruth 93
Bunbury, Enrique 192
Burdon, Eric 135 see also War and/or The Animals
Bustamante, Cruz (Lieutenant Governor) 3–4
Byrd, Roy (or, Professor Longhair) 93
Byrds, The 39, 128
Byrne, David 91, 163, 166, 168, 176 see also Talking Heads

Café Tacuba 5, 144, 161, 169, 171, 173, 176–7, 191
Caifanes 143, 162
Cake 39, 44
Calexico 40, 44, 53, 172, 184–5, 189
Calloway, Cab 57
Canned Heat 101, 121, 130–1 see also 'Fito' de la Parra
Cannibal and the Headhunters 77, 103 see also Eastside Sound
Cano, Eddie 58
Capitols, The 97
Captain Hook 43
Carrasco, Joe 'King' see Joe 'King' Carrasco & the Crowns
Carter Family 41–2
Cash, Johnny 29–30, 43–4, 184
Cash, June Carter 31 see also Carter Family
Castañeda, Carlos 113
Chambao 192
Champs, The 47, 95
Chan Romero and the Carlos Brothers 74
Charles, Ray 94
Chávez, César 69–70, 127, 134, 157 see also Chicano – movement
Chávez Ravine 76
Cherry Poppin' Daddies 84
Chicano (or, Chicana)
  chicanismo 2 see also MEChA
  the 'Chicano wave' in Texas 78, 132
  discourse 133
  identity 2, 65–6, 70–1, 77, 79, 98, 100, 108, 110, 133–4, 154–5, 157–8, 166, 170, 187, 189, 192–4
  movement 69–70, 77–8, 131–2, 133–4, 157, 184
'Chicano' song 79
chicha music 183
Chile (or, Chilean) 127, 176–7, 149–50, 159–60, 165, 174, 185
cholo style (or, chola style) 82, 87
Clapton, Eric 36, 54
Clark, Roy 40
Clash, The 105, 110, 152–3, 164–5
class (or, socioeconomic status) 4, 64, 80, 84, 90, 92, 116–17, 120, 125–6, 137, 142–3, 148–9, 153, 159, 169, 195, 199–202
Clinton, Bill (President) 72–3
Coasters, The 38, 93–4
Cobain, Kurt see Nirvana
Colombia 152, 160, 165, 168, 174
colonialism 3 see also cultural imperialism
compound bimusicality 130, 132
Concrete Blonde 166–7
Cooder, Ry 76, 176
Cooke, Sam 96
Cordero 185–6
'Corrido de Delano' song 69
Cortez, Bobby 91
Cortez, Dave 'Baby' 97
country music 24, 41, 45–6, 49, 190–1, 194
  country rock 24, 39, 43, 81, 85, 128, 130, 184–5, 192
Creedence Clearwater Revival 192
Crosby, Bing 15, 42, 44
Crosby, Stills & Nash 130
Cuarteto Don Ramon Sr 58
cultural imperialism 9, 11, 112, 122, 124, 128, 137, 144, 151, 196
cultural nationalism 132, 143, 151, 153–4, 193
Cuba (or, Cuban) 2, 16, 34, 49, 72, 104, 108, 118, 130–1, 152, 167, 173, 176–7, 191, 198
  Afro-Cuban music 46–7, 131, 76–7, 93–6, 99, 108, 114, 131, 167, 200
Cuca 165
Cugat, Xavier 104
Cure, The (or, Robert Smith) 39, 165, 181
Cypress Hill 167

Dale, Dick 40
Dallas music scene 37, 101
Damn Yankees 33
Danzig 158
Darío, Ruben 114

Index

'Davey Crockett' song 68
Day of the Dead iconography/death imagery 128, 159, 167
de la Parra, Adolfo 'Fito' 121, 130–1 *see also* Canned Heat
Dean, James 81
Decemberists, The 40
Descendents, The 158
Detroit music scene 57, 129, 153, 168, 192
DeVotchka 44
dialogue (or, music as dialogue) 20–1
Diamond, Neil 97
diaspora 1, 9, 18–20, 25, 198, 200
    doubly and triply diasporic 198
    Latin diaspora/pan-Latin 1, 18, 71, 198–202
    'Latin Rock Diaspora' 25–7, 169–70, 173–6, 180, 188, 190–4, 198, 200
Díaz, Junot 146–7
Díaz, Raul 58
Diddley, Bo 38, 47, 93, 110 *see also* 'Bo Diddley Beat'
Dion, Celine 106
Dominican Republic (*or*, Dominican) 146
Domino, Antoine 'Fats' (*or*, Fats Domino) 16, 67, 93–4, 104
'Don Tosti' (*or*, Edmundo Martínez Tostado) 56, 59–60, 176
Don Tosti's Quartet 65
Doors, The 97, 128–9, 165 *see also* Morrison, Jim
Dorsey, Tommy (Tommy Dorsey Orchestra) 58
Downs, Lila 191–2
Drifters, The 96
ducktail haircut (*or*, Argentine ducktail, etc) 80–1
Dylan, Bob (*or*, Dylan-like) 113, 122, 127, 148

Eagles, The 39, 81–2, 128
Eastside Sound 73, 77, 128, 143
Echeverri, Andrea 168–9 *see also* Aterciopelados
El Chicano band 78, 133–4, 154, 174 *see also* Eastside Sound
El Gran Silencio 176
El Monte Legion Stadium 74
'El Monte' song 75
El Paso-Juárez music scene (*or*, Juárez-El Paso scene) 38, 46, 55–6, 59, 105, 202
El Salvador 118, 176
El TRI/Three Souls in My Mind 112, 122–4, 126, 138, 143 *see also* Lora, Alex
'El Vez' (*or*, Robert Lopez) 1, 80, 155, 157, 190
Electric Light Orchestra (*or*, ELO) 39
Ellen DeGeneres TV program 29
'Elvis Perez' song 72

Emeralds, The 77 *see also* Eastside Sound
Eno, Brian 177
Epumer, Mar'a Gabriela 169
Escovedo, Alejandro 156
Etheridge, Melissa 166
ethnocentrism 4, 90, 117, 141, 175 *see also* anglocentrism
European Americans 3, 16, 24, 59, 81, 90, 98, 114, 117, 136, 142, 181, 190, 195, 199–200 *see also* Anglo Americans

Fabulosos Cadillacs 163–4, 182 *see also* Señor Flavio
Fats Domino *see* Domino, Antoine 'Fats'
Feliciano, José 130, 184
Fender, Freddy 43, 96, 100
Fiestas, The 96, 104
Fifth Dimension, The 75
films (*or*, movies) 13–15, 81, 93, 98, 129, 193
    film soundtracks 38, 71, 102, 157, 166–7, 174, 177–8, 192–3
Flores, Lysa 165, 168
France 83, 149, 176, 183
Franco, Francisco (General) 127
Freed, Alan 94
Fuentes, Carlos 113, 118–19
Fuller, Bobby (*or*, Bobby Fuller Four) 38, 48, 105, 110

Garcia, Billy 91
García, Charly 143, 149, 151
Garcia, Danny 91
García, Erica 168
Garcia, Jerry 128 *see also* Grateful Dead
García Marquez, Gabriel 114, 165
García Saldaña, Parménides 113
gay/lesbian
    community slang 73
    GLBT youth 159
    sexual orientation 109, 180–3, 199–200, 201
Gayle, Crystal 43
gender
    feminist critique/subversion 136, 154, 168, 179–80, 191
    gendered language/discourse 136, 154, 199–202
    masculinity 80–1, 84, 136, 159, 194
    norms/roles 64, 168–9, 179–80
    politics 109, 154, 169, 179–80, 199–202
    sexism 137
Genitallica 52–3
genres
    identity signifiers as a speech genre 9, 193
    literary genres 114, 196

genres (*continued*)
  music genres and industry categories 5, 9, 22, 31, 33–4, 37, 41, 46, 55, 73, 80, 112, 114, 153, 157–60, 168, 179, 181, 183, 186, 190, 193, 203
Gillespie, Dizzy 104
Gipsy Kings 167
Girl In A Coma 44–5, 180, 190, 203
Glenn, Lloyd 93
globalization 7–9, 18–19, 33, 140, 165, 170, 196, 199
Goldstein, Jerry 135
Gonzalez, Bob 91
González, José 191
González, Rock-drigo 122–3, 126
Gotan Project 185
Graham, Bill 131
Grammy Awards 6–7, 31, 42–3, 87–8, 106, 157–8, 168–9, 173
  Latin Grammy Awards 5, 7, 158, 168, 173
Grateful Dead 42, 47, 110, 128, 167
Great Depression 67
Great Migration 37–8
Griffith, D W 11, 13
Guatemala 176, 183, 189
Guerrero, 'Lalo' (*or*, Eduardo Guerrero) 56, 60, 67–73, 128
Guerrero, Mark 73
Guerrero, Tommy 183–4
Guns N' Roses (*or*, guitarist Slash) 39–40
Guzmán, Alejandra 168

Haggard, Merle 45
Haley & the Comets, Bill *see* Bill Haley & the Comets
Hargrove, Linda 43
Harptones, The 94
Hatfield, Bobby *see* Righteous Brothers
heavy metal 24, 39, 52, 98, 112, 132, 134–5, 156–7, 159–60, 187–8
'Hey Pachuco!' song 84
Higgins, Chuck 92–3
'Himno Chicano' song 69
hip-hop (*or*, rap music) 37
Hispanic 1, 133 *see also* Latino
Hendrix, Jimi 38, 101, 130
Holly, Buddy 38, 46–8, 110
Hollywood Argyles, The 96
Hooker, John Lee 73–4
Hopkins, Lightin' 45
'Hotel California' song 81–2, 167 *see also* Eagles, The
Houston music scene 79, 85, 162–3, 183
Huerta, Baldemar *see* Fender, Freddy

Huerta, Dolores 69–70
Hunter, Long John 38, 46
Huntington, Samuel P 4, 7–8, 140–1
  critiques of 4
Hurt, Mississippi John 38

Iglesias, Enrique 87
Illya Kuryaki and the Valderramas 172
immigrants/immigration 3–4, 50, 53, 60, 108–9, 128, 147, 154, 161, 187, 194
  and anti-immigrant sentiment 64, 187
Incubus 39
intercultural communication (*or*, multiculturalism) 31, 35, 40, 48, 50, 58, 61, 63–4, 66–7, 71, 73, 74, 82, 89–90, 92, 105, 120, 128, 130, 135, 139–40, 147, 158, 164, 166, 170, 175–7, 180–3, 189–92, 193, 198, 202
Isley Brothers, The 97

Jackson, Michael 88
Jagger, Mick *see* Rolling Stones
Jane's Addiction (*or*, Juana's Adicción) 167
jazz 15, 35–6, 42–3, 57–8, 60–1, 64–5, 71, 84, 94–5, 99, 104, 108, 131–3, 135, 148–9, 157–8, 184, 186, 194
Jefferson, Blind Lemon 35–6, 40
Jefferson Airplane 130
Jewish (*or*, Jewish Americans) 43, 74, 76, 90, 95, 200–1
  Jerry Leiber and Mike Stoller 74, 94–6, 200–1
Jiménez, 'Flaco' 100, 177
Joan Jett & the Blackhearts 101
Joe 'King' Carrasco and the Crowns 83
Johnson, Lonnie 36
Johnson, Robert 36–7, 38, 40
Jones, Quincy 168
Joplin, Janis 121
Juanes 89, 169
jump blues/jump-type shuffle 58, 73, 194 *see also* boogie woogie

King Changó 163
Kingsmen, The 97–8
Kinks, The 98
Kinky 172, 189, 198, 203

La Mala Rodríguez 177
La Revolución de Emilano Zapata 121, 177
'Land of a Thousand Dances' 77 *see also* Cannibal and the Headhunters
Lanegan, Mark 3 9
Las Hermanas Barraza 37
Latin alternative label 89, 147, 152, 160–2, 168–74, 177, 181–3, 187, 189, 193, 197, 202

Index

Latin Alternative Music Conference 170, 187, 202
Latin Grammy Awards *see* Grammy Awards
Latin music explosion (*or*, Latin 'craze'/Latin 'boom') 89–90, 107–8, 140–1, 196
Latino/Latin identity 1, 71–2, 98, 110, 132, 152, 155–8, 166–7, 170, 175, 179–89, 192–4, 198 *see also* Hispanic
Leadbelly *see* Ledbetter, Huddie
Led Zeppelin 39, 128, 134–5, 145, 180–1, 187–8
Ledbetter, Huddie (*or*, Leadbelly) 35–6, 39, 40
Leiber, Jerry *see* Jewish/Jewish Americans
Lennon, John 75–6, 184 *see also* Beatles, The
'Little Joe' Hernández 78–9, 132–3, 143, 174
'Little Richard' (*or*, Ricardo Wayne Penniman/Richard Wayne Penniman) 16, 73, 104
London 152–3
López, Israel 'Cachao' 97, 131
Lopez, Jennifer 87
Lopez, John 91
Lopez, Robert *see* El Vez
Lora, Alejandro/Alex 123–4, 126, 137–9 *see also* El TRI/Three Souls in My Mind
Los Amigos Invisibles 168
Los Angeles Dodgers 76
Los Angeles music scene 59, 66, 68–9, 73–7, 80, 82, 92–5, 99, 128, 133–5, 152–9, 163, 166–8, 170–1, 174, 182, 189, 191–2
Los Black Jeans 121
Los Bravos 91, 190–1
Los Cheyenes 91
Los Chijuas 91
Los de Abajo 168
Los Dos 121
Los Dug Dug's 119, 121, 126, 138
Los Enanitos Verdes 170
Los Hooligans 121
Los Illegals 165
Los Kumbia Queers 181–2, 192–3
Los Lobos 5, 7, 73, 101, 110, 134, 156–8, 161, 170, 173–4, 187, 191–2
Los Locos del Ritmo 121
Los Lonely Boys 44, 184, 189, 203
Los Mockers 91
Los Profetas 121
Los Rebeldes de Rock 121
Los Shakers 91
Los Sleepers 121
Los Straitjackets 190–1
Los Super Seven (*or*, Los Super 7) 30–4, 46, 48–9, 54, 185, 190
Los Teen Tops 121
Los Tigres del Norte 173, 178
Los TJ's 121
Los Tres 177
Los Vaqueros del Oeste 44
Los Yaki 121
Louie and the Lovers 192
'Louie Louie' 97–8
Love 130
Lovett, Lyle 41
Lowriders (*or*, car cruising) 77, 80, 134–5
Lowrider magazine 7
Lymon, Frankie 94, 186 *see also* Teenagers, The

Maldita Vecindad (*or*, Maldita Vecindad y Los Hijos del Quinto Patio) 52, 83–5, 143
Malo (band) 5, 77, 133, 170, 178
Malo, Raul 34, 49, 190
Manu Chao (*or*, Mano Negra) 83, 172, 176–7
Manzanera, Phil 152
Mariachi El Bronx 54
mariachi music
    mariachi legacy in rock 'n' roll 42–4, 49–50, 52–4, 77, 130, 184–5
    mariachi project and *mariachi* renaissance 104–7
Marin, Cheech 70–1
Mars Volta 170, 185–7, 203
Martin, Ricky 87
Martínez, Rudy *see* Question Mark and the Mysterians
Masked Phantom Band, The 96
Mavericks, The 49 *see also* Malo, Raul
McCoys, The 97
McNeely, Big Jay 74, 93
McTell, Blind Willie 36, 45
McVea, Jack 73
MEChA 3–4 *see also* chicanismo
media
    and nationalism 11–17, 32
    representation 8–9, 13, 20, 24, 32, 70, 132, 166
Medley, Bill *see* Righteous Brothers
melting pot theory/metaphor 14–5, 98, 155
Mendez Hamlin, Rosalie 75 *see also* 'Angel Baby' song
mestizaje (mixture) 17, 118, 172
'Mexican Radio' song 189
Mexican revolution (*or*, revolutionary period) 112, 142–3
'Mexicans' 2, 56–7, 60–2, 81, 94, 133, 157–8, 161, 177
Mexico City music scene 52, 55, 72, 112, 115, 117, 121, 123–4, 126, 130–1, 142–4, 161, 166, 175–6, 181
Meyers, Augie 100
Mickey & Sylvia 96
Midniters *see* Thee Midniters
migration *see* immigration

Index

Miller, Jerry 105
Mingus, Charles 58
minstrelsy (*or*, counter minstrelsy) 15, 64
Minutemen (band) 40, 184–5, 203
minutemen (vigilante group), 187
Mira, Vince 29–30
Misfits, The 158
Mitch Ryder and the Detroit Wheels 129
MOJO magazine 104, 192
Monsivaís, Carlos 113
Montalvo, Francisco 37
Monte Negro 182, 192
Monterrey, México music scene 189
Moré, Benny 72
Morrison, Jim 112, 114, 128–9 *see also* Doors, The
Morrison, Van 97
Morrissey, Stephen Patrick 53–4, 190 *see also* Smiths, The
movies *see* films
Mudhoney 187
Muldaur, Maria 43
music as politics (*or*, music as political discourse) 27, 48, 64, 68, 70, 79–80, 83, 106–7, 124, 127, 142–3, 148–51, 153–4, 171, 179–82, 184, 187, 192
    humorous music as political discourse 69, 154
music as public discourse 14–16, 20, 29–32, 48, 126, 198

Nelson, Willie 45
Neruda, Pablo 114
Neutral Milk Hotel 44
New York Dolls 152
New York music scene 47, 72, 76, 94, 127, 131–3, 152–3, 167–8, 170, 181, 186–7
Nicaragua 2, 8, 153, 176
Nirvana (*or*, Kurt Cobain) 39, 51, 91, 174, 186–7
North American Free Trade Agreement (f) 18, 161
'Not Fade Away' song 44, 47, 97, 110, 128

O'Daniel, W Lee 'Pappy' 36–7
Orozco, José Clemente 165
Os Mutantes 91, 168
Otis, Johnny 58
Owens, Buck 46
'Oye Como Va' song 131
Ozomatli 189
Ozuna, Sunny *see* Sunny and the Sunliners/Sunglows

'Pachuco hop' song (*or*, 'Patchuko Hop') 83
'Pachuco' song 83 *see also* Vecindad, Maldita

Páez, Fito 151, 168
Page, Patti 44
Palmer, Robert 93–4, 104
Panamá 183
'Pancho Lopez' song 68
Paraguay 183
Pavarotti, Luciano 168
Penguins, The 74
Penniman, Ricardo/Richard Wayne Penniman *see* 'Little Richard'
Perón, Evita 12, 149
Perón, Juan 12, 148–9
Peru (*or*, Peruvian) 130, 183, 192
Phillips, Michelle 43
Pink Floyd 187
Pinochet, Augusto (General) 127, 149
Pistolera 187–8
Pixies, The 167, 174, 178
Plastilina Mosh 84–5
Platters, The 75
Poniatowska, Elena 113
Portastatic 91
Prado, Pérez 72, 131
Premiers, The 77, 91 *see also* Eastside Sound
Presley, Elvis 38, 44, 50, 74, 78, 80–1, 121, 123, 144
Price, Lloyd 104
Puente, Tito 99, 131, 172
Puerto Rican rock scene 133
Puerto Rico (*or*, Puerto Rican) 2, 8, 16, 72, 94, 130–1, 133, 147, 152, 158, 160, 165, 170–1, 186
punk rock 24, 27, 40, 44, 54, 77, 81, 83, 87, 91, 96, 98, 102–3, 105, 110–11, 116, 142–4, 146–7, 152–9, 161, 164, 166–7, 169, 174–5, 179–80, 183, 185, 190, 196–7

Queen 39, 165
Question Mark and the Mysterians (*or*, ? and the Mysterians) 102–3, 110, 157, 196

R&B 6, 31, 38, 67, 73–4, 93–4, 95–7, 99, 102, 120, 156–7, 194–5, 200
Rábago Pérez, Andrés *see* Russell, Andy
racial passing 58–9, 64, 94, 96, 103, 107, 110, 195 *see also* whiteness
Raconteurs, The 44
radio
    border radio (*or*, X stations) 30–3, 36–7, 41–2, 44–6, 48–50, 55, 120, 185, 194
    internet radio 181–3
    lack of airplay 151, 162–3 *see also* media representation
    radio and nationalism 11–13, 32
    talk radio 4
Rage Against The Machine 40

Index

Ramone, Phil 167-8
Ramones, The 90, 98, 152, 157
Rascals, The 97
Recall election in California (2003) 3, 194
Red Hot Chili Peppers 39, 167, 171
REM 39
retro-swing movement 84
Rey, Bobby 94, 96
Rhythm Rockers, The 94-5, 99 see also Rillera Brothers, The
Richardson, J. P. (or, The Big Bopper) 46
Righteous Brothers, The 95
Rillera Brothers, The 94-5 see also Rhythm Rockers, The
Robbins, Marty 41-2
Robins, The 94
rock en español 5, 27, 47, 52, 83-4, 88-9, 91, 96, 138, 152, 156, 160-75, 177, 181, 183, 187, 189, 191, 193, 197, 202 see also Latin alternative
Rock en Tu Idioma (slogan) 143, 160-1, 169, 174
rock music (definitions) 22-5
Rodrigo y Gabriela 187-8
Rodriguez, Johnny 43
'Rodriguez' (or, Sixto Rodriguez) 192
Rolling Stone magazine 100, 104, 184, 192
Rolling Stones 44, 47, 97, 110, 113, 121, 123
Romancers, The 77 see also Eastside Sound
Ronstadt, Linda 43, 71, 73, 106, 127-8, 157-8
Royal Crown Revue 84
Roxy Music 152 see also Manzanera, Phil
Russell, Andy (or, Andrés Rábago Pérez) 58-9, 76

Sahm, Doug 49, 99-101, 189, 192 see also Sir Douglas Quintet
Saínz, Gustavo 113
Saldivar, Mingo 44
Sam the Sham and the Pharaohs (or, Domingo Samudio) 101-2, 108, 100, 157, 190
San Antonio music scene 38, 41, 42, 78, 100, 155, 179
San Francisco music scene 128, 131-2, 163, 168, 181
Santana, Carlos 5-6, 87-8, 120-1, 131-3, 170, 184
  Santana band 5, 77, 131-2, 156, 159, 172, 191
Santaolalla, Gustavo 151-2, 156, 161, 166, 168
Sapo 77 see also Eastside Sound
Schifrin, Lalo 129
Schwarzenegger, Arnold (Governor) 3-4
Searchers, The 128
Seattle music scene 98, 144, 161
Secada, Jon 168
Señor Flavio 163-4 see also Fabulosos Cadillacs
Sepultura 159

Sesma, Chico 58
Setzer, Brian (or, Brian Setzer Orchestra) 40, 84, 177
Shakira 88, 168
'She's About A Mover' song 101
Shins, The 40
Simon and Garfunkel 130
Sinatra, Frank 15-16, 168
Sir Douglas Quintet 39, 49, 99-101, 79, 92, 99-103, 108 see also Sahm, Doug
Skarnales, Los 85, 163
Slash see Guns n' Roses
'Sleepy Lagoon' song 75
Smiths, The 39, 187, 190 see also Morrissey
Soda Stereo 143
Solís, Javier 67
Sonics, The 38, 105, 110
Sosa, Mercedes 192
Spain (or, Spanish music) 1, 2, 47, 72, 83, 91, 104, 127-8, 130, 143, 152, 160-2, 165, 171-2, 176-7, 183, 185, 189, 191-2, 199, 201
  flamenco 35, 40, 58, 177, 159-60, 167, 172, 187-9
  Spanish guitar 130, 135, 177, 152, 159-60, 167, 185, 187-9
Spencer Davis Group 129
Spoon 44, 52
Springsteen, Bruce 39
Squirrel Nut Zippers 84
Steely Dan 130
Stefani, Gwen (or, No Doubt) 82, 87
Stereolab 91
Steve Miller Band 38-9
Stevens, Sufjan 44
Stoller, Mike see Jewish/Jewish Americans
Stone Poneys, The 128 see also Ronstadt, Linda
Stone Temple Pilots 39
Strait, George 45-6
Strangeloves, The 92, 104
Stray Cats, The 177 see also Setzer, Brian
'Suavecito' song 169-70
Sublime (or, Bradley Nowell) 81
Sunny and the Sunglows/Sunliners 49, 78
Superchunk 91
Swinging Blue Jeans, The 74
System Of A Down 40

'Talk to Me' song 79
Talking Heads 164, 168 see also Byrne, David
Taylor, James 168
Teenagers, The 94 see also Lymon, Frankie
Texas Tornados 33
Thee Midniters 77, 133 see also Eastside Sound
Thornton, Big Mama 74

Index

Tierra 77, 133, 154, 156, 174 *see also* Eastside Sound
Tijuana music scene 43, 120–1, 128–9, 131, 164, 189
Tijuana NO! 145, 161, 164–5, 178
Tillis, Mel 43
'Tin Tan' (*or*, German Valdes) 55, 83
Tom Petty & the Heartbreakers 39
Tostado, Edmundo Martínez *see* 'Don Tosti'
Toussaint, Cecilia 126–7
Touzet, René 99
transnationalism 7, 9, 18–19, 72, 108, 112–3, 188, 122, 126, 140, 145–7, 152–3, 161, 164–6, 173, 175–7, 182–3, 191–3
Traveling Wilburys 33
Treviño, Rick 49
Trío Los Panchos 67
Triple (band) 162
Troggs, The 98
Trujillo, Robert Agustín 159–60
Tucson music scene 60, 67, 73, 128, 172
twelve-string guitar 35–6, 39–40 *see also* bajo sexto

Uriah Heep 130
US Census
    2000 Census 1, 2, 30, 89, 193–4, 199
    1970 Census 2
    1950–60 Census 2
    1930 Census 2, 64
    census brief on Hispanic population 1
U2 101

Valdez, Luis 71 *see also Zoot Suit* play
Valens, Ritchie 40, 46–8, 74, 93, 96, 98–9, 108, 121–2, 134–5, 144, 153, 157, 192
Vallejo 172, 189

Van Halen 40
Van Zandt, Townes 45
Vega, Arturo 152
Velez, Gerry 130
Velvet Revolver 33
Velvet Underground, The 102
Venezuela 152, 160, 165, 189–90, 192
Villa, Pancho 11, 68 *see also* Mexican revolution
Village Voice 122
VIPs, The *see* El Chicano
Vocaleers, The 94
Voodoo Glow Skulls 5, 167

Walker, T-Bone 67
War 135 *see also* Burdon, Eric
We All Together 91
White, Barry 75
White, Jack 53, 183, 185 *see also* White Stripes, The
White Stripes, The (*or*, Las Rayas Blancas) 44, 53–4, 183
whiteness 59, 64 *see also* racial passing
Whitman, Walt 14–16
Who, The 39
Wilco 44
Willis, Chuck 94
Woodstock 130–1
'Wooly Bully' song 101
Wonder, Stevie 130

Yardbirds, The 38
Yo La Tengo 91, 96

Zappa, Frank (*or*, Frank Zappa and the Mothers of Invention) 74–5, 176–7
Zoot Suit play 71 *see also* Valdez, Luis
'Zoot Suit Riot' song 84
ZZ Top 31, 39, 49

Acknowledgments

First and foremost, I want to acknowledge and thank my family, those who have sacrificed as much as I have and who had to deal with every one of the pressures, problems, and struggles along with me. My wife, Olguita, deserves a great deal of recognition because much of this would never have been written without my conversations with her. Likewise, much of this would have never been completed without her dedication to our children and allowing me to close doors to keep noise down and work late nights. Our daughter, Sofía, deserves more thanks than I can give for being a wonderful child, enriching my life ever since the day she was born, and making me want to try harder to make a better life for her and us. Our son, Diego, has made things more complicated, utterly difficult, and sometimes impossible. I can smile now as I think back to how he always seemed to be against my work habits, and to how, because of him, I often thought that I would never be able to finish my doctoral studies, my dissertation, and my current research. But his spirit and personality are radiant, and he often makes me reconsider what I think I know about myself, and life in general. And I am so happy to have him in my life, and I'm looking forward to making music with him. Our third child, Daniela (la bebé), also deserves credit, just for being such a good baby and bringing us so many smiles and so much happiness, and especially for making us smile with her dancing. Like all children, mine always seem to forgive me for my shortcomings, and I hope I can repay them with time and affection.

At the same time, there are other members of my family, Mom and Dad (Granma and Granpa), who deserve credit for their love and support throughout the several years of writing. There are obviously many other family members and friends who have also been supportive throughout the process, but they are too numerous to list here. But I do want to recognize their love and support, and express my gratitude.

Beyond this I want to thank Professor Leonard C. Hawes from the Department of Communication at the University of Utah, who was a major part of this academic journey from the beginning, essentially making this research project possible for me by supporting me in various forms along the way, sticking with me throughout the worst of times, and coming through for me in more ways than one. Likewise, I will also never forget the support and influence of several professors from the University of Utah, my many graduate student friends (and now new professors) that I met while at Utah, others from my time at the University of Texas at El Paso (UTEP), and others from elsewhere around the US who have all been a part of the process and kept me going with their friendship over the years.

Lastly, I wish to recognize others who were immensely supportive and without whom my professional life at Boston College would have been much more difficult — Professor Elfriede Fürsich and Professor Michael Keith. Without them and other supportive colleagues at Boston College, things would have seemed insurmountable. With their support, I was able to carry on and finish my research. There are many more friends, colleagues, and others who surely deserve thanks for all the love and support. I will have to carry on with the expectation of thanking people individually when I talk to them again.

Thanks also to the publishers for permission to reprint my previously published articles, as well as friends, artists, musicians, and other professionals who allowed me to use their images in this book. Thanks also to Paul Dryden (and the Latin Alternative Music Conference) for help and support of this project. Finally, thanks, of course, to Katie Gallof for her labor, support, and kindness, and to Continuum for taking a chance and making this book possible.

www.ingramcontent.com/pod-product-compliance
Lightning Source LLC
Chambersburg PA
CBHW052035300426
44117CB00012B/1837